Natsume's
BOOK of FRIENDS

Shojo Beat

Natsume's BOOK of FRIENDS

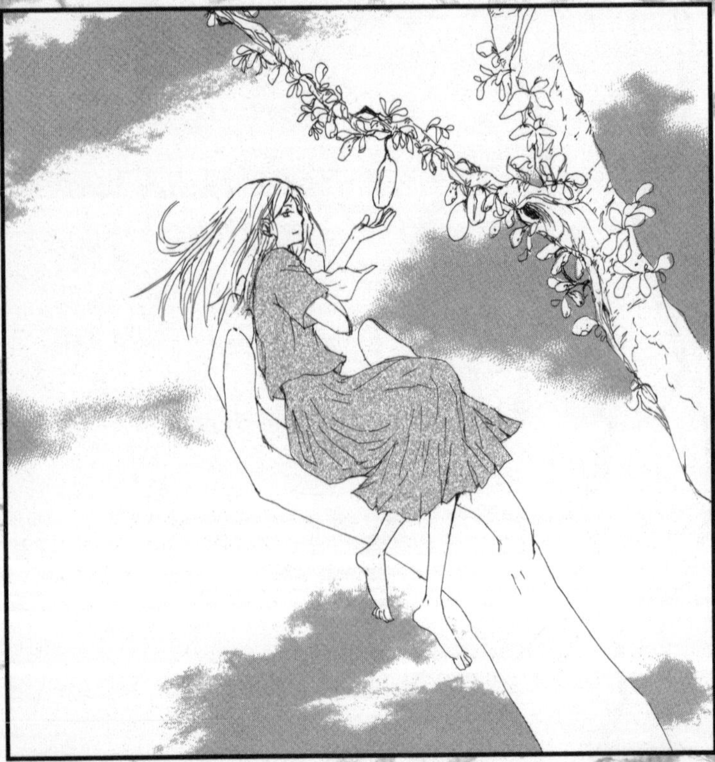

STORY and ART by
Yuki Midorikawa

VOLUME 15

Natsume's BOOK of FRIENDS

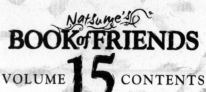

VOLUME 15 CONTENTS

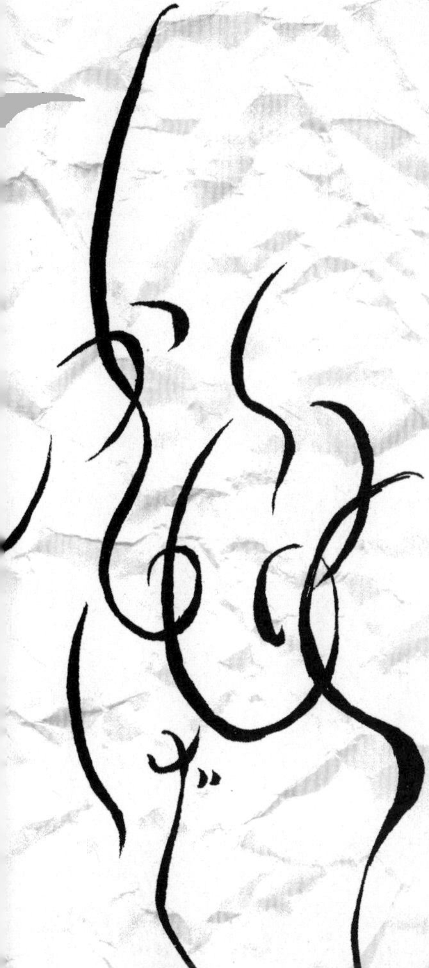

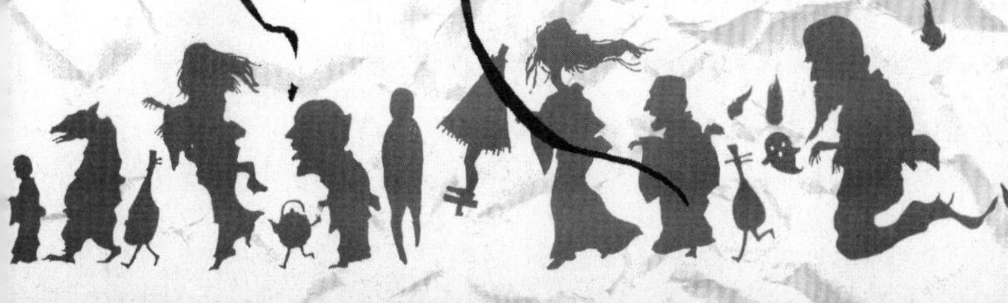

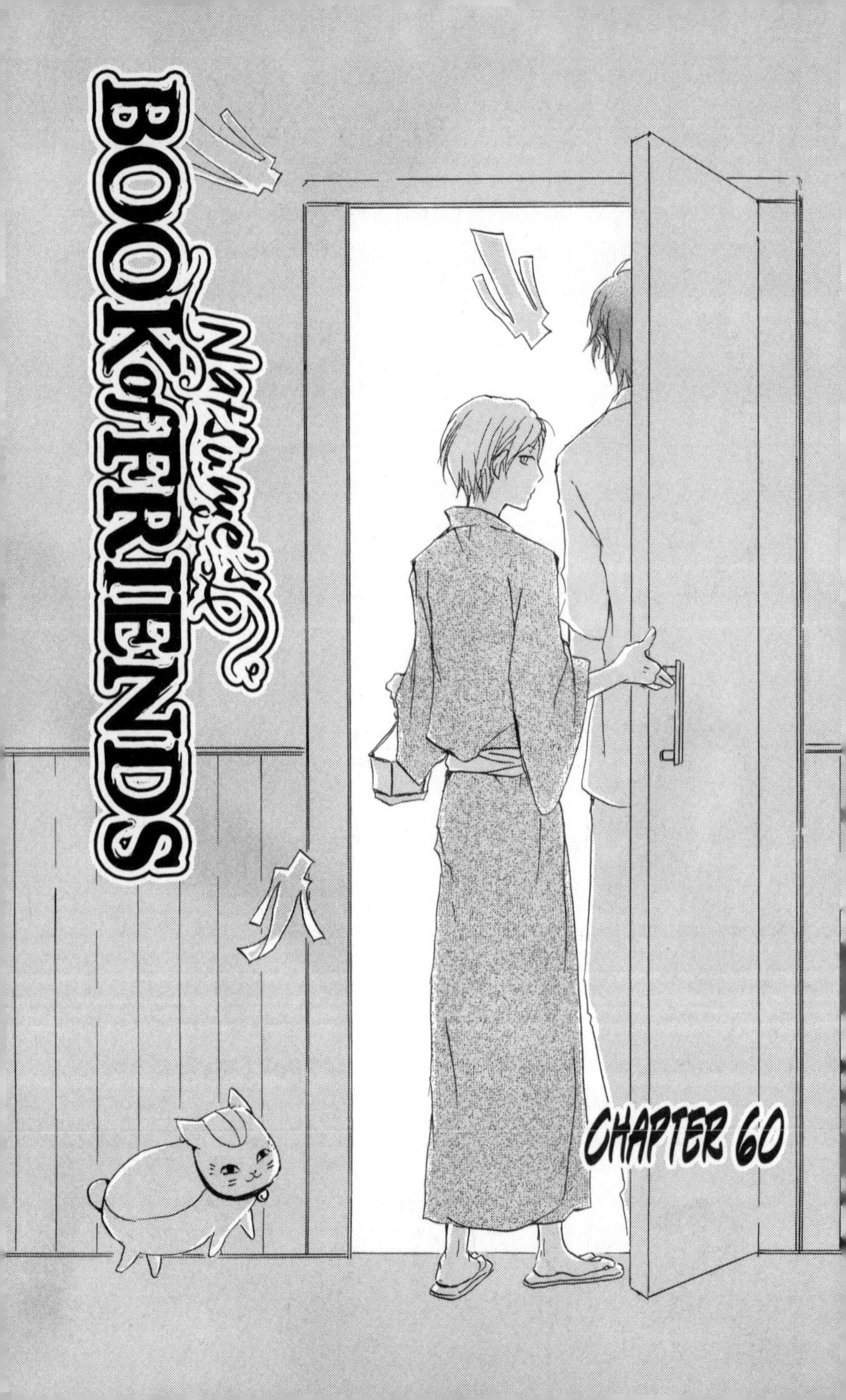
Natsume's
BOOK of FRIENDS
CHAPTER 60

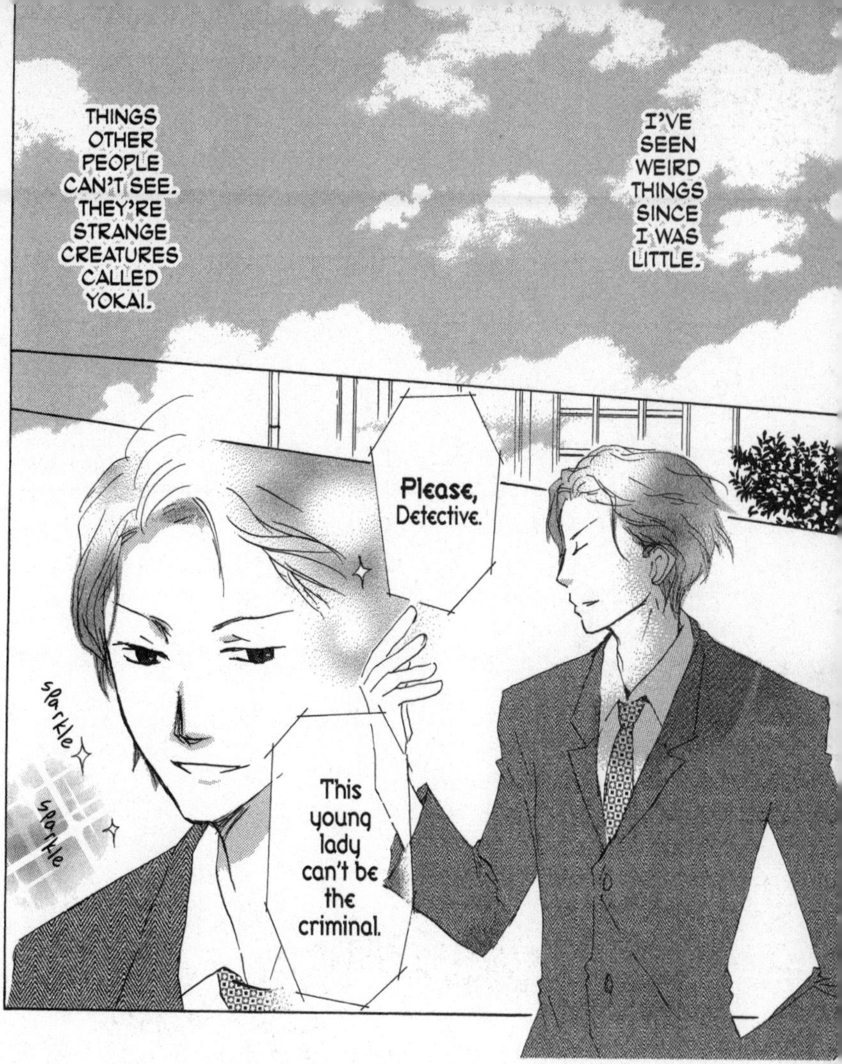
I'VE SEEN WEIRD THINGS SINCE I WAS LITTLE.
THINGS OTHER PEOPLE CAN'T SEE. THEY'RE STRANGE CREATURES CALLED YOKAI.
Please, Detective.
This young lady can't be the criminal.
sparkle
sparkle

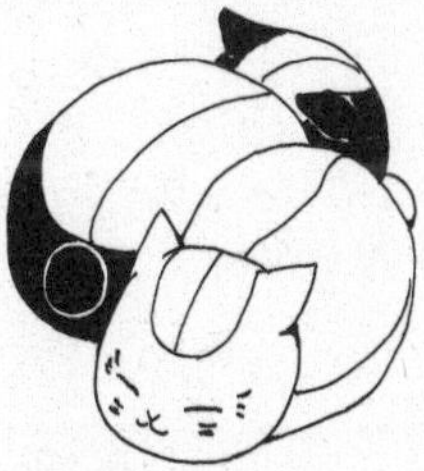

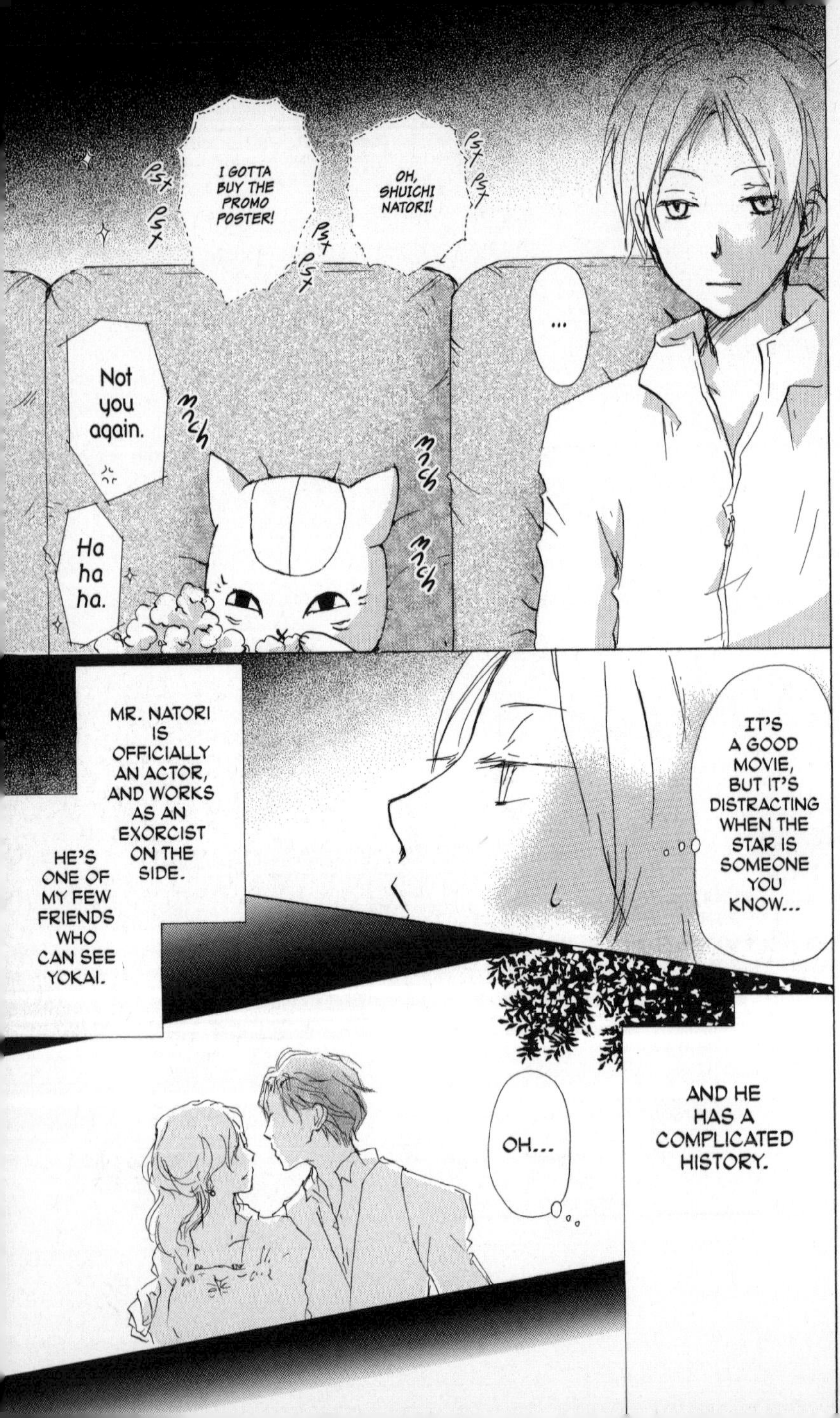
...
Pst pst
OH, SHUICHI NATORI!
Pst pst
I GOTTA BUY THE PROMO POSTER!
Pst pst
mnch mnch mnch
Not you again.
Ha ha ha.
IT'S A GOOD MOVIE, BUT IT'S DISTRACTING WHEN THE STAR IS SOMEONE YOU KNOW...
MR. NATORI IS OFFICIALLY AN ACTOR, AND WORKS AS AN EXORCIST ON THE SIDE.
HE'S ONE OF MY FEW FRIENDS WHO CAN SEE YOKAI.
AND HE HAS A COMPLICATED HISTORY.
OH...

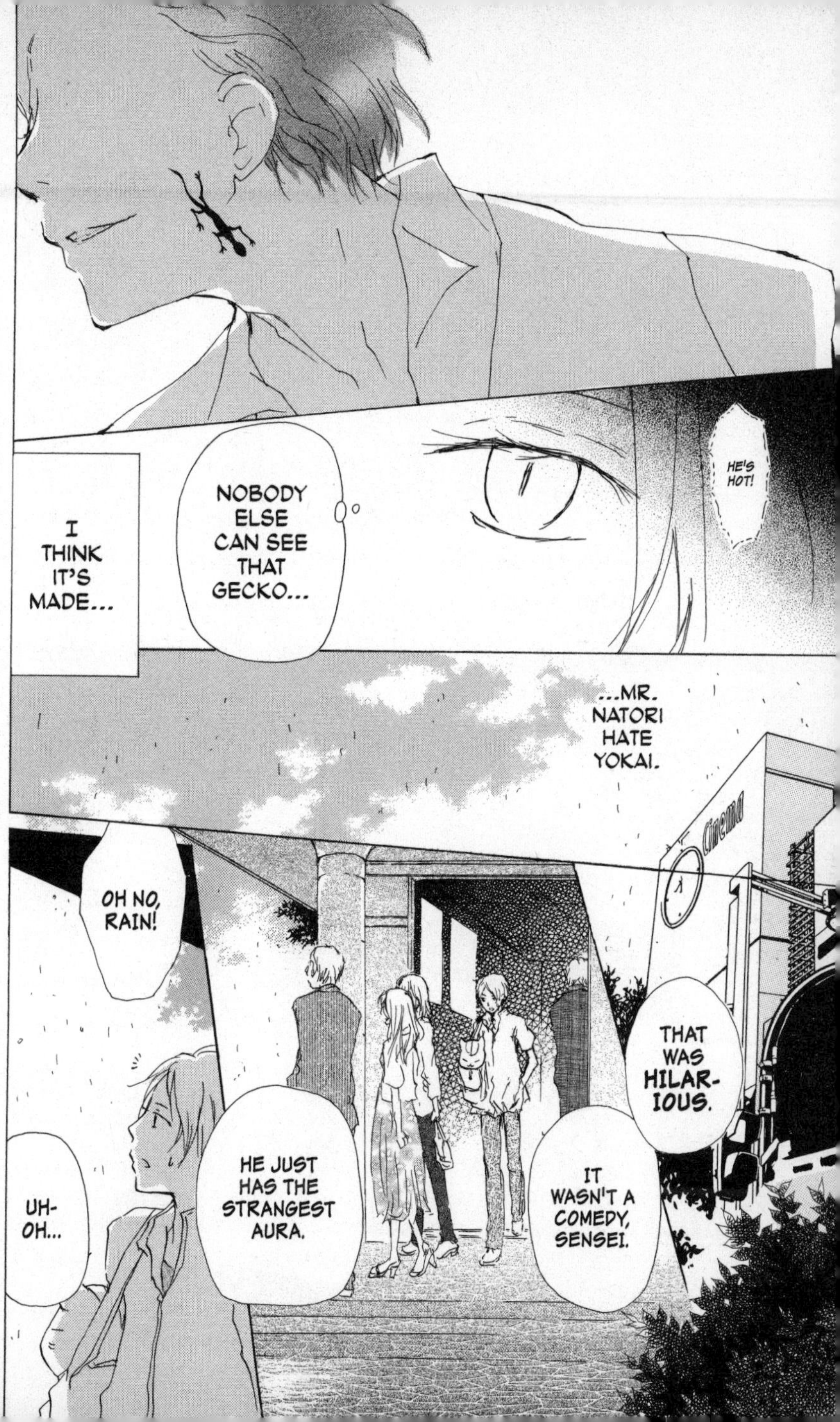
HE'S HOT!
NOBODY ELSE CAN SEE THAT GECKO...
I THINK IT'S MADE...
...MR. NATORI HATE YOKAI.
Cinema
THAT WAS HILAR-IOUS.
IT WASN'T A COMEDY, SENSEI.
HE JUST HAS THE STRANGEST AURA.
OH NO, RAIN!
UH-OH...

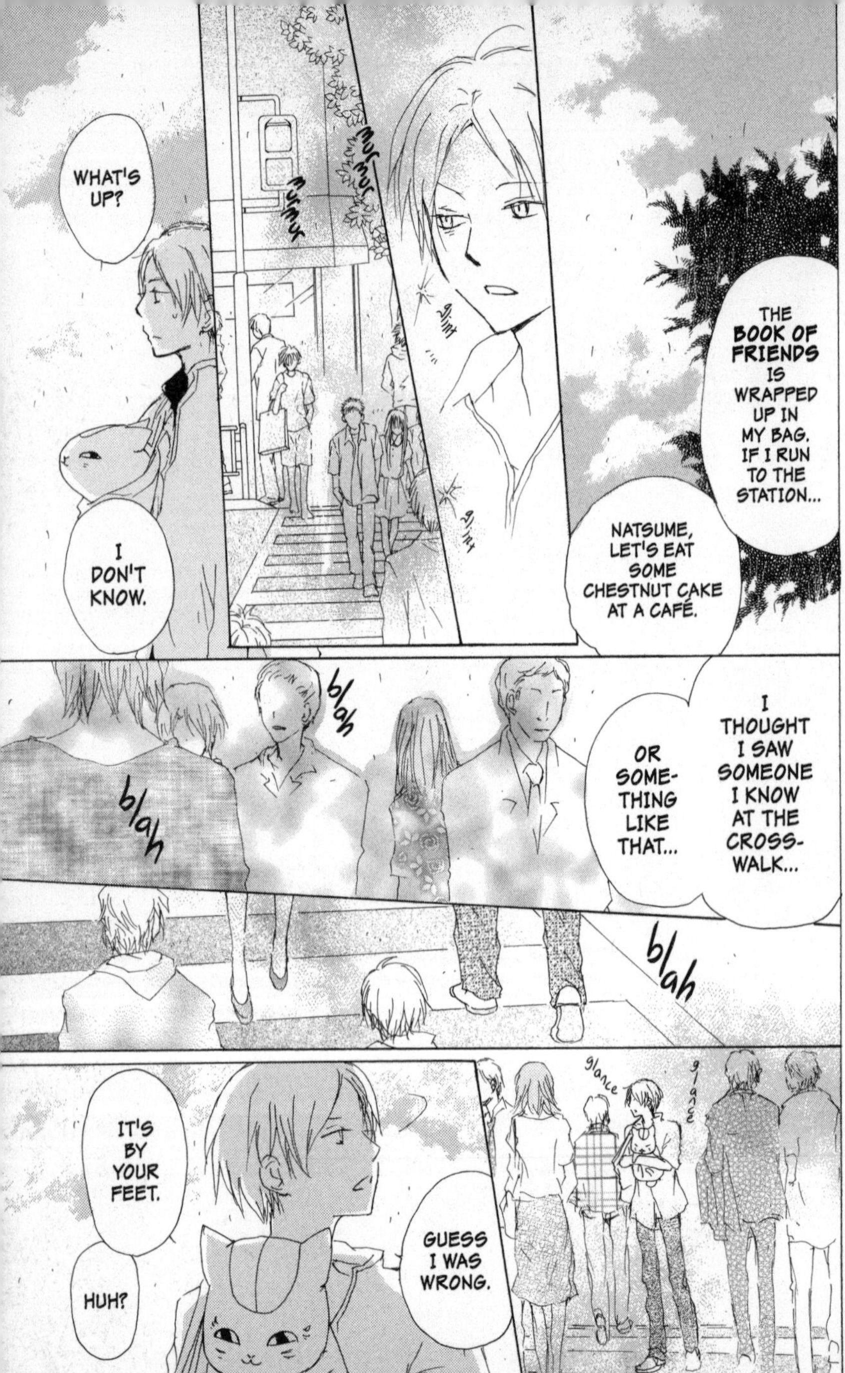
THE BOOK OF FRIENDS IS WRAPPED UP IN MY BAG. IF I RUN TO THE STATION...
NATSUME, LET'S EAT SOME CHESTNUT CAKE AT A CAFÉ.
glint
glint
murmur
murmur
murmur
WHAT'S UP?
I DON'T KNOW.
I THOUGHT I SAW SOMEONE I KNOW AT THE CROSS-WALK...
OR SOME-THING LIKE THAT...
blah
blah
blah
glance
glance
GUESS I WAS WRONG.
IT'S BY YOUR FEET.
HUH?

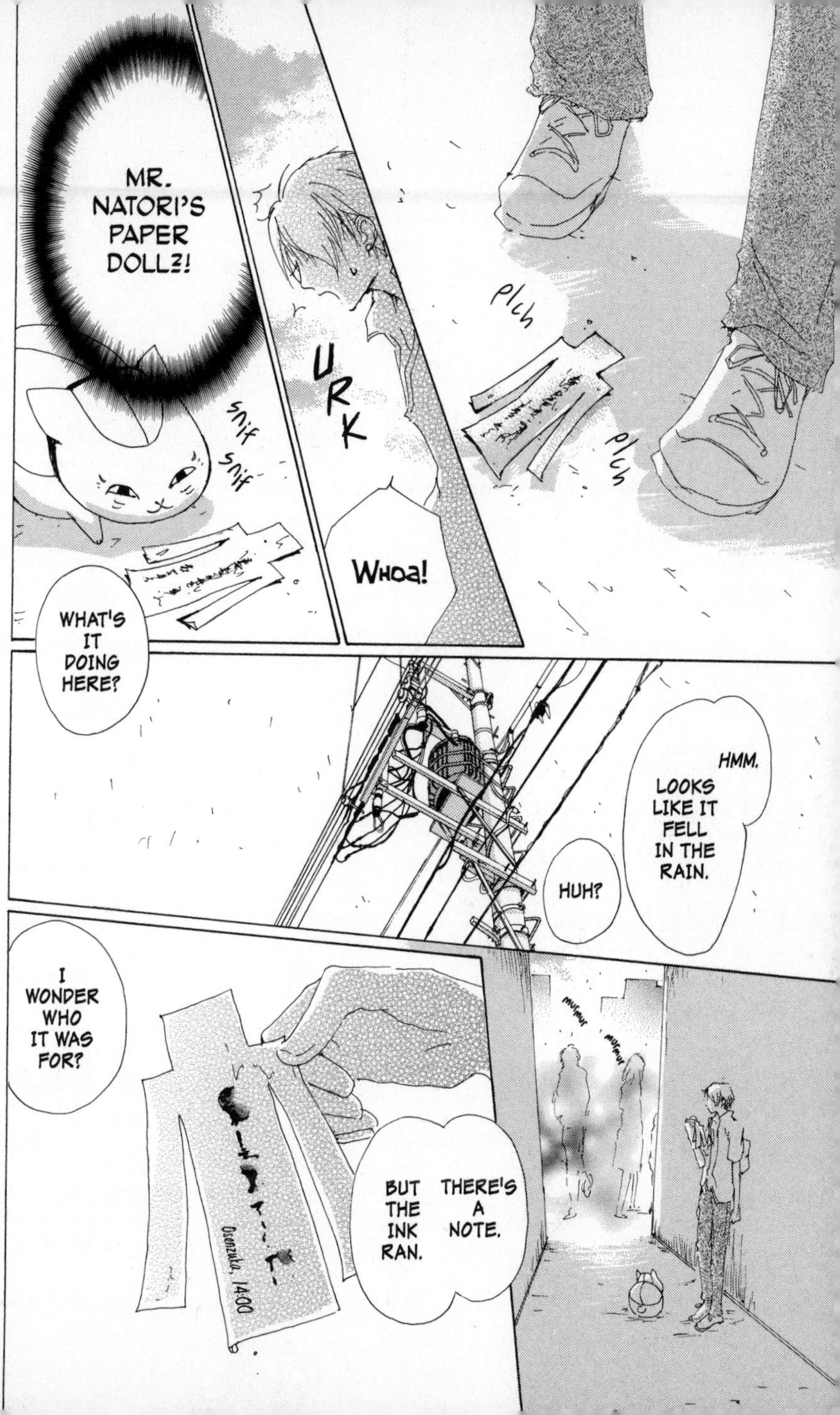
plch
plch
URK
Whoa!
MR. NATORI'S PAPER DOLL?!
snif snif
WHAT'S IT DOING HERE?
HMM. LOOKS LIKE IT FELL IN THE RAIN.
HUH?
murmur
murmur
THERE'S A NOTE.
BUT THE INK RAN.
Osenzuka, 14:00
I WONDER WHO IT WAS FOR?

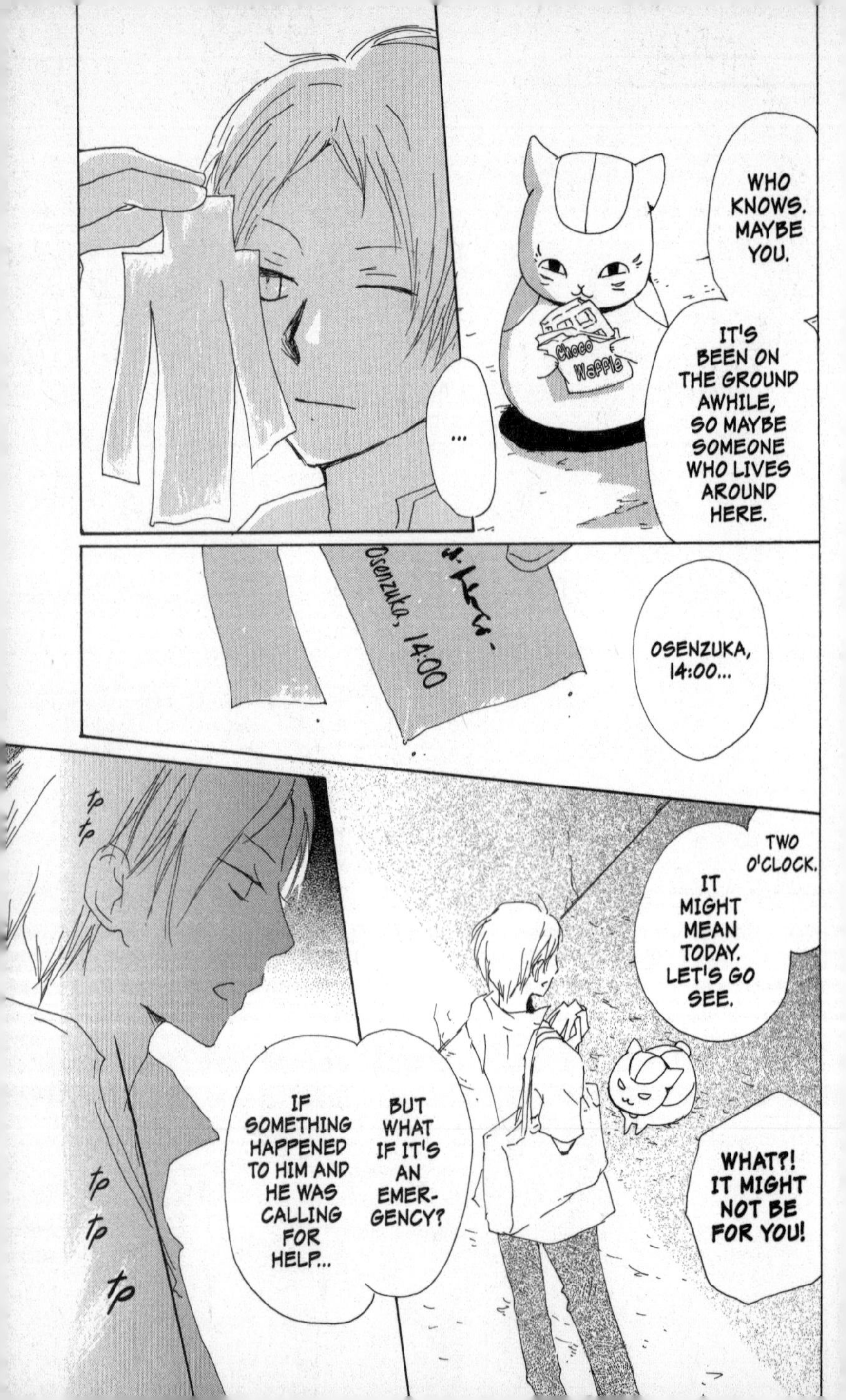
WHO KNOWS. MAYBE YOU.
IT'S BEEN ON THE GROUND AWHILE, SO MAYBE SOMEONE WHO LIVES AROUND HERE.
Choco Waffle
...
OSENZUKA, 14:00...
Osenzuka, 14:00
TWO O'CLOCK.
IT MIGHT MEAN TODAY. LET'S GO SEE.
WHAT?! IT MIGHT NOT BE FOR YOU!
BUT WHAT IF IT'S AN EMERGENCY?
IF SOMETHING HAPPENED TO HIM AND HE WAS CALLING FOR HELP...
tp tp
tp tp tp

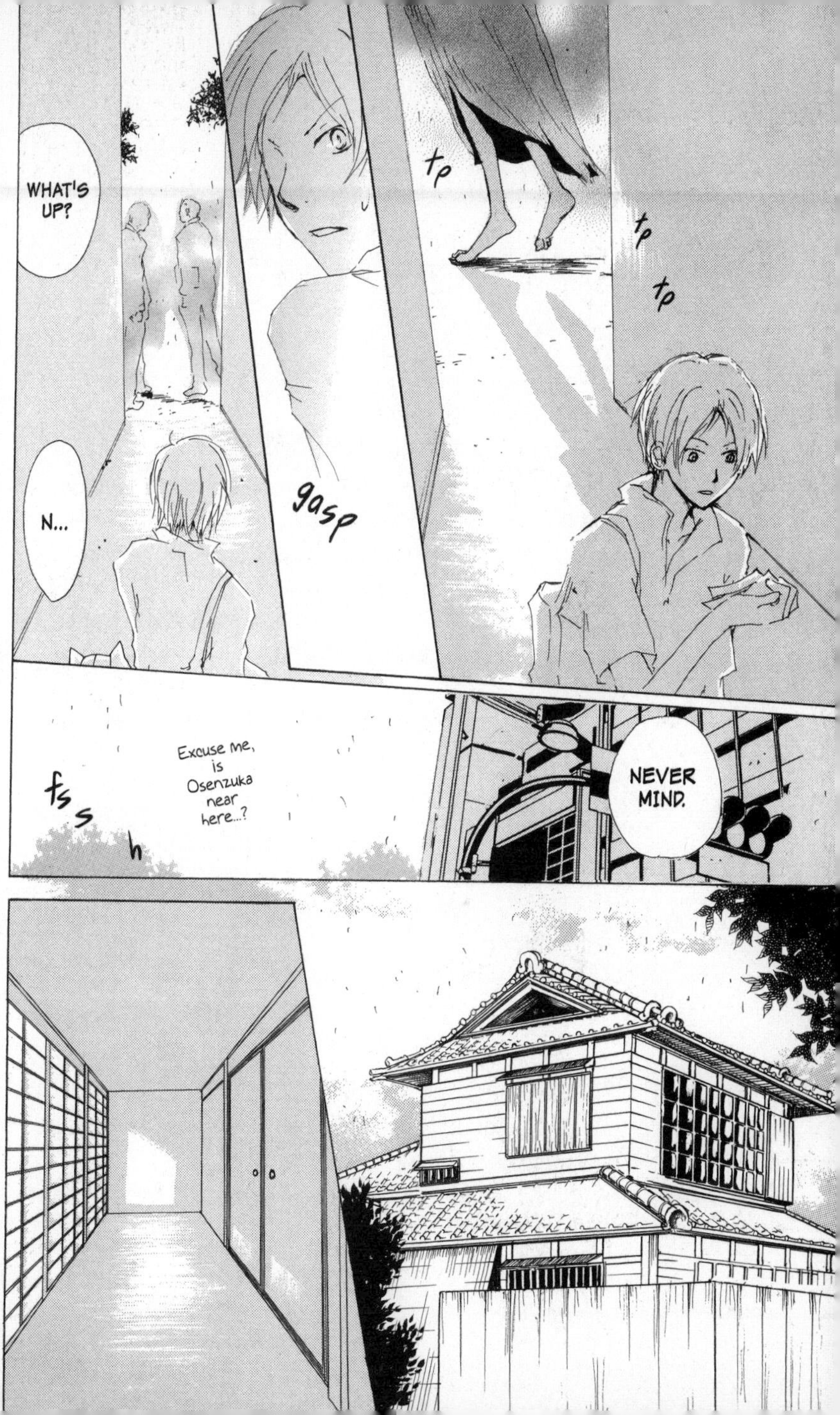
tp
tp
tp
gasp
WHAT'S UP?
N...
NEVER MIND.
Excuse me, is Osenzuka near here...?
fssh

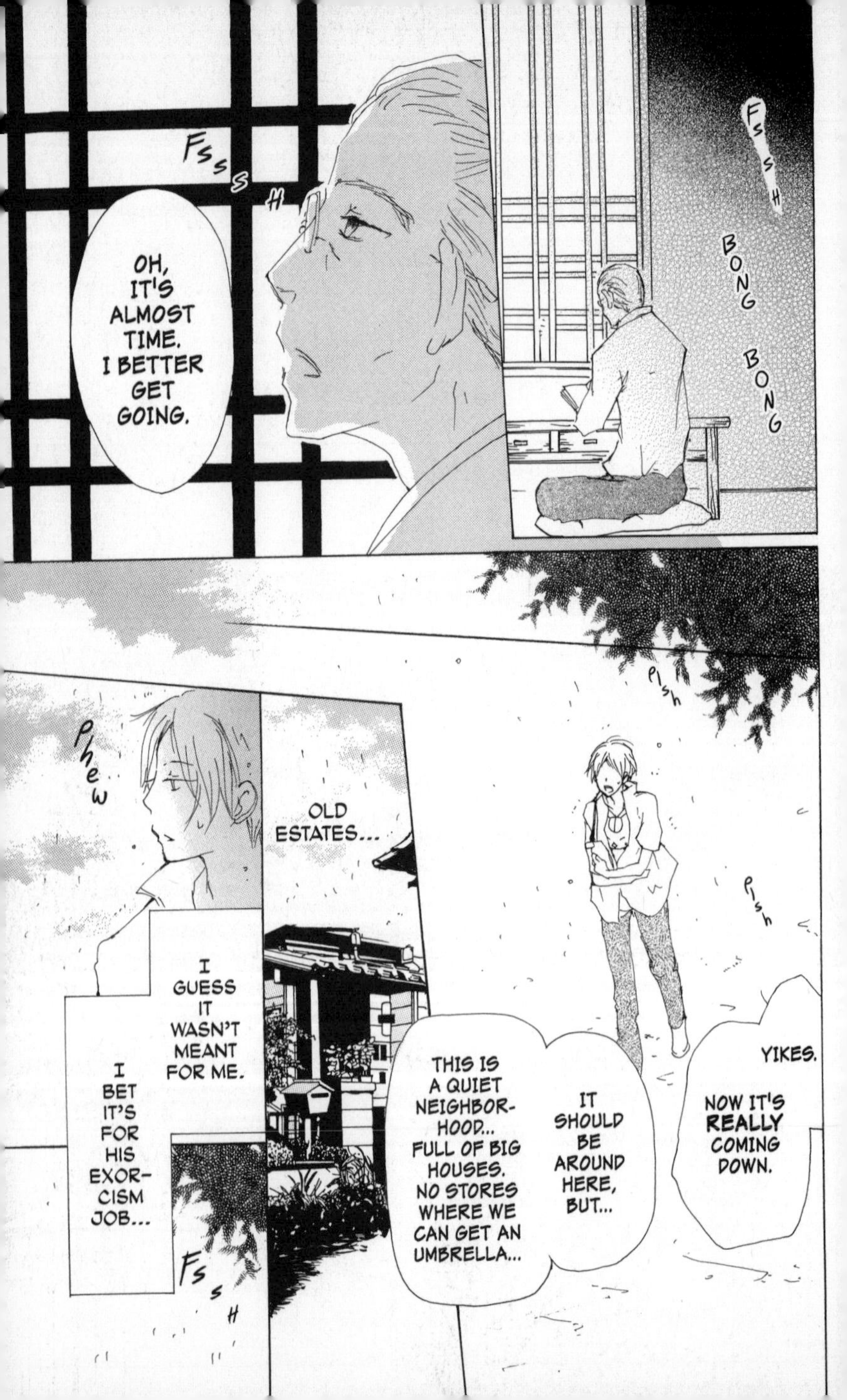
FSSH
BONG
BONG
FSSSH
OH, IT'S ALMOST TIME. I BETTER GET GOING.
PLSH
PLSH
YIKES.
NOW IT'S REALLY COMING DOWN.
IT SHOULD BE AROUND HERE, BUT...
THIS IS A QUIET NEIGHBOR-HOOD... FULL OF BIG HOUSES. NO STORES WHERE WE CAN GET AN UMBRELLA...
OLD ESTATES...
PHEW
I GUESS IT WASN'T MEANT FOR ME.
I BET IT'S FOR HIS EXOR-CISM JOB...
FSSH

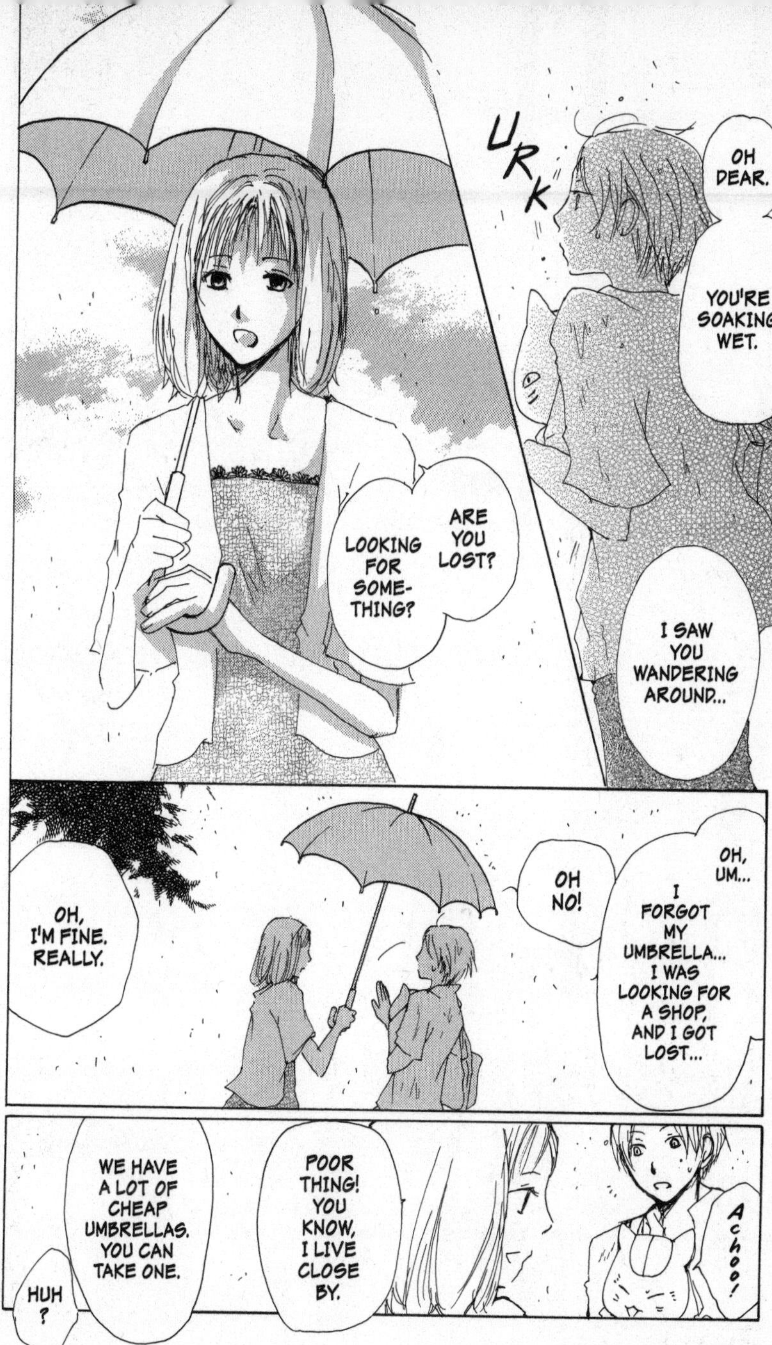
URK
OH DEAR.
YOU'RE SOAKING WET.
I SAW YOU WANDERING AROUND...
ARE YOU LOST?
LOOKING FOR SOME-THING?
OH, UM...
I FORGOT MY UMBRELLA... I WAS LOOKING FOR A SHOP, AND I GOT LOST...
OH NO!
OH, I'M FINE. REALLY.
Achoo!
POOR THING! YOU KNOW, I LIVE CLOSE BY.
WE HAVE A LOT OF CHEAP UMBRELLAS. YOU CAN TAKE ONE.
HUH?

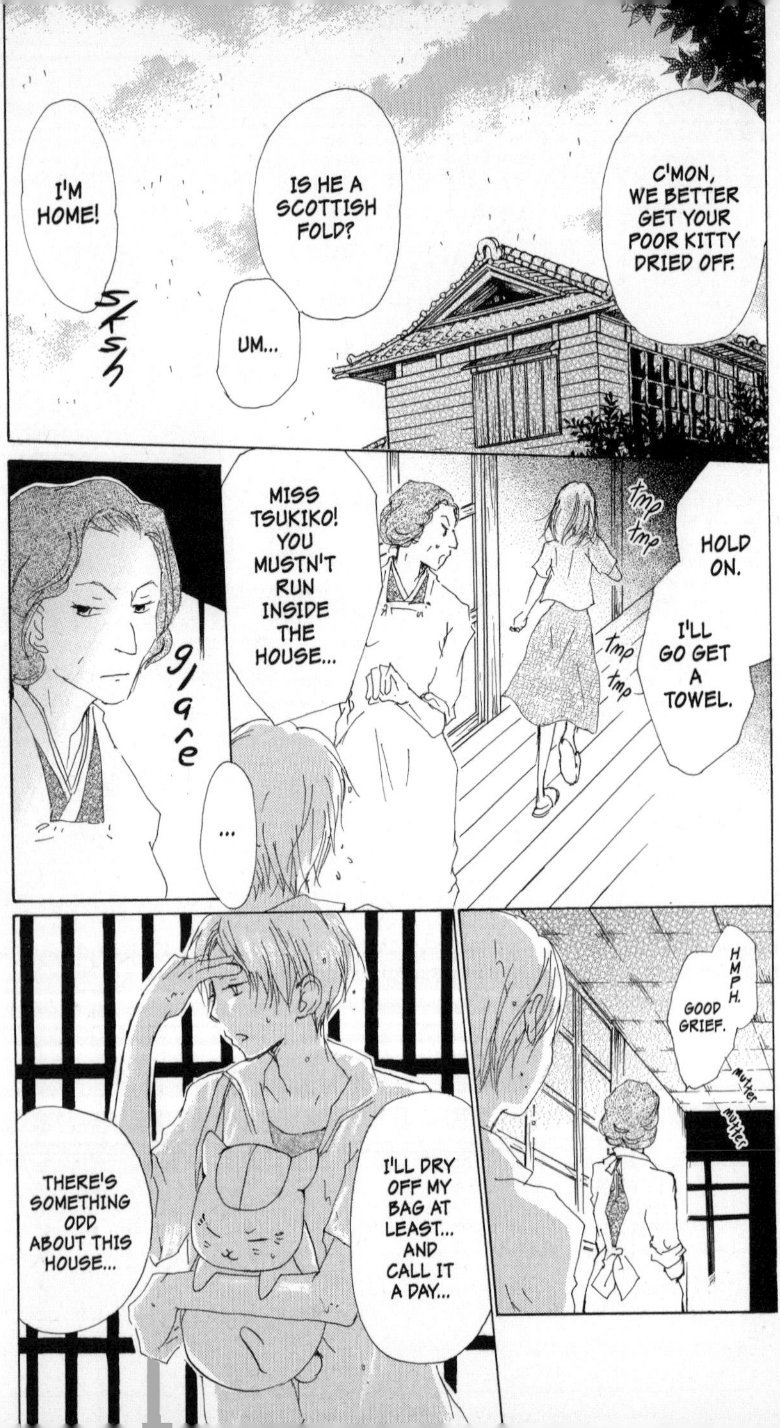
C'MON, WE BETTER GET YOUR POOR KITTY DRIED OFF.
IS HE A SCOTTISH FOLD?
UM...
I'M HOME!
sksh
tmp tmp
HOLD ON.
I'LL GO GET A TOWEL.
tmp tmp
MISS TSUKIKO! YOU MUSTN'T RUN INSIDE THE HOUSE...
...
glare
HMPH.
GOOD GRIEF.
mutter mutter
I'LL DRY OFF MY BAG AT LEAST... AND CALL IT A DAY...
THERE'S SOMETHING ODD ABOUT THIS HOUSE...

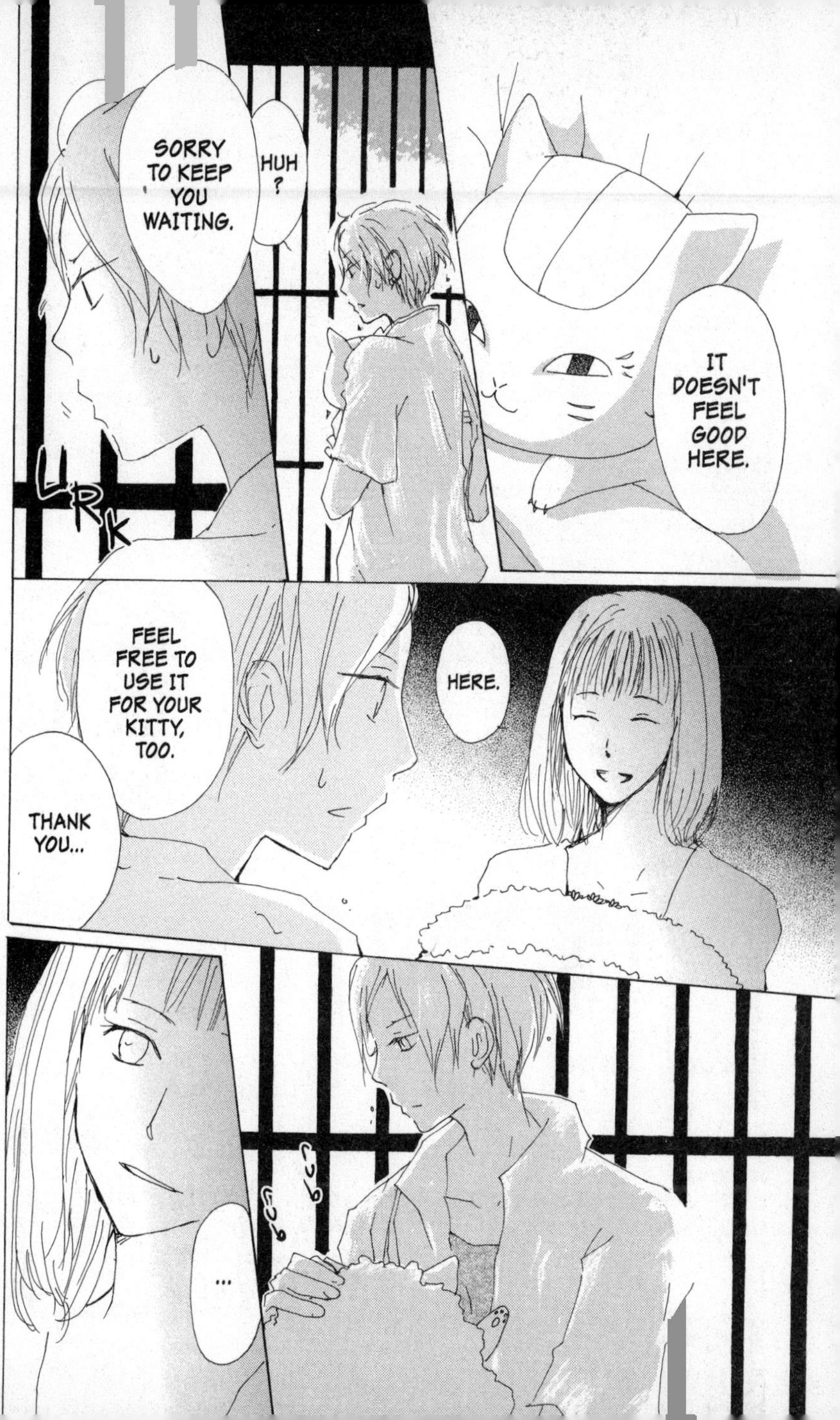
IT DOESN'T FEEL GOOD HERE.
HUH?
SORRY TO KEEP YOU WAITING.
LRK
HERE.
FEEL FREE TO USE IT FOR YOUR KITTY, TOO.
THANK YOU...
...

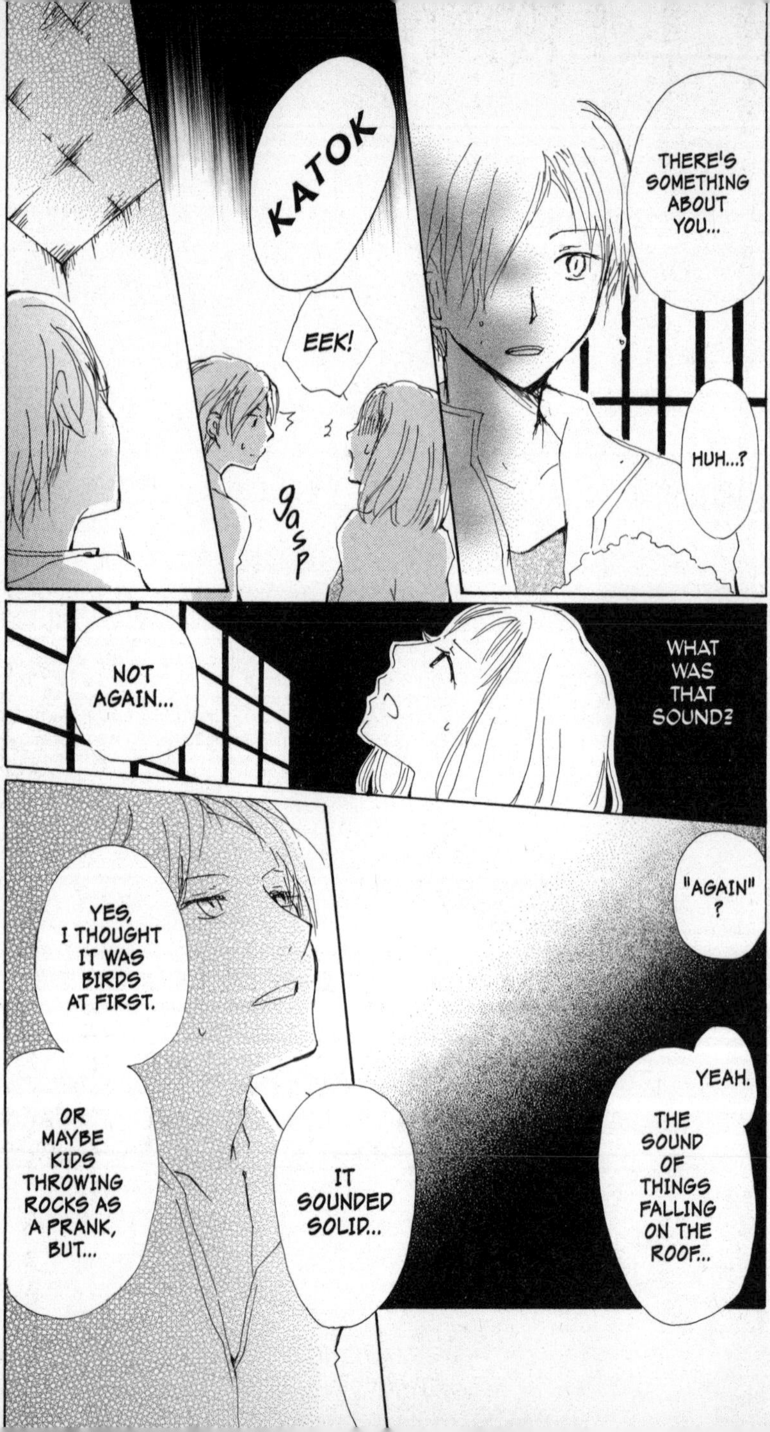
THERE'S SOMETHING ABOUT YOU...
HUH...?
KATOK
EEK!
gasp
WHAT WAS THAT SOUND?
NOT AGAIN...
"AGAIN"?
YEAH.
THE SOUND OF THINGS FALLING ON THE ROOF...
YES, I THOUGHT IT WAS BIRDS AT FIRST.
OR MAYBE KIDS THROWING ROCKS AS A PRANK, BUT...
IT SOUNDED SOLID...

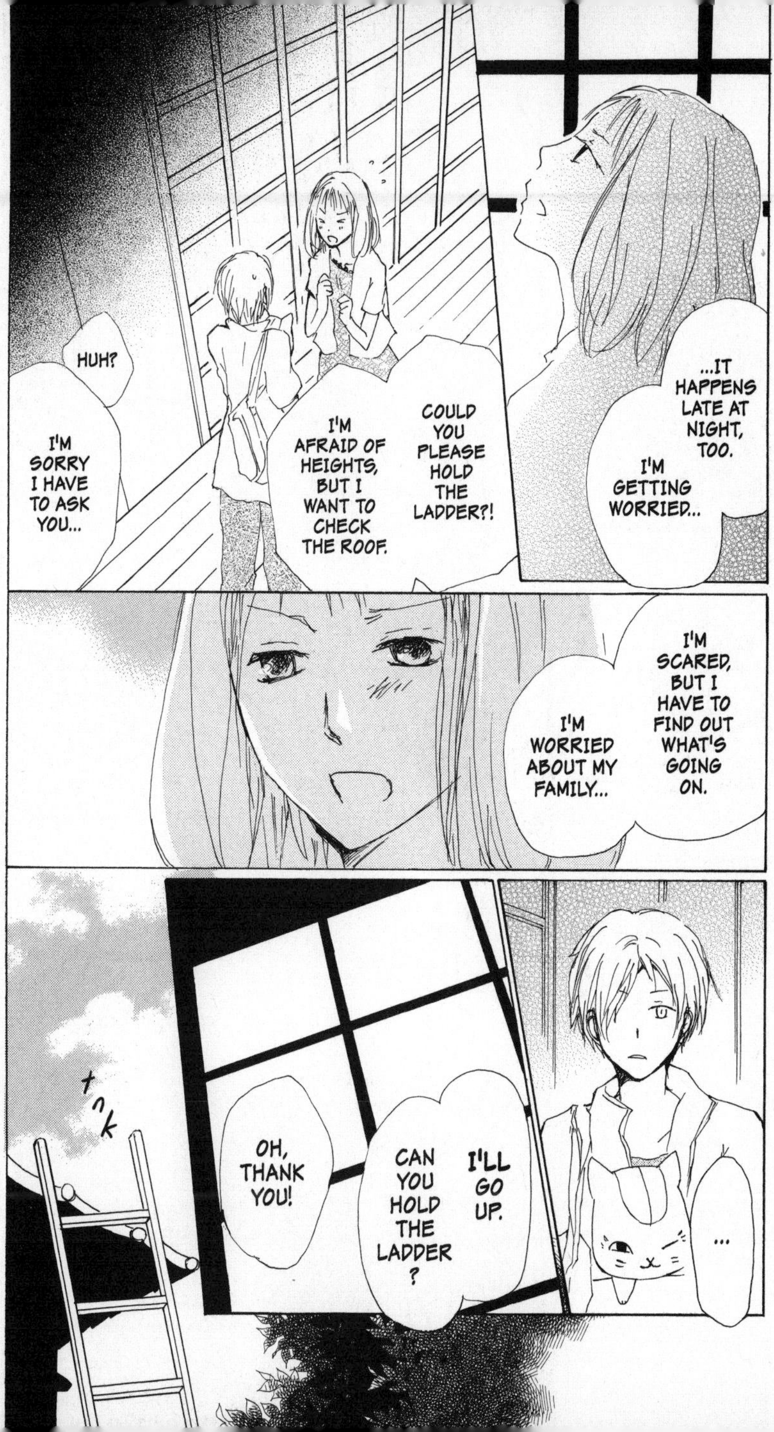
...IT HAPPENS LATE AT NIGHT, TOO.
I'M GETTING WORRIED...
COULD YOU PLEASE HOLD THE LADDER?!
I'M AFRAID OF HEIGHTS, BUT I WANT TO CHECK THE ROOF.
HUH?
I'M SORRY I HAVE TO ASK YOU...
I'M SCARED, BUT I HAVE TO FIND OUT WHAT'S GOING ON.
I'M WORRIED ABOUT MY FAMILY...
...
I'LL GO UP.
CAN YOU HOLD THE LADDER?
OH, THANK YOU!

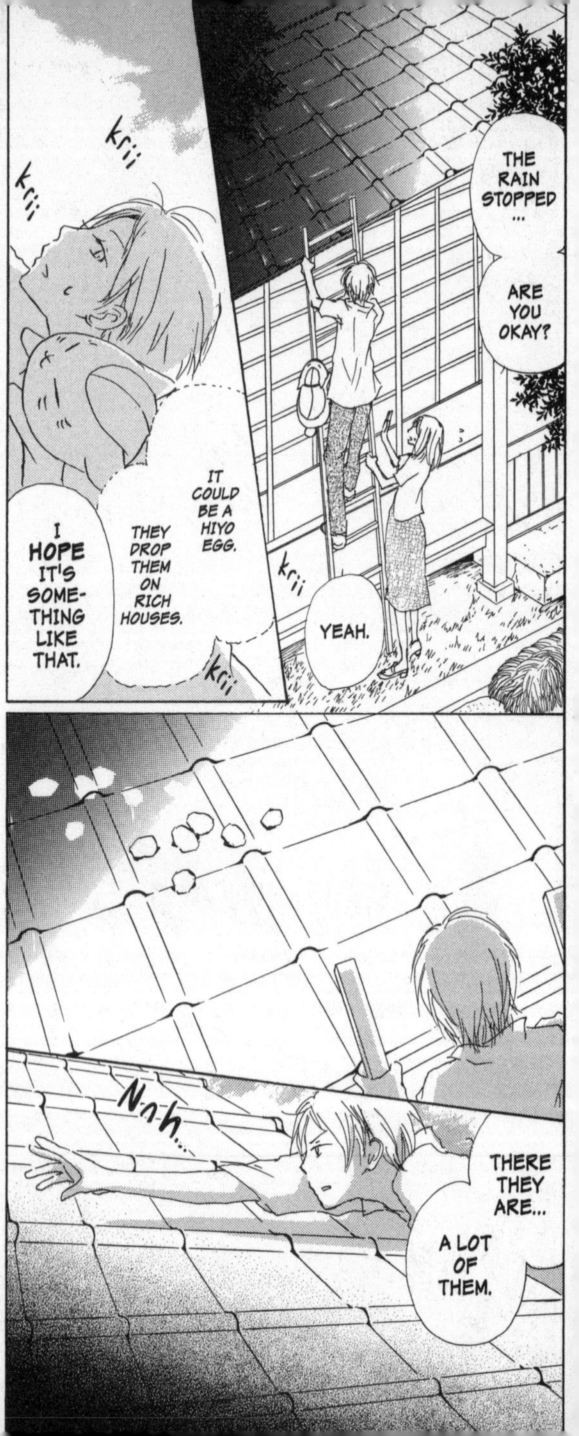
THE RAIN STOPPED ...
ARE YOU OKAY?
YEAH.
krii
IT COULD BE A HIYO EGG.
THEY DROP THEM ON RICH HOUSES.
I HOPE IT'S SOMETHING LIKE THAT.
krii
krii
krii
Nnh...
THERE THEY ARE...
A LOT OF THEM.

01

Hello, I'm Midorikawa. This is the 15th volume of Natsume's Book of Friends.

Each episode is exciting and fun for me to draw. I'm so happy that I get to continue to work on Natsume. Thank you so much.

I probably haven't changed much, but I'll work hard to continue going forward while respecting my initial goals. Thank you for your support.

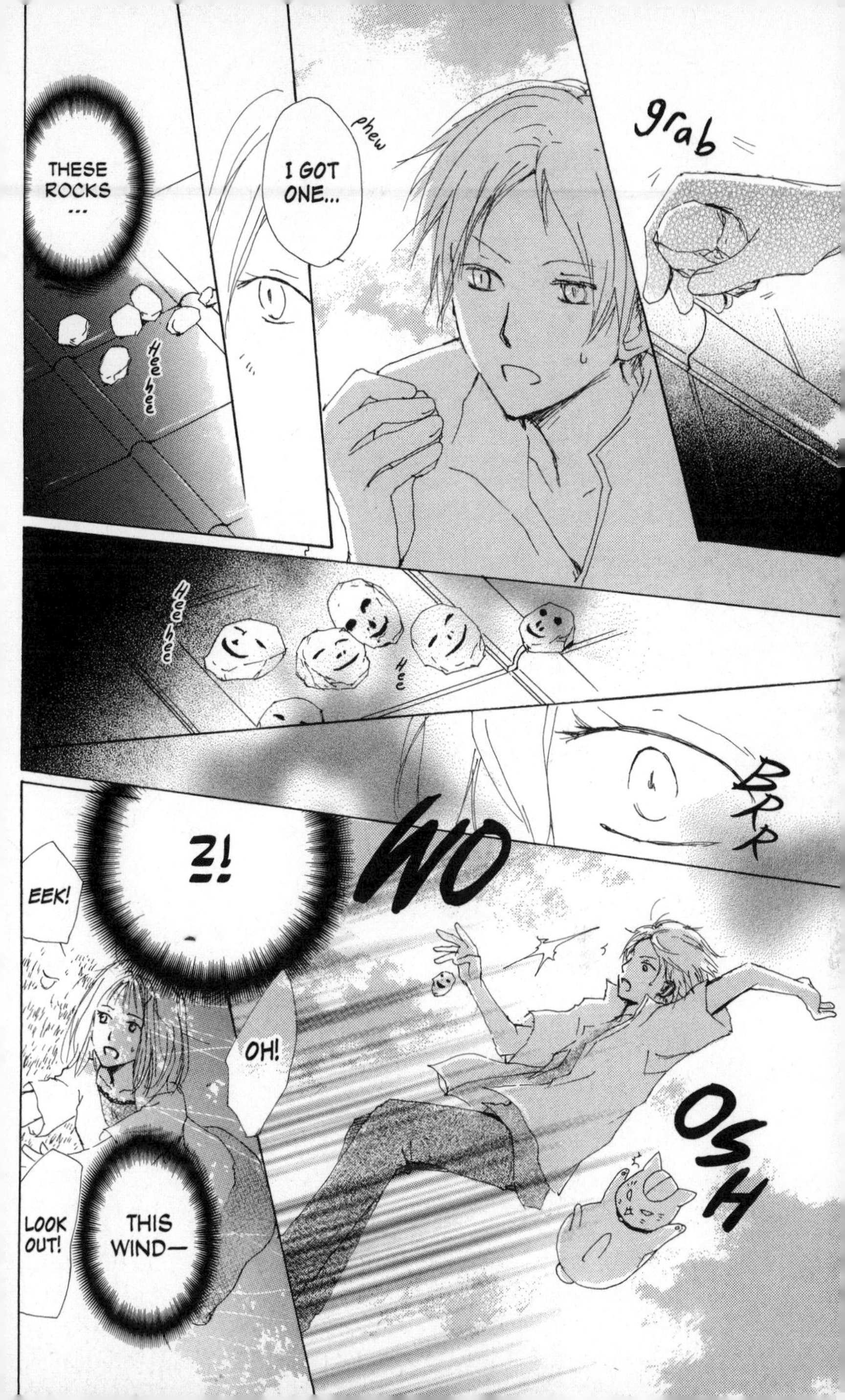
grab
phew
I GOT ONE...
THESE ROCKS ...
Hee hee
Hee hee
Hee
BRR
WO
OSH
!?
OH!
EEK!
THIS WIND—
LOOK OUT!

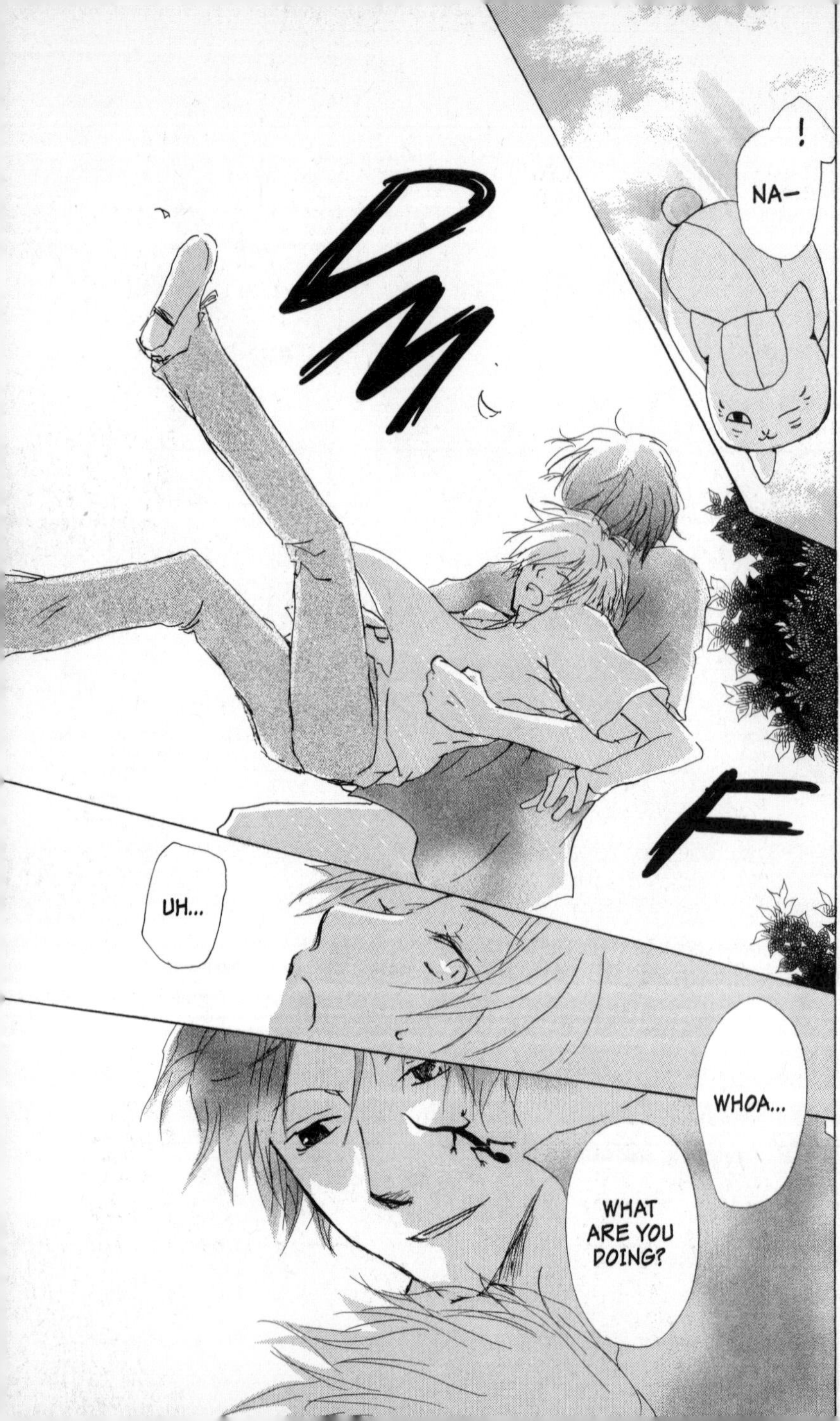
!
NA—
DM
F
UH...
WHOA...
WHAT ARE YOU DOING?

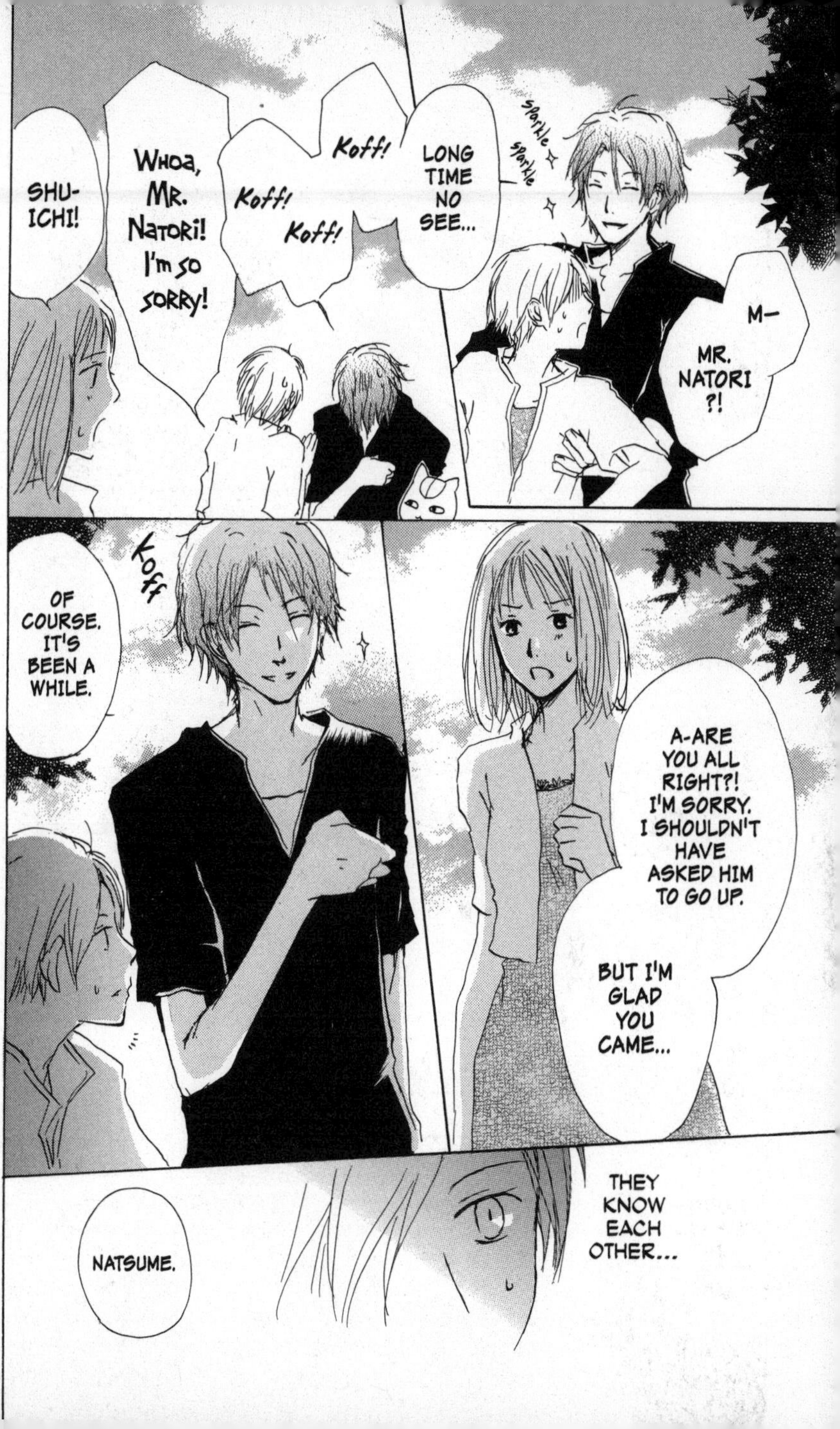
M— MR. NATORI?!
sparkle sparkle
LONG TIME NO SEE...
Koff!
Koff!
Koff!
Whoa, Mr. Natori! I'm so sorry!
SHUICHI!
A-ARE YOU ALL RIGHT?! I'M SORRY. I SHOULDN'T HAVE ASKED HIM TO GO UP.
BUT I'M GLAD YOU CAME...
Koff
OF COURSE. IT'S BEEN A WHILE.
THEY KNOW EACH OTHER...
NATSUME.

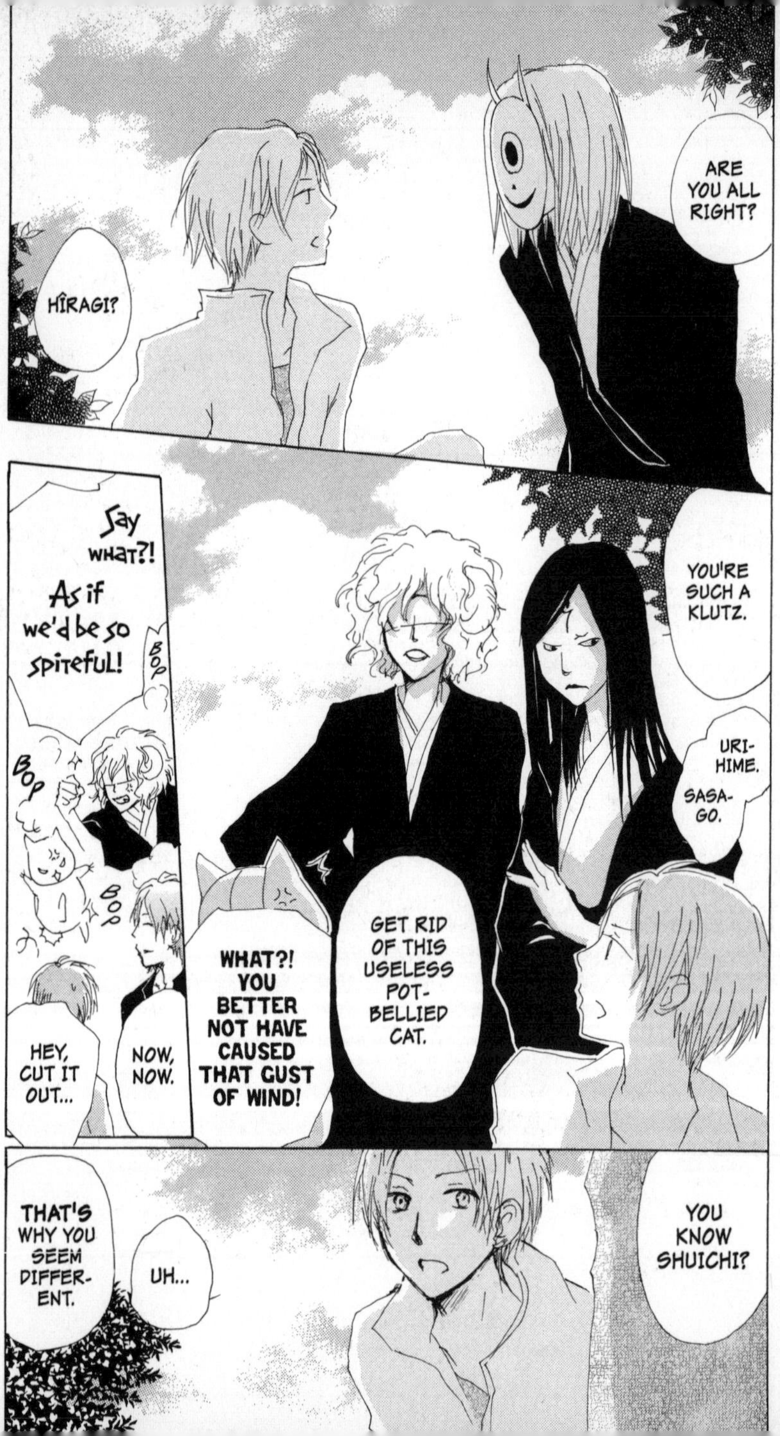
ARE YOU ALL RIGHT?
HÎRAGI?
YOU'RE SUCH A KLUTZ.
URI-HIME.
SASA-GO.
GET RID OF THIS USELESS POT-BELLIED CAT.
WHAT?! YOU BETTER NOT HAVE CAUSED THAT GUST OF WIND!
Say what?!
As if we'd be so spiteful!
BOP
BOP
BOP
NOW, NOW.
HEY, CUT IT OUT...
YOU KNOW SHUICHI?
UH...
THAT'S WHY YOU SEEM DIFFER-ENT.

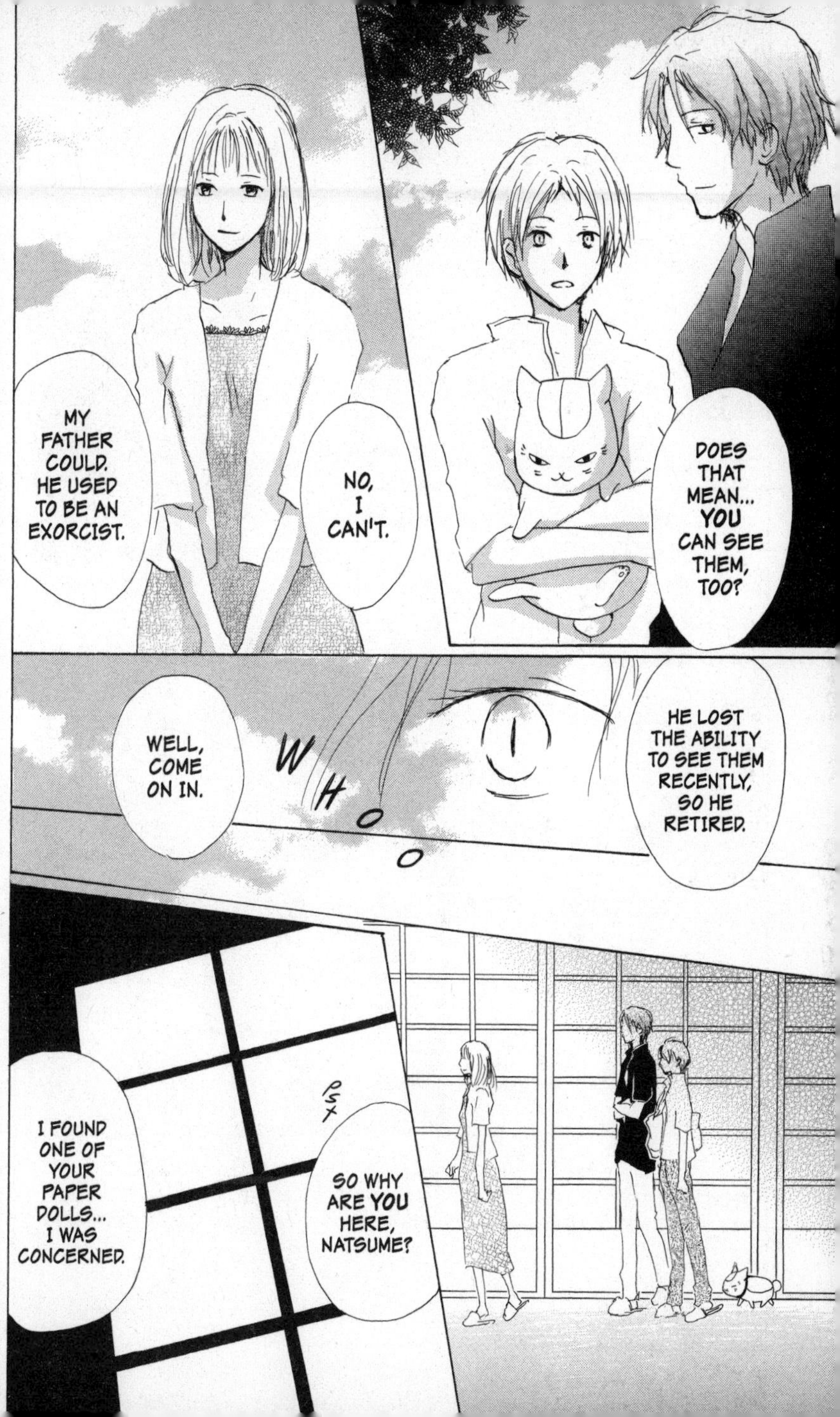
DOES THAT MEAN... YOU CAN SEE THEM, TOO?
NO, I CAN'T.
MY FATHER COULD. HE USED TO BE AN EXORCIST.
HE LOST THE ABILITY TO SEE THEM RECENTLY, SO HE RETIRED.
WHOO
WELL, COME ON IN.
SO WHY ARE YOU HERE, NATSUME?
I FOUND ONE OF YOUR PAPER DOLLS... I WAS CONCERNED.

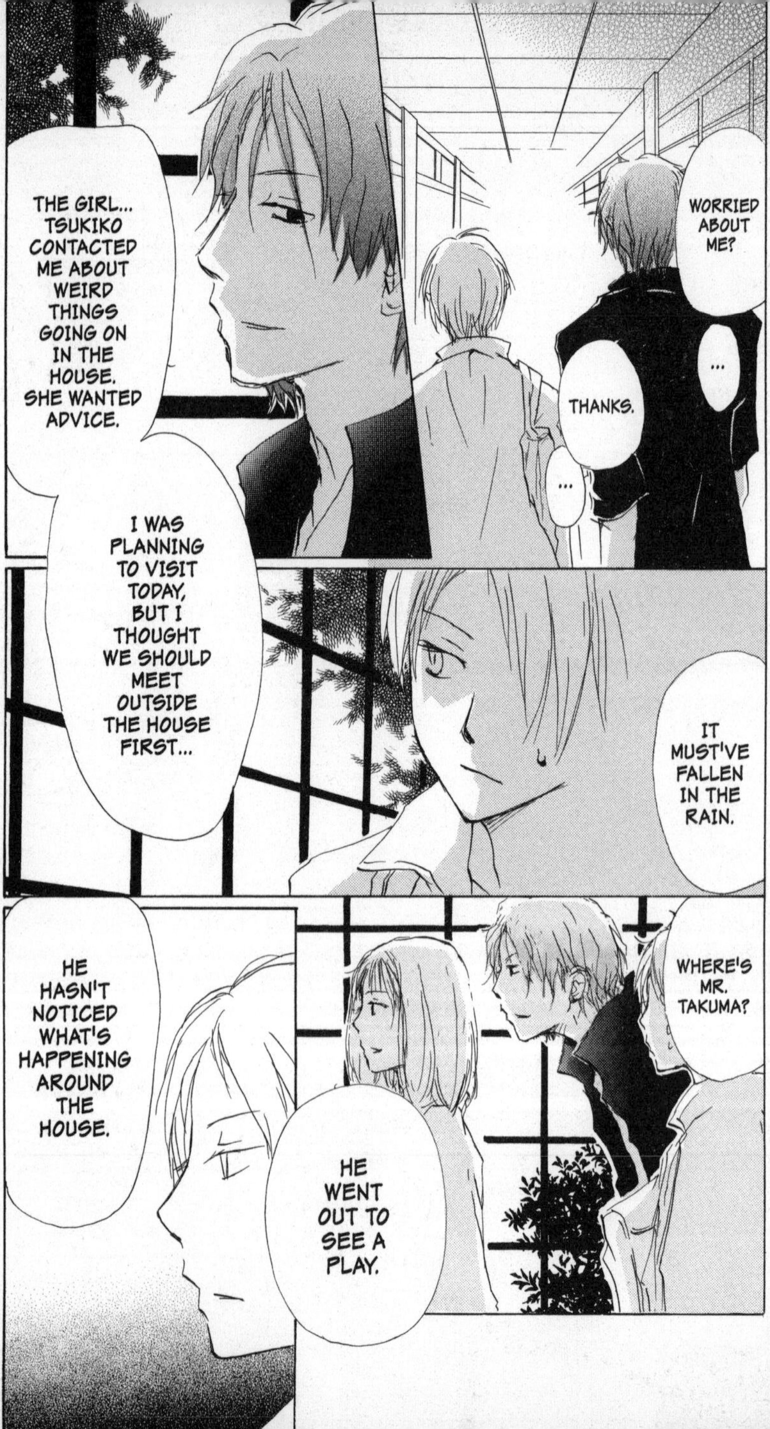
WORRIED ABOUT ME?
...
THANKS.
...
THE GIRL... TSUKIKO CONTACTED ME ABOUT WEIRD THINGS GOING ON IN THE HOUSE. SHE WANTED ADVICE.
I WAS PLANNING TO VISIT TODAY, BUT I THOUGHT WE SHOULD MEET OUTSIDE THE HOUSE FIRST...
IT MUST'VE FALLEN IN THE RAIN.
WHERE'S MR. TAKUMA?
HE WENT OUT TO SEE A PLAY.
HE HASN'T NOTICED WHAT'S HAPPENING AROUND THE HOUSE.

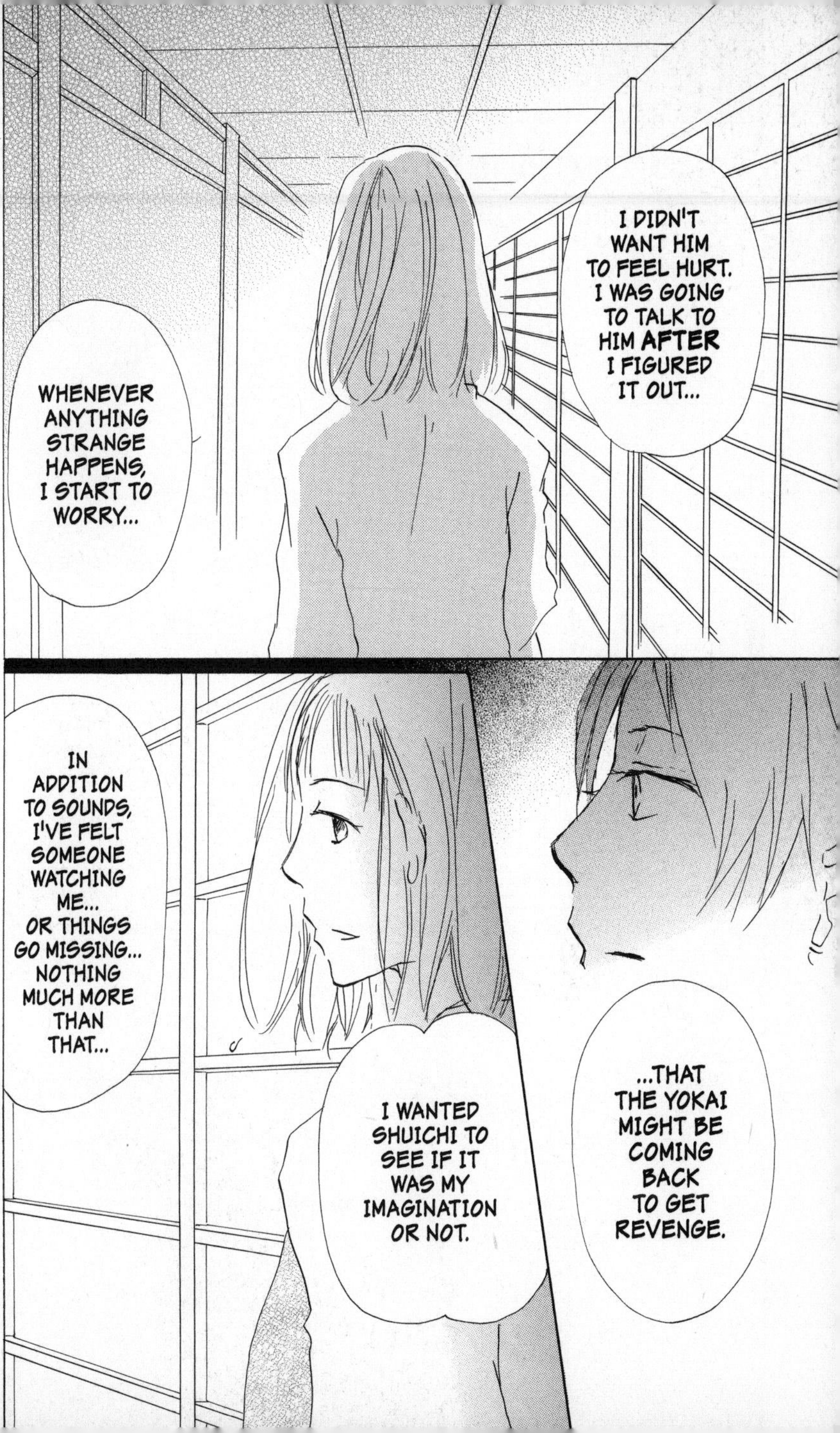
I DIDN'T WANT HIM TO FEEL HURT. I WAS GOING TO TALK TO HIM **AFTER** I FIGURED IT OUT...
WHENEVER ANYTHING STRANGE HAPPENS, I START TO WORRY...
...THAT THE YOKAI MIGHT BE COMING BACK TO GET REVENGE.
I WANTED SHUICHI TO SEE IF IT WAS MY IMAGINATION OR NOT.
IN ADDITION TO SOUNDS, I'VE FELT SOMEONE WATCHING ME... OR THINGS GO MISSING... NOTHING MUCH MORE THAN THAT...

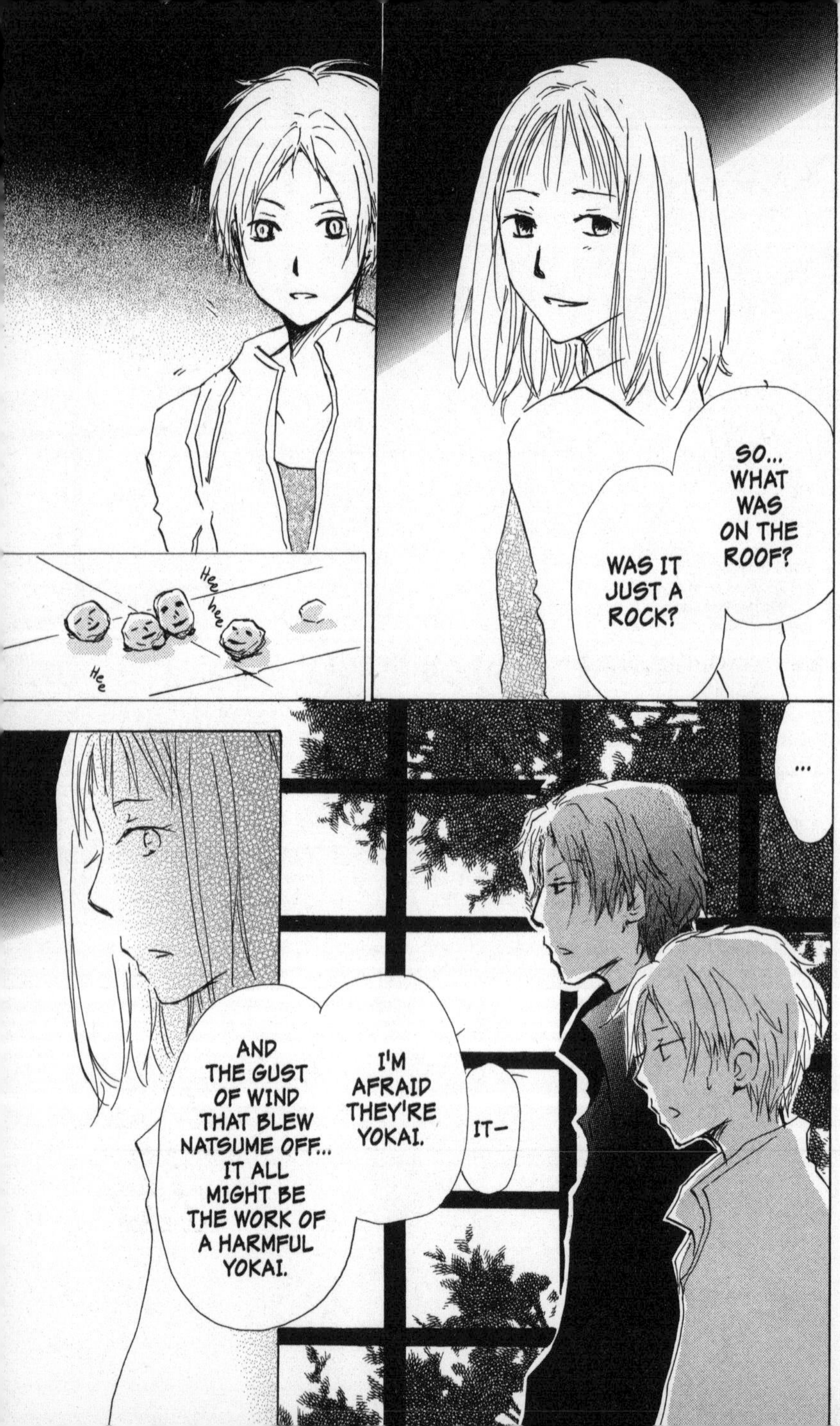
SO... WHAT WAS ON THE ROOF?
WAS IT JUST A ROCK?
Hee hee
Hee
...
IT—
I'M AFRAID THEY'RE YOKAI.
AND THE GUST OF WIND THAT BLEW NATSUME OFF... IT ALL MIGHT BE THE WORK OF A HARMFUL YOKAI.

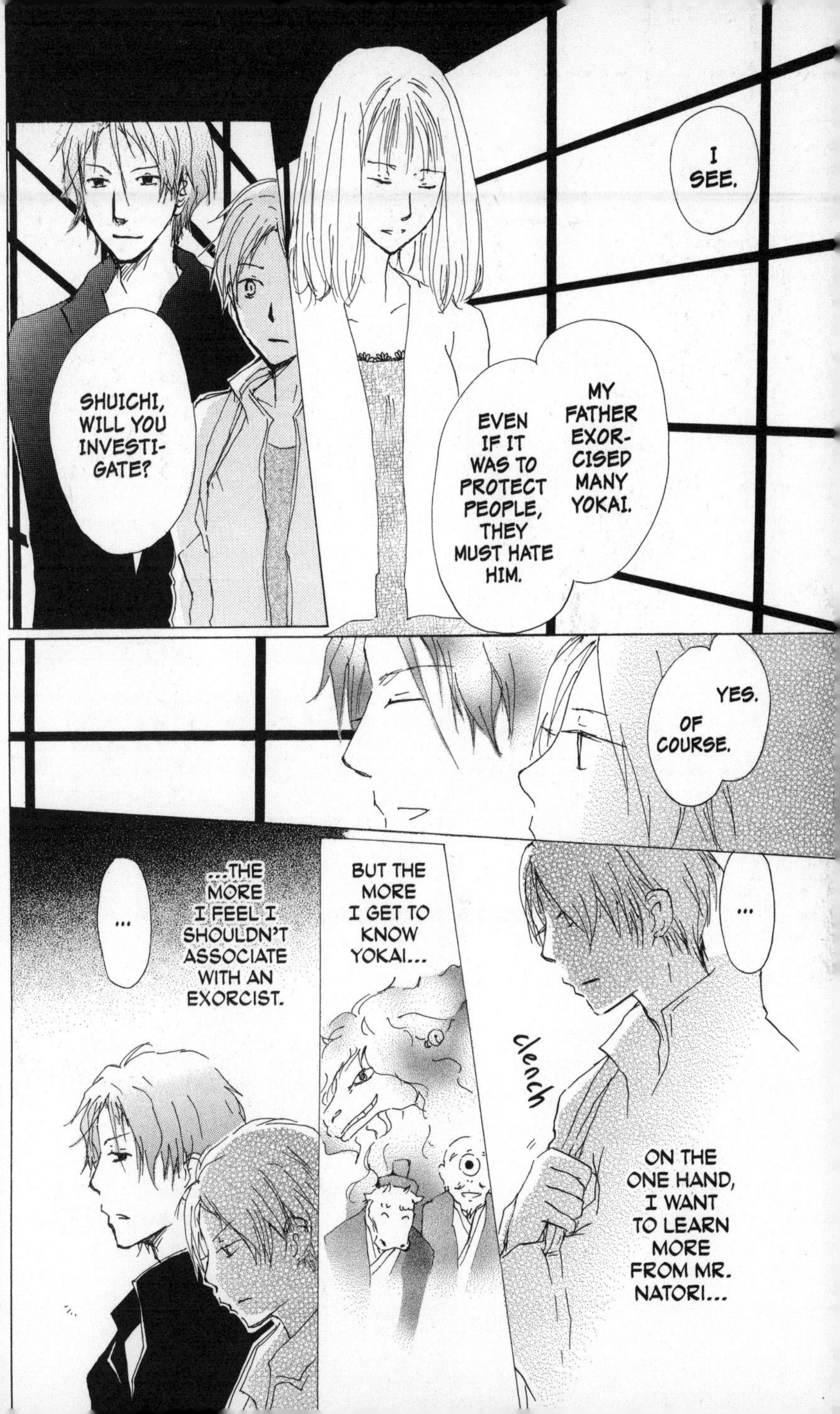
I SEE.
MY FATHER EXORCISED MANY YOKAI. EVEN IF IT WAS TO PROTECT PEOPLE, THEY MUST HATE HIM.
SHUICHI, WILL YOU INVESTIGATE?
YES. OF COURSE.
...
clench
ON THE ONE HAND, I WANT TO LEARN MORE FROM MR. NATORI...
BUT THE MORE I GET TO KNOW YOKAI...
...THE MORE I FEEL I SHOULDN'T ASSOCIATE WITH AN EXORCIST.
...

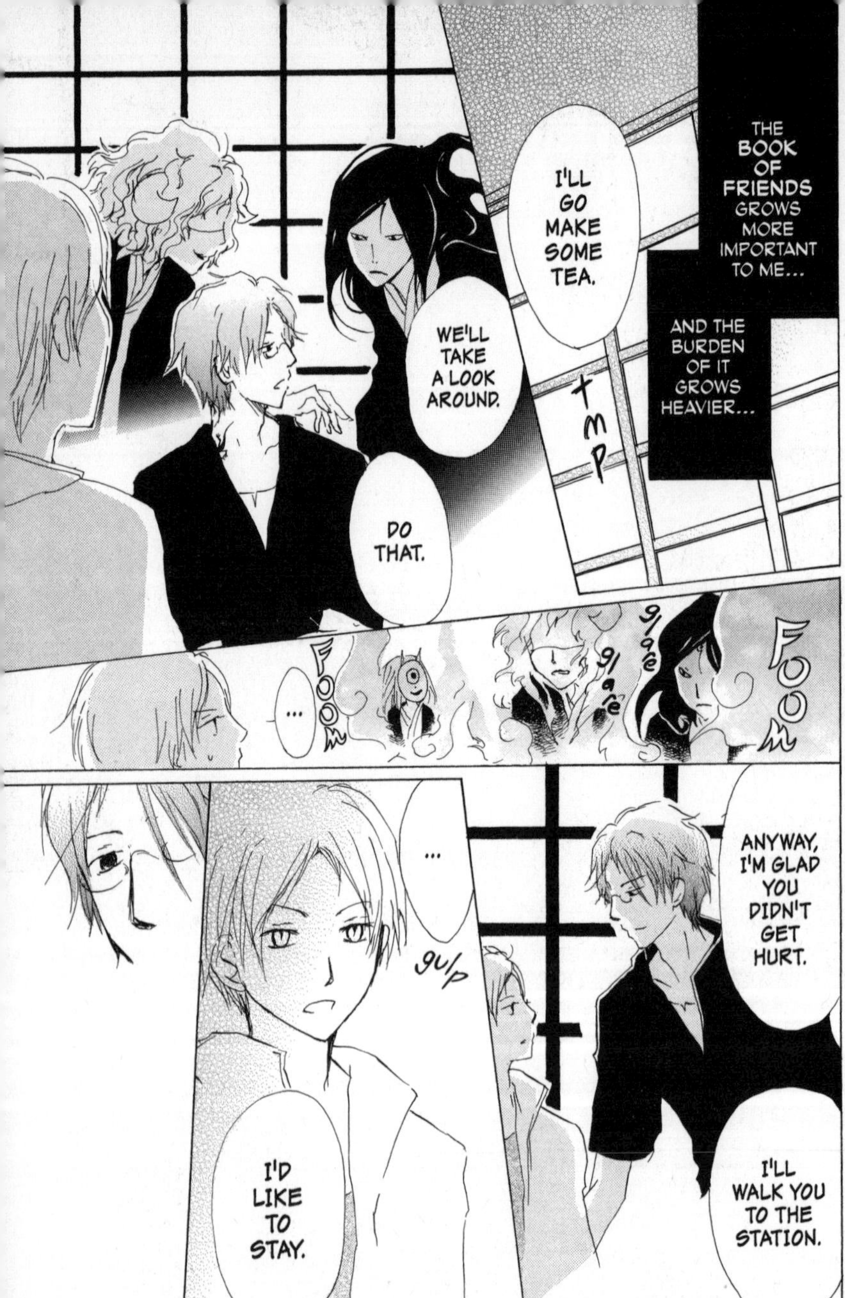
THE BOOK OF FRIENDS GROWS MORE IMPORTANT TO ME...
AND THE BURDEN OF IT GROWS HEAVIER...
I'LL GO MAKE SOME TEA.
tmp
WE'LL TAKE A LOOK AROUND.
DO THAT.
FOOOM
glare
glare
FOOOM
...
ANYWAY, I'M GLAD YOU DIDN'T GET HURT.
I'LL WALK YOU TO THE STATION.
...
gulp
I'D LIKE TO STAY.

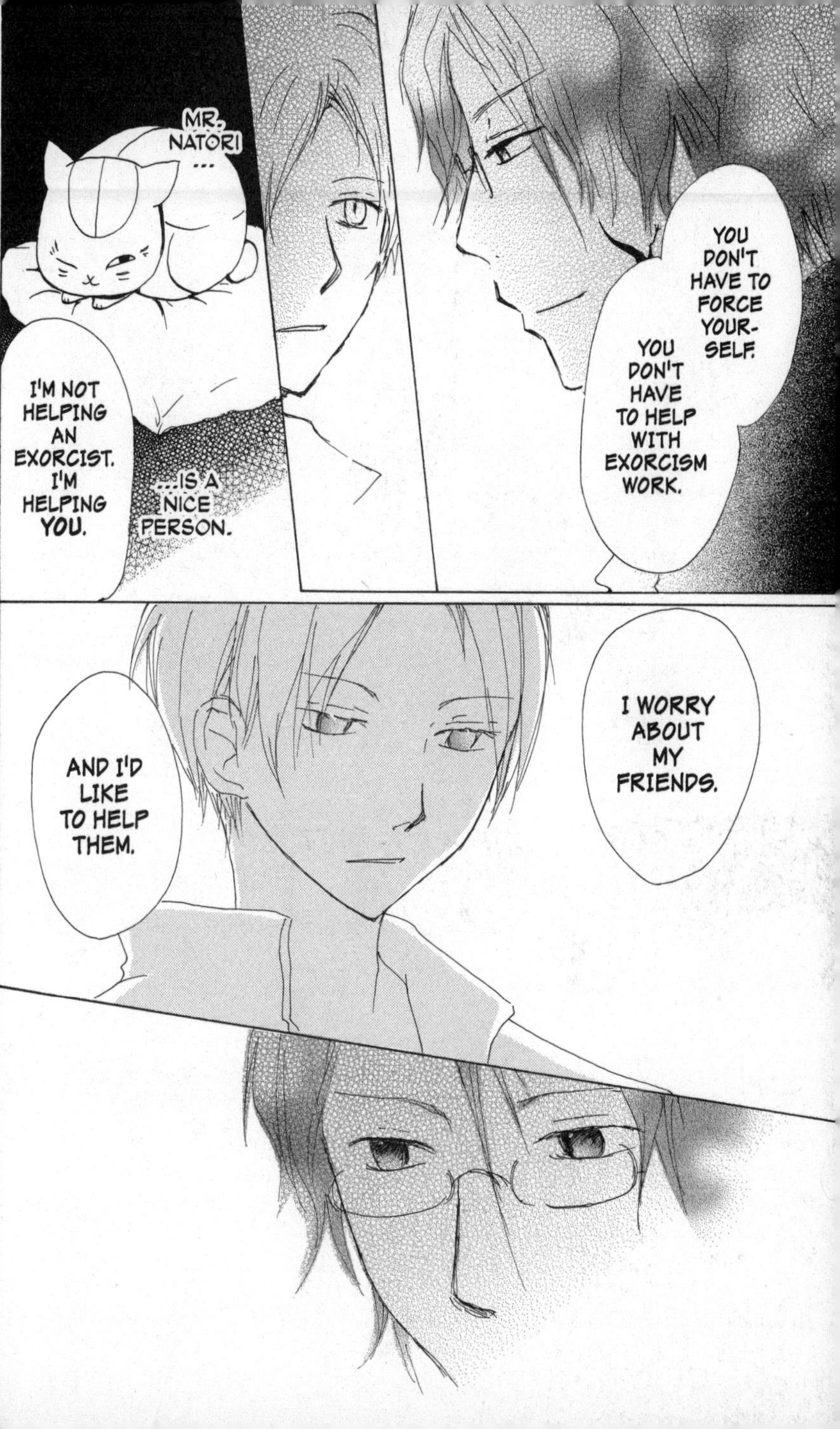
YOU DON'T HAVE TO FORCE YOUR-SELF.
YOU DON'T HAVE TO HELP WITH EXORCISM WORK.
MR. NATORI ...
...IS A NICE PERSON.
I'M NOT HELPING AN EXORCIST. I'M HELPING YOU.
I WORRY ABOUT MY FRIENDS.
AND I'D LIKE TO HELP THEM.

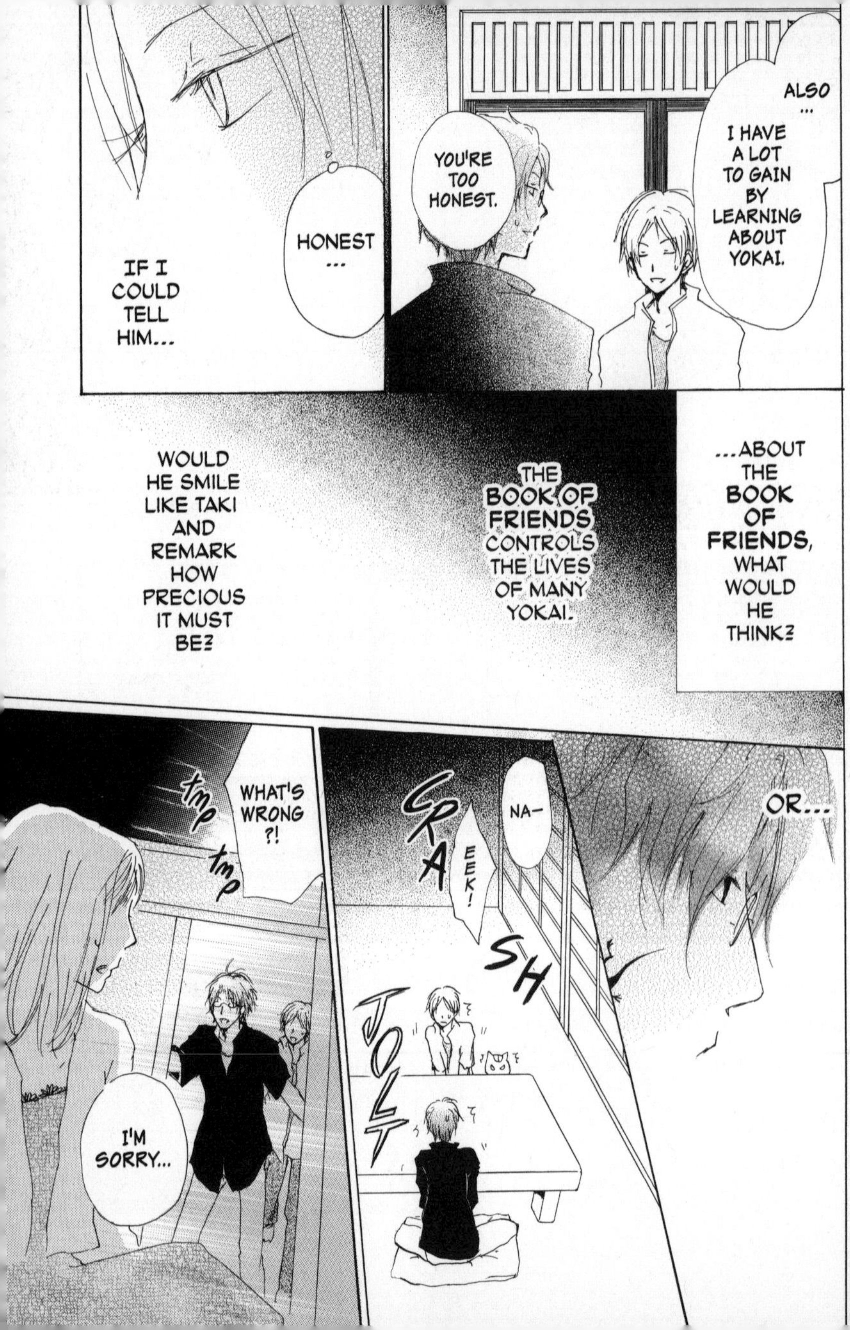

ALSO... I HAVE A LOT TO GAIN BY LEARNING ABOUT YOKAI.
YOU'RE TOO HONEST.
HONEST...
IF I COULD TELL HIM...
...ABOUT THE BOOK OF FRIENDS, WHAT WOULD HE THINK?
THE BOOK OF FRIENDS CONTROLS THE LIVES OF MANY YOKAI.
WOULD HE SMILE LIKE TAKI AND REMARK HOW PRECIOUS IT MUST BE?
OR...
NA—
EEK!
CRASH
JOLT
WHAT'S WRONG?!
tmp tmp
I'M SORRY...

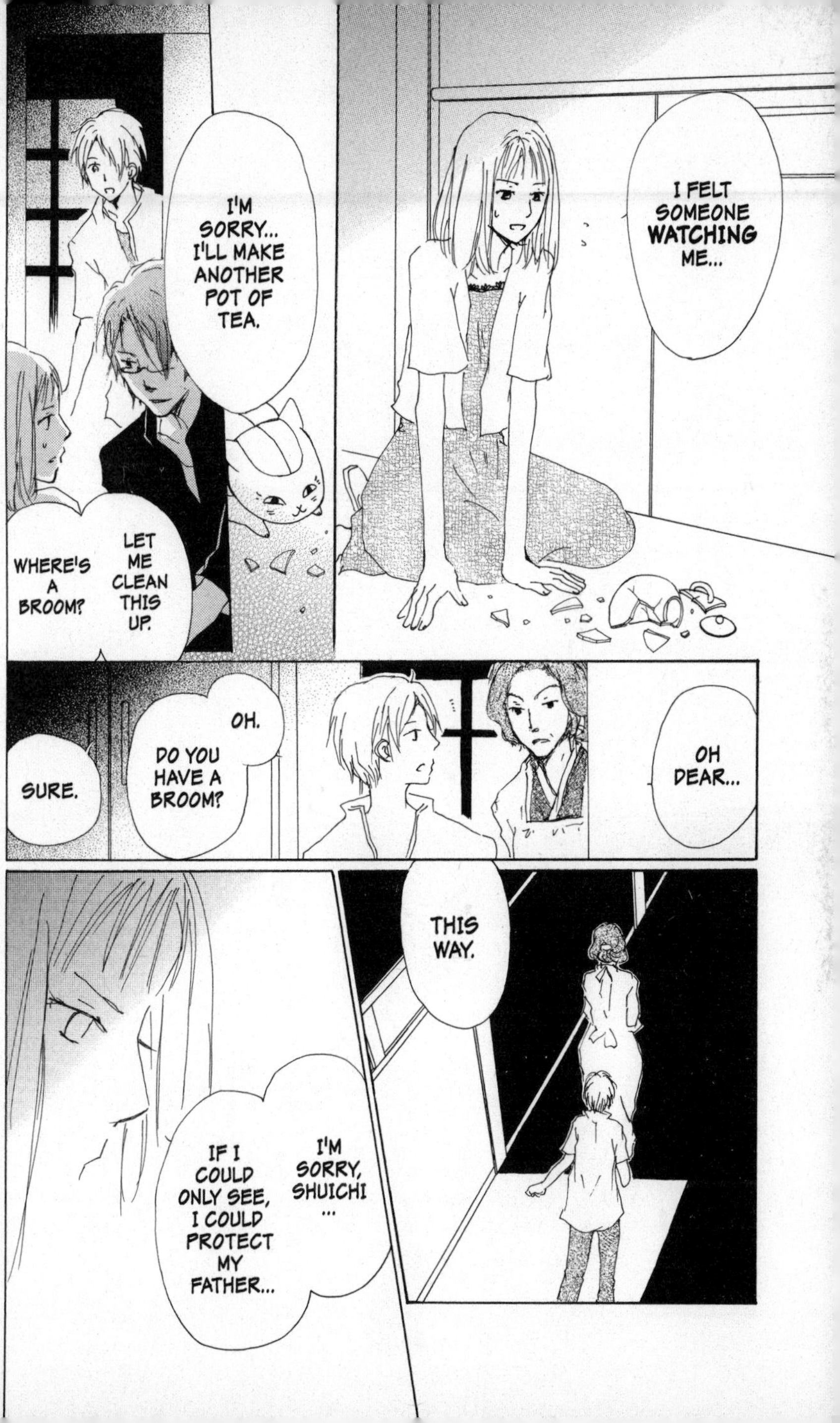
I FELT SOMEONE WATCHING ME...
I'M SORRY... I'LL MAKE ANOTHER POT OF TEA.
LET ME CLEAN THIS UP.
WHERE'S A BROOM?
OH DEAR...
OH.
DO YOU HAVE A BROOM?
SURE.
THIS WAY.
I'M SORRY, SHUICHI...
IF I COULD ONLY SEE, I COULD PROTECT MY FATHER...

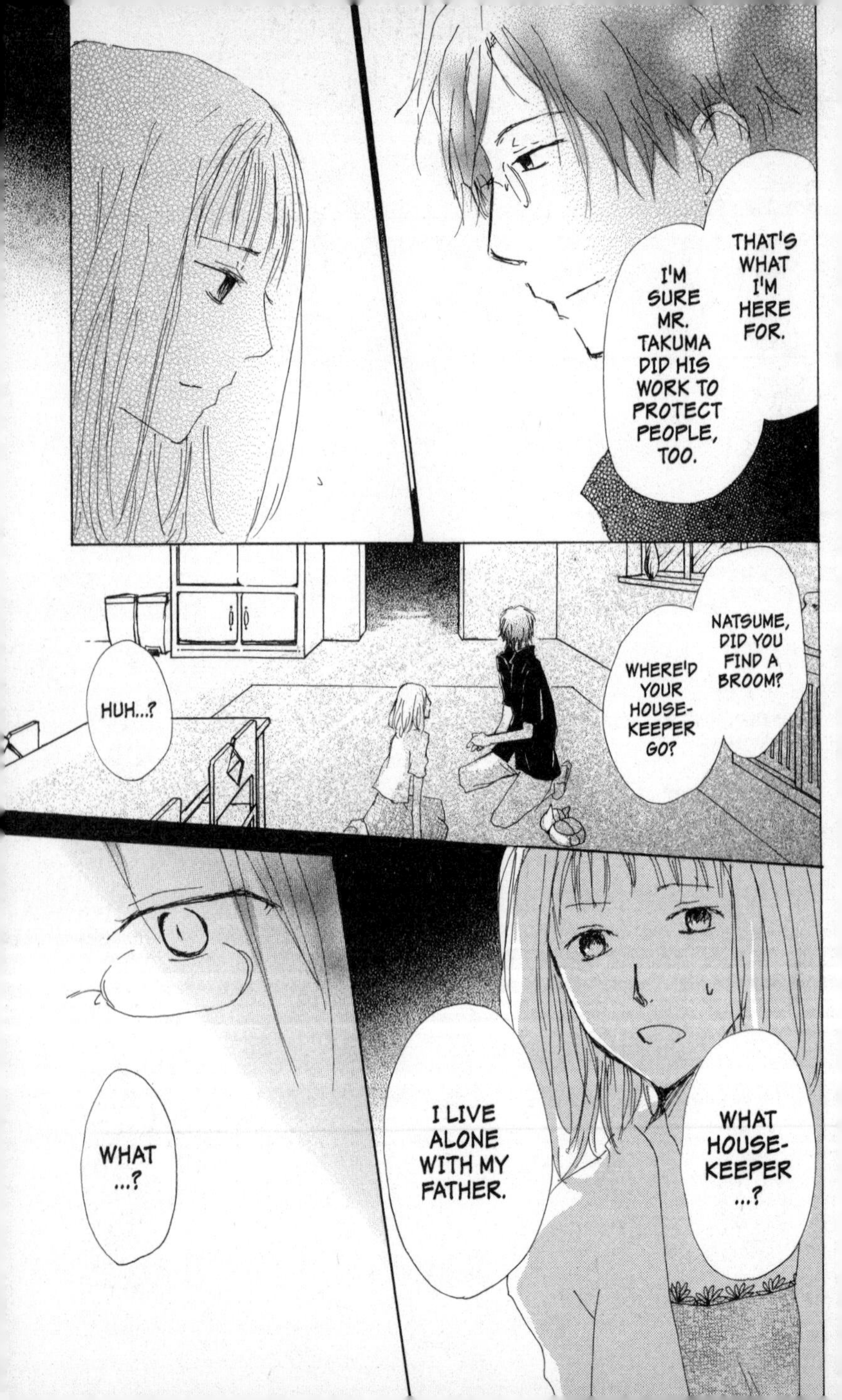
THAT'S WHAT I'M HERE FOR.
I'M SURE MR. TAKUMA DID HIS WORK TO PROTECT PEOPLE, TOO.
NATSUME, DID YOU FIND A BROOM?
WHERE'D YOUR HOUSE-KEEPER GO?
HUH...?
WHAT HOUSE-KEEPER ...?
I LIVE ALONE WITH MY FATHER.
WHAT ...?

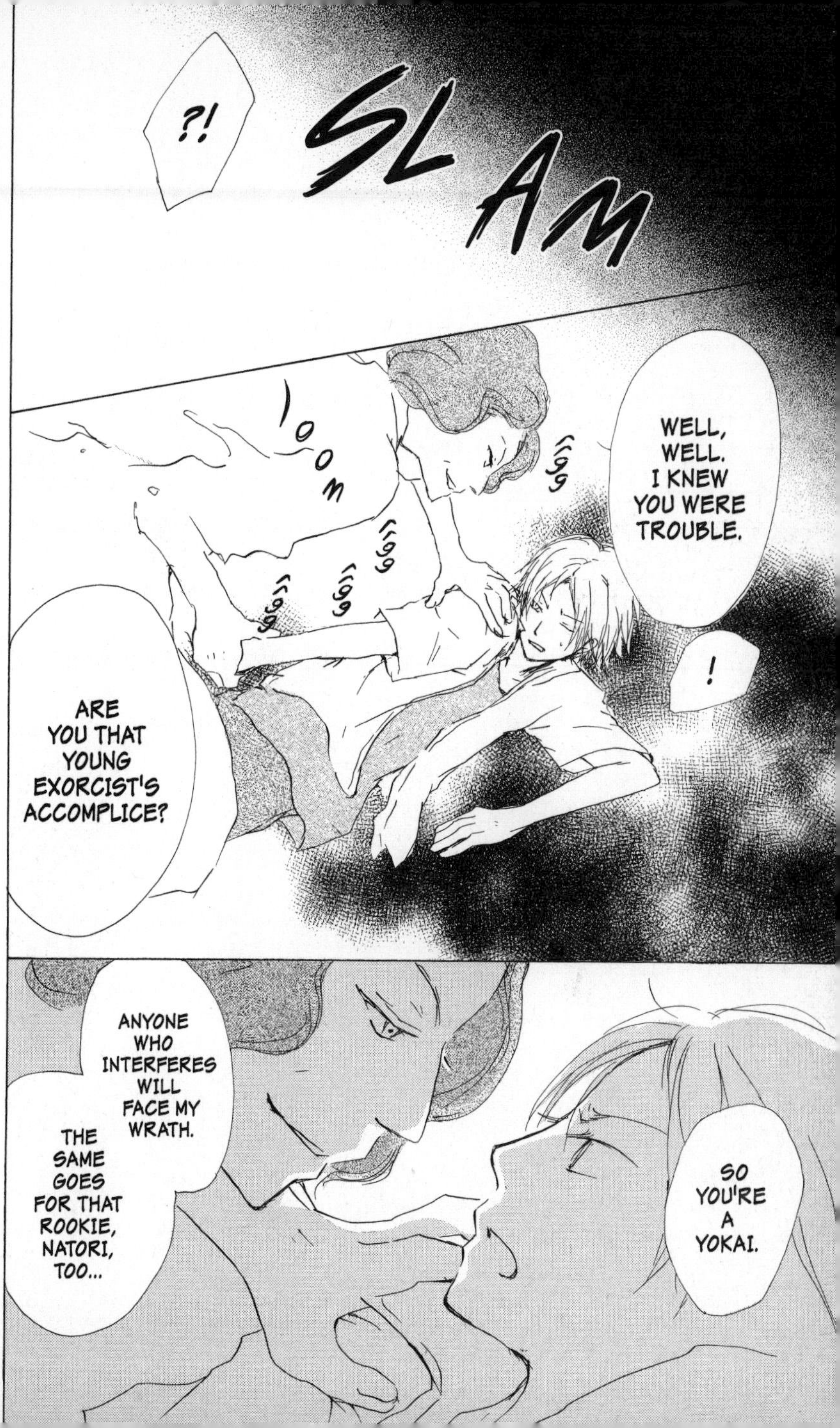
SLAM
?!
WELL, WELL. I KNEW YOU WERE TROUBLE.
!
gg
gg
gg
gg
VOOM
ARE YOU THAT YOUNG EXORCIST'S ACCOMPLICE?
SO YOU'RE A YOKAI.
ANYONE WHO INTERFERES WILL FACE MY WRATH.
THE SAME GOES FOR THAT ROOKIE, NATORI, TOO...

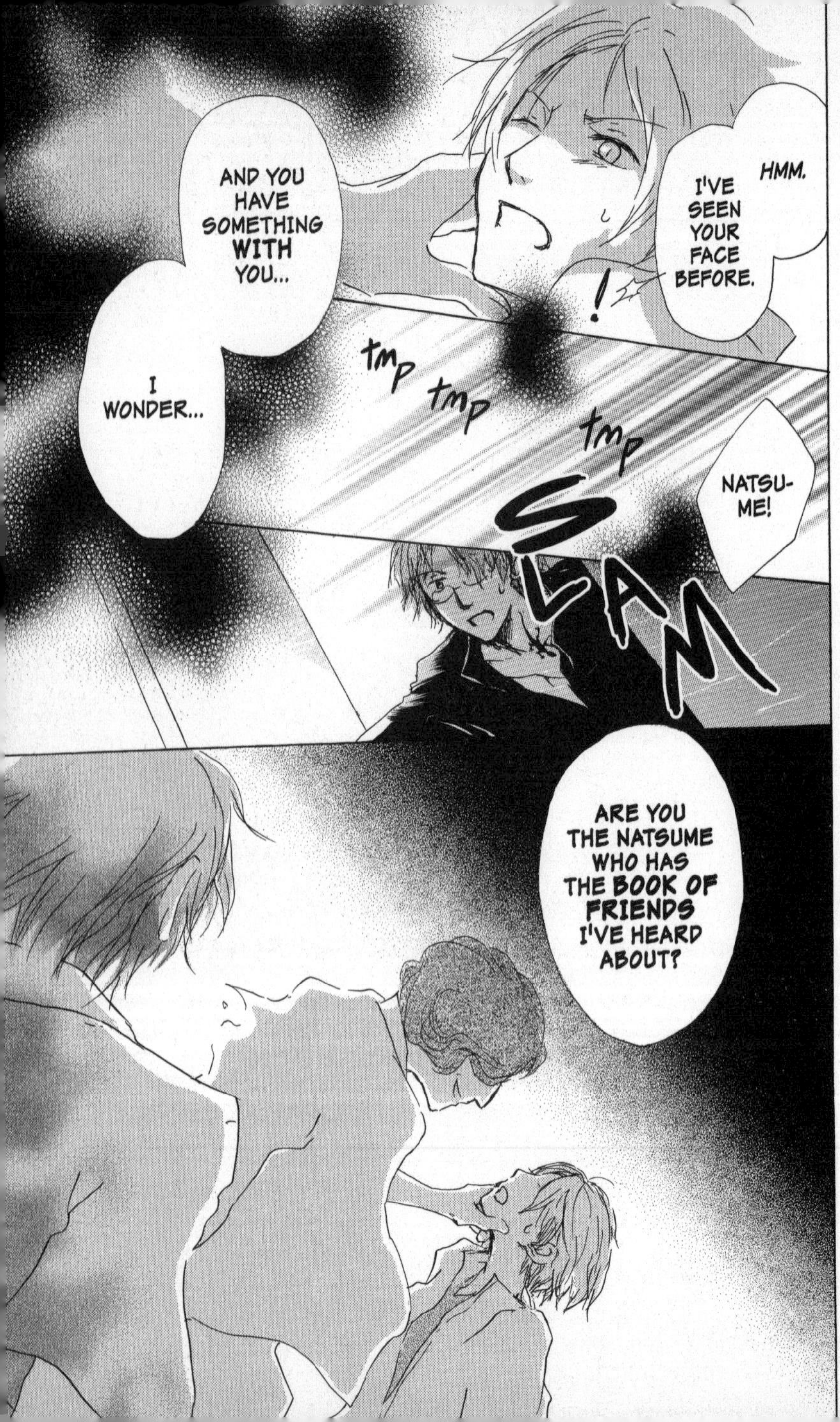
HMM. I'VE SEEN YOUR FACE BEFORE.
!
AND YOU HAVE SOMETHING WITH YOU...
I WONDER...
NATSU-ME!
tmp tmp tmp
SLAM
ARE YOU THE NATSUME WHO HAS THE BOOK OF FRIENDS I'VE HEARD ABOUT?

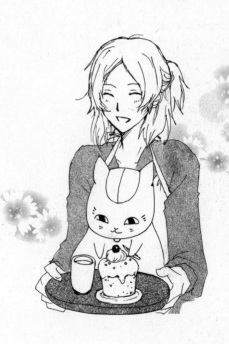

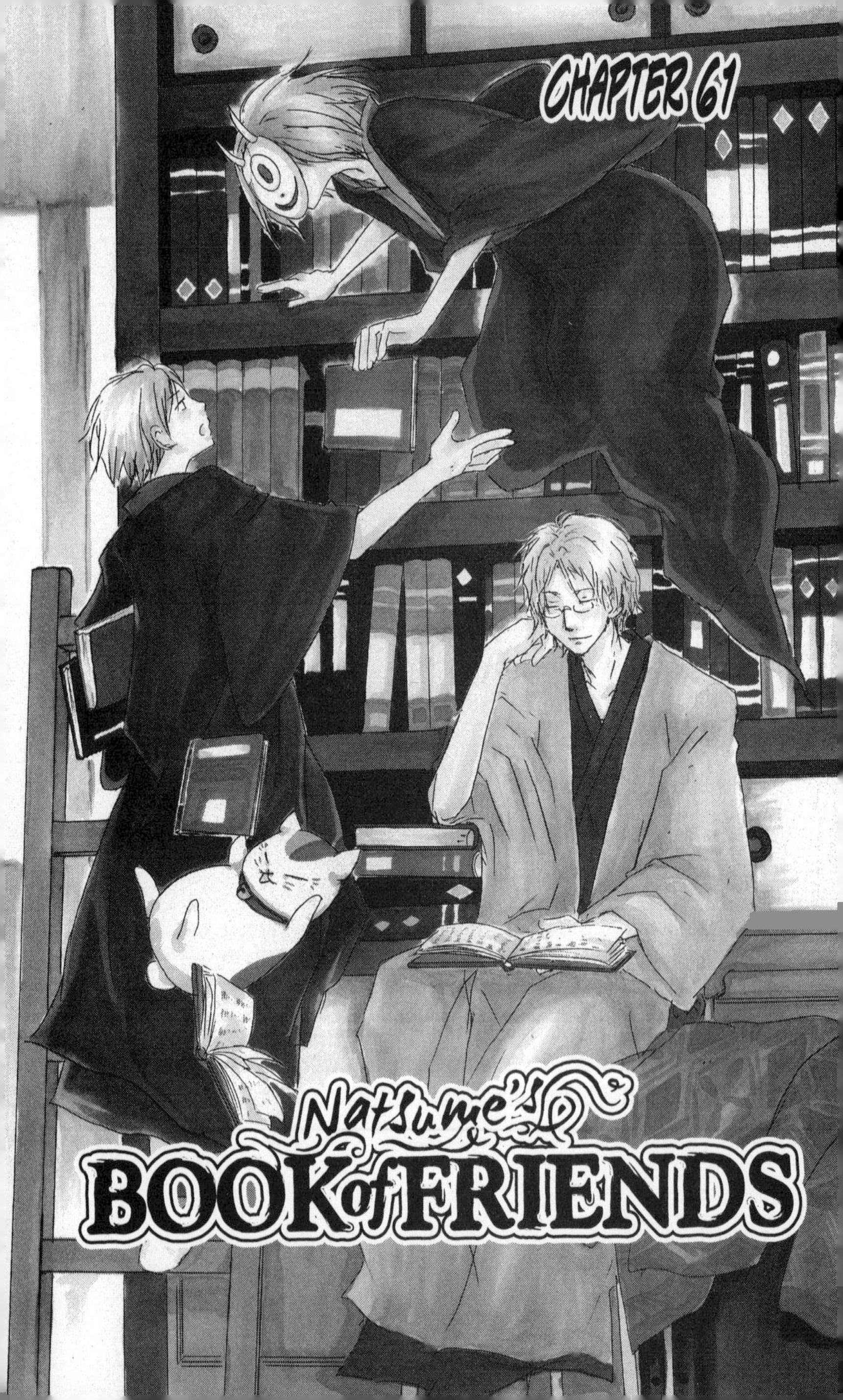
CHAPTER 61
Natsume's
BOOK of FRIENDS

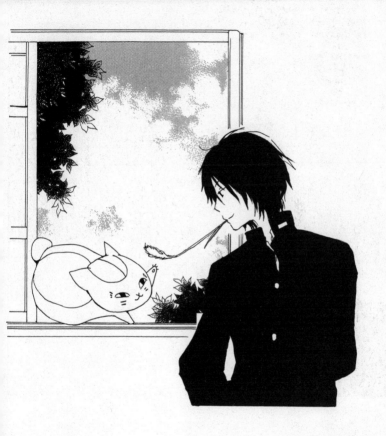

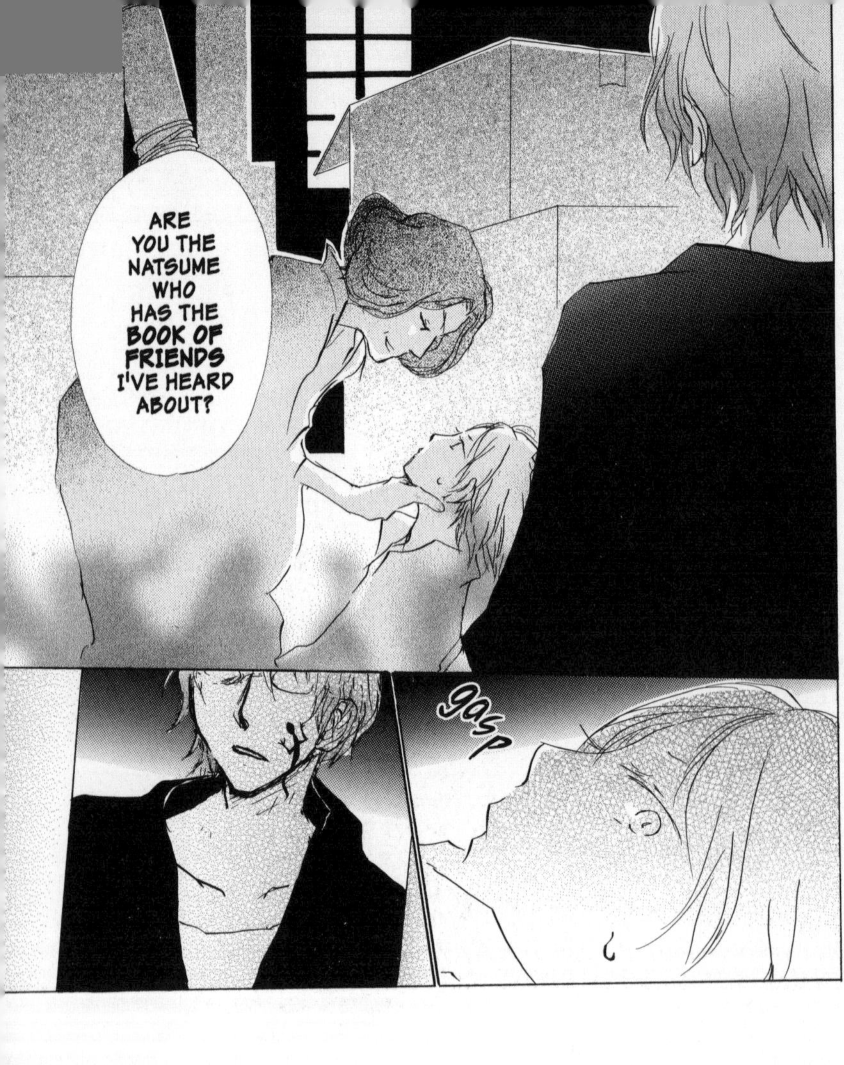
ARE YOU THE NATSUME WHO HAS THE BOOK OF FRIENDS I'VE HEARD ABOUT?
gasp

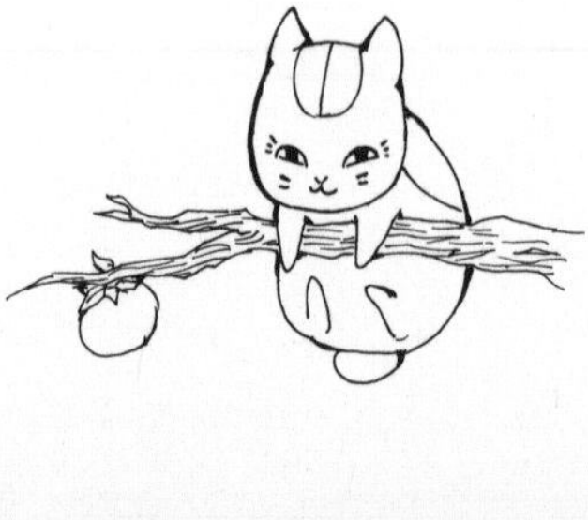

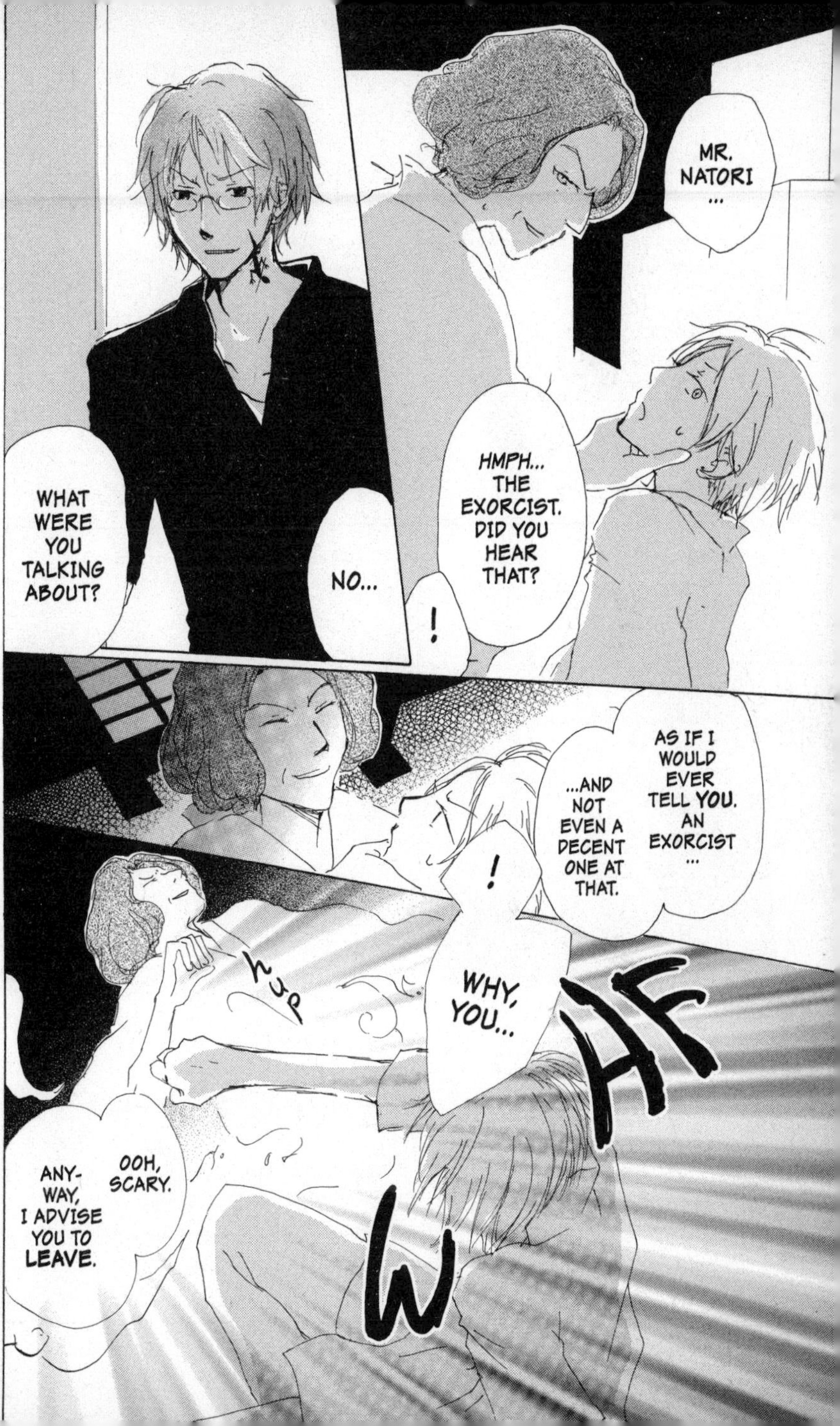
MR. NATORI ...
HMPH... THE EXORCIST. DID YOU HEAR THAT?
!
WHAT WERE YOU TALKING ABOUT?
NO...
AS IF I WOULD EVER TELL **YOU**. AN EXORCIST ...
...AND NOT EVEN A DECENT ONE AT THAT.
!
WHY, YOU...
hup
WHF
OOH, SCARY.
ANY-WAY, I ADVISE YOU TO **LEAVE**.

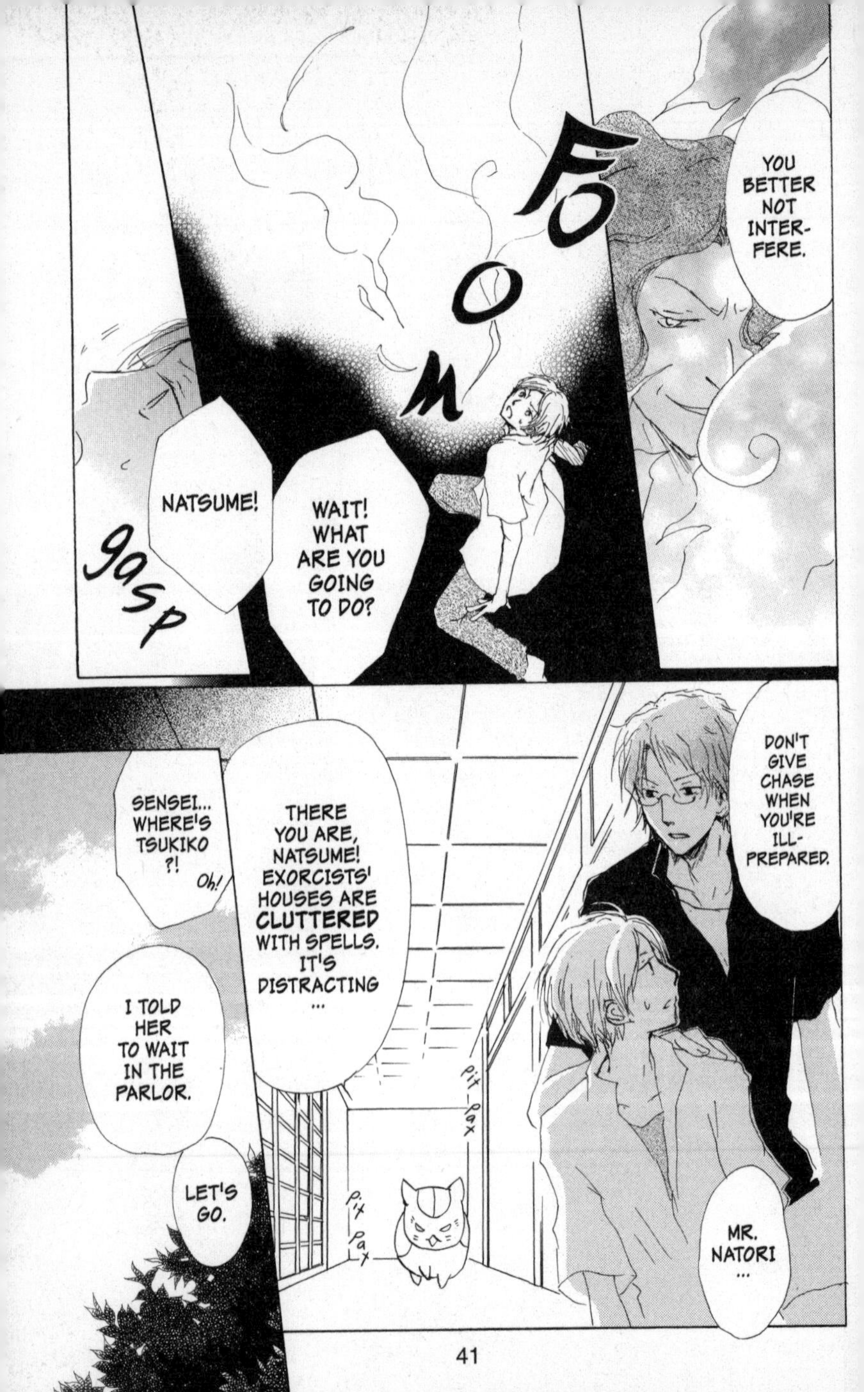
YOU BETTER NOT INTER-FERE.
FOOM
WAIT! WHAT ARE YOU GOING TO DO?
NATSUME!
gasp
DON'T GIVE CHASE WHEN YOU'RE ILL-PREPARED.
MR. NATORI ...
THERE YOU ARE, NATSUME! EXORCISTS' HOUSES ARE **CLUTTERED** WITH SPELLS. IT'S DISTRACTING ...
pit pat
SENSEI... WHERE'S TSUKIKO ?!
Oh!
I TOLD HER TO WAIT IN THE PARLOR.
LET'S GO.
pit pat

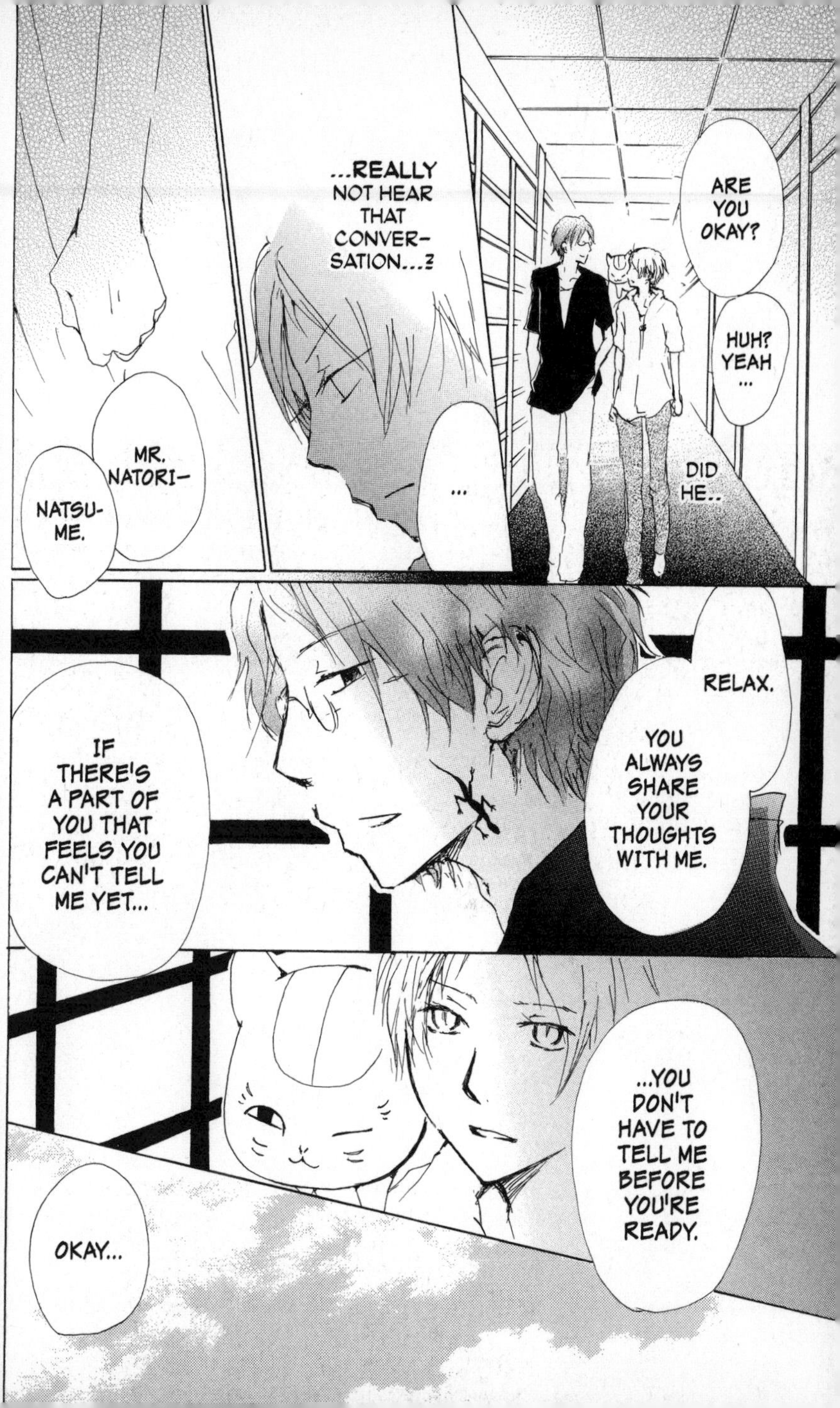
ARE YOU OKAY?
HUH? YEAH ...
DID HE..
...REALLY NOT HEAR THAT CONVERSATION...?
...
MR. NATORI—
NATSU-ME.
RELAX.
YOU ALWAYS SHARE YOUR THOUGHTS WITH ME.
IF THERE'S A PART OF YOU THAT FEELS YOU CAN'T TELL ME YET...
...YOU DON'T HAVE TO TELL ME BEFORE YOU'RE READY.
OKAY...

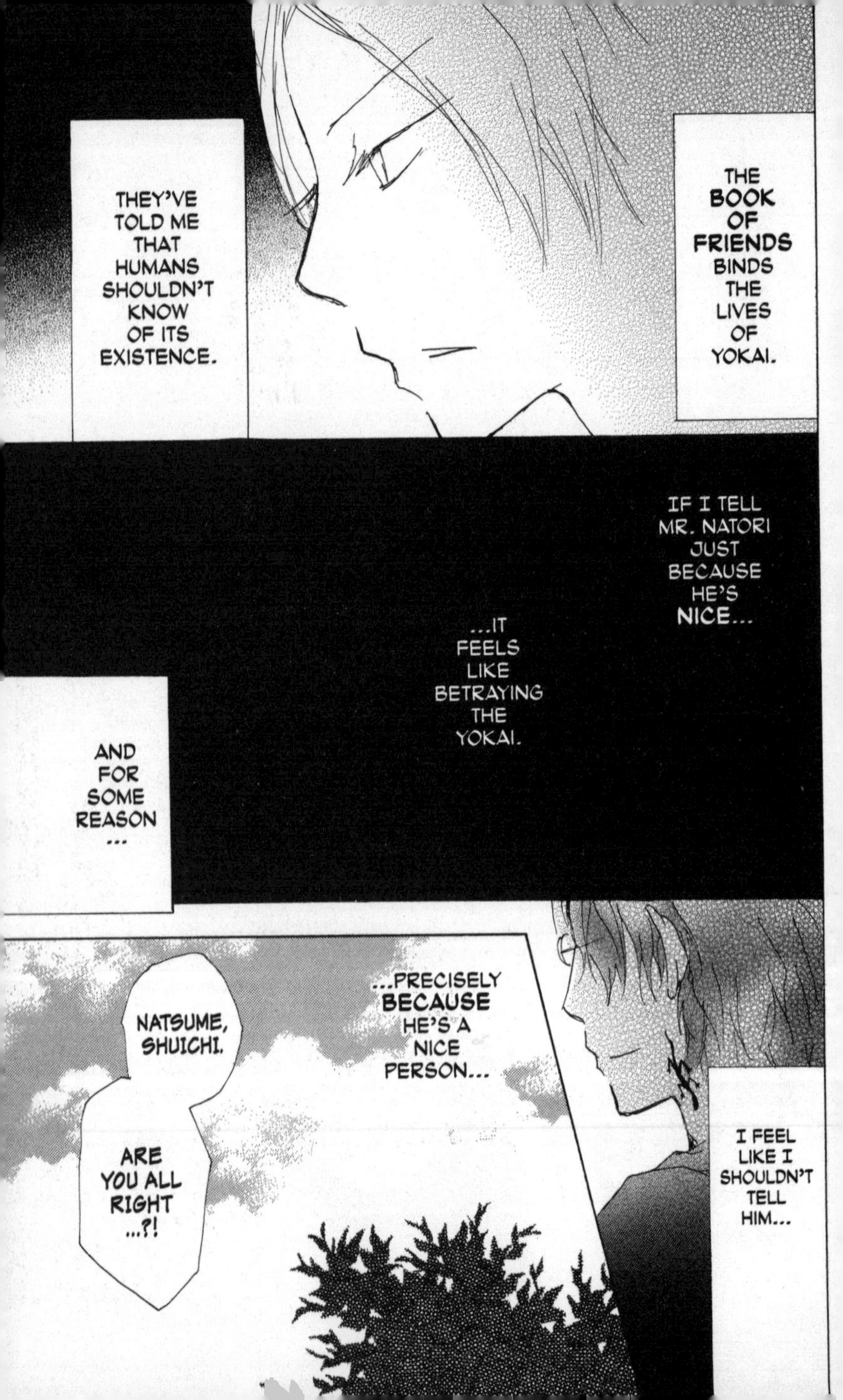
THE BOOK OF FRIENDS BINDS THE LIVES OF YOKAI.
THEY'VE TOLD ME THAT HUMANS SHOULDN'T KNOW OF ITS EXISTENCE.
IF I TELL MR. NATORI JUST BECAUSE HE'S NICE...
...IT FEELS LIKE BETRAYING THE YOKAI.
AND FOR SOME REASON...
I FEEL LIKE I SHOULDN'T TELL HIM...
...PRECISELY BECAUSE HE'S A NICE PERSON...
NATSUME, SHUICHI.
ARE YOU ALL RIGHT...?!

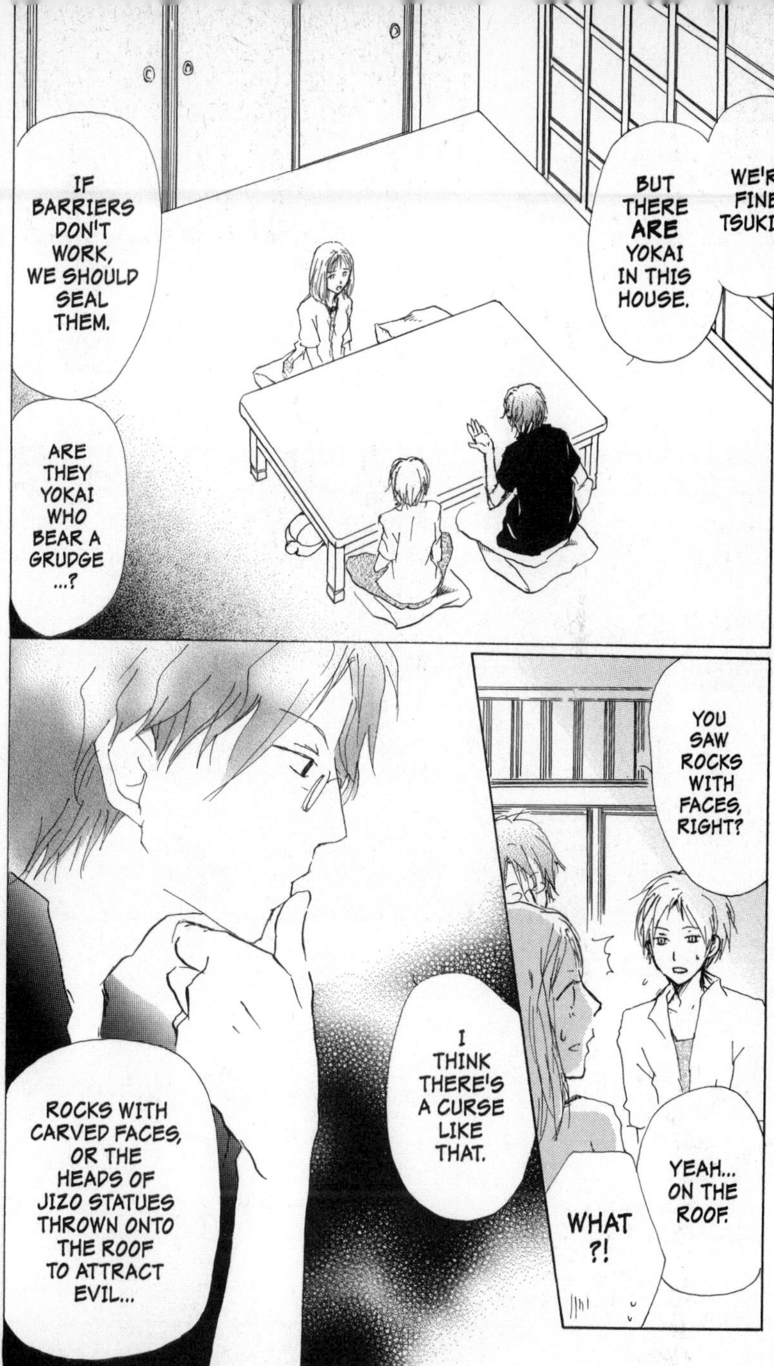
WE'RE FINE, TSUKIKO.
BUT THERE ARE YOKAI IN THIS HOUSE.
IF BARRIERS DON'T WORK, WE SHOULD SEAL THEM.
ARE THEY YOKAI WHO BEAR A GRUDGE ...?
YOU SAW ROCKS WITH FACES, RIGHT?
YEAH... ON THE ROOF.
WHAT ?!
I THINK THERE'S A CURSE LIKE THAT.
ROCKS WITH CARVED FACES, OR THE HEADS OF JIZO STATUES THROWN ONTO THE ROOF TO ATTRACT EVIL...

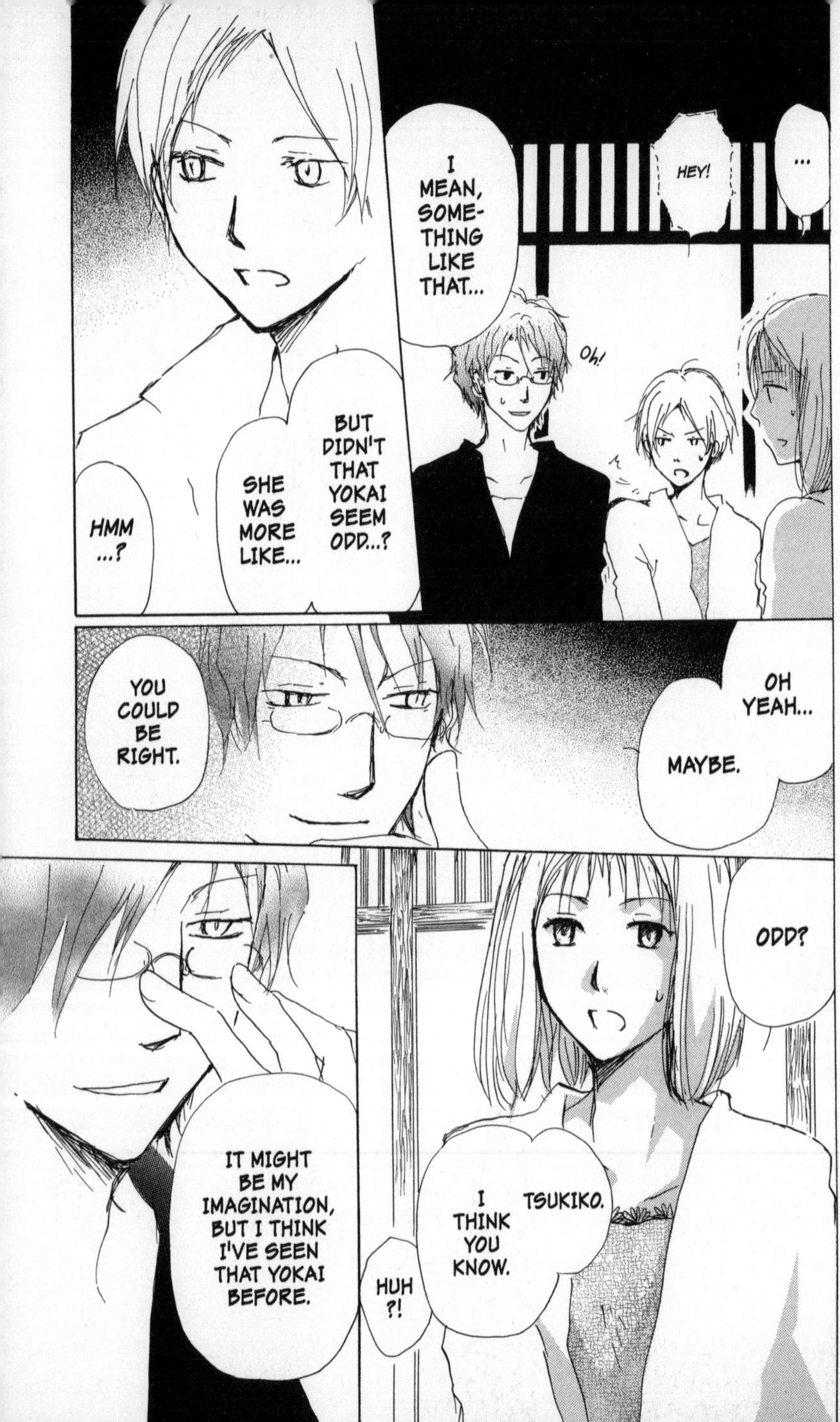
...
HEY!
I MEAN, SOMETHING LIKE THAT...
Oh!
BUT DIDN'T THAT YOKAI SEEM ODD...?
SHE WAS MORE LIKE...
HMM...?
OH YEAH... MAYBE.
YOU COULD BE RIGHT.
ODD?
TSUKIKO.
I THINK YOU KNOW.
HUH?!
IT MIGHT BE MY IMAGINATION, BUT I THINK I'VE SEEN THAT YOKAI BEFORE.

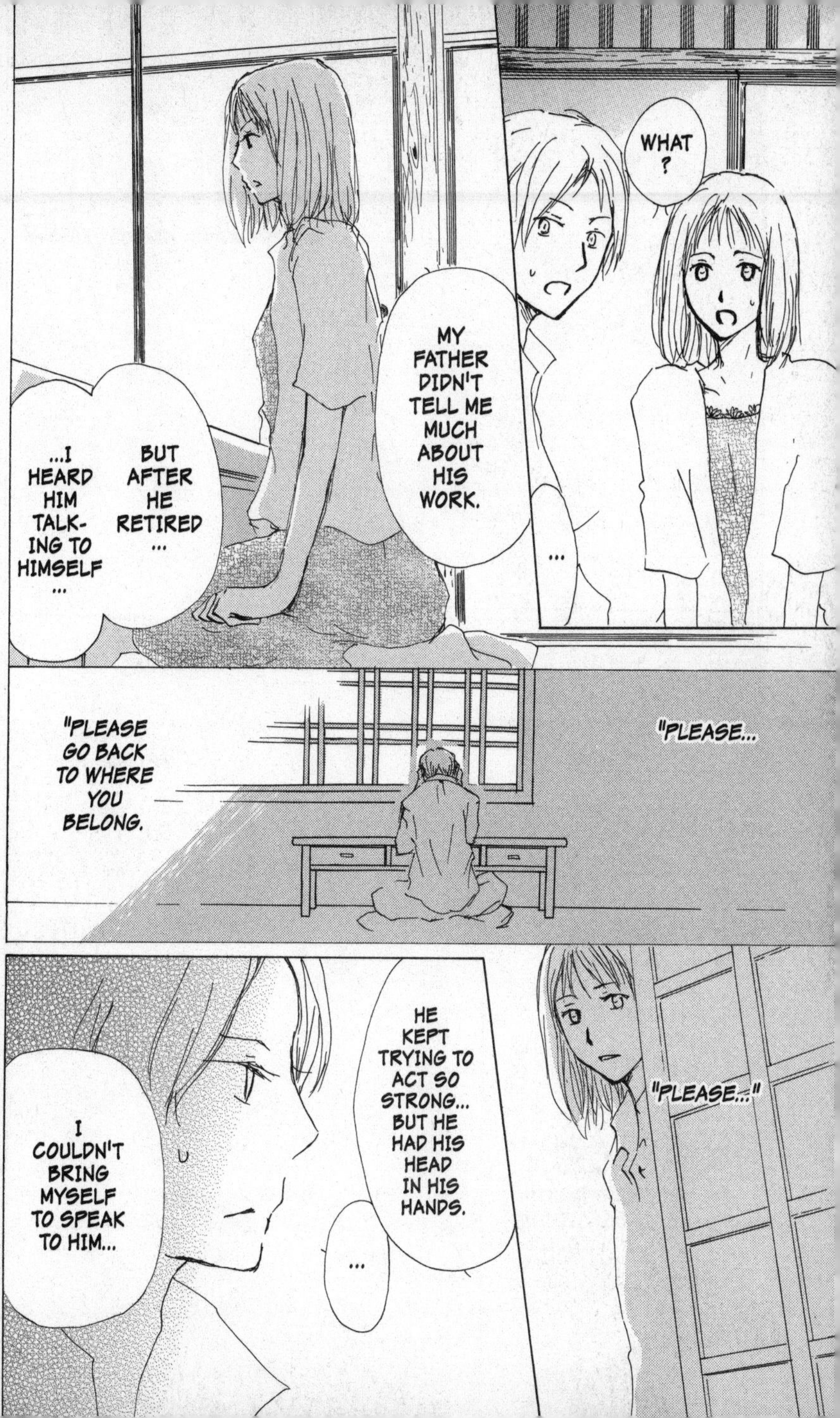
WHAT?
...
MY FATHER DIDN'T TELL ME MUCH ABOUT HIS WORK.
BUT AFTER HE RETIRED...
...I HEARD HIM TALKING TO HIMSELF...
"PLEASE...
"PLEASE GO BACK TO WHERE YOU BELONG.
"PLEASE..."
HE KEPT TRYING TO ACT SO STRONG... BUT HE HAD HIS HEAD IN HIS HANDS.
...
I COULDN'T BRING MYSELF TO SPEAK TO HIM...

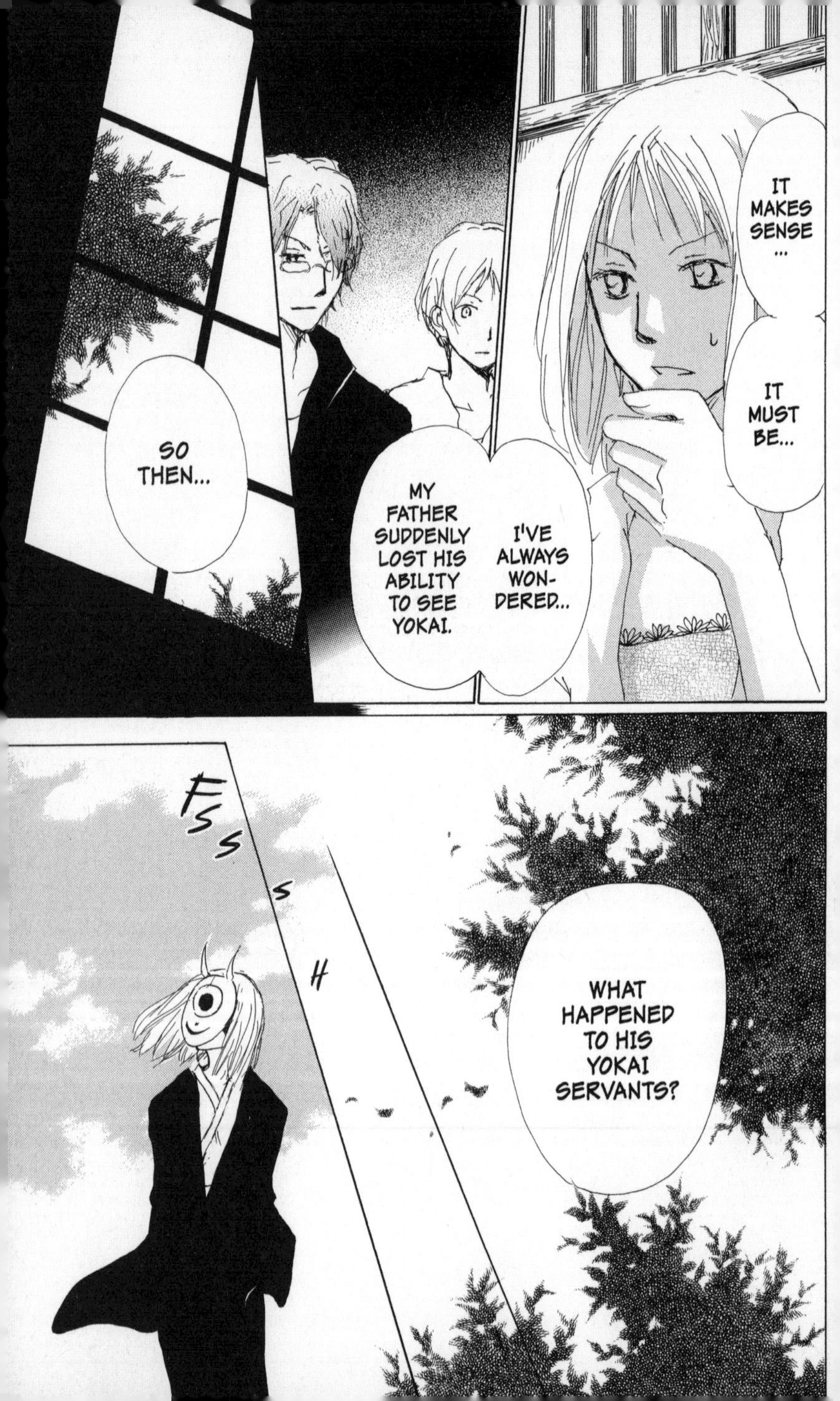
IT MAKES SENSE...
IT MUST BE...
I'VE ALWAYS WONDERED...
MY FATHER SUDDENLY LOST HIS ABILITY TO SEE YOKAI.
SO THEN...
WHAT HAPPENED TO HIS YOKAI SERVANTS?
FSSSH

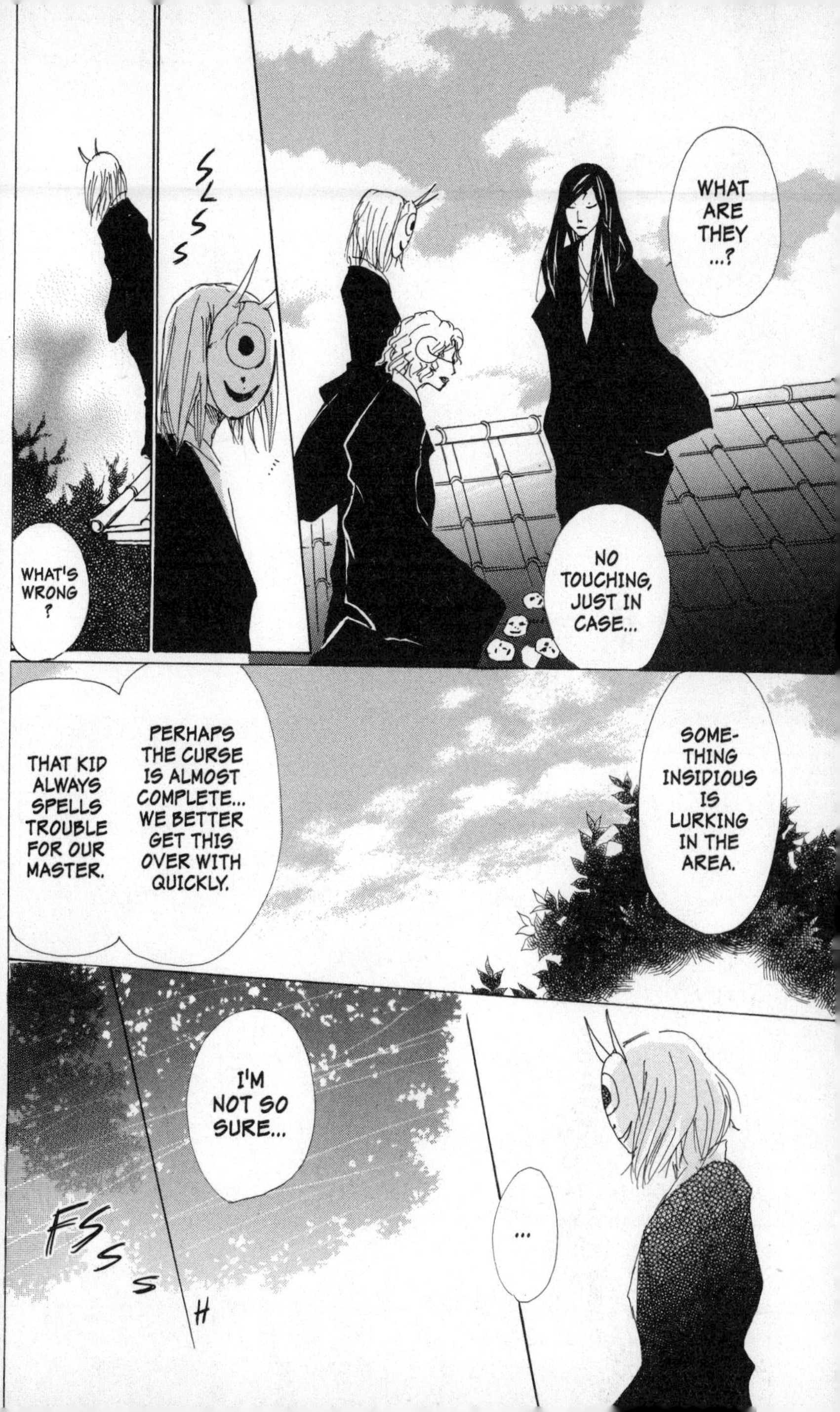
WHAT ARE THEY ...?
NO TOUCHING, JUST IN CASE...
SLSSS
WHAT'S WRONG?
SOME-THING INSIDIOUS IS LURKING IN THE AREA.
PERHAPS THE CURSE IS ALMOST COMPLETE... WE BETTER GET THIS OVER WITH QUICKLY.
THAT KID ALWAYS SPELLS TROUBLE FOR OUR MASTER.
...
I'M NOT SO SURE...
FSSSH

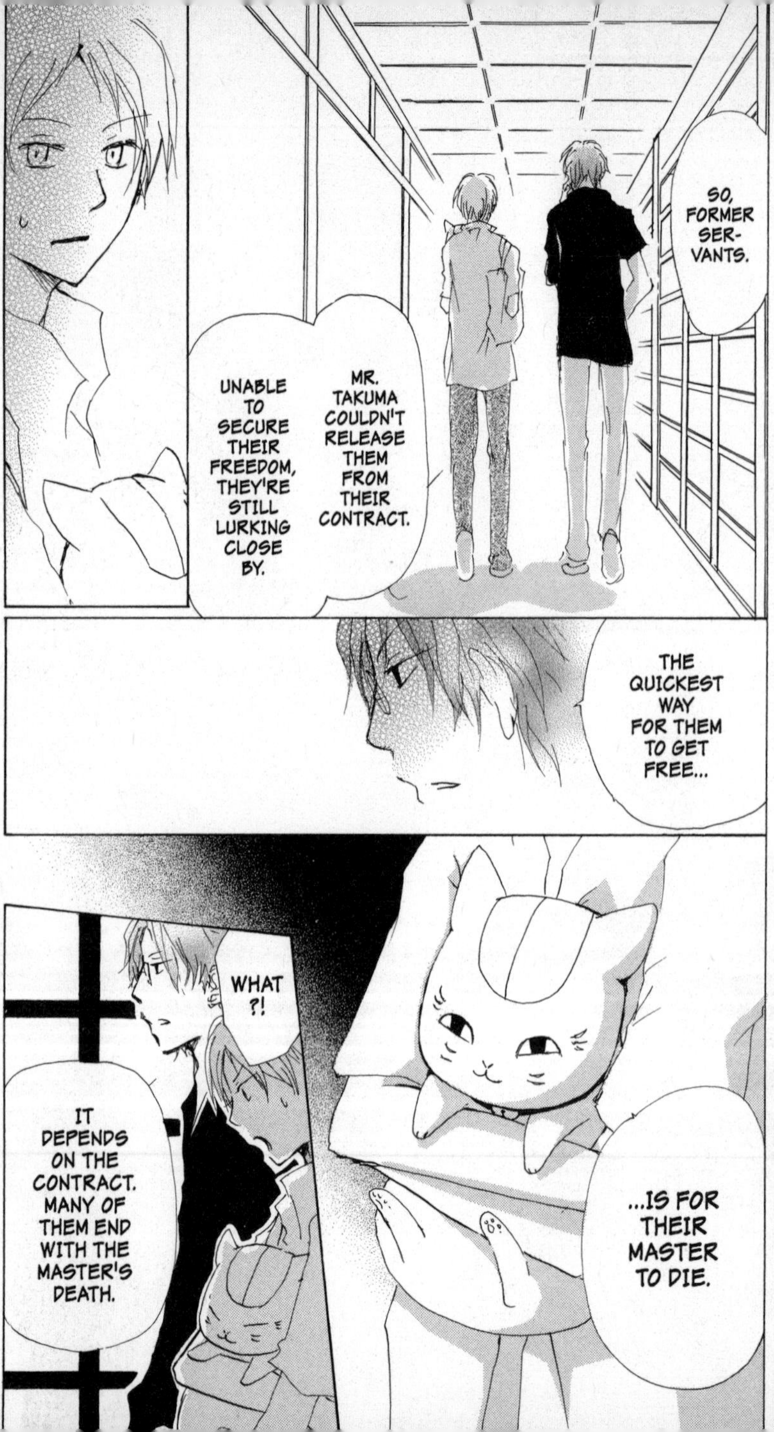
SO, FORMER SER-VANTS.
MR. TAKUMA COULDN'T RELEASE THEM FROM THEIR CONTRACT.
UNABLE TO SECURE THEIR FREEDOM, THEY'RE STILL LURKING CLOSE BY.
THE QUICKEST WAY FOR THEM TO GET FREE...
...IS FOR THEIR MASTER TO DIE.
WHAT?!
IT DEPENDS ON THE CONTRACT. MANY OF THEM END WITH THE MASTER'S DEATH.

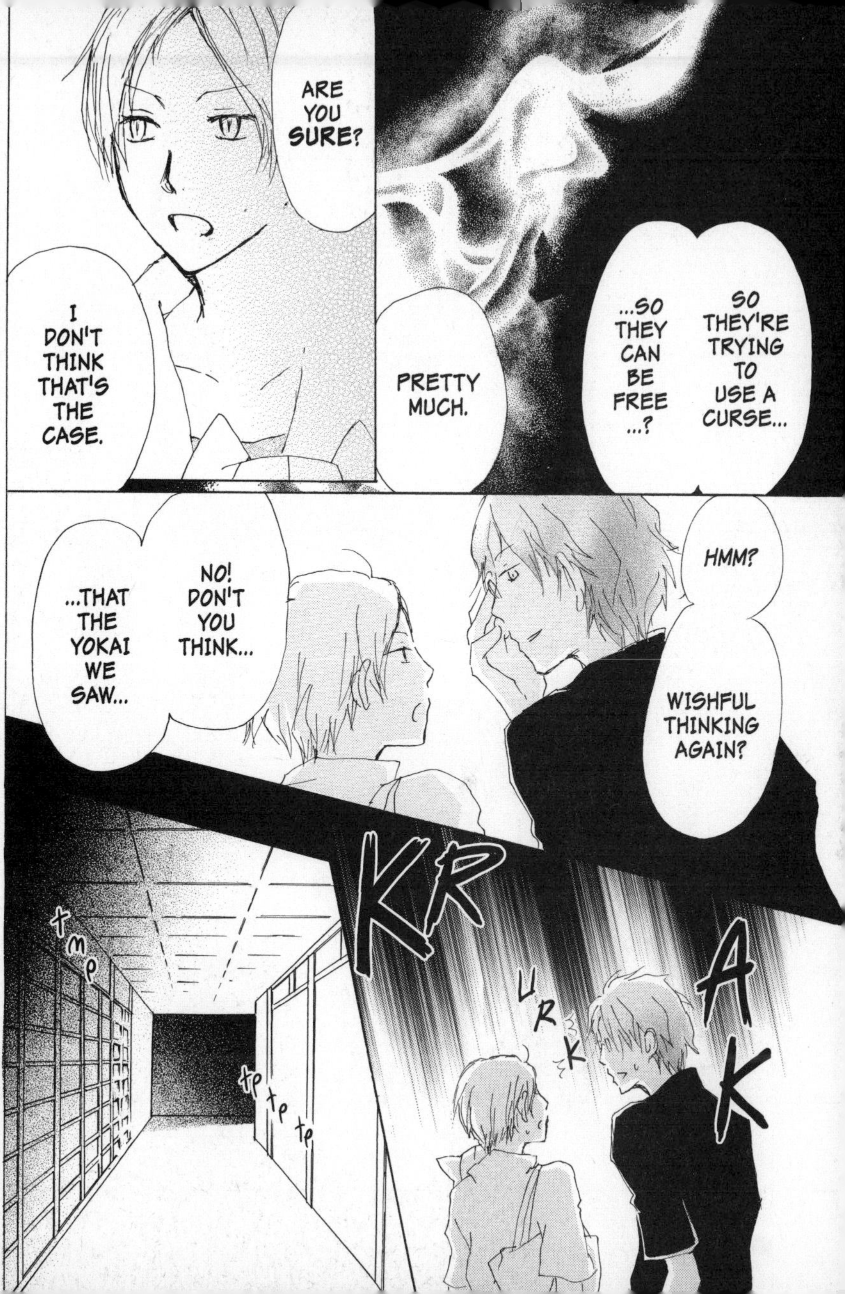
SO THEY'RE TRYING TO USE A CURSE...
...SO THEY CAN BE FREE...?
PRETTY MUCH.
ARE YOU SURE?
I DON'T THINK THAT'S THE CASE.
HMM?
WISHFUL THINKING AGAIN?
NO! DON'T YOU THINK...
...THAT THE YOKAI WE SAW...
KRAK
URK
tp tp tp
tmp

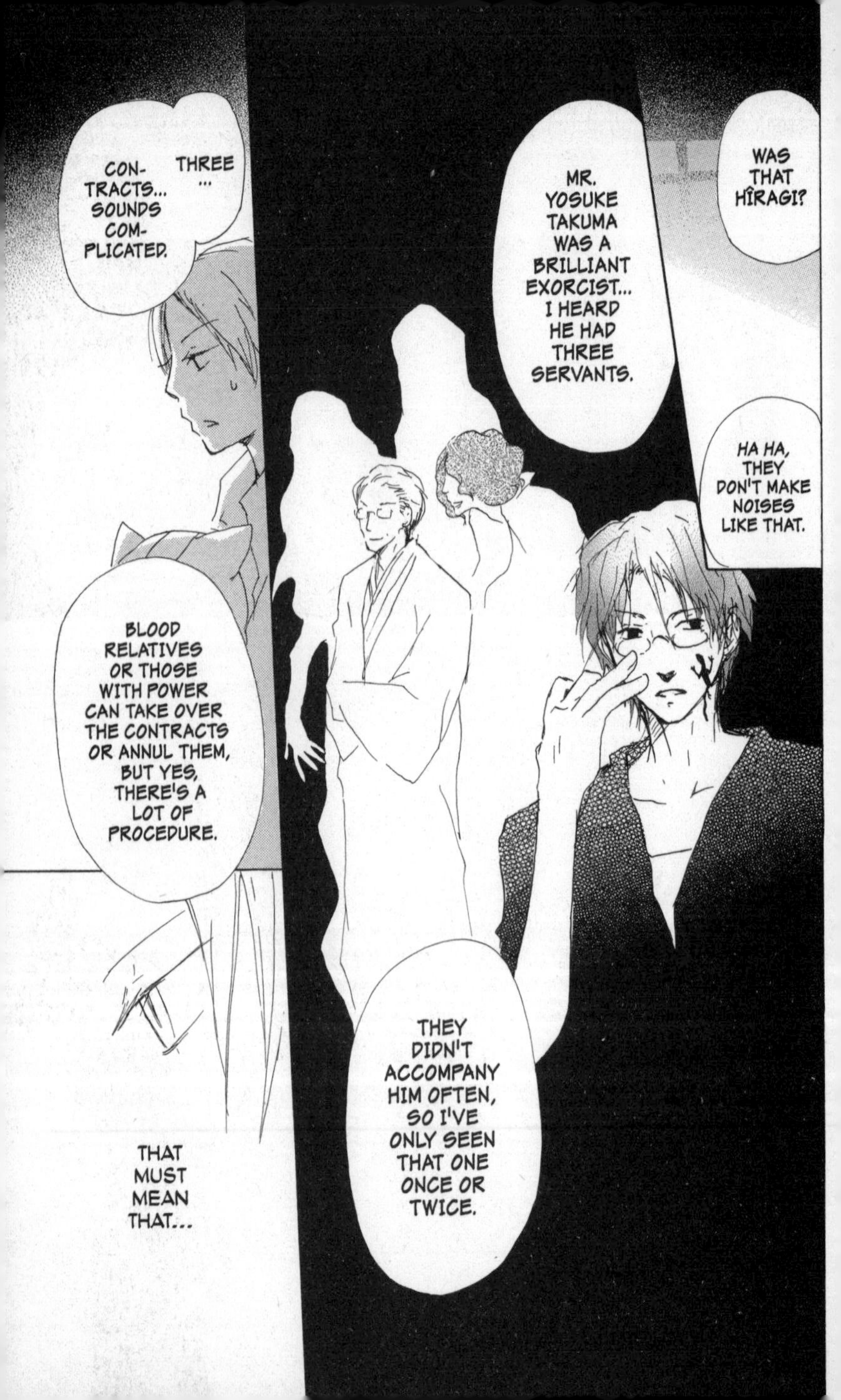
WAS THAT HÎRAGI?
MR. YOSUKE TAKUMA WAS A BRILLIANT EXORCIST... I HEARD HE HAD THREE SERVANTS.
HA HA, THEY DON'T MAKE NOISES LIKE THAT.
THEY DIDN'T ACCOMPANY HIM OFTEN, SO I'VE ONLY SEEN THAT ONE ONCE OR TWICE.
THREE ...
CON-TRACTS... SOUNDS COM-PLICATED.
BLOOD RELATIVES OR THOSE WITH POWER CAN TAKE OVER THE CONTRACTS OR ANNUL THEM, BUT YES, THERE'S A LOT OF PROCEDURE.
THAT MUST MEAN THAT...

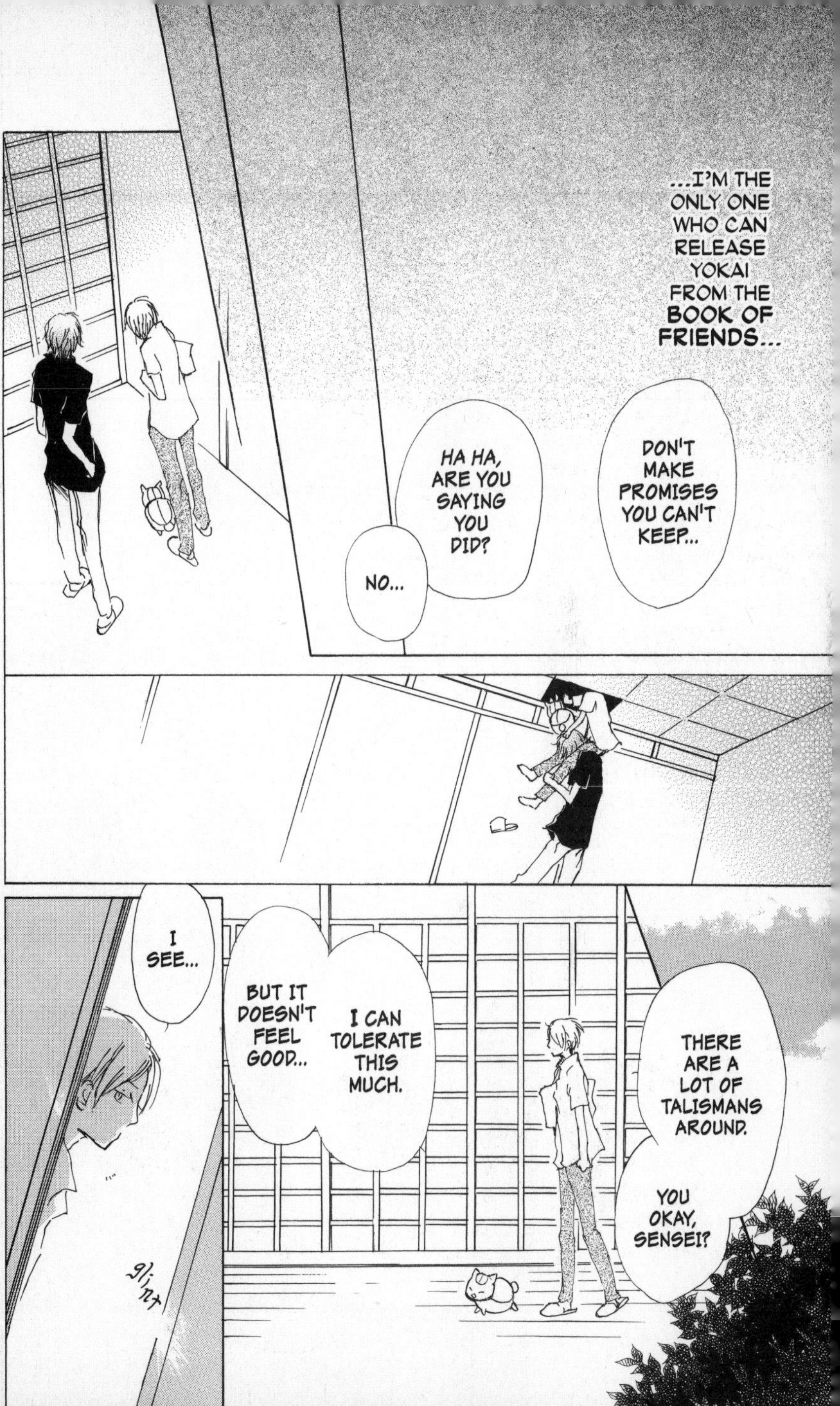
...I'M THE ONLY ONE WHO CAN RELEASE YOKAI FROM THE BOOK OF FRIENDS...
DON'T MAKE PROMISES YOU CAN'T KEEP...
HA HA, ARE YOU SAYING YOU DID?
NO...
THERE ARE A LOT OF TALISMANS AROUND.
YOU OKAY, SENSEI?
I CAN TOLERATE THIS MUCH.
BUT IT DOESN'T FEEL GOOD...
I SEE...
glint

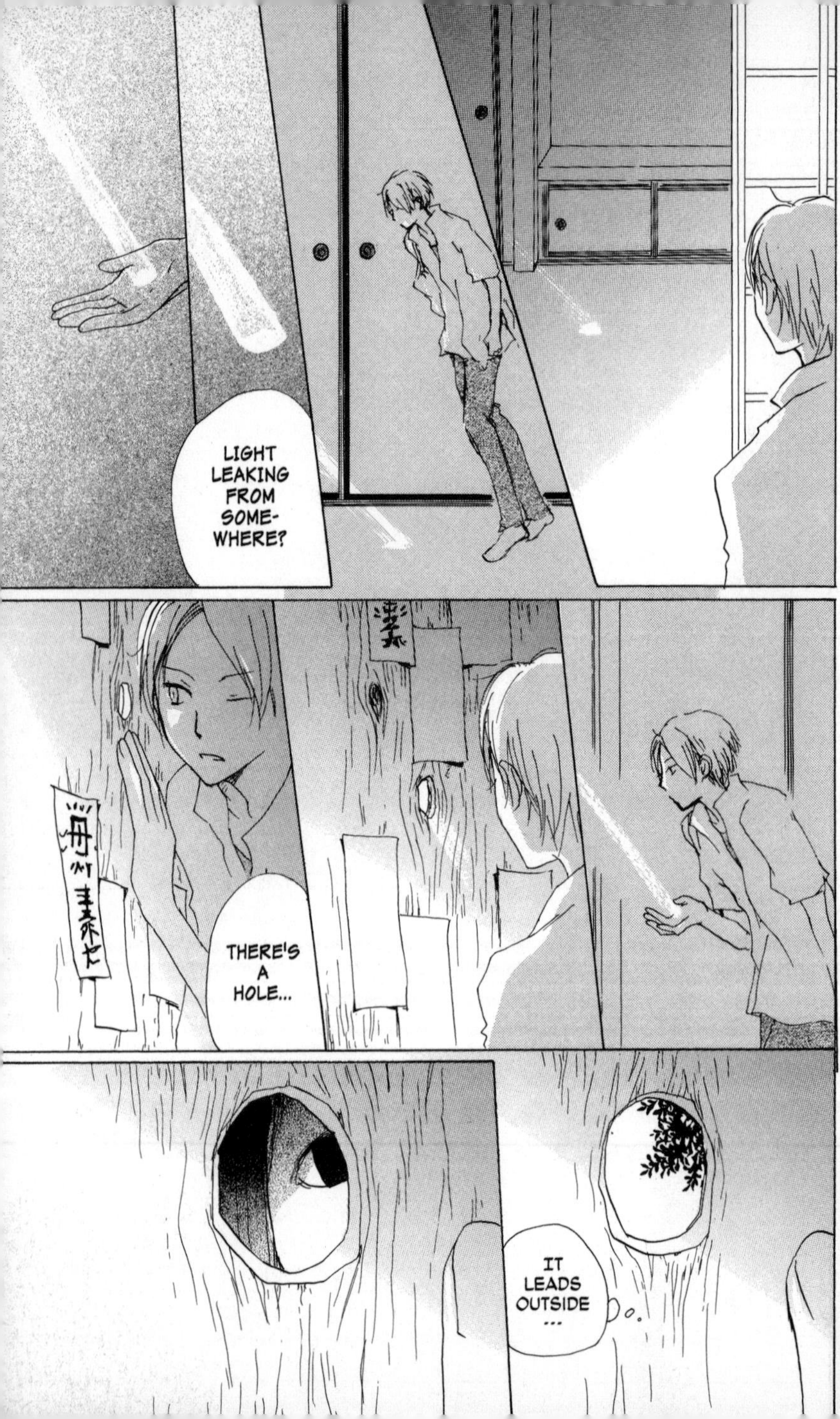
LIGHT LEAKING FROM SOME-WHERE?
THERE'S A HOLE...
IT LEADS OUTSIDE ...

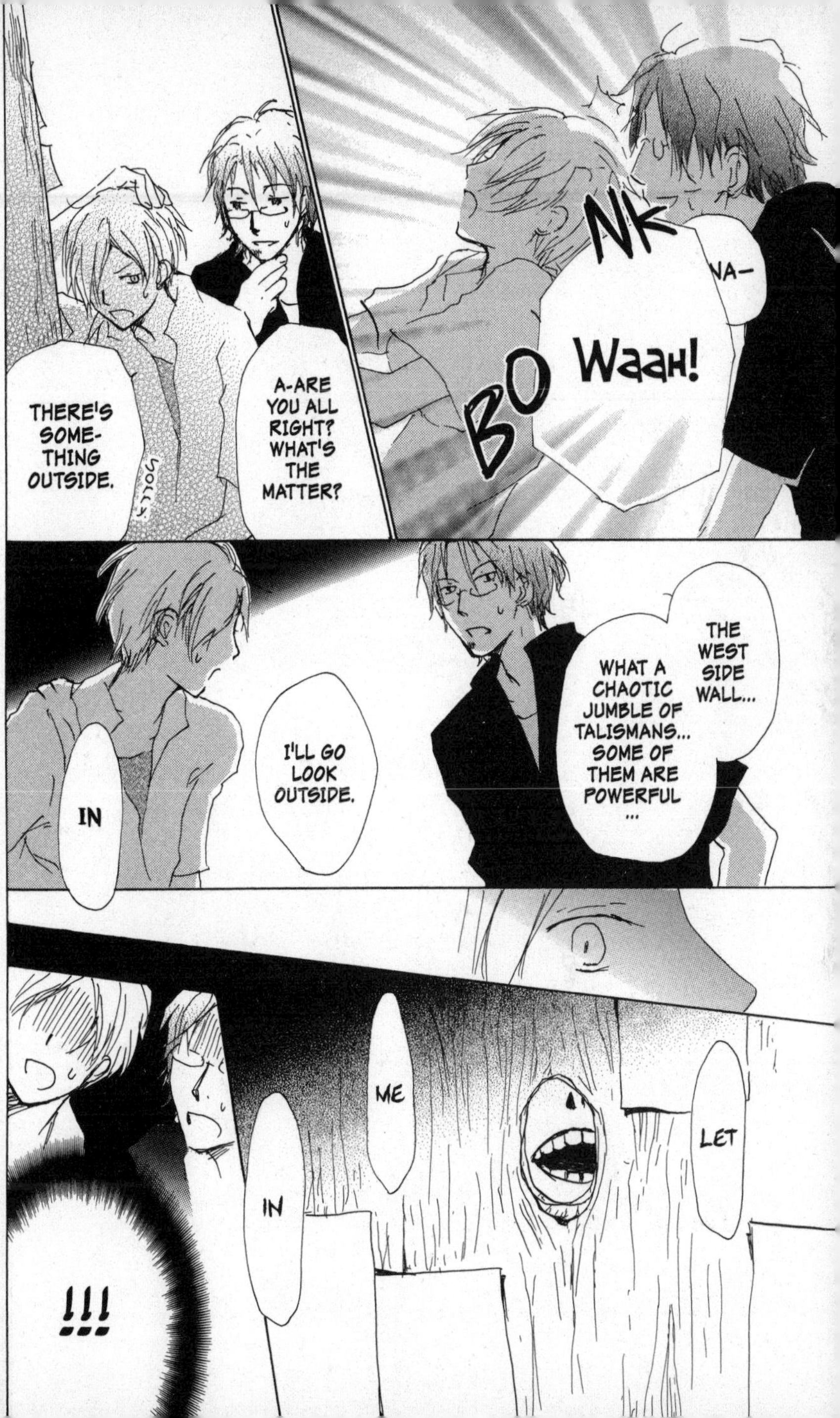
NA—
BONK
Waah!
A-ARE YOU ALL RIGHT? WHAT'S THE MATTER?
THERE'S SOMETHING OUTSIDE.
sorry.
THE WEST SIDE WALL...
WHAT A CHAOTIC JUMBLE OF TALISMANS... SOME OF THEM ARE POWERFUL ...
I'LL GO LOOK OUTSIDE.
IN
LET
ME
IN
!!!

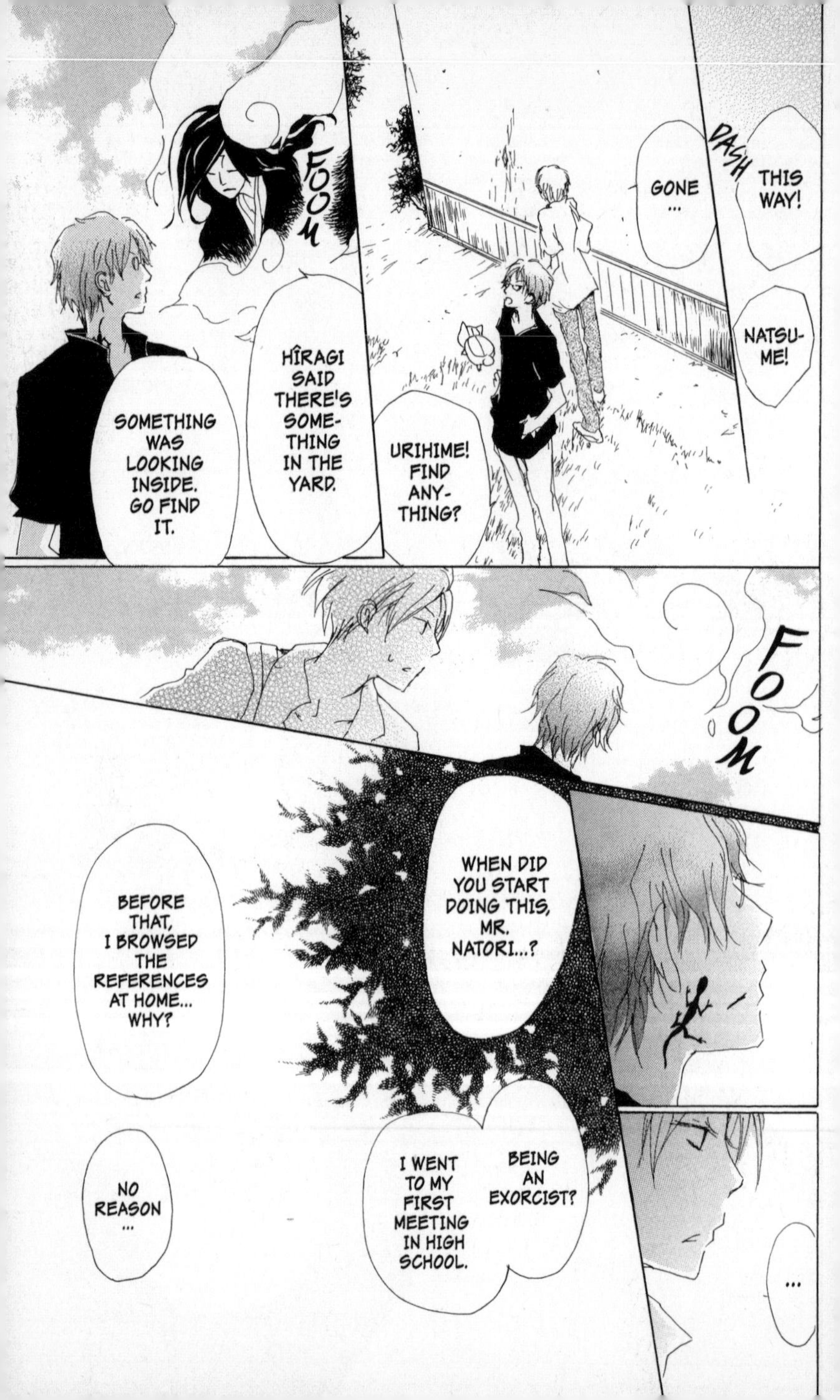
THIS WAY!
DASH
GONE ...
NATSUME!
URIHIME! FIND ANYTHING?
HÎRAGI SAID THERE'S SOMETHING IN THE YARD.
FOOM
SOMETHING WAS LOOKING INSIDE. GO FIND IT.
FOOM
WHEN DID YOU START DOING THIS, MR. NATORI...?
BEING AN EXORCIST?
I WENT TO MY FIRST MEETING IN HIGH SCHOOL.
BEFORE THAT, I BROWSED THE REFERENCES AT HOME... WHY?
...
NO REASON ...

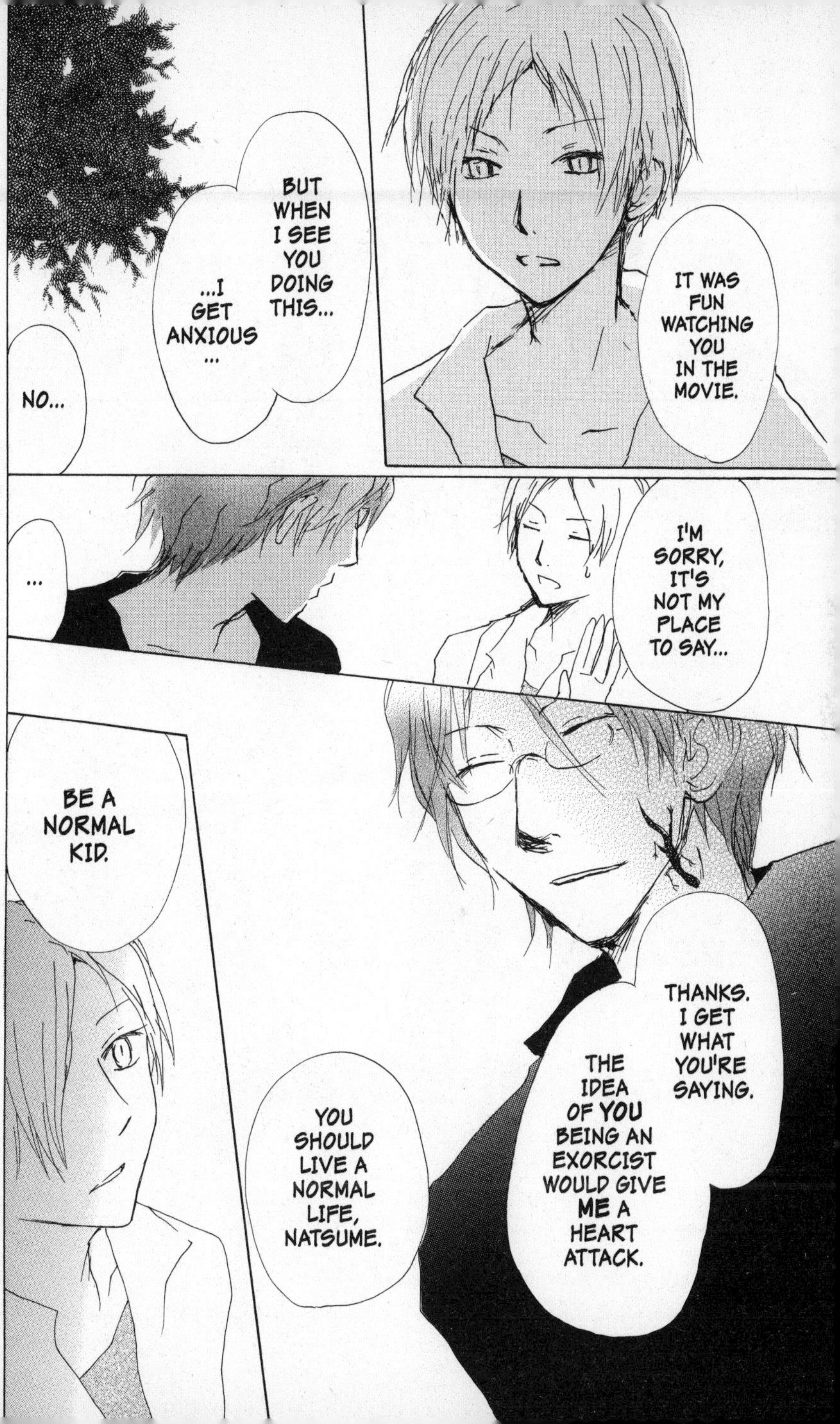
IT WAS FUN WATCHING YOU IN THE MOVIE.
BUT WHEN I SEE YOU DOING THIS...
...I GET ANXIOUS ...
NO...
I'M SORRY, IT'S NOT MY PLACE TO SAY...
...
THANKS. I GET WHAT YOU'RE SAYING.
THE IDEA OF YOU BEING AN EXORCIST WOULD GIVE ME A HEART ATTACK.
YOU SHOULD LIVE A NORMAL LIFE, NATSUME.
BE A NORMAL KID.

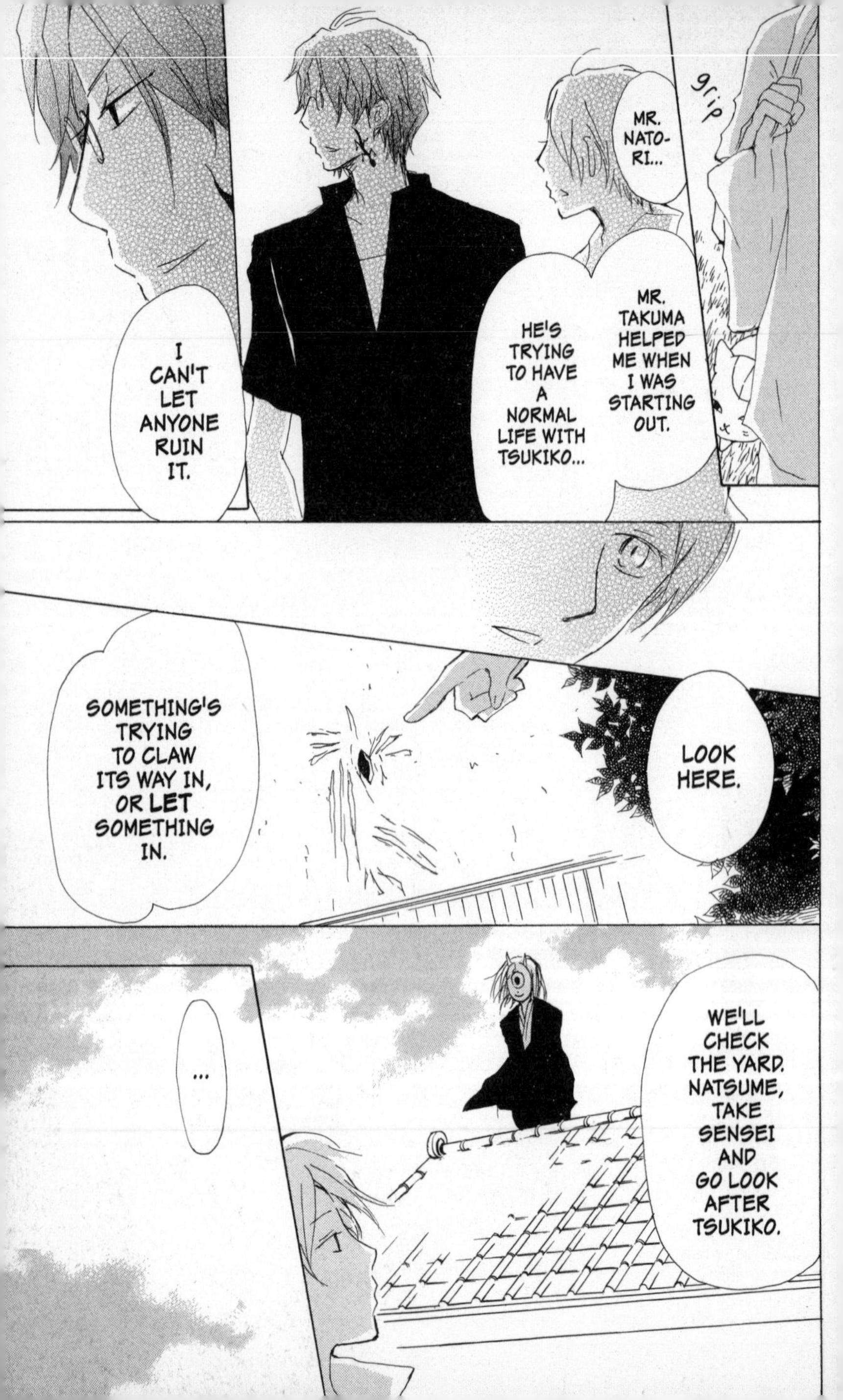
grip
MR. NATO-RI...
MR. TAKUMA HELPED ME WHEN I WAS STARTING OUT.
HE'S TRYING TO HAVE A NORMAL LIFE WITH TSUKIKO...
I CAN'T LET ANYONE RUIN IT.
LOOK HERE.
SOMETHING'S TRYING TO CLAW ITS WAY IN, OR LET SOMETHING IN.
WE'LL CHECK THE YARD. NATSUME, TAKE SENSEI AND GO LOOK AFTER TSUKIKO.
...

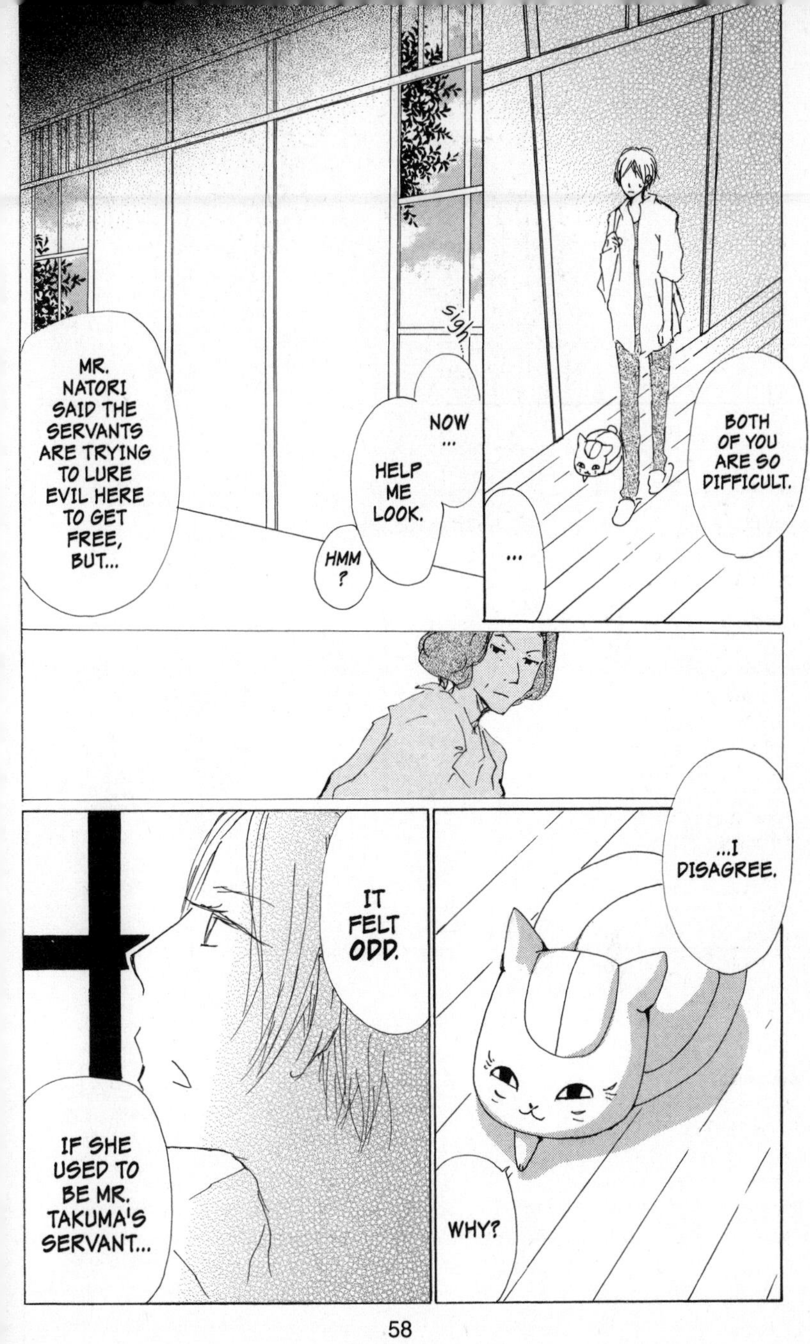
BOTH OF YOU ARE SO DIFFICULT.
...
sigh...
NOW ... HELP ME LOOK.
HMM?
MR. NATORI SAID THE SERVANTS ARE TRYING TO LURE EVIL HERE TO GET FREE, BUT...
...I DISAGREE.
WHY?
IT FELT ODD.
IF SHE USED TO BE MR. TAKUMA'S SERVANT...

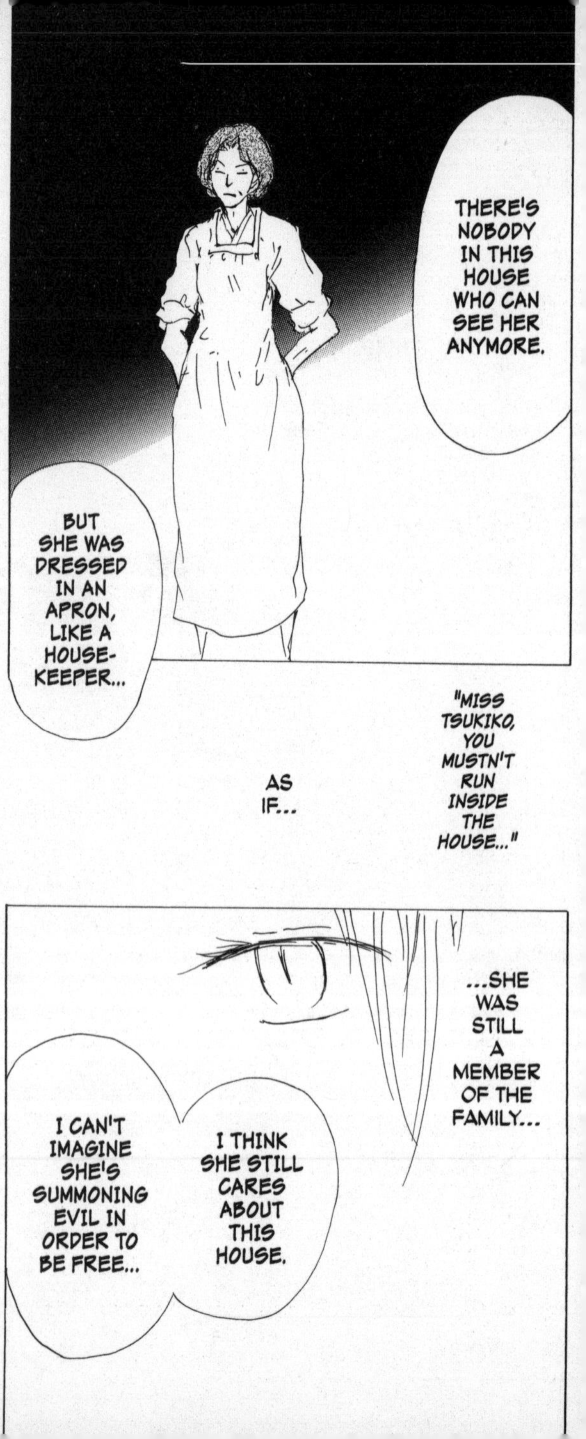
THERE'S NOBODY IN THIS HOUSE WHO CAN SEE HER ANYMORE.
BUT SHE WAS DRESSED IN AN APRON, LIKE A HOUSE-KEEPER...
"MISS TSUKIKO, YOU MUSTN'T RUN INSIDE THE HOUSE..."
AS IF...
...SHE WAS STILL A MEMBER OF THE FAMILY...
I THINK SHE STILL CARES ABOUT THIS HOUSE.
I CAN'T IMAGINE SHE'S SUMMONING EVIL IN ORDER TO BE FREE...

02

❋Natsume's Book of Friends Novel

They're publishing a prose book of short stories for *Natsume's Book of Friends*, due to be released in Japan at the same time as this volume. The author is Sadayuki Murai, the script writer and series planner for the third and fourth seasons of the anime. He wrote some mysterious and delicate stories.

The book includes two stories that he contributed for a magazine called *Natsume's Book of Friends: Selected Stories* (summer and winter issues), plus two brand new stories. They're multi-layered, vivid and wonderful. I'm so happy. I'm so excited and hope that many people will read it. Please check it out.

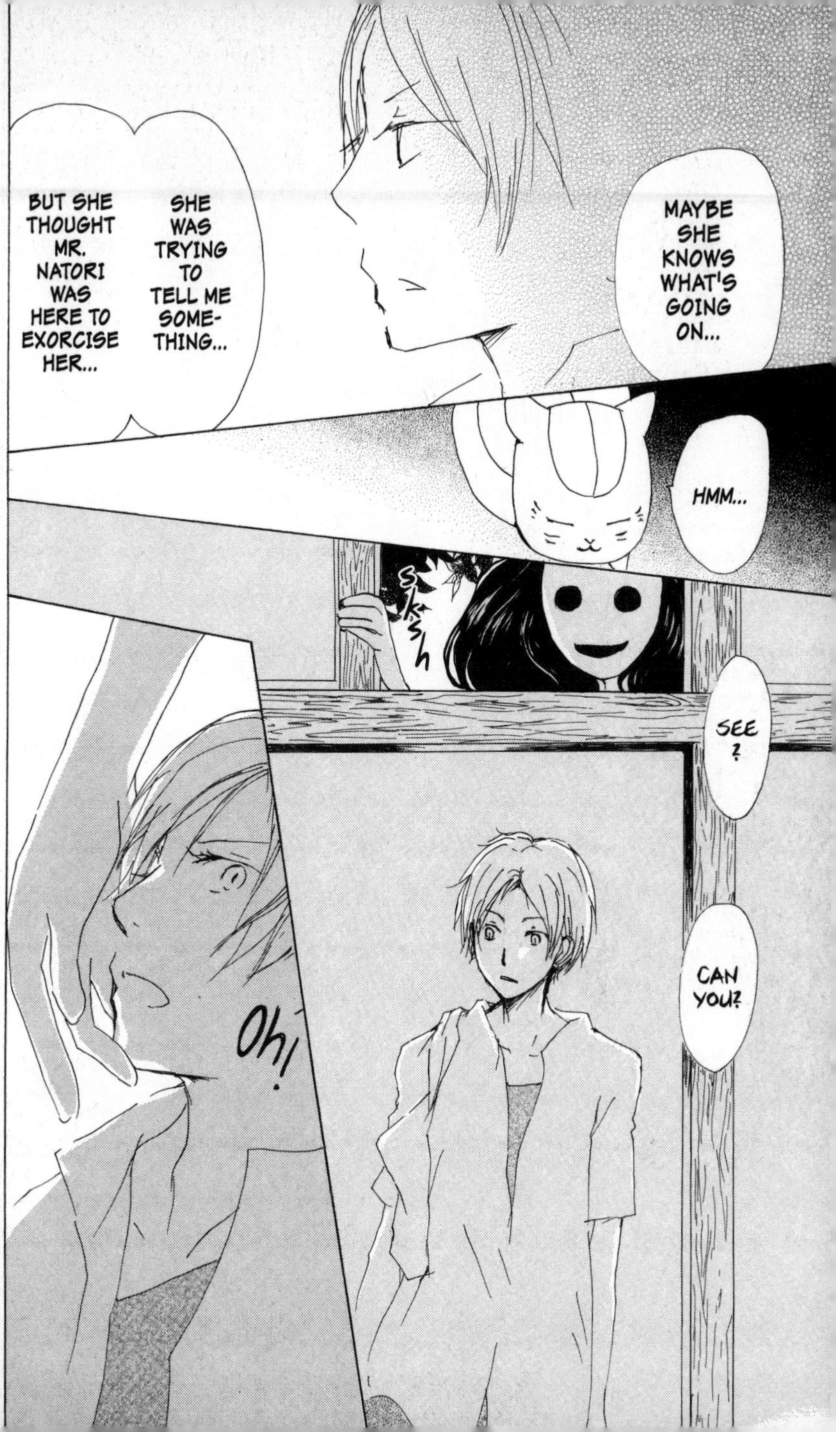
MAYBE SHE KNOWS WHAT'S GOING ON...
SHE WAS TRYING TO TELL ME SOME-THING...
BUT SHE THOUGHT MR. NATORI WAS HERE TO EXORCISE HER...
HMM...
SKSH
SEE?
CAN YOU?
Oh!

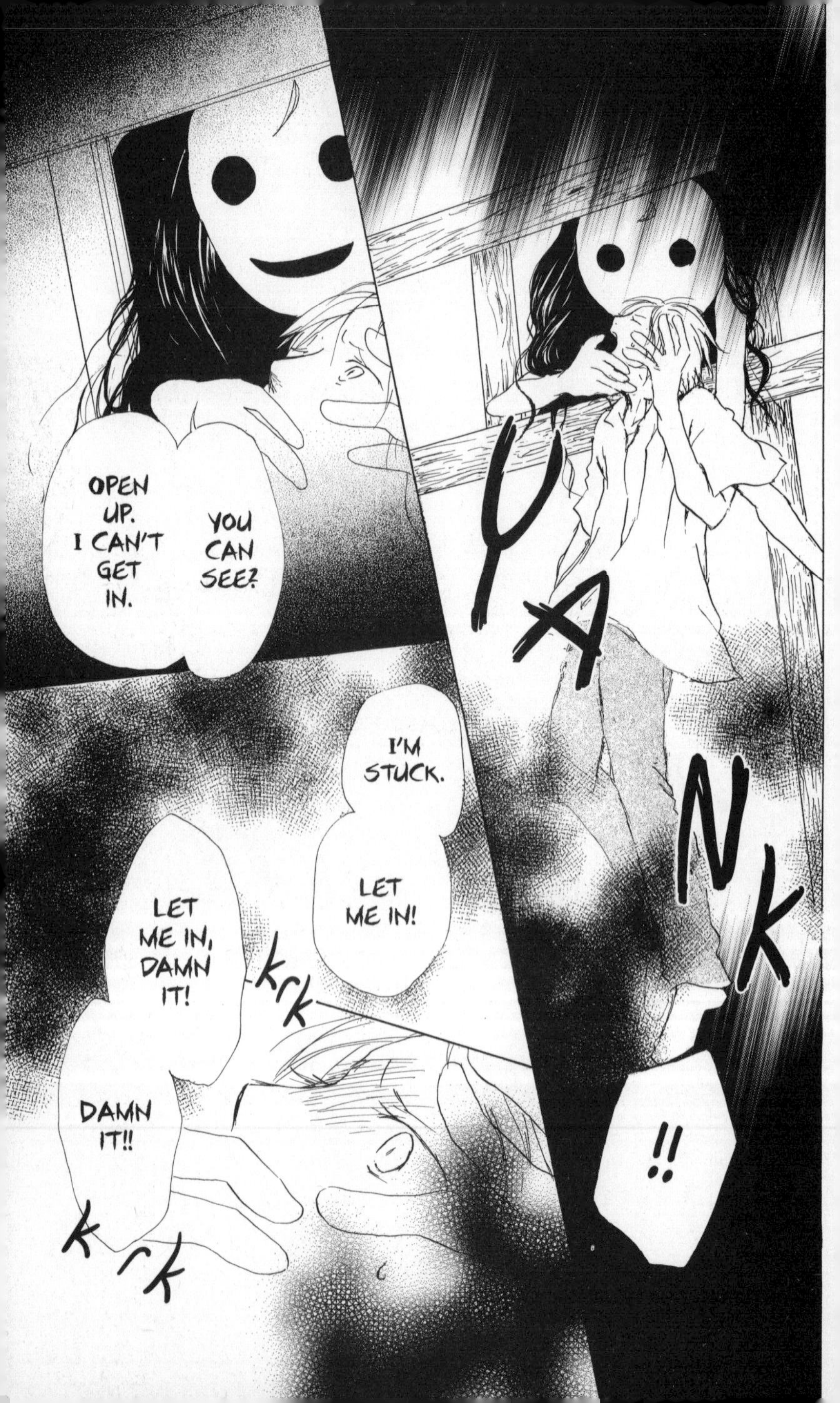
YANK
!!
YOU CAN SEE?
OPEN UP. I CAN'T GET IN.
I'M STUCK.
LET ME IN!
LET ME IN, DAMN IT!
KRK
DAMN IT!!
KRK

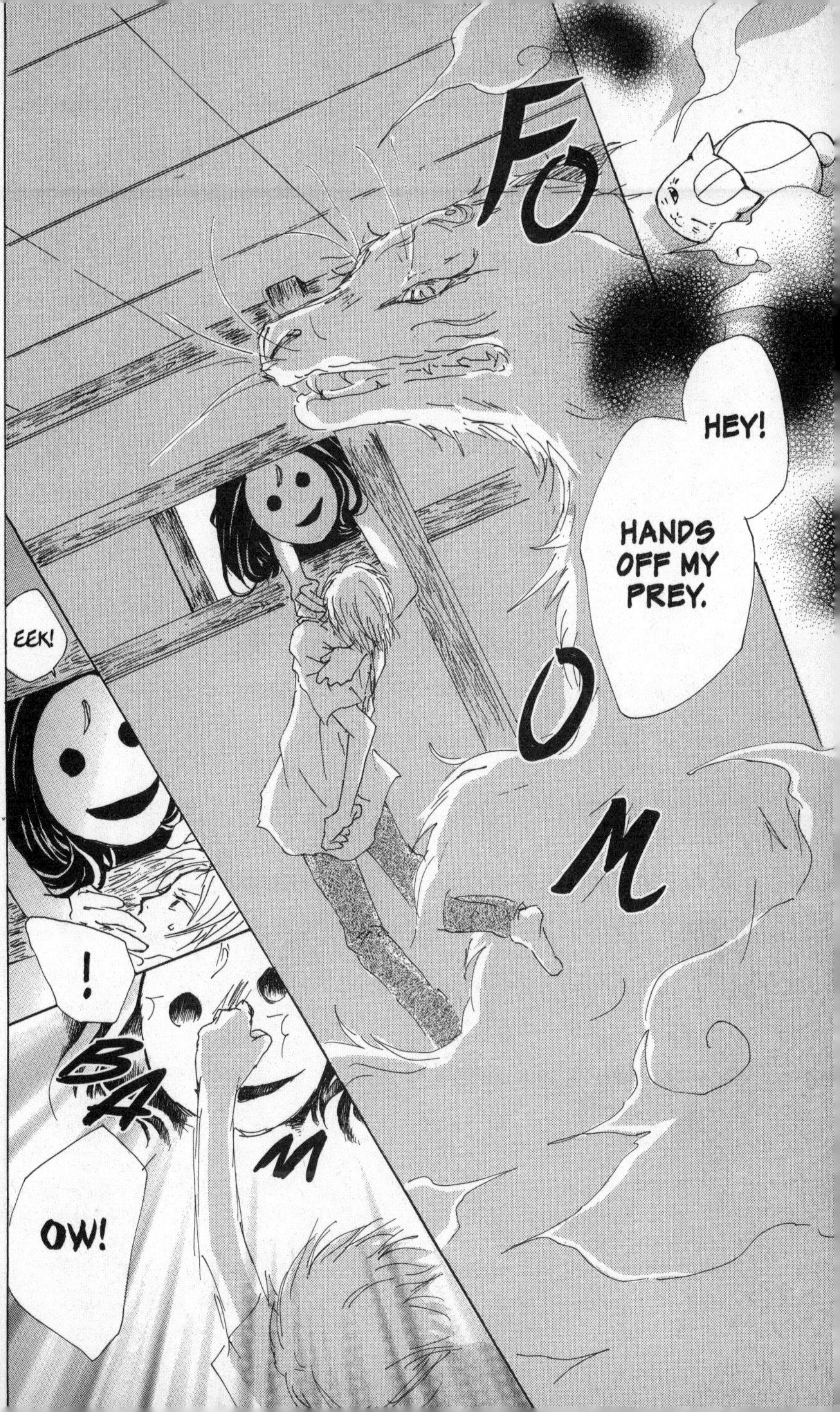
FOOM
HEY!
HANDS OFF MY PREY.
EEK!
!
BAM
OW!

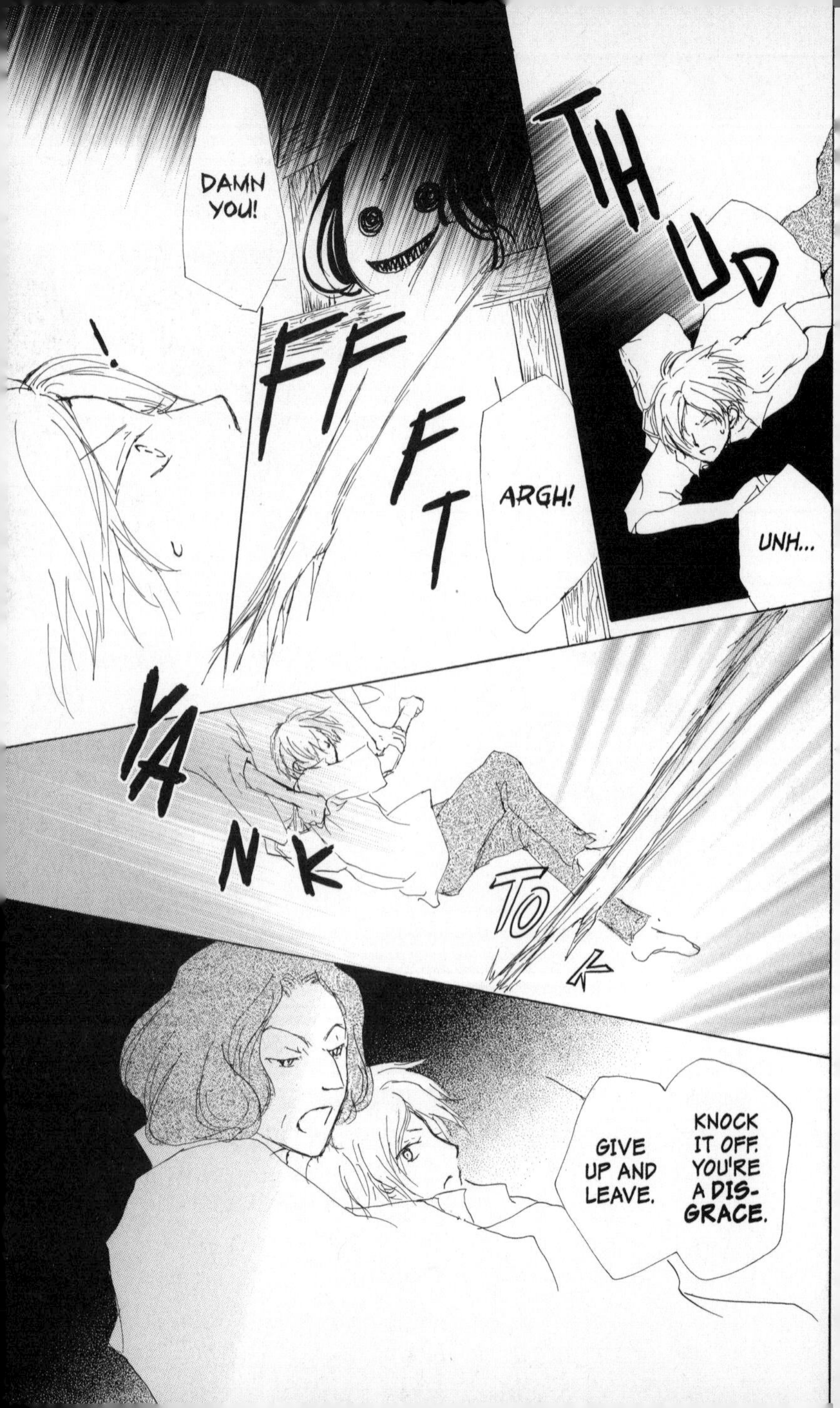
THUD
UNH...
DAMN YOU!
FFFT
ARGH!
!
YANK
TOK
KNOCK IT OFF. YOU'RE A DISGRACE.
GIVE UP AND LEAVE.

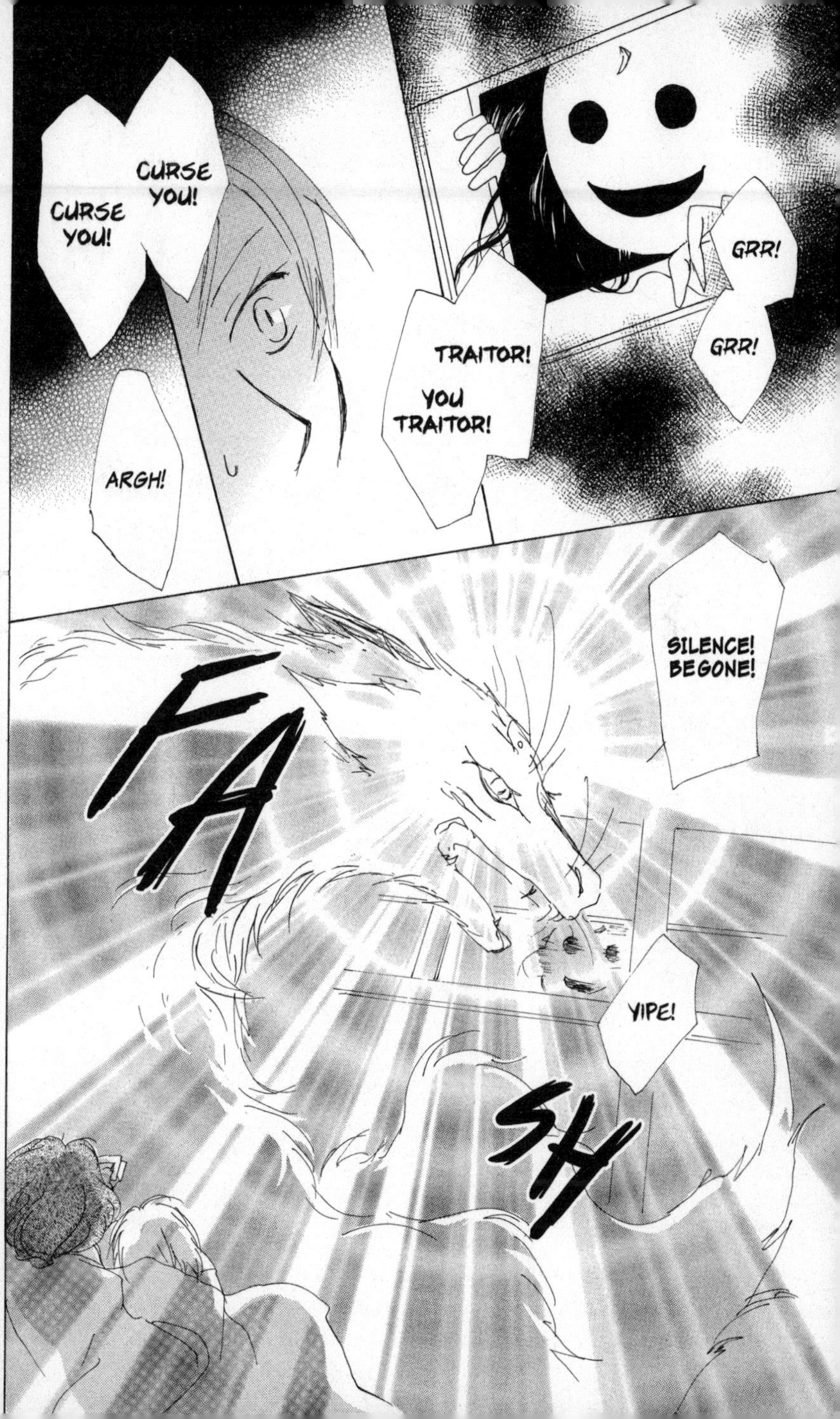
GRR!
GRR!
TRAITOR!
YOU TRAITOR!
CURSE YOU!
CURSE YOU!
ARGH!
SILENCE! BEGONE!
FA
YIPE!
SH

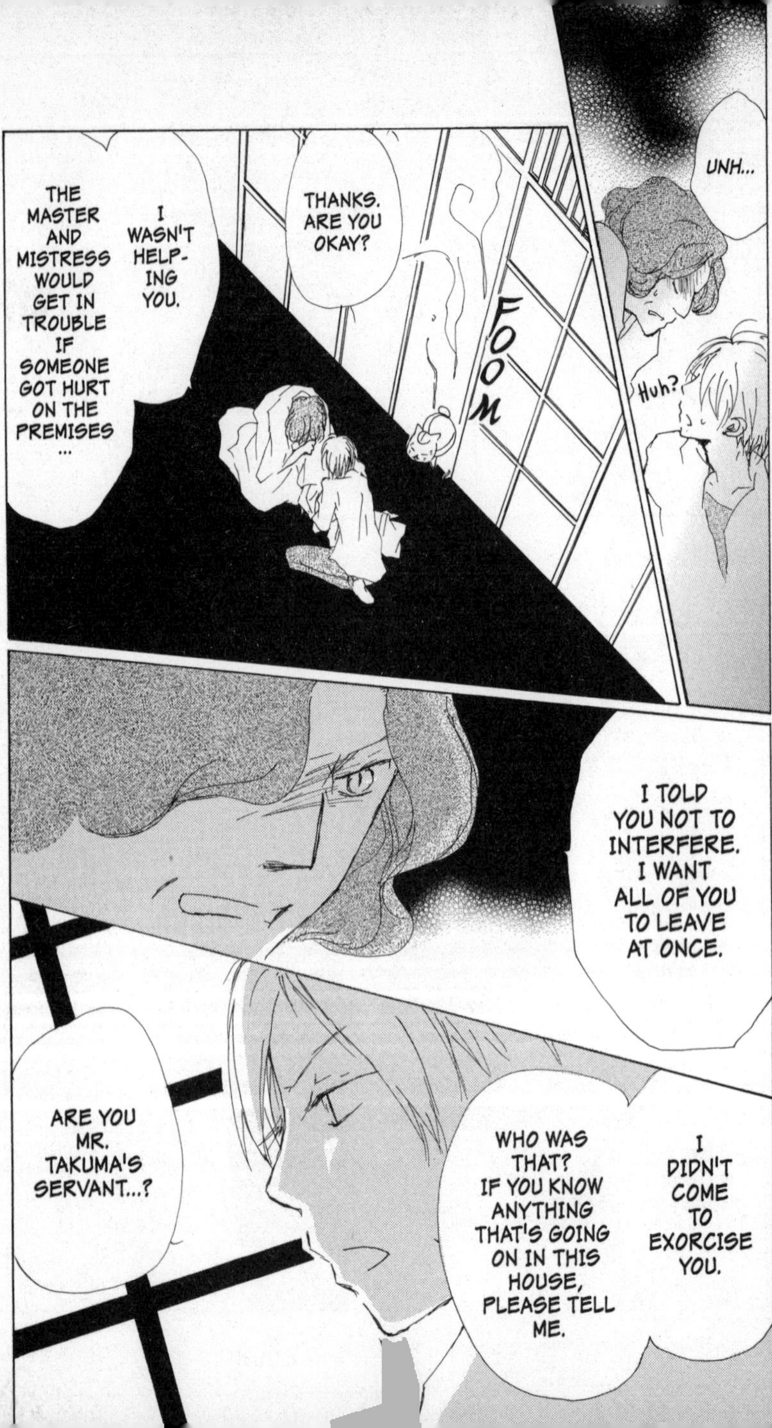
UNH...
Huh?
FOOM
THANKS. ARE YOU OKAY?
I WASN'T HELPING YOU.
THE MASTER AND MISTRESS WOULD GET IN TROUBLE IF SOMEONE GOT HURT ON THE PREMISES...
I TOLD YOU NOT TO INTERFERE. I WANT ALL OF YOU TO LEAVE AT ONCE.
I DIDN'T COME TO EXORCISE YOU.
WHO WAS THAT? IF YOU KNOW ANYTHING THAT'S GOING ON IN THIS HOUSE, PLEASE TELL ME.
ARE YOU MR. TAKUMA'S SERVANT...?

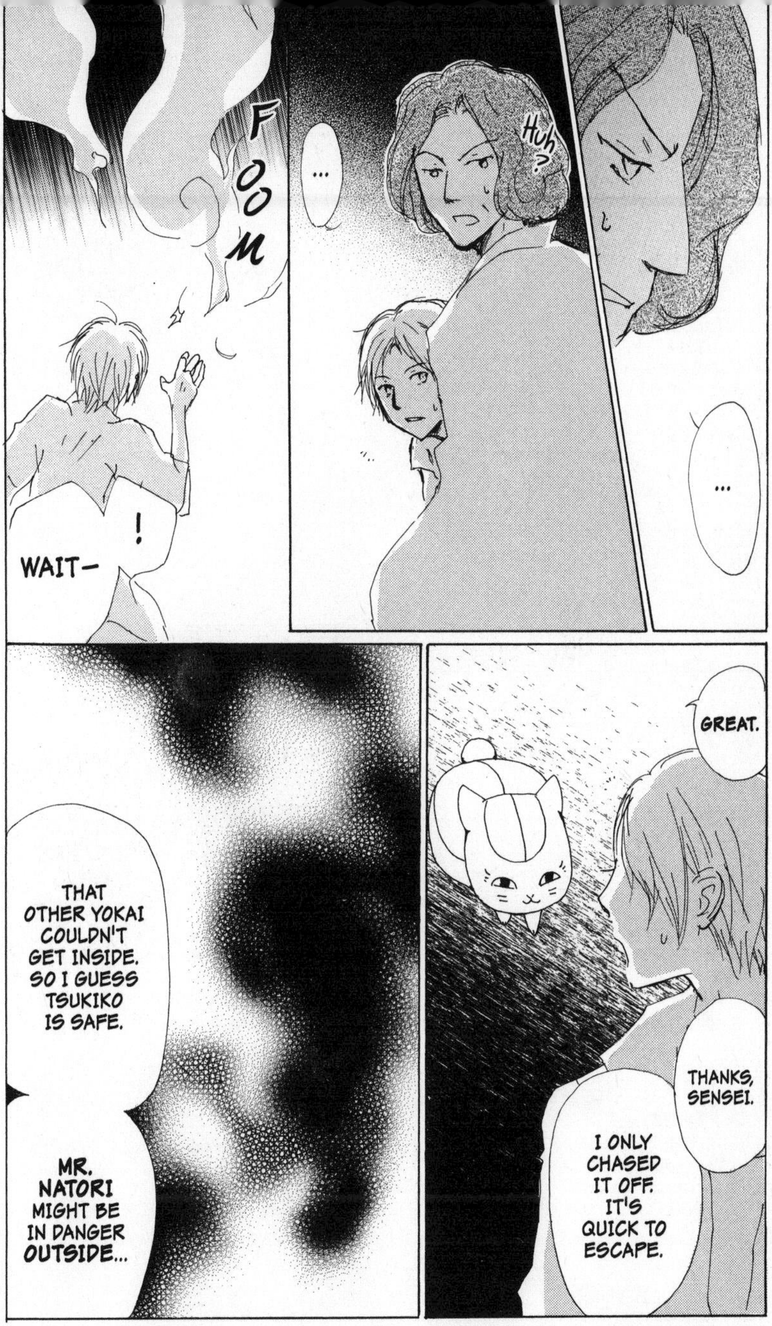
...
Huh?
...
FOOM
!
WAIT—
GREAT.
THANKS, SENSEI.
I ONLY CHASED IT OFF. IT'S QUICK TO ESCAPE.
THAT OTHER YOKAI COULDN'T GET INSIDE. SO I GUESS TSUKIKO IS SAFE.
MR. NATORI MIGHT BE IN DANGER OUTSIDE...

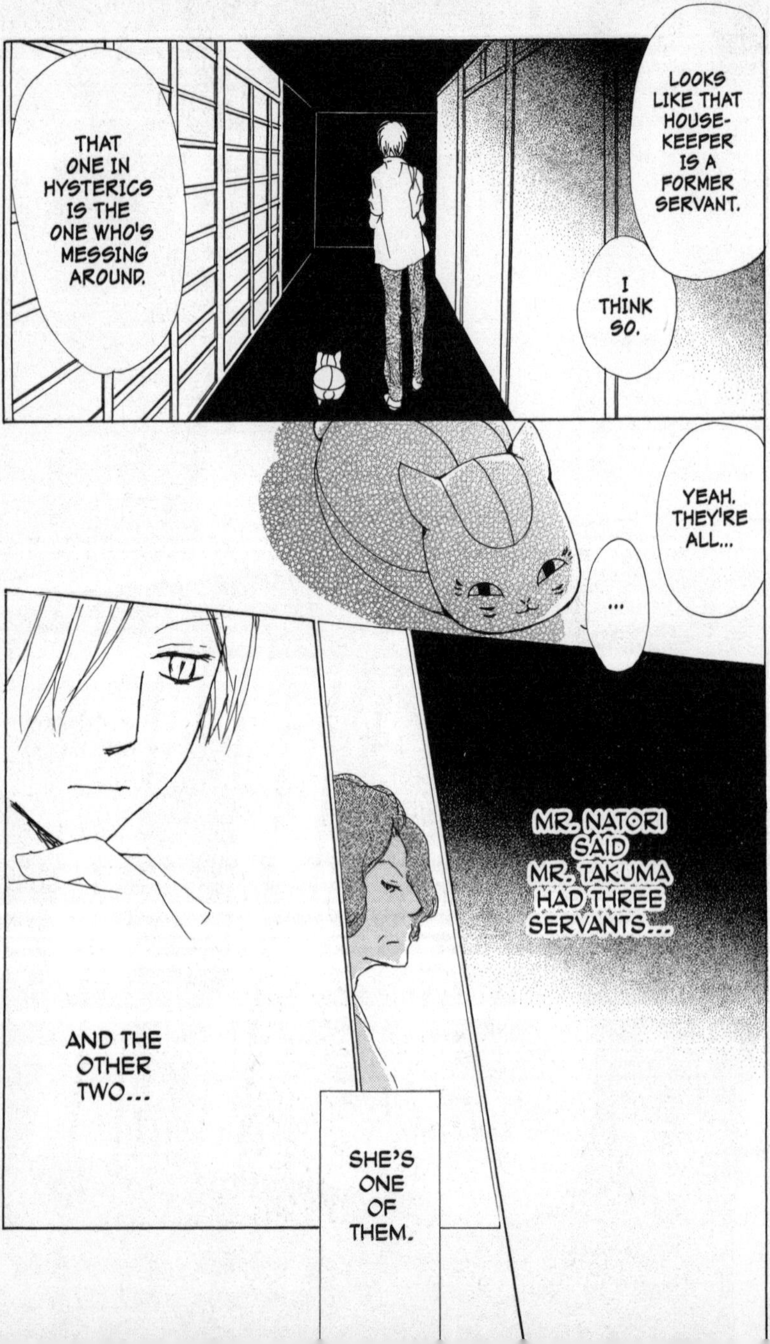
LOOKS LIKE THAT HOUSE-KEEPER IS A FORMER SERVANT.
I THINK SO.
THAT ONE IN HYSTERICS IS THE ONE WHO'S MESSING AROUND.
YEAH. THEY'RE ALL...
...
MR. NATORI SAID MR. TAKUMA HAD THREE SERVANTS...
SHE'S ONE OF THEM.
AND THE OTHER TWO...

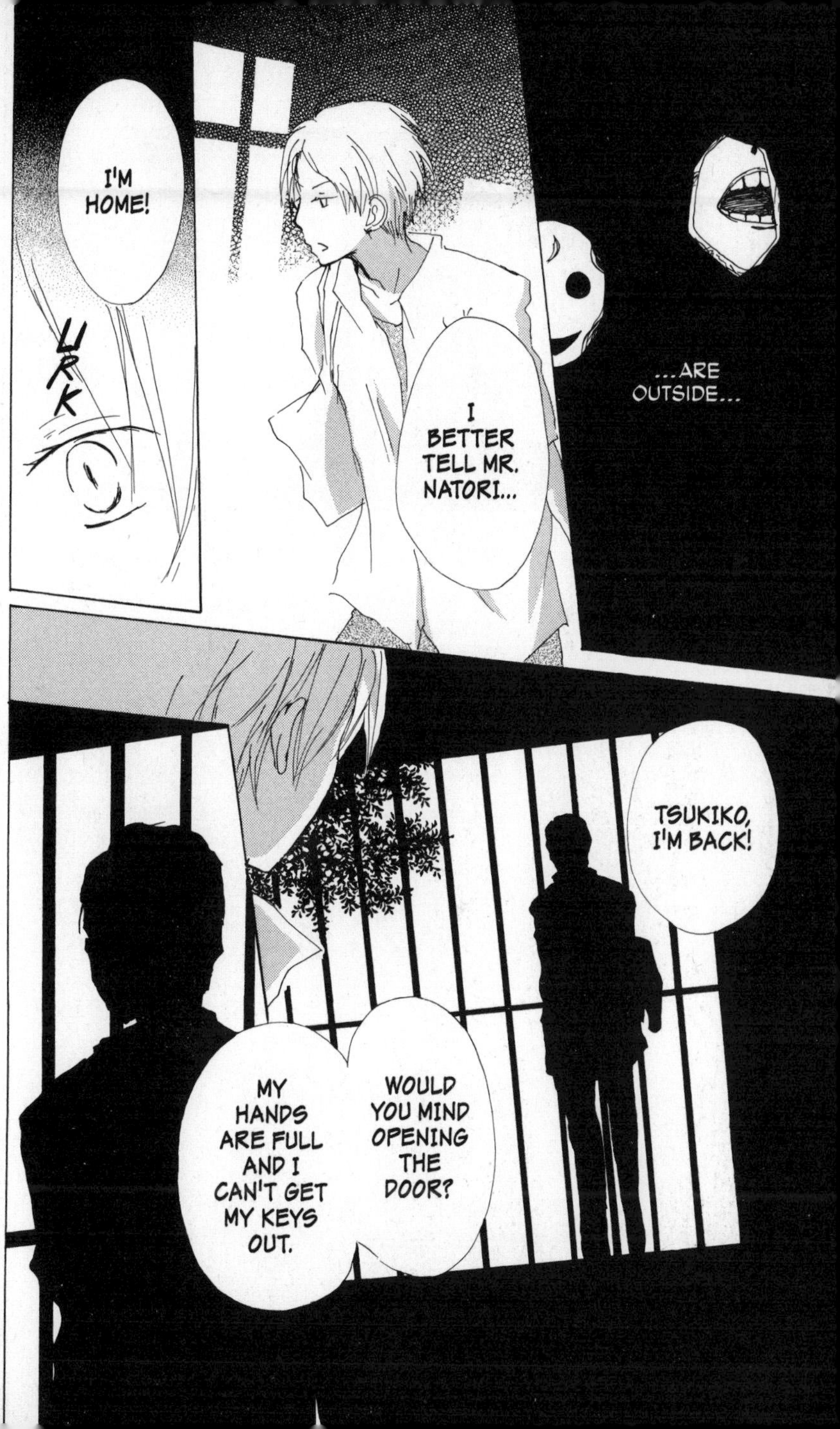
...ARE OUTSIDE...
I BETTER TELL MR. NATORI...
I'M HOME!
URK
TSUKIKO, I'M BACK!
WOULD YOU MIND OPENING THE DOOR?
MY HANDS ARE FULL AND I CAN'T GET MY KEYS OUT.

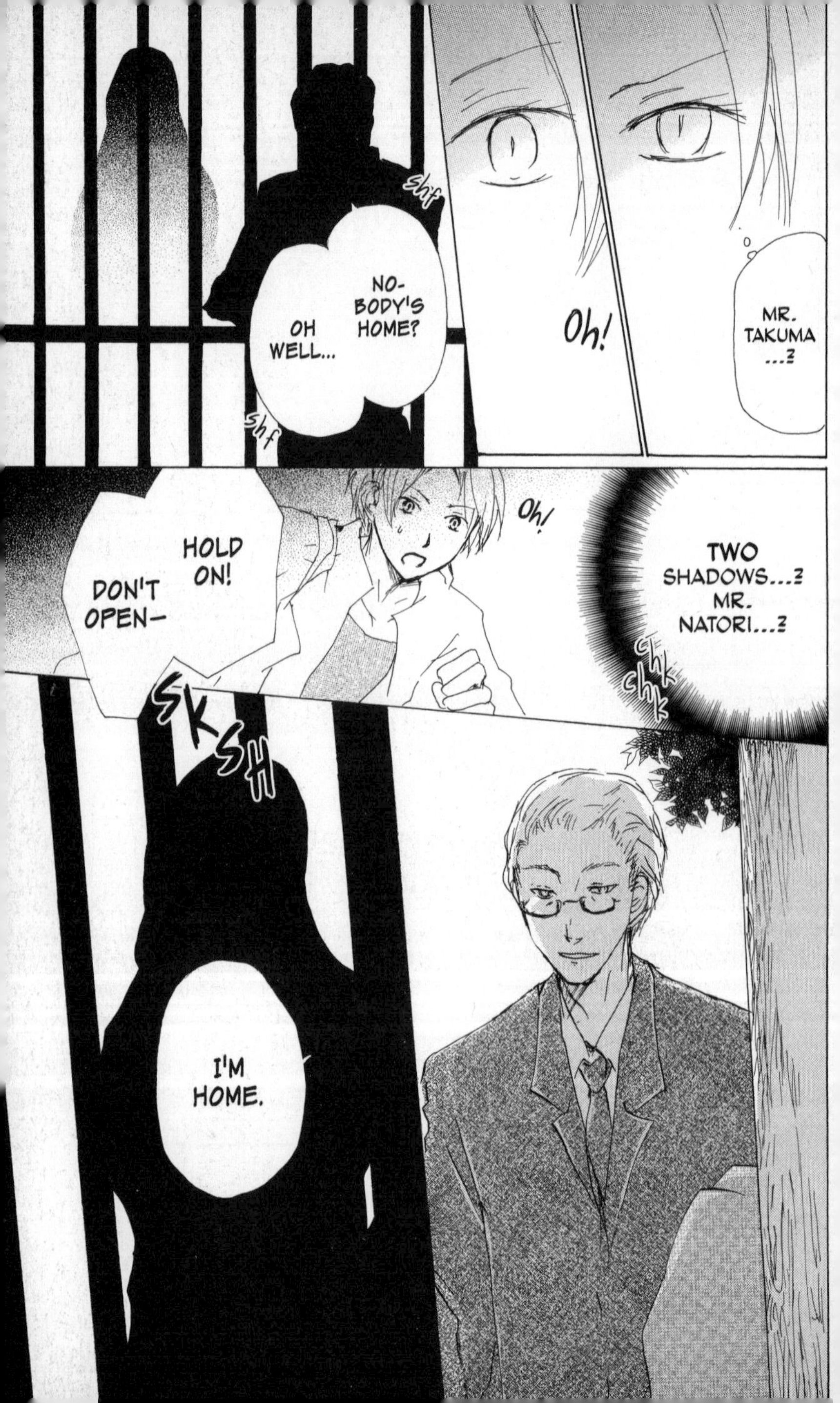
MR. TAKUMA...?
Oh!
shf
NO-BODY'S HOME? OH WELL...
shf
TWO SHADOWS...? MR. NATORI...?
chk chk
Oh!
HOLD ON! DON'T OPEN—
SKSH
I'M HOME.

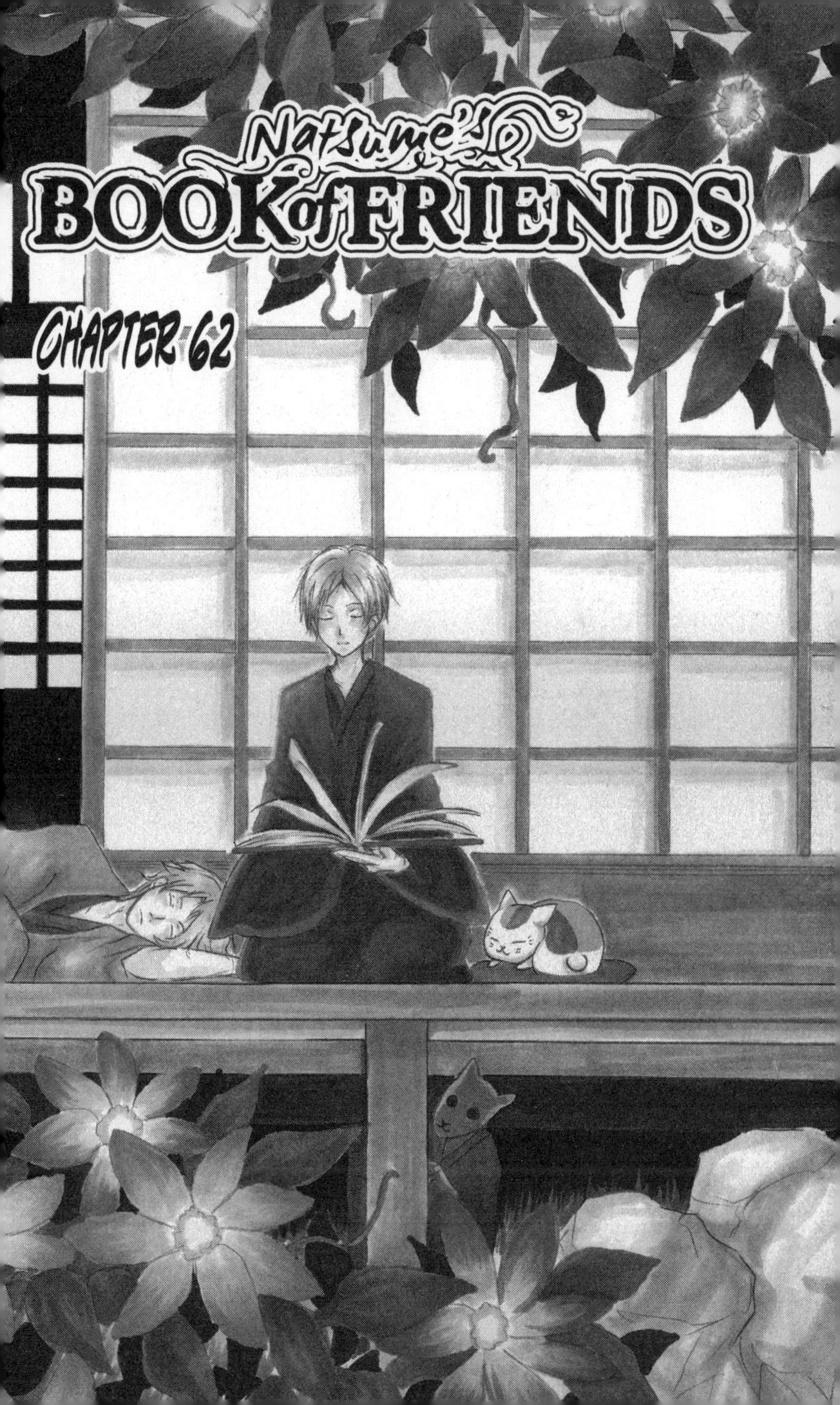
Natsume's
BOOK of FRIENDS
CHAPTER 62

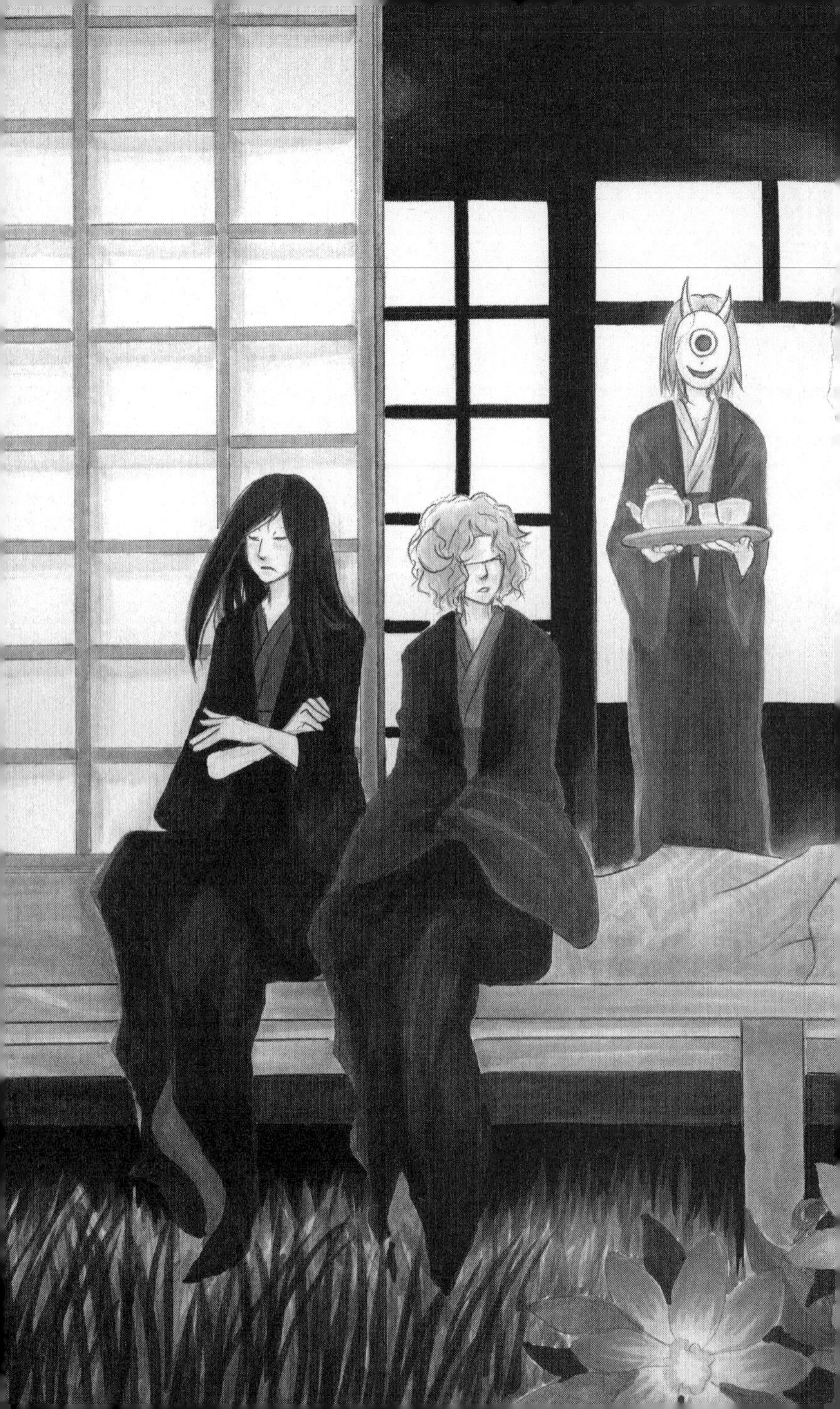

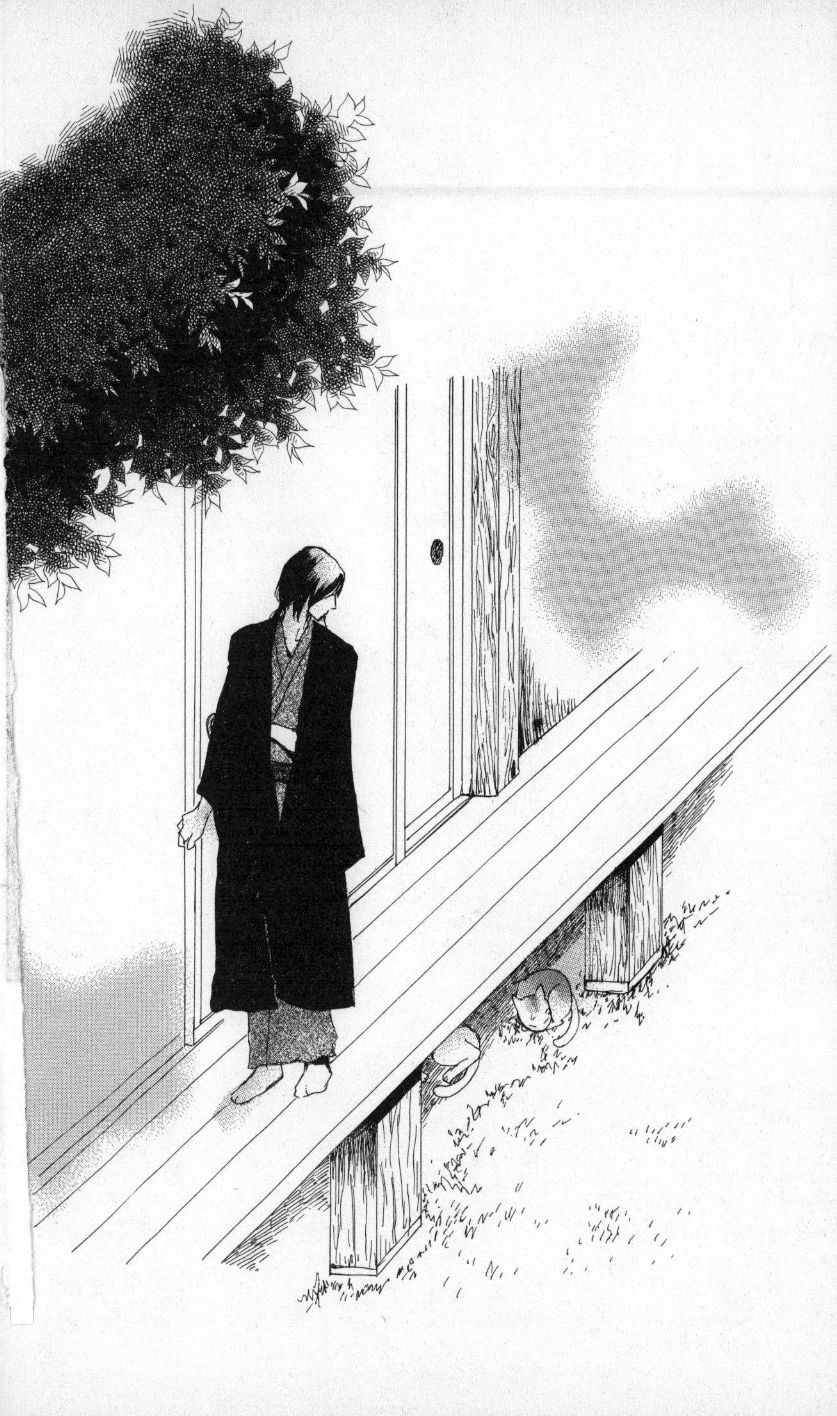

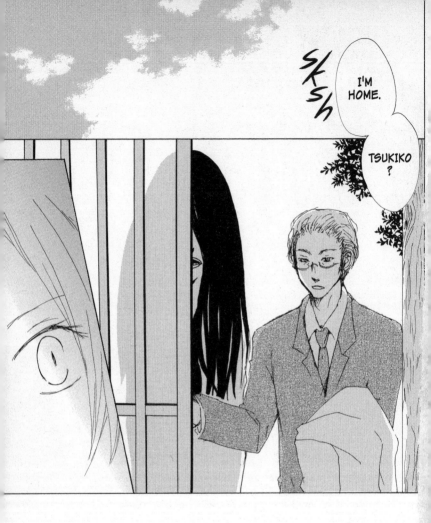

SK
SH

I'M HOME.

TSUKIKO?

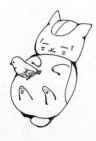

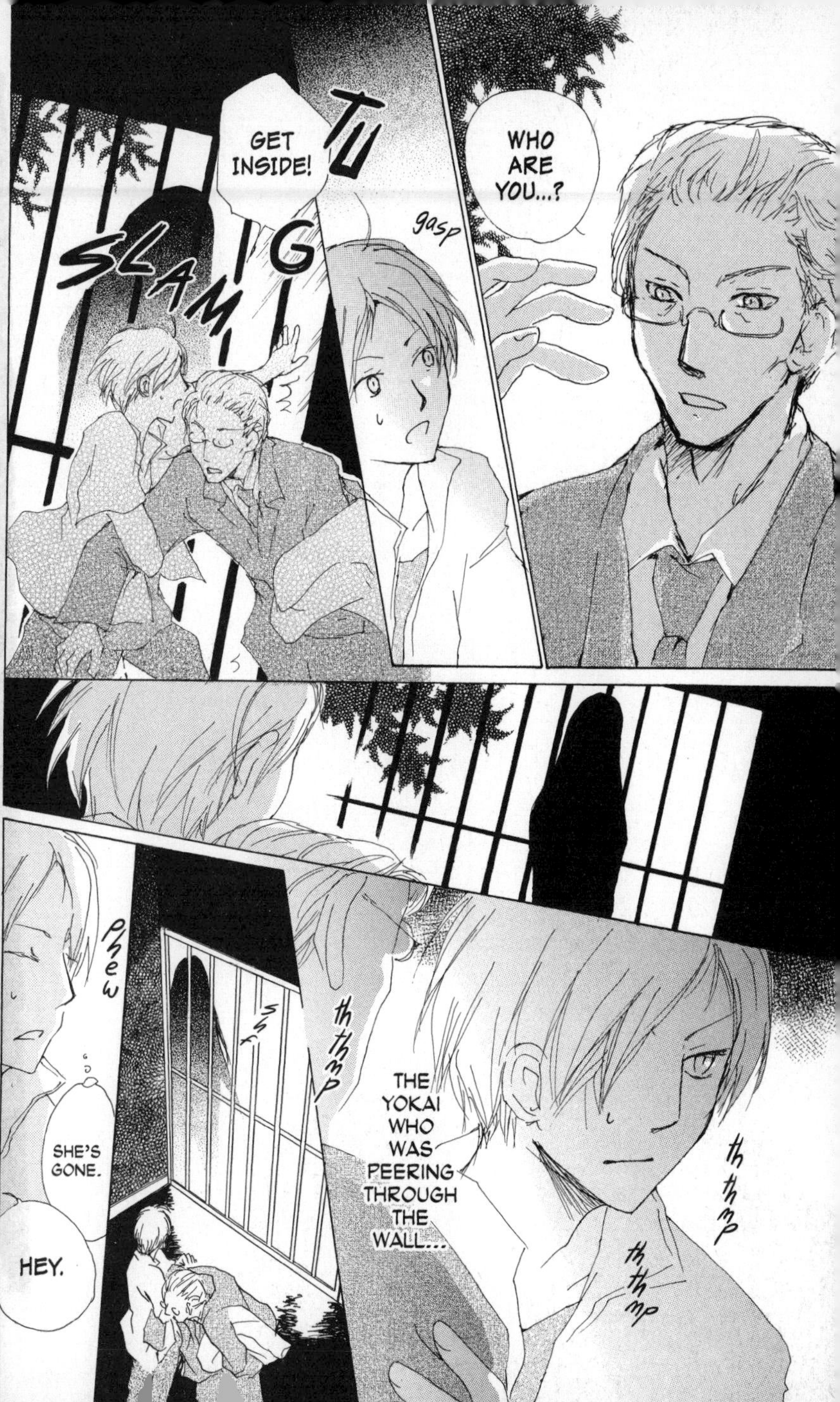
WHO ARE YOU...?
gasp
TUG
GET INSIDE!
SLAM
th thmp
th thmp
THE YOKAI WHO WAS PEERING THROUGH THE WALL...
th thmp
sf
Phew
SHE'S GONE.
HEY.

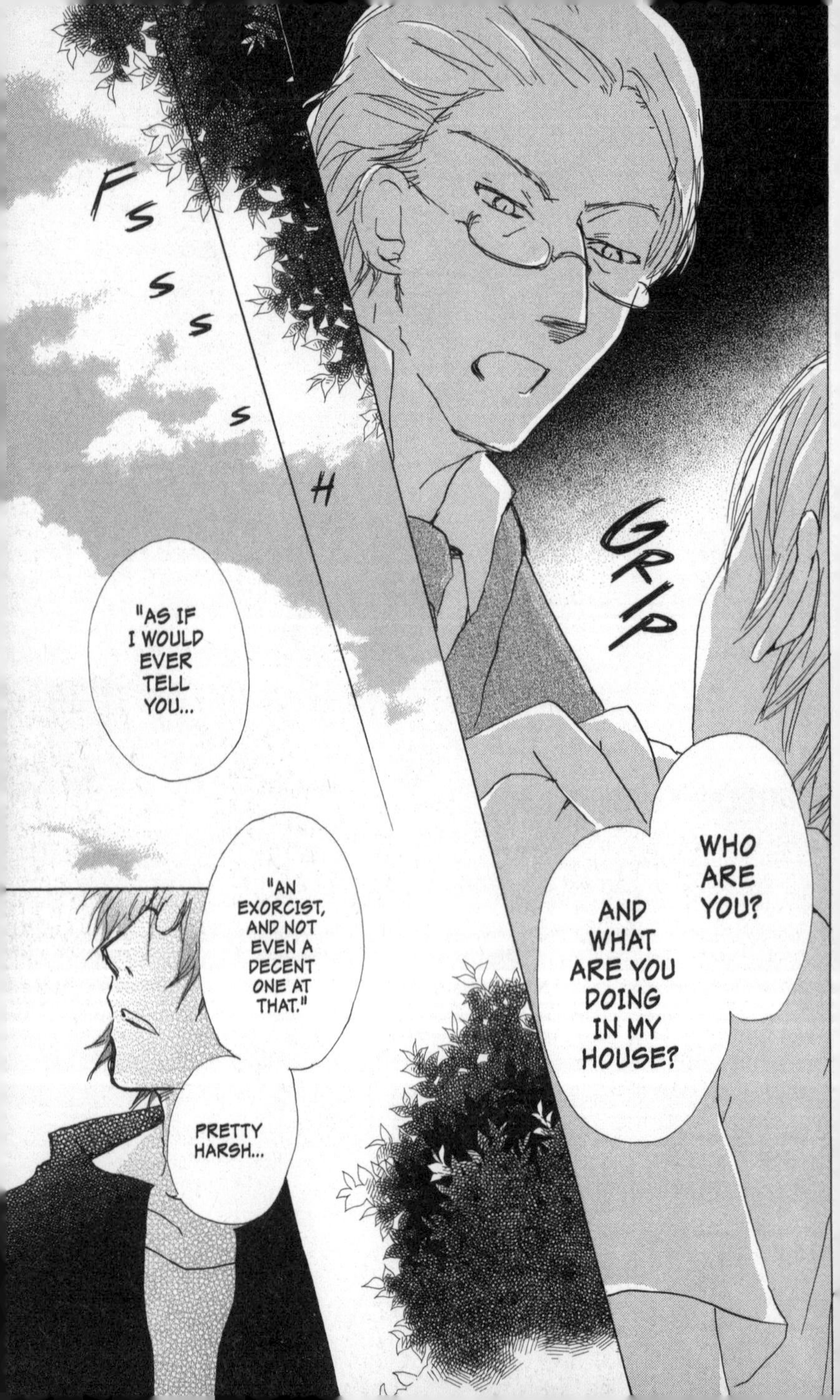
FSSSSH
GRIP
WHO ARE YOU?
AND WHAT ARE YOU DOING IN MY HOUSE?
"AS IF I WOULD EVER TELL YOU...
"AN EXORCIST, AND NOT EVEN A DECENT ONE AT THAT."
PRETTY HARSH...

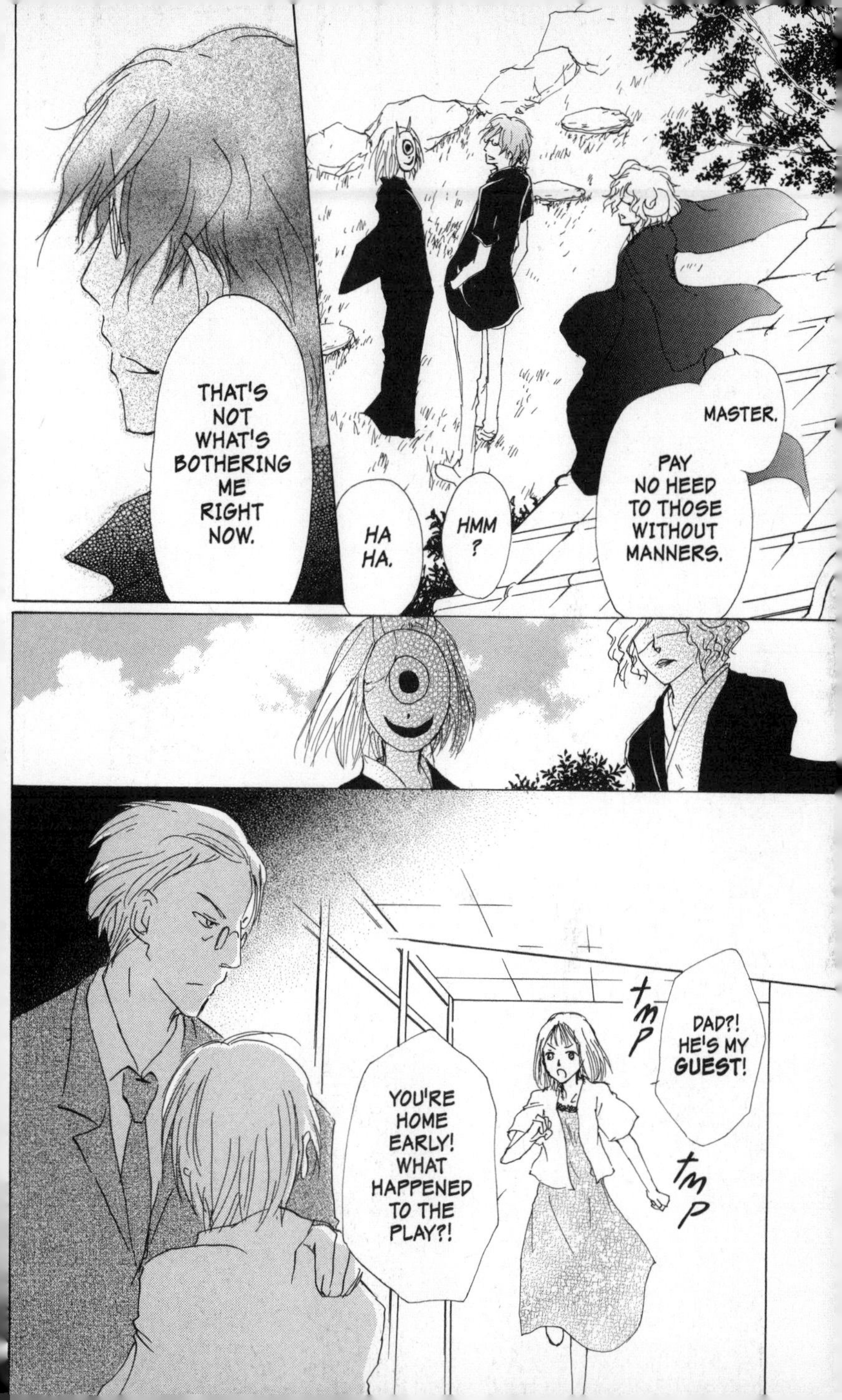
MASTER.
PAY NO HEED TO THOSE WITHOUT MANNERS.
HMM?
HA HA.
THAT'S NOT WHAT'S BOTHERING ME RIGHT NOW.
DAD?! HE'S MY GUEST!
tmp
tmp
YOU'RE HOME EARLY! WHAT HAPPENED TO THE PLAY?!

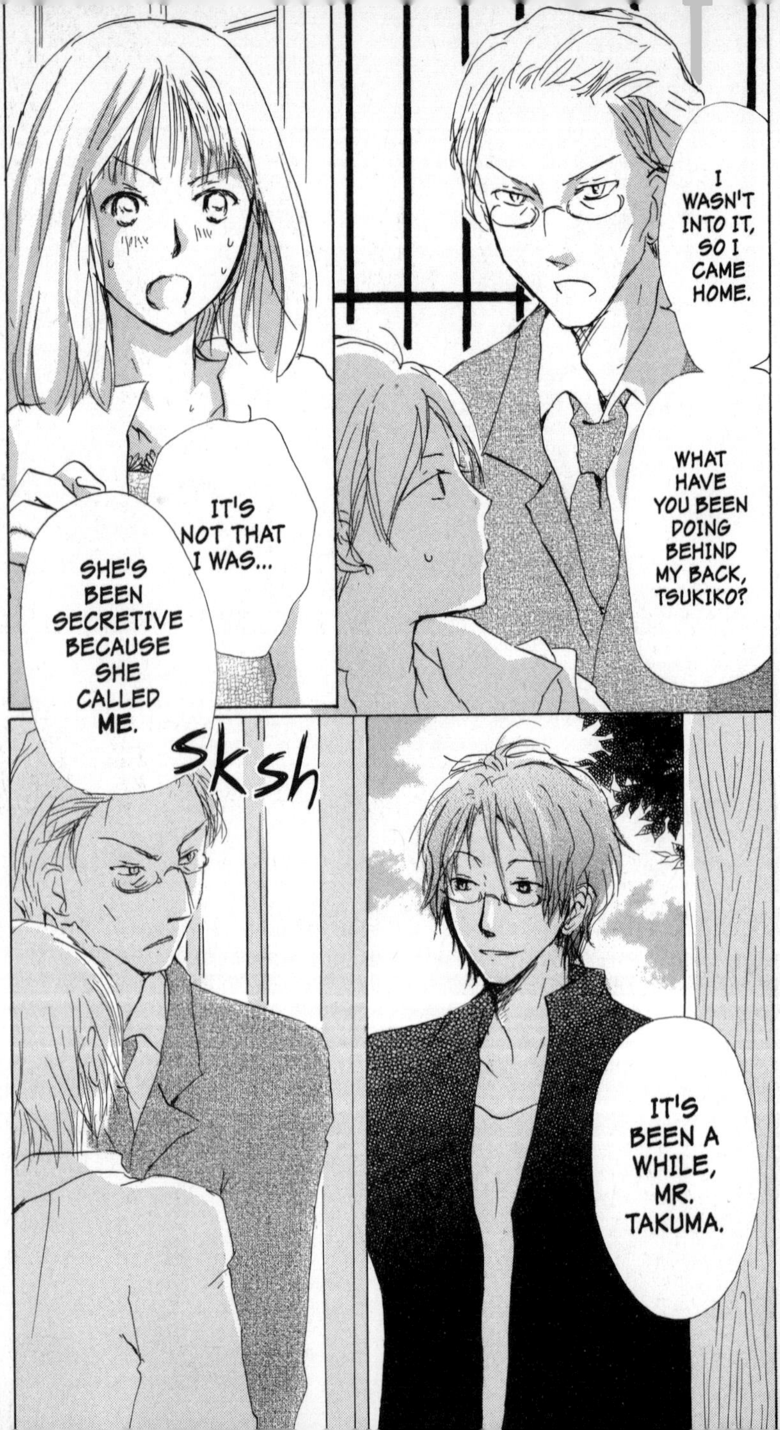
I WASN'T INTO IT, SO I CAME HOME.
WHAT HAVE YOU BEEN DOING BEHIND MY BACK, TSUKIKO?
IT'S NOT THAT I WAS...
IT'S BEEN A WHILE, MR. TAKUMA.
SHE'S BEEN SECRETIVE BECAUSE SHE CALLED ME.
Sksh

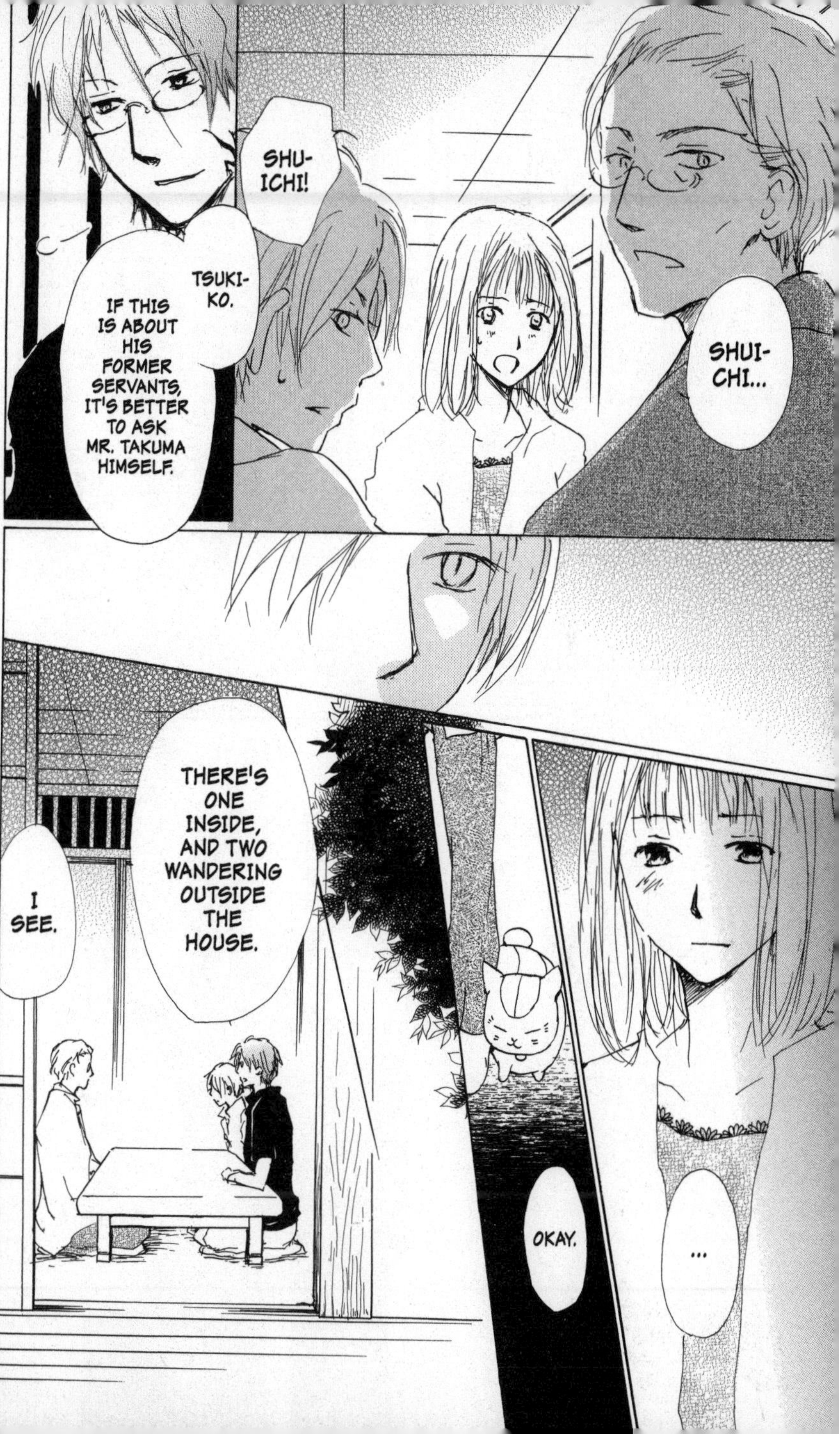
SHUI-CHI...
SHU-ICHI!
TSUKI-KO.
IF THIS IS ABOUT HIS FORMER SERVANTS, IT'S BETTER TO ASK MR. TAKUMA HIMSELF.
...
OKAY.
THERE'S ONE INSIDE, AND TWO WANDERING OUTSIDE THE HOUSE.
I SEE.

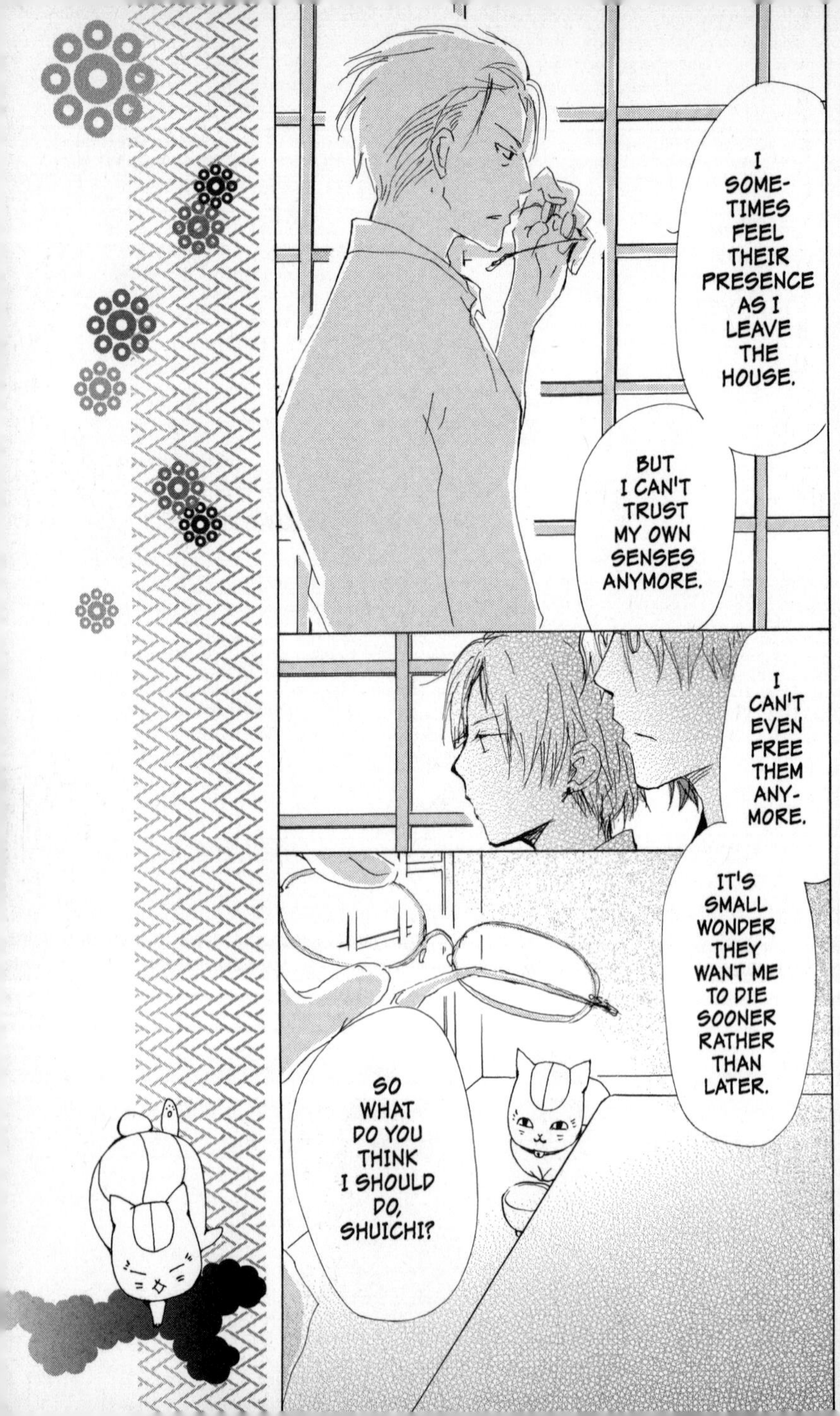
I SOMETIMES FEEL THEIR PRESENCE AS I LEAVE THE HOUSE.
BUT I CAN'T TRUST MY OWN SENSES ANYMORE.
I CAN'T EVEN FREE THEM ANYMORE.
IT'S SMALL WONDER THEY WANT ME TO DIE SOONER RATHER THAN LATER.
SO WHAT DO YOU THINK I SHOULD DO, SHUICHI?

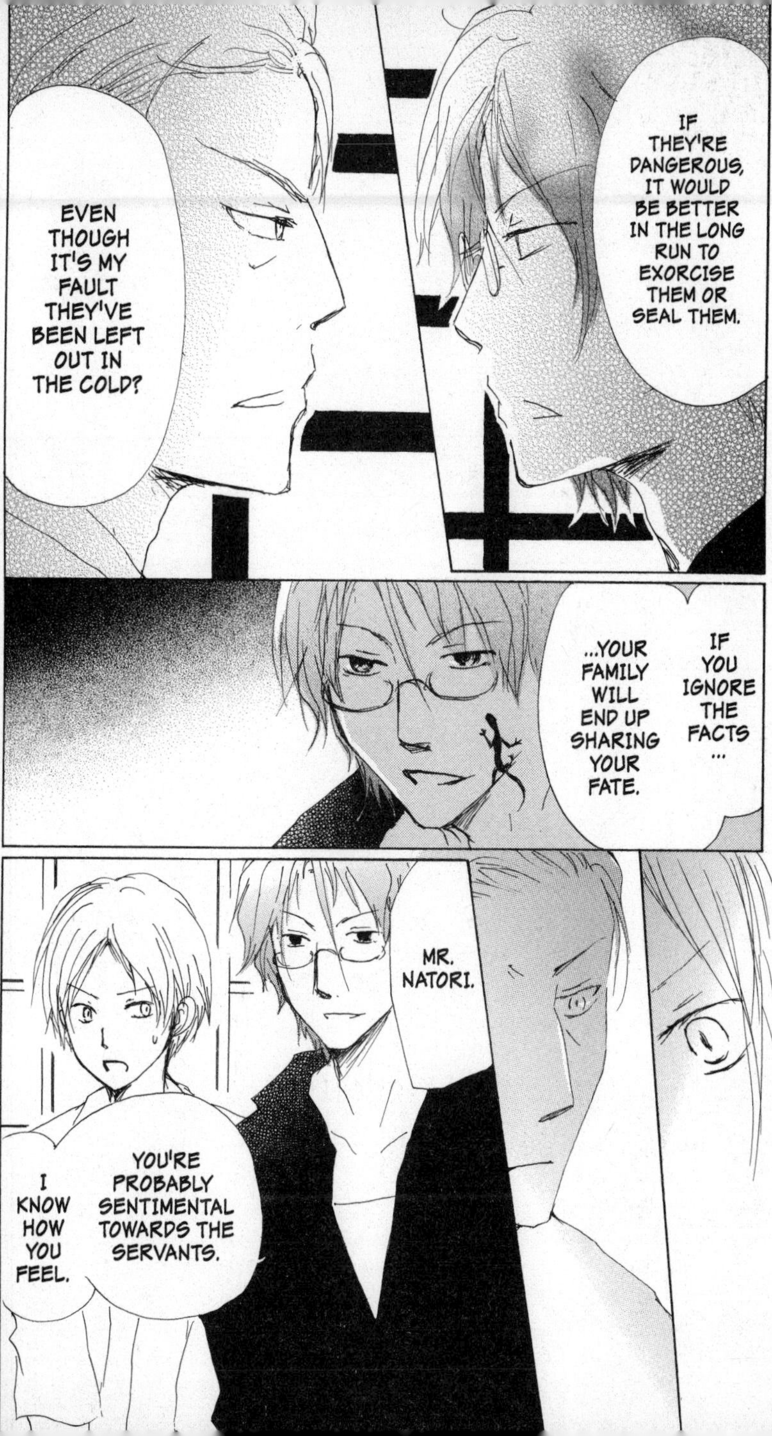
IF THEY'RE DANGEROUS, IT WOULD BE BETTER IN THE LONG RUN TO EXORCISE THEM OR SEAL THEM.
EVEN THOUGH IT'S MY FAULT THEY'VE BEEN LEFT OUT IN THE COLD?
IF YOU IGNORE THE FACTS...
...YOUR FAMILY WILL END UP SHARING YOUR FATE.
MR. NATORI.
YOU'RE PROBABLY SENTIMENTAL TOWARDS THE SERVANTS.
I KNOW HOW YOU FEEL.

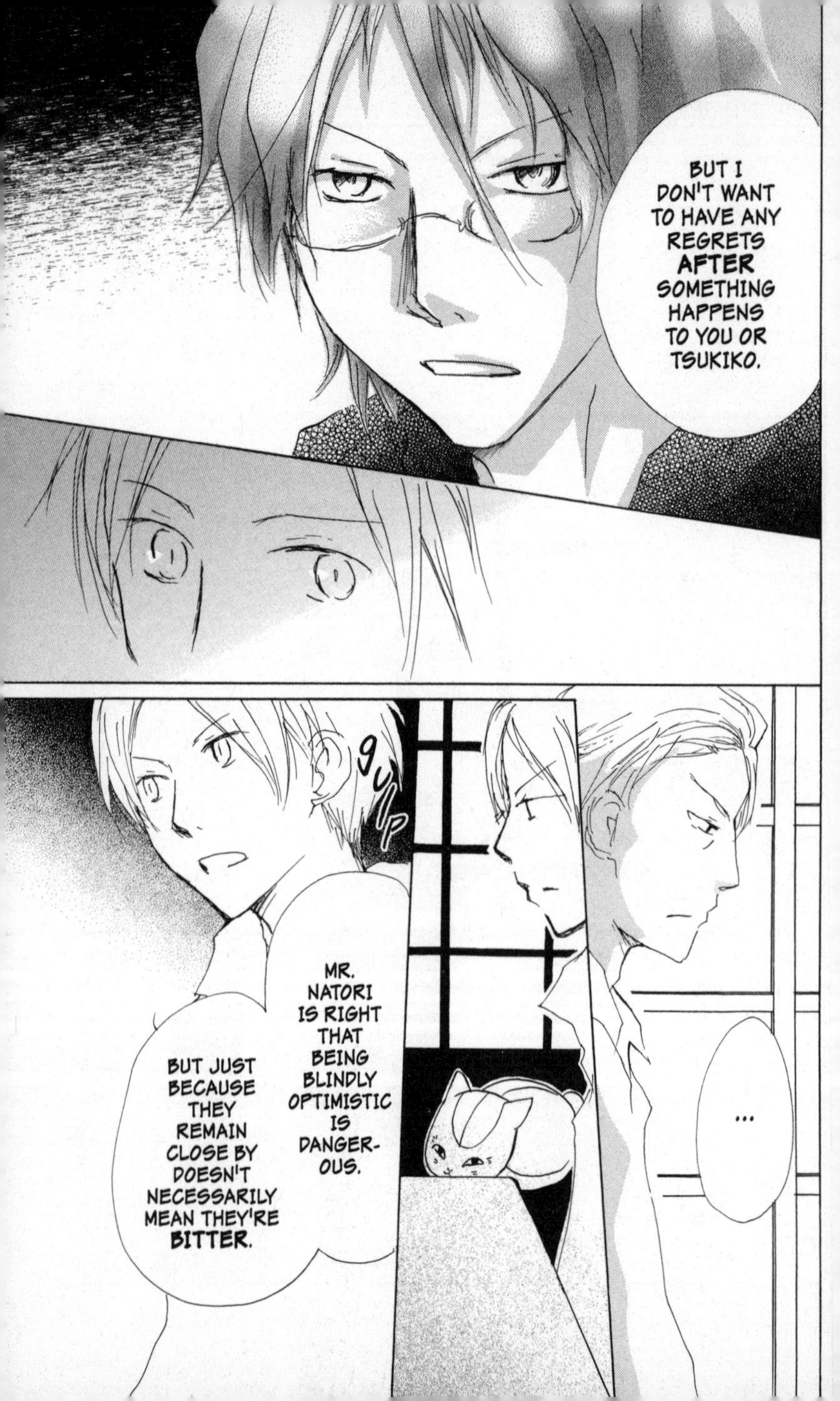

BUT I DON'T WANT TO HAVE ANY REGRETS **AFTER** SOMETHING HAPPENS TO YOU OR TSUKIKO.
...
GULP
MR. NATORI IS RIGHT THAT BEING BLINDLY OPTIMISTIC IS DANGER-OUS.
BUT JUST BECAUSE THEY REMAIN CLOSE BY DOESN'T NECESSARILY MEAN THEY'RE **BITTER**.

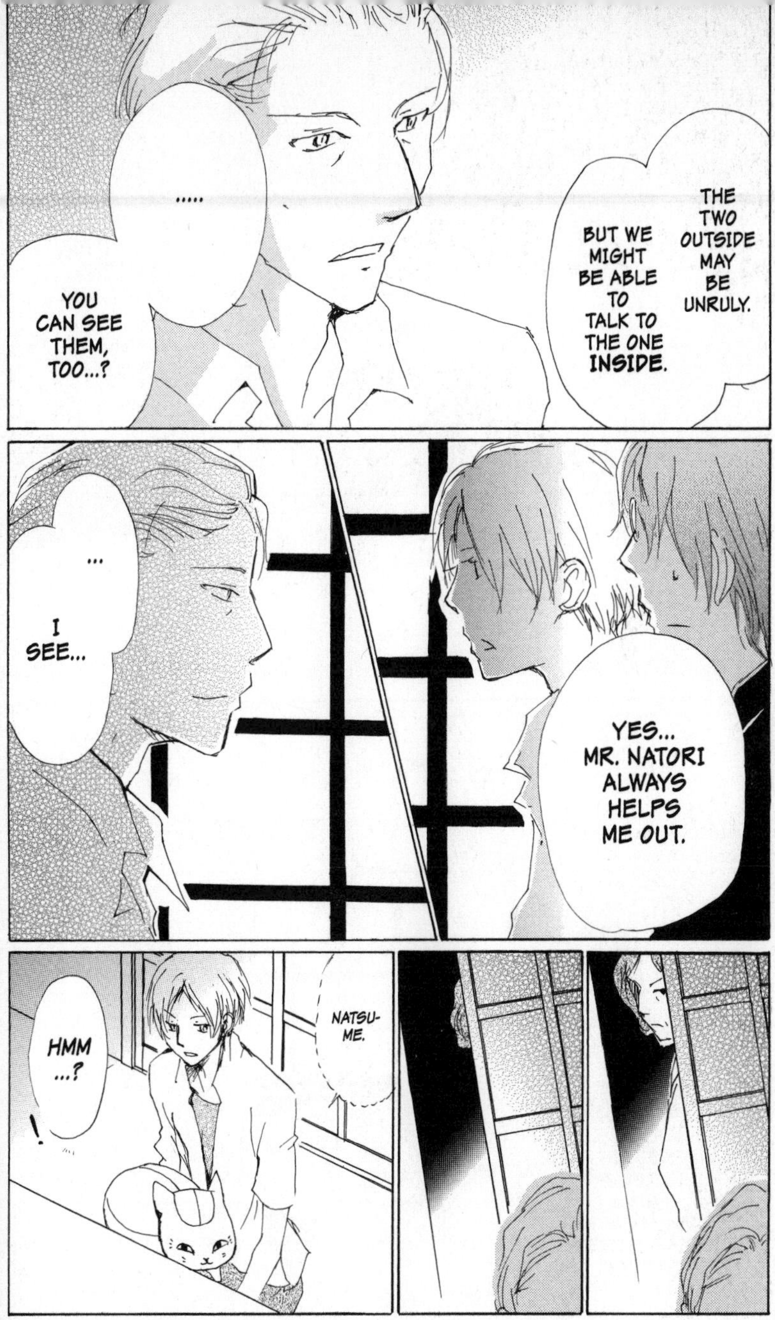
THE TWO OUTSIDE MAY BE UNRULY.
BUT WE MIGHT BE ABLE TO TALK TO THE ONE INSIDE.
.....
YOU CAN SEE THEM, TOO...?
YES... MR. NATORI ALWAYS HELPS ME OUT.
...
I SEE...
NATSU-ME.
HMM ...?
!

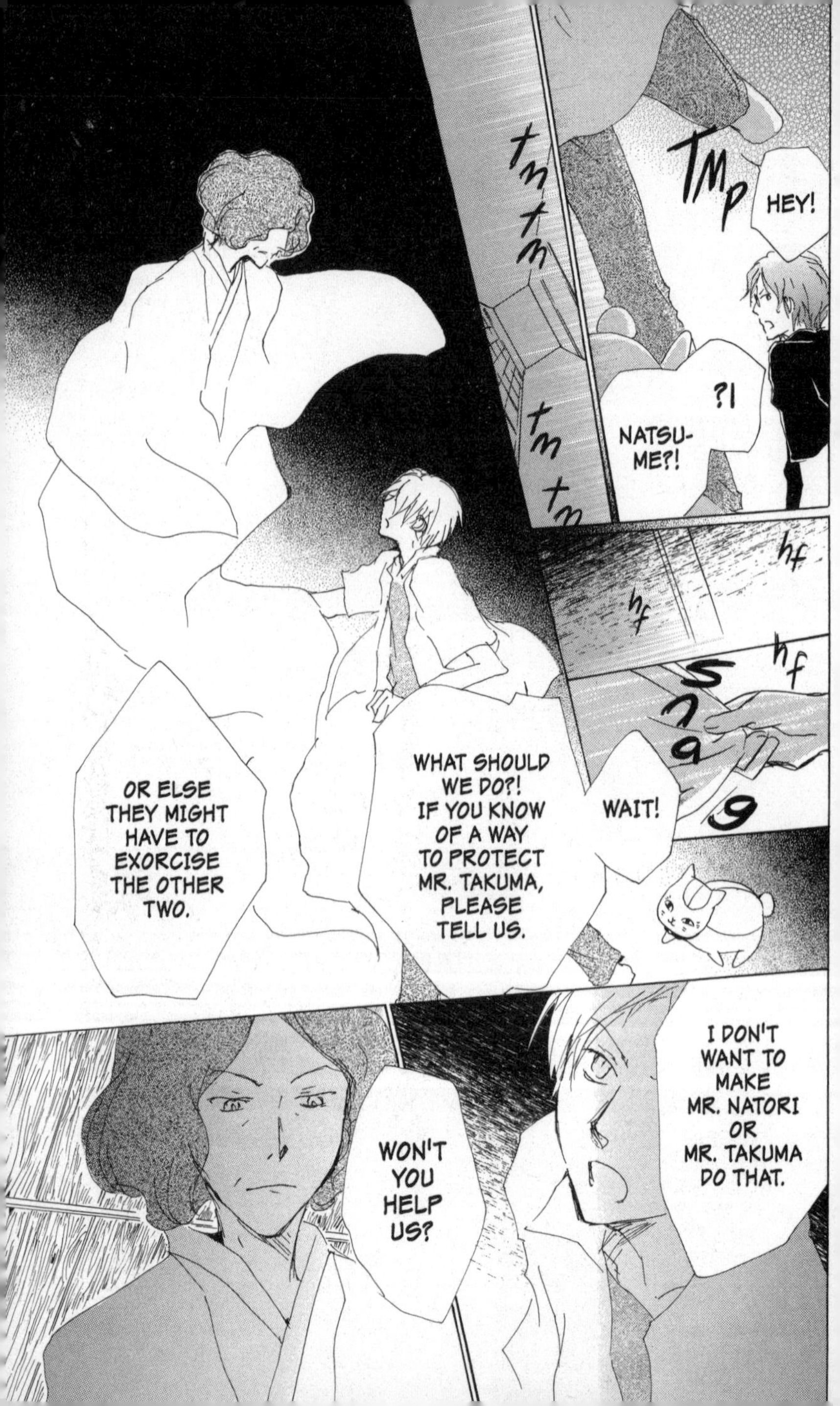
TMP
HEY!
tm tm tm tm
tm tm tm
?!
NATSU-
ME?!
hf
hf
hf
SNAG
WAIT!
WHAT SHOULD WE DO?! IF YOU KNOW OF A WAY TO PROTECT MR. TAKUMA, PLEASE TELL US.
OR ELSE THEY MIGHT HAVE TO EXORCISE THE OTHER TWO.
I DON'T WANT TO MAKE MR. NATORI OR MR. TAKUMA DO THAT.
WON'T YOU HELP US?

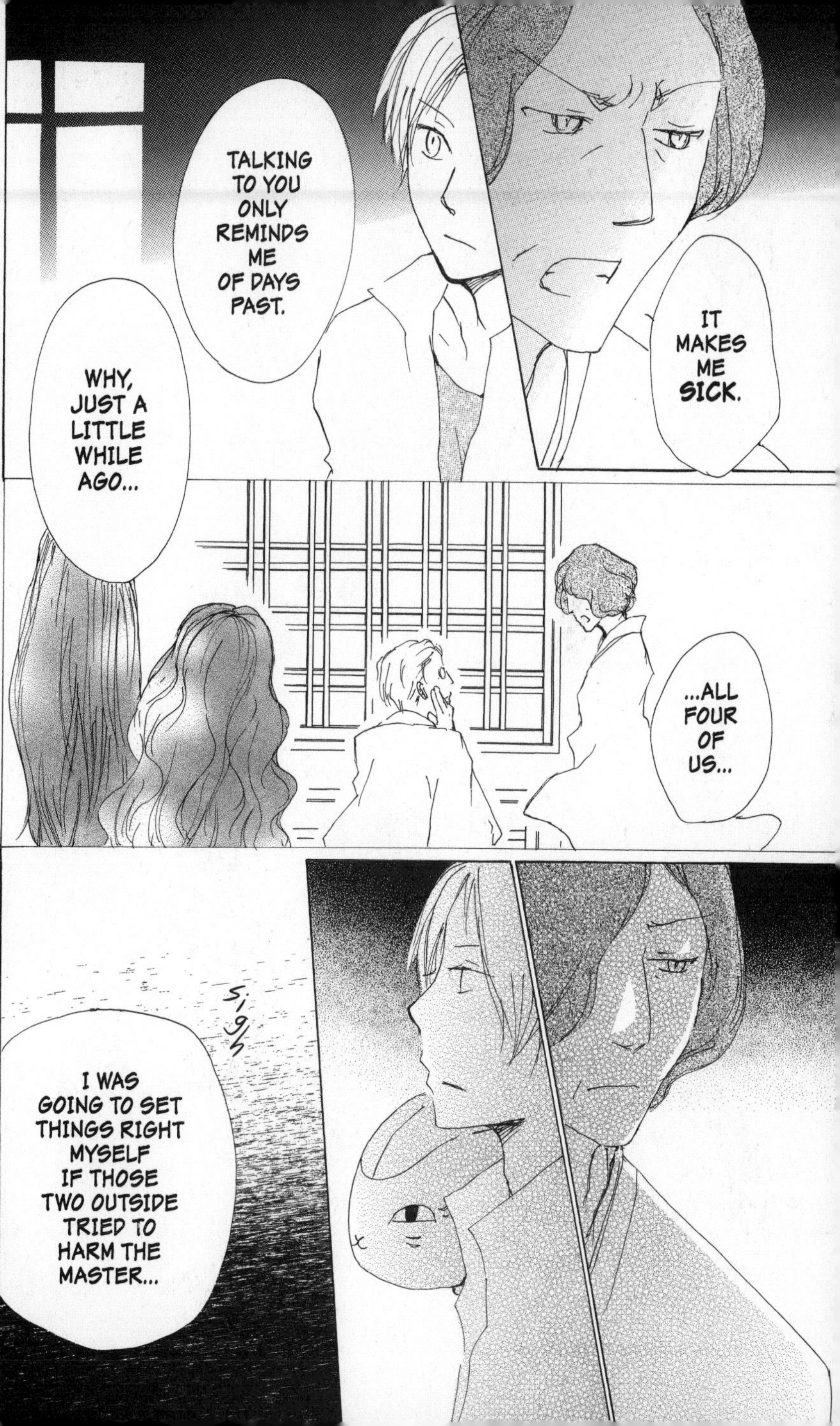
TALKING TO YOU ONLY REMINDS ME OF DAYS PAST.
IT MAKES ME SICK.
WHY, JUST A LITTLE WHILE AGO...
...ALL FOUR OF US...
sigh
I WAS GOING TO SET THINGS RIGHT MYSELF IF THOSE TWO OUTSIDE TRIED TO HARM THE MASTER...

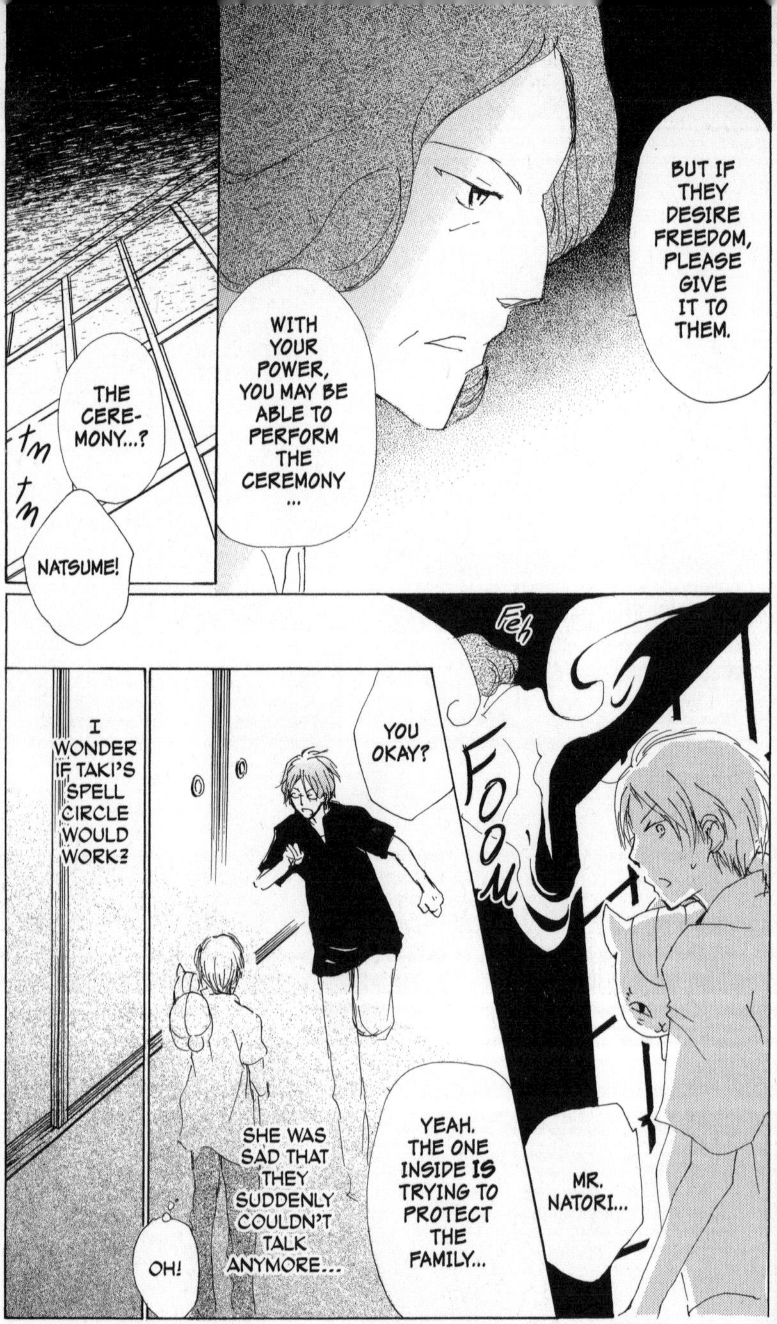
BUT IF THEY DESIRE FREEDOM, PLEASE GIVE IT TO THEM.
WITH YOUR POWER, YOU MAY BE ABLE TO PERFORM THE CEREMONY...
THE CERE-MONY...?
tm tm
NATSUME!
Feh
FOOM
MR. NATORI...
YEAH. THE ONE INSIDE IS TRYING TO PROTECT THE FAMILY...
YOU OKAY?
I WONDER IF TAKI'S SPELL CIRCLE WOULD WORK?
SHE WAS SAD THAT THEY SUDDENLY COULDN'T TALK ANYMORE...
OH!

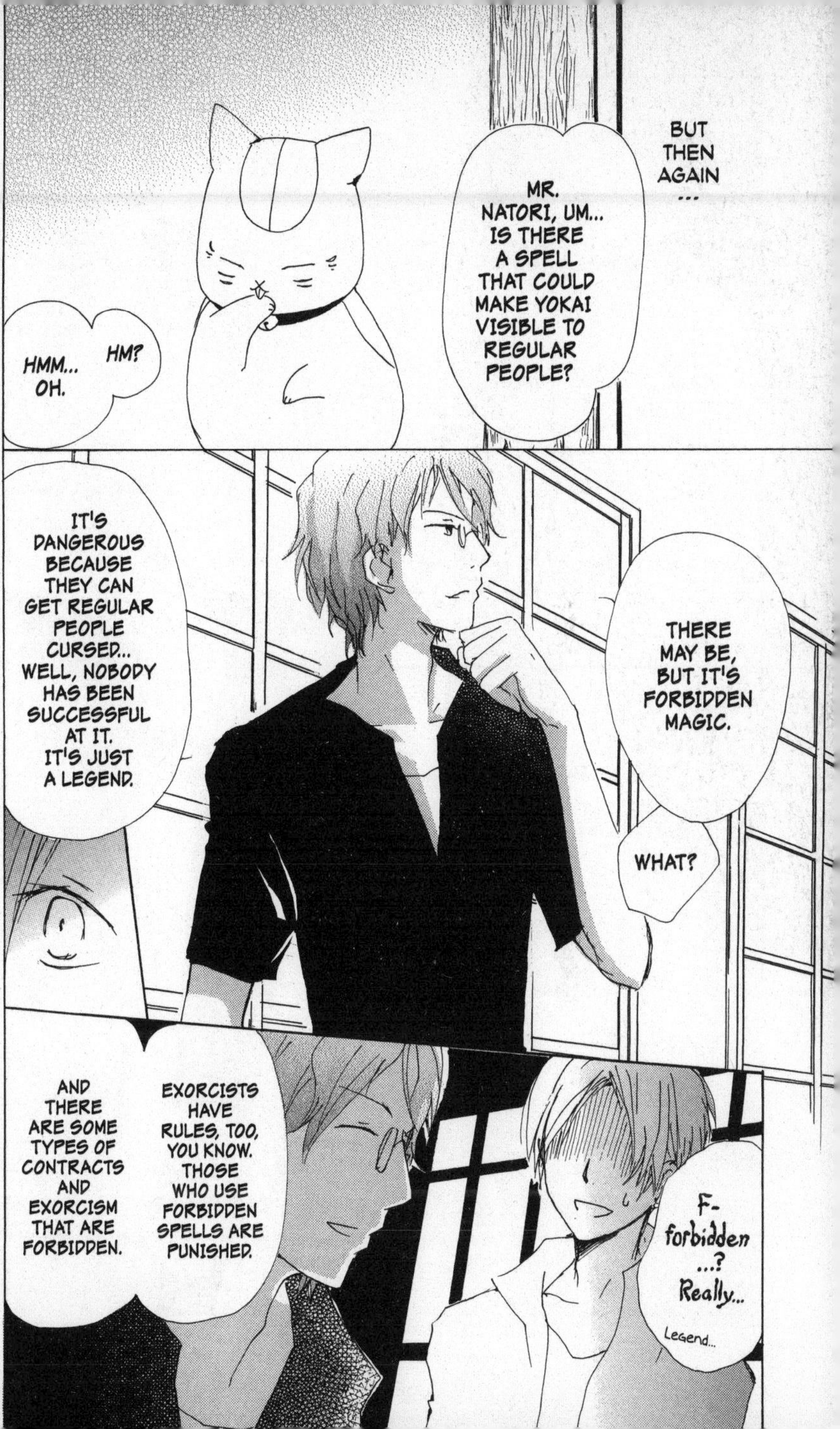
BUT THEN AGAIN ...
MR. NATORI, UM... IS THERE A SPELL THAT COULD MAKE YOKAI VISIBLE TO REGULAR PEOPLE?
HM?
HMM... OH.
THERE MAY BE, BUT IT'S FORBIDDEN MAGIC.
WHAT?
IT'S DANGEROUS BECAUSE THEY CAN GET REGULAR PEOPLE CURSED... WELL, NOBODY HAS BEEN SUCCESSFUL AT IT. IT'S JUST A LEGEND.
F-forbidden ...? Really...
Legend...
EXORCISTS HAVE RULES, TOO, YOU KNOW. THOSE WHO USE FORBIDDEN SPELLS ARE PUNISHED.
AND THERE ARE SOME TYPES OF CONTRACTS AND EXORCISM THAT ARE FORBIDDEN.

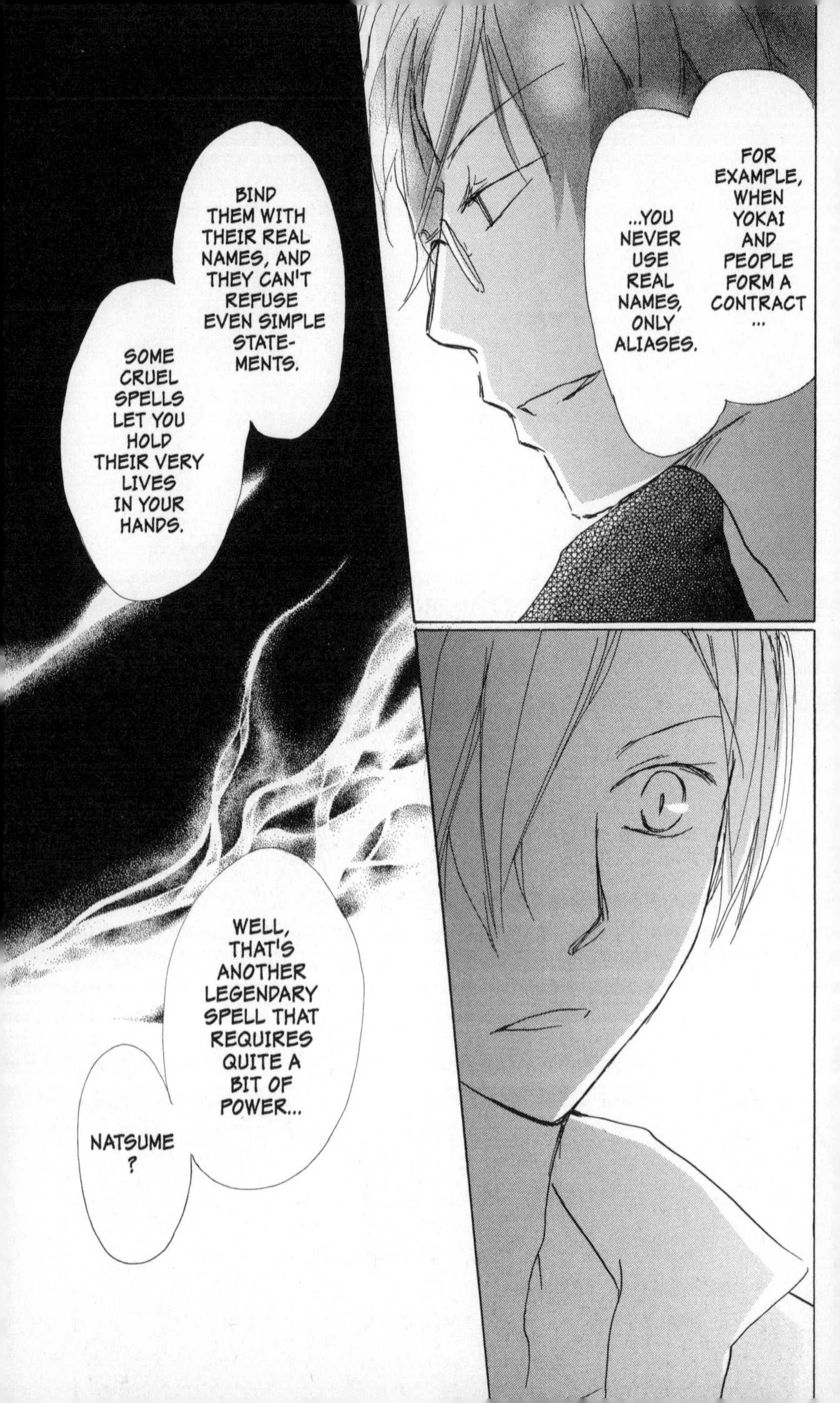
FOR EXAMPLE, WHEN YOKAI AND PEOPLE FORM A CONTRACT...
...YOU NEVER USE REAL NAMES, ONLY ALIASES.
BIND THEM WITH THEIR REAL NAMES, AND THEY CAN'T REFUSE EVEN SIMPLE STATE-MENTS.
SOME CRUEL SPELLS LET YOU HOLD THEIR VERY LIVES IN YOUR HANDS.
WELL, THAT'S ANOTHER LEGENDARY SPELL THAT REQUIRES QUITE A BIT OF POWER...
NATSUME?

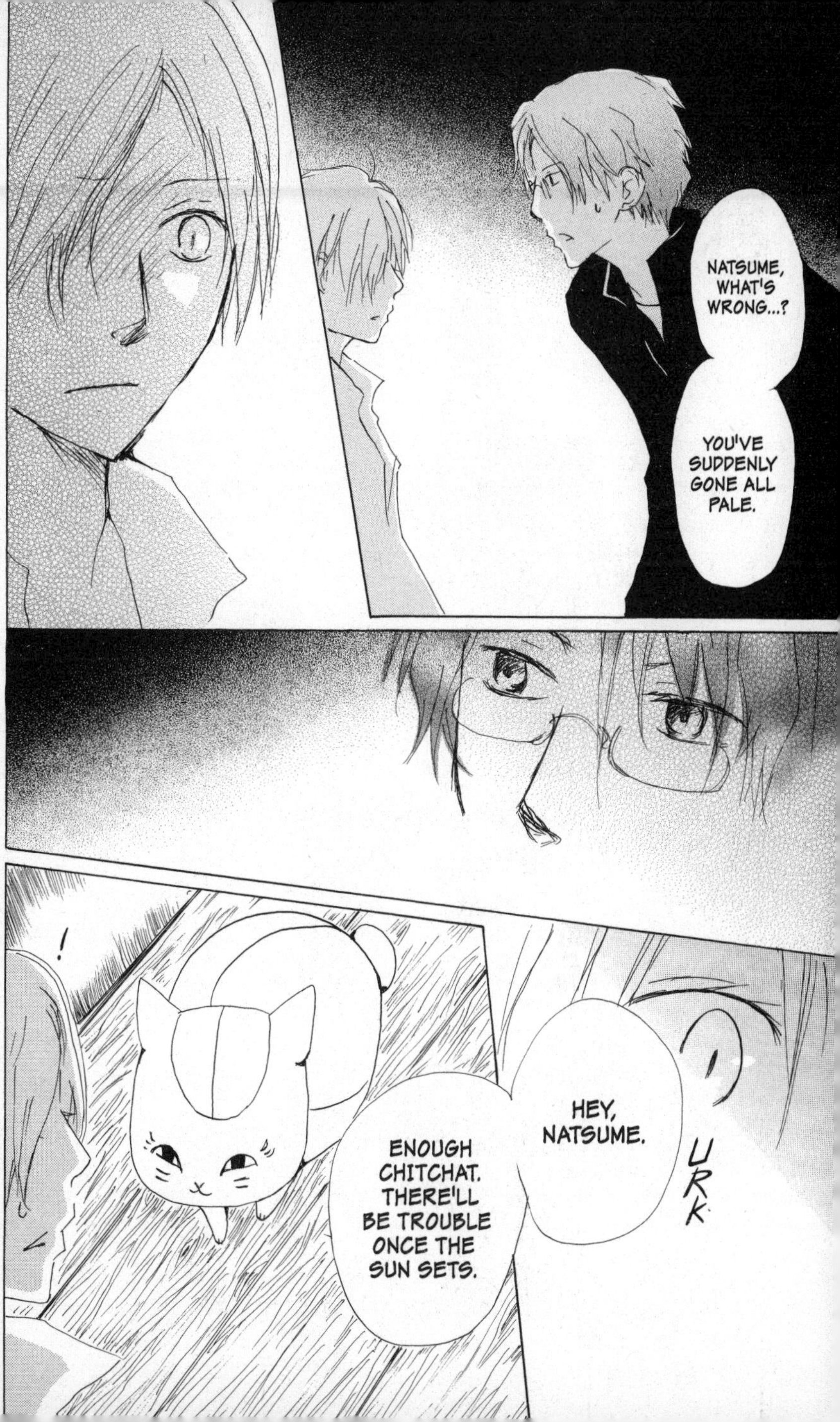
NATSUME, WHAT'S WRONG...?
YOU'VE SUDDENLY GONE ALL PALE.
!
HEY, NATSUME.
ENOUGH CHITCHAT. THERE'LL BE TROUBLE ONCE THE SUN SETS.
URK

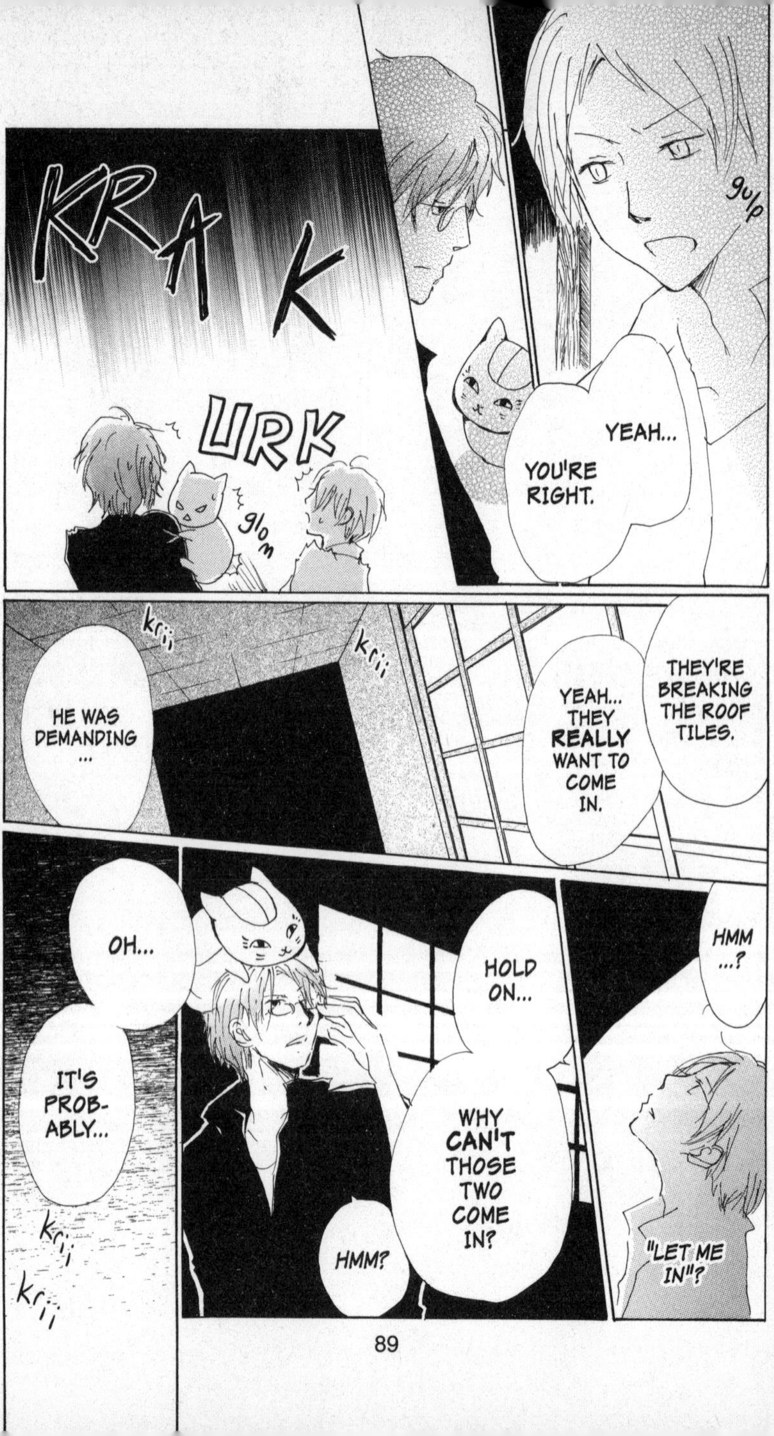

gulp
YEAH... YOU'RE RIGHT.
KRAK
URK
glom
THEY'RE BREAKING THE ROOF TILES.
YEAH... THEY **REALLY** WANT TO COME IN.
krii
HE WAS DEMANDING ...
krii
HMM ...?
"LET ME IN"?
HOLD ON...
WHY **CAN'T** THOSE TWO COME IN?
HMM?
OH...
IT'S PROB- ABLY...
krii
krii

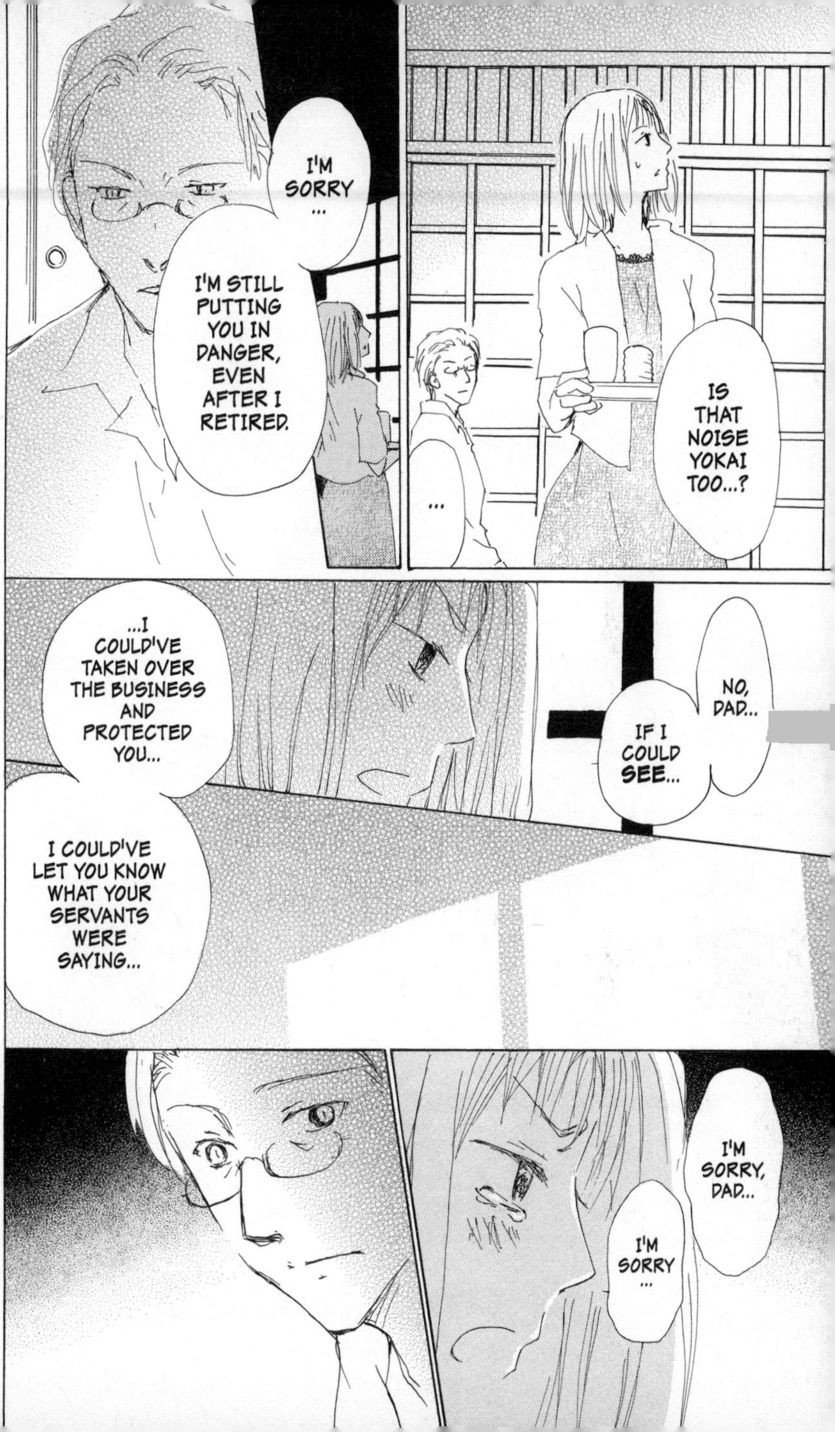
IS THAT NOISE YOKAI TOO...?
...
I'M SORRY ...
I'M STILL PUTTING YOU IN DANGER, EVEN AFTER I RETIRED.
NO, DAD...
IF I COULD SEE...
...I COULD'VE TAKEN OVER THE BUSINESS AND PROTECTED YOU...
I COULD'VE LET YOU KNOW WHAT YOUR SERVANTS WERE SAYING...
I'M SORRY, DAD...
I'M SORRY ...

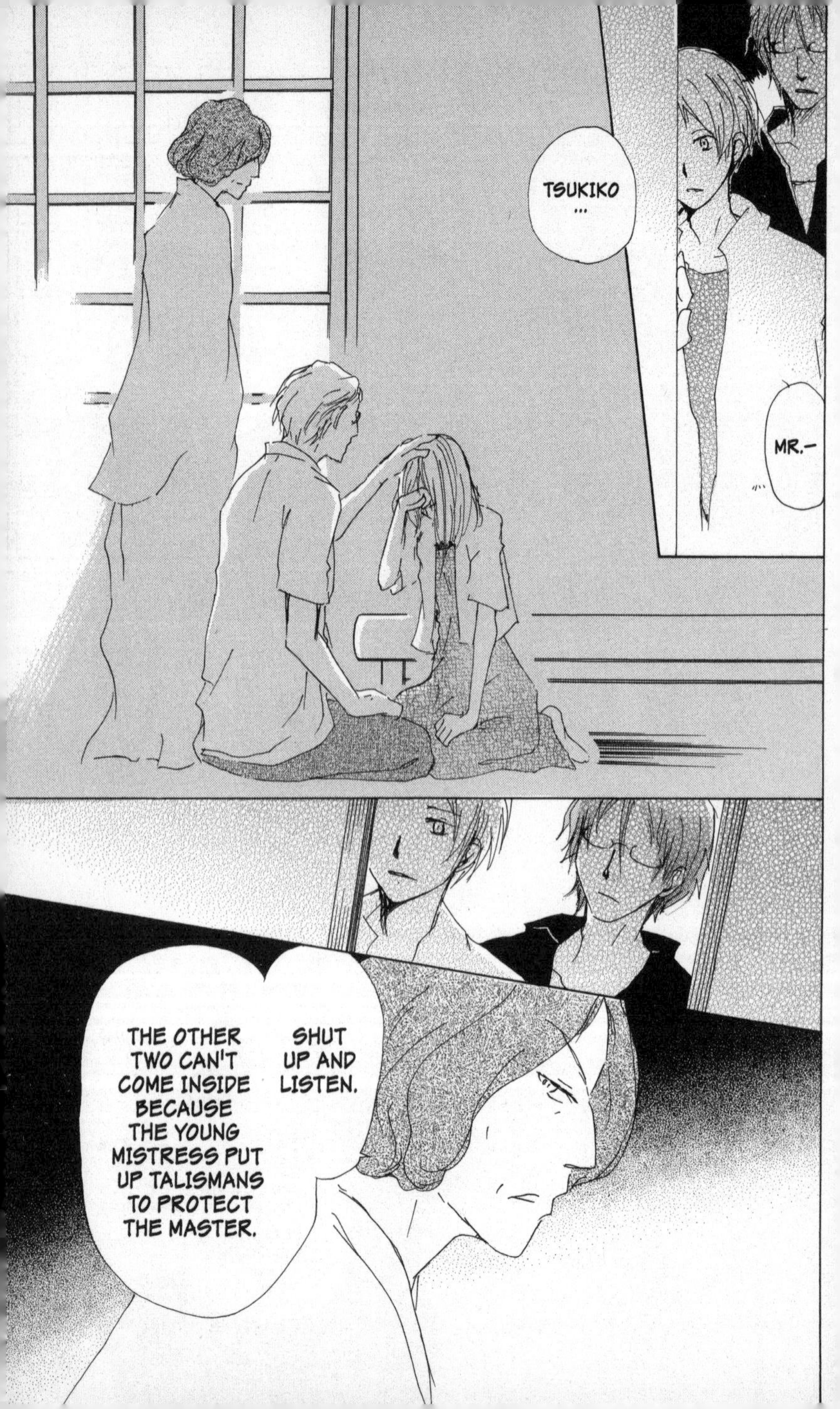

MR.–
TSUKIKO ...
SHUT UP AND LISTEN.
THE OTHER TWO CAN'T COME INSIDE BECAUSE THE YOUNG MISTRESS PUT UP TALISMANS TO PROTECT THE MASTER.

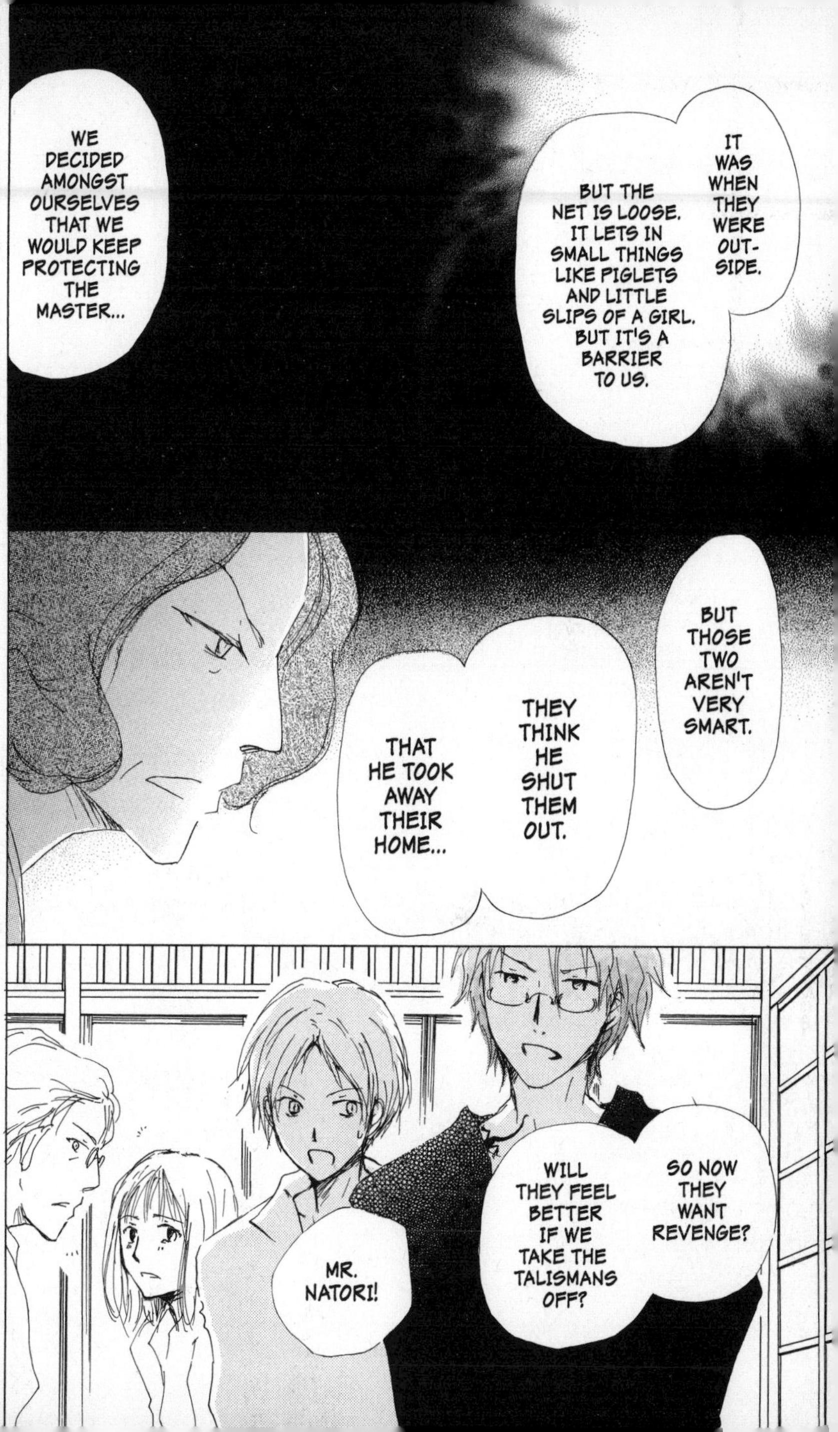
IT WAS WHEN THEY WERE OUT-SIDE.
BUT THE NET IS LOOSE. IT LETS IN SMALL THINGS LIKE PIGLETS AND LITTLE SLIPS OF A GIRL. BUT IT'S A BARRIER TO US.
WE DECIDED AMONGST OURSELVES THAT WE WOULD KEEP PROTECTING THE MASTER...
BUT THOSE TWO AREN'T VERY SMART.
THEY THINK HE SHUT THEM OUT.
THAT HE TOOK AWAY THEIR HOME...
SO NOW THEY WANT REVENGE?
WILL THEY FEEL BETTER IF WE TAKE THE TALISMANS OFF?
MR. NATORI!

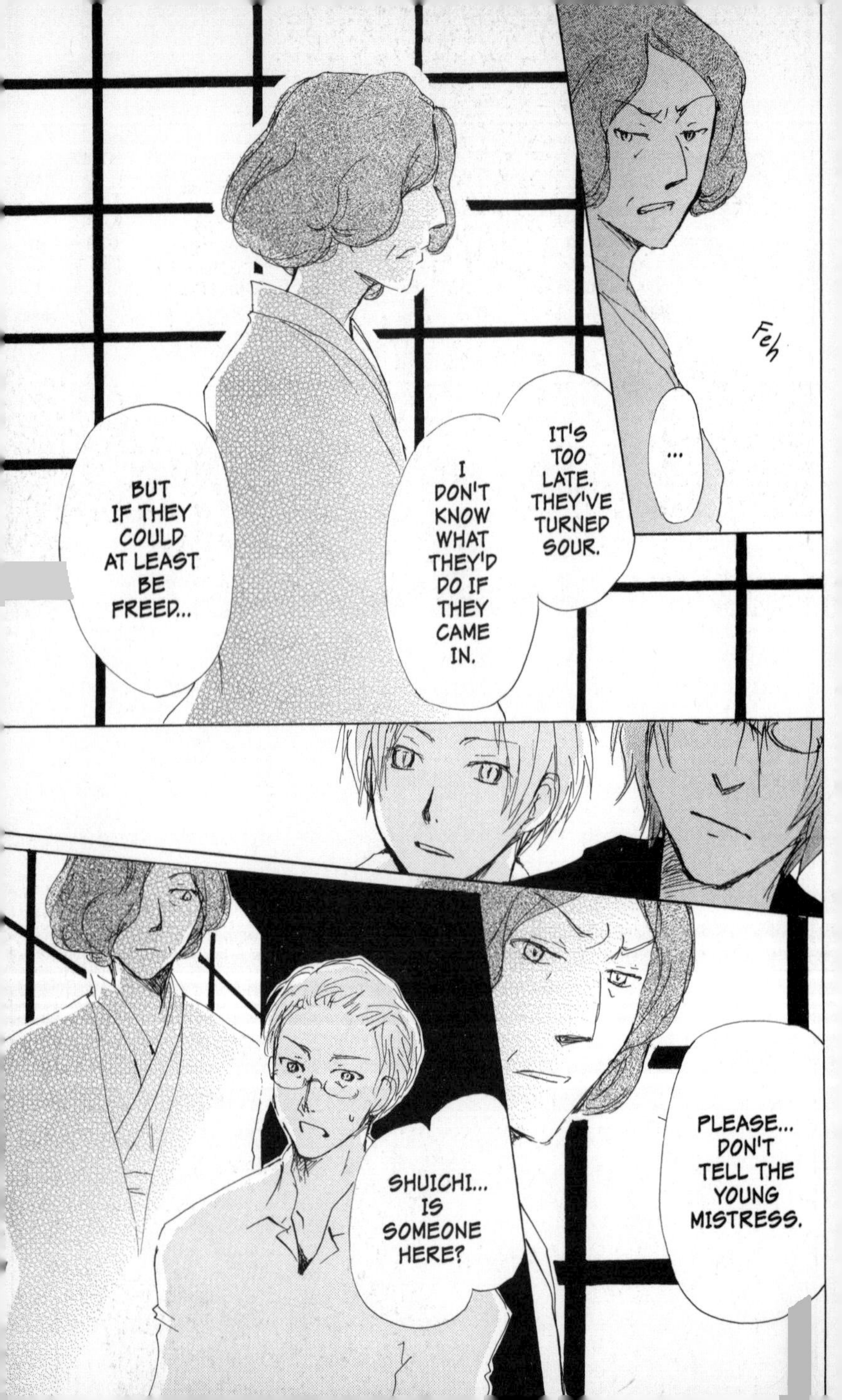
Feh
...
IT'S TOO LATE. THEY'VE TURNED SOUR.
I DON'T KNOW WHAT THEY'D DO IF THEY CAME IN.
BUT IF THEY COULD AT LEAST BE FREED...
PLEASE... DON'T TELL THE YOUNG MISTRESS.
SHUICHI... IS SOMEONE HERE?

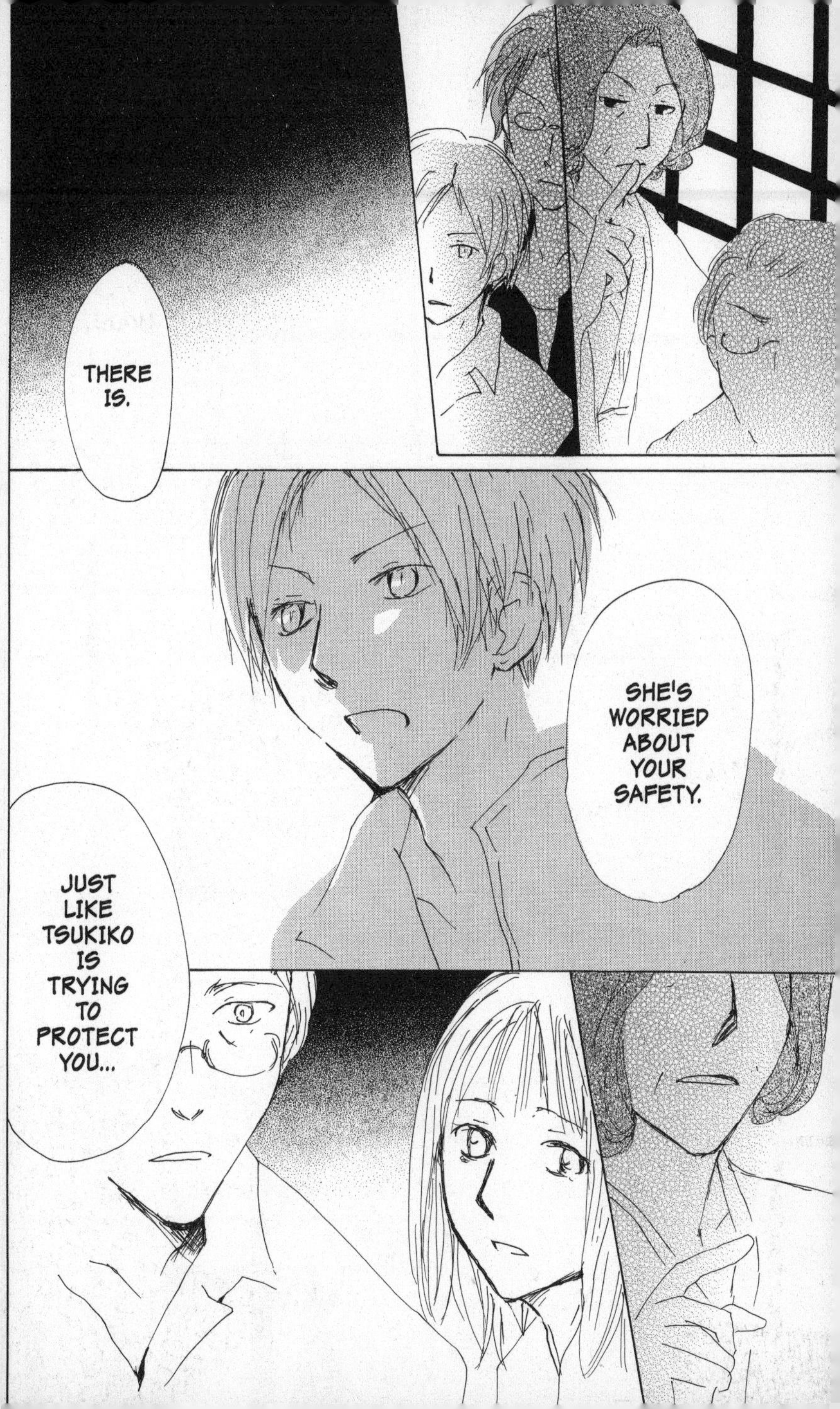
THERE IS.
SHE'S WORRIED ABOUT YOUR SAFETY.
JUST LIKE TSUKIKO IS TRYING TO PROTECT YOU...

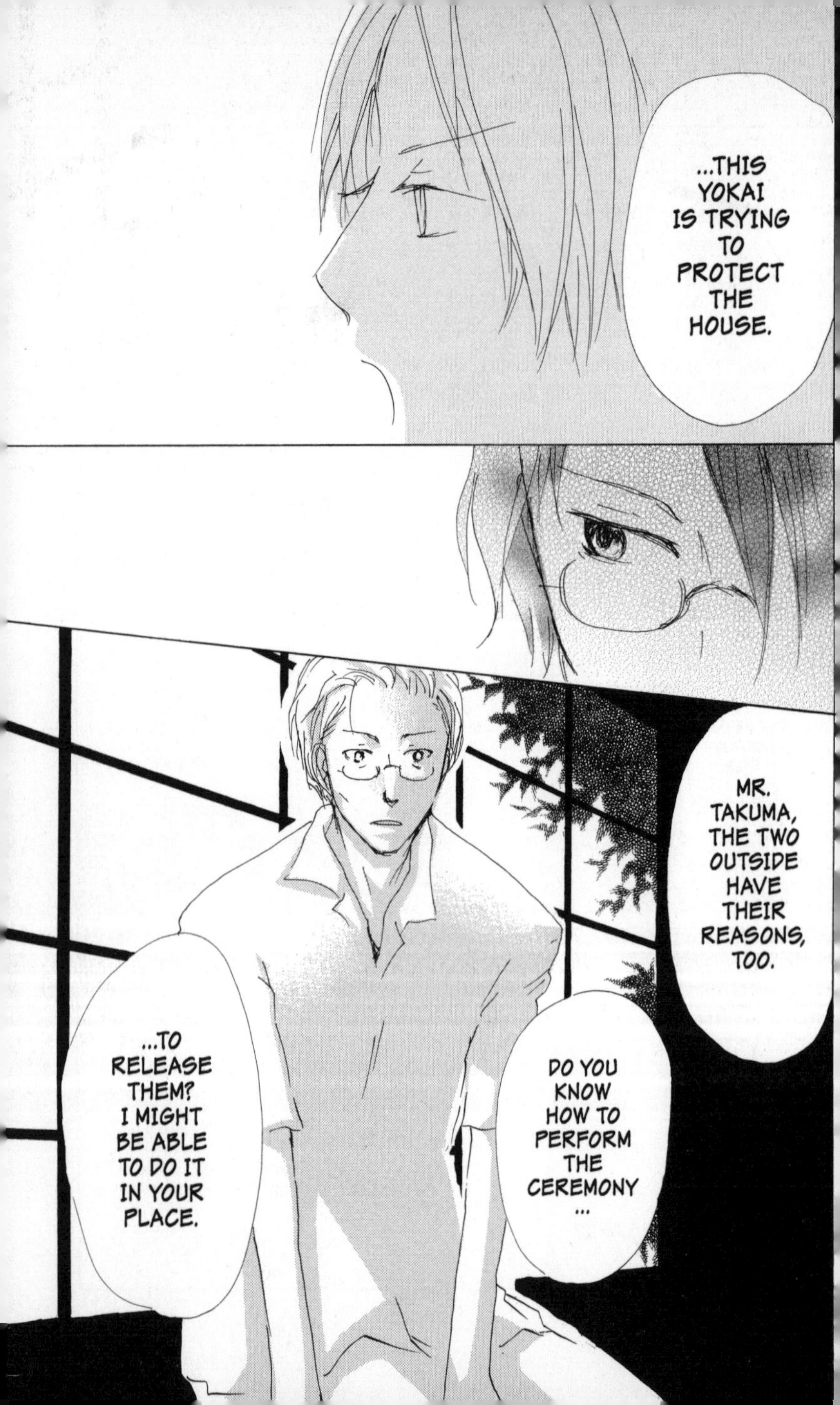
...THIS YOKAI IS TRYING TO PROTECT THE HOUSE.
MR. TAKUMA, THE TWO OUTSIDE HAVE THEIR REASONS, TOO.
DO YOU KNOW HOW TO PERFORM THE CEREMONY ...
...TO RELEASE THEM? I MIGHT BE ABLE TO DO IT IN YOUR PLACE.

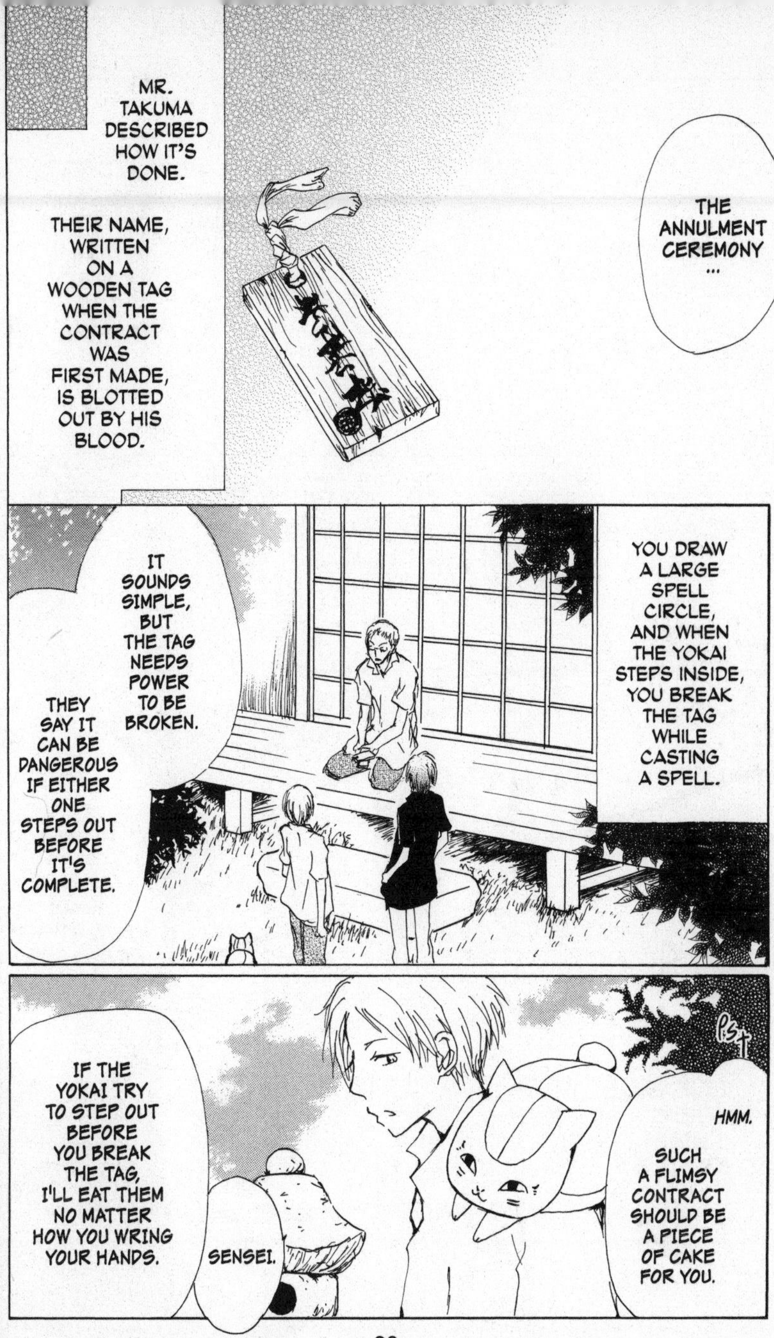
THE ANNULMENT CEREMONY ...
MR. TAKUMA DESCRIBED HOW IT'S DONE.
THEIR NAME, WRITTEN ON A WOODEN TAG WHEN THE CONTRACT WAS FIRST MADE, IS BLOTTED OUT BY HIS BLOOD.
YOU DRAW A LARGE SPELL CIRCLE, AND WHEN THE YOKAI STEPS INSIDE, YOU BREAK THE TAG WHILE CASTING A SPELL.
IT SOUNDS SIMPLE, BUT THE TAG NEEDS POWER TO BE BROKEN.
THEY SAY IT CAN BE DANGEROUS IF EITHER ONE STEPS OUT BEFORE IT'S COMPLETE.
PSST
HMM.
SUCH A FLIMSY CONTRACT SHOULD BE A PIECE OF CAKE FOR YOU.
SENSEI.
IF THE YOKAI TRY TO STEP OUT BEFORE YOU BREAK THE TAG, I'LL EAT THEM NO MATTER HOW YOU WRING YOUR HANDS.

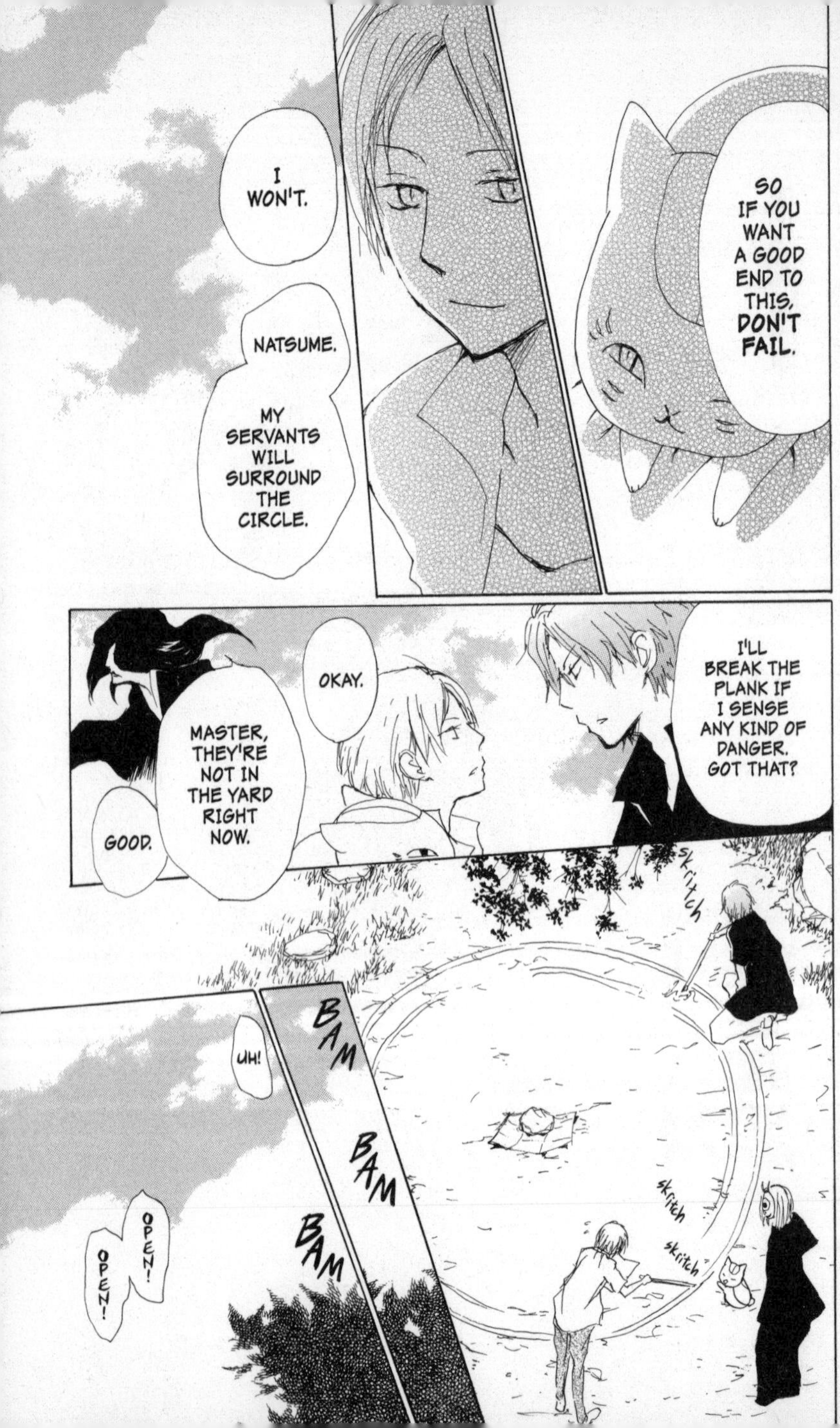

SO IF YOU WANT A GOOD END TO THIS, **DON'T FAIL.**
I WON'T.
NATSUME.
MY SERVANTS WILL SURROUND THE CIRCLE.
I'LL BREAK THE PLANK IF I SENSE ANY KIND OF DANGER. GOT THAT?
OKAY.
MASTER, THEY'RE NOT IN THE YARD RIGHT NOW.
GOOD.
skritch
skritch
skritch
BAM
BAM
BAM
UH!
OPEN!
OPEN!

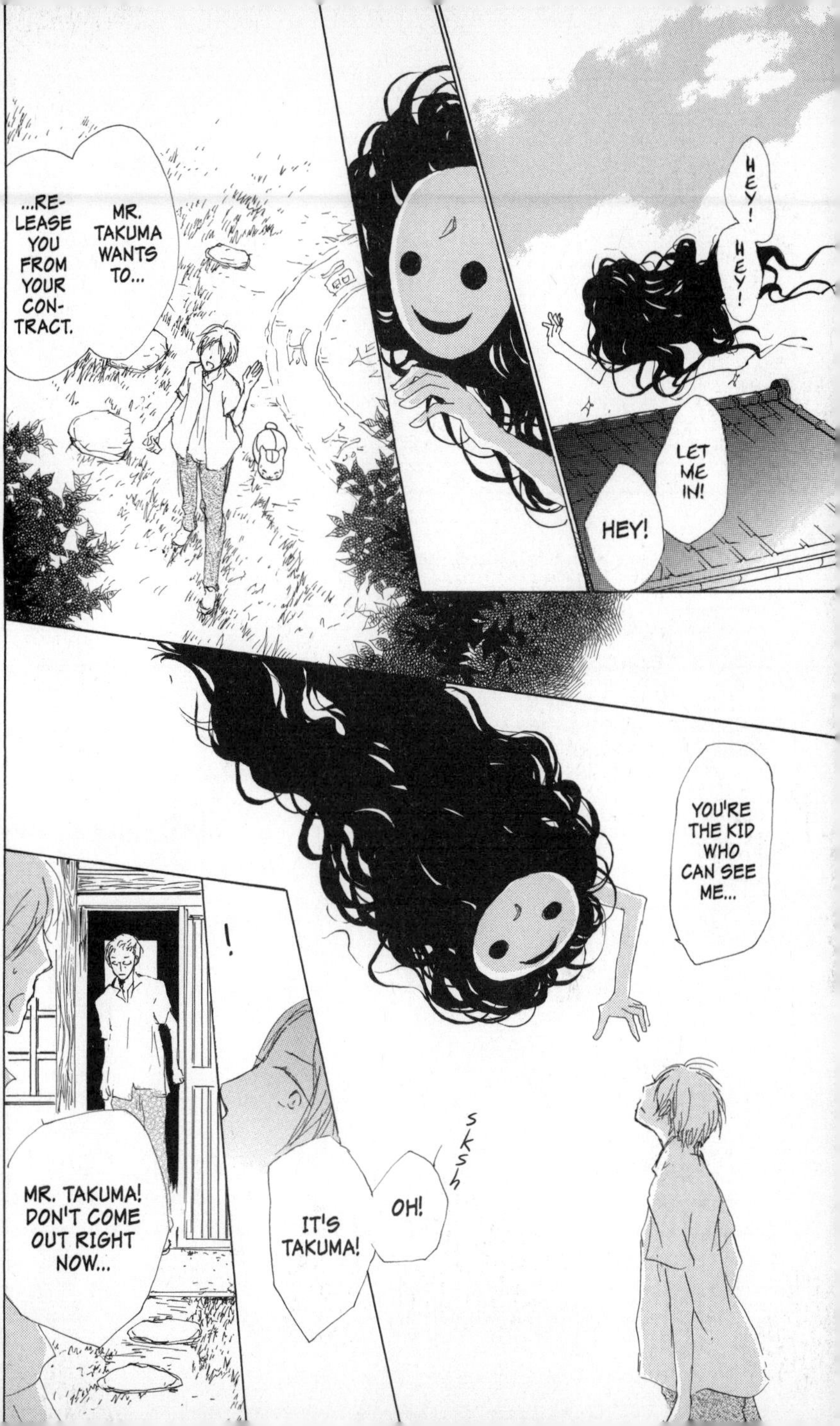
HEY! HEY!
LET ME IN!
HEY!
MR. TAKUMA WANTS TO...
...RE-LEASE YOU FROM YOUR CON-TRACT.
YOU'RE THE KID WHO CAN SEE ME...
SKSH
OH!
IT'S TAKUMA!
!
MR. TAKUMA! DON'T COME OUT RIGHT NOW...

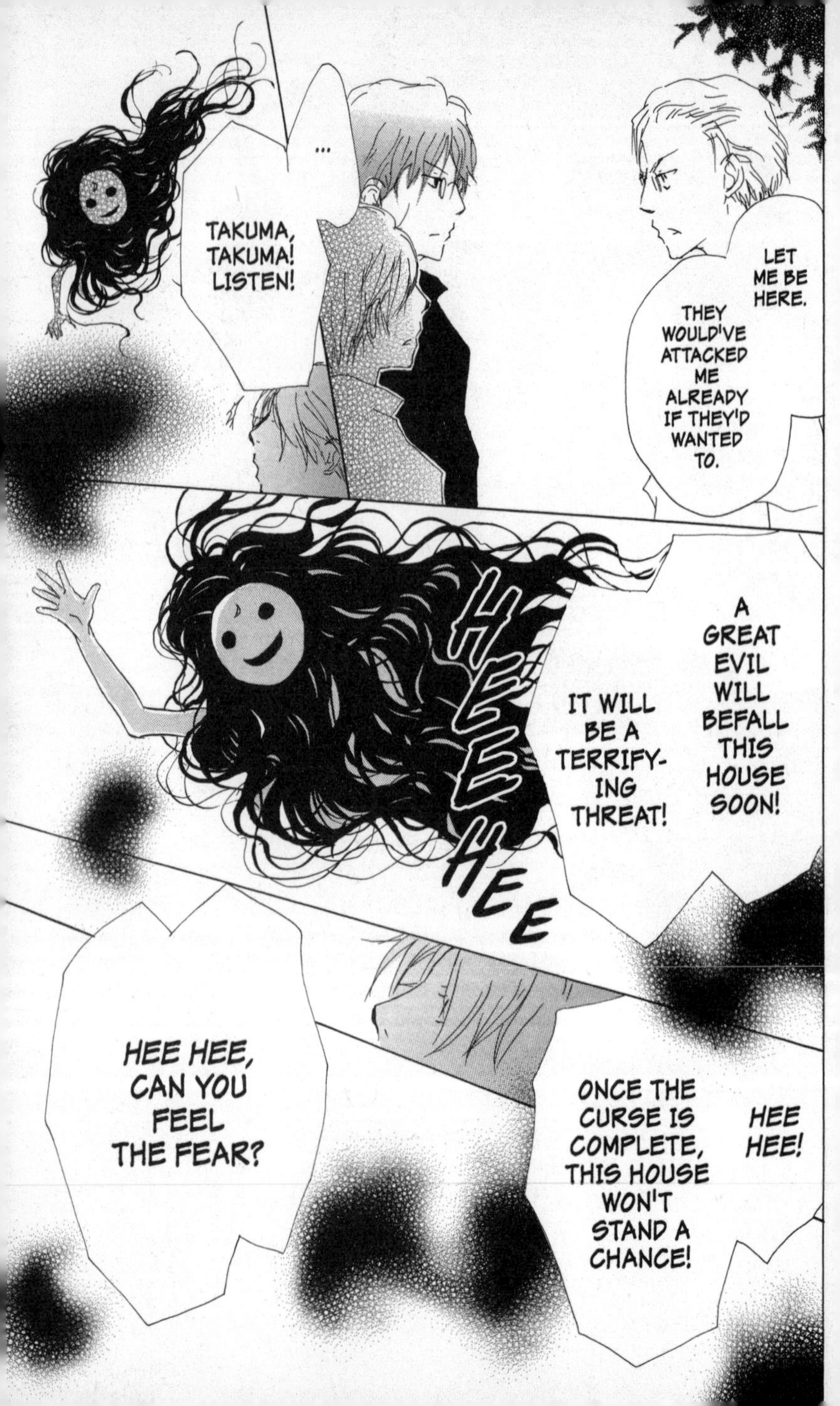
LET ME BE HERE.
THEY WOULD'VE ATTACKED ME ALREADY IF THEY'D WANTED TO.
...
TAKUMA, TAKUMA! LISTEN!
A GREAT EVIL WILL BEFALL THIS HOUSE SOON!
IT WILL BE A TERRIFY-ING THREAT!
HEE HEE HEE
HEE HEE!
ONCE THE CURSE IS COMPLETE, THIS HOUSE WON'T STAND A CHANCE!
HEE HEE, CAN YOU FEEL THE FEAR?

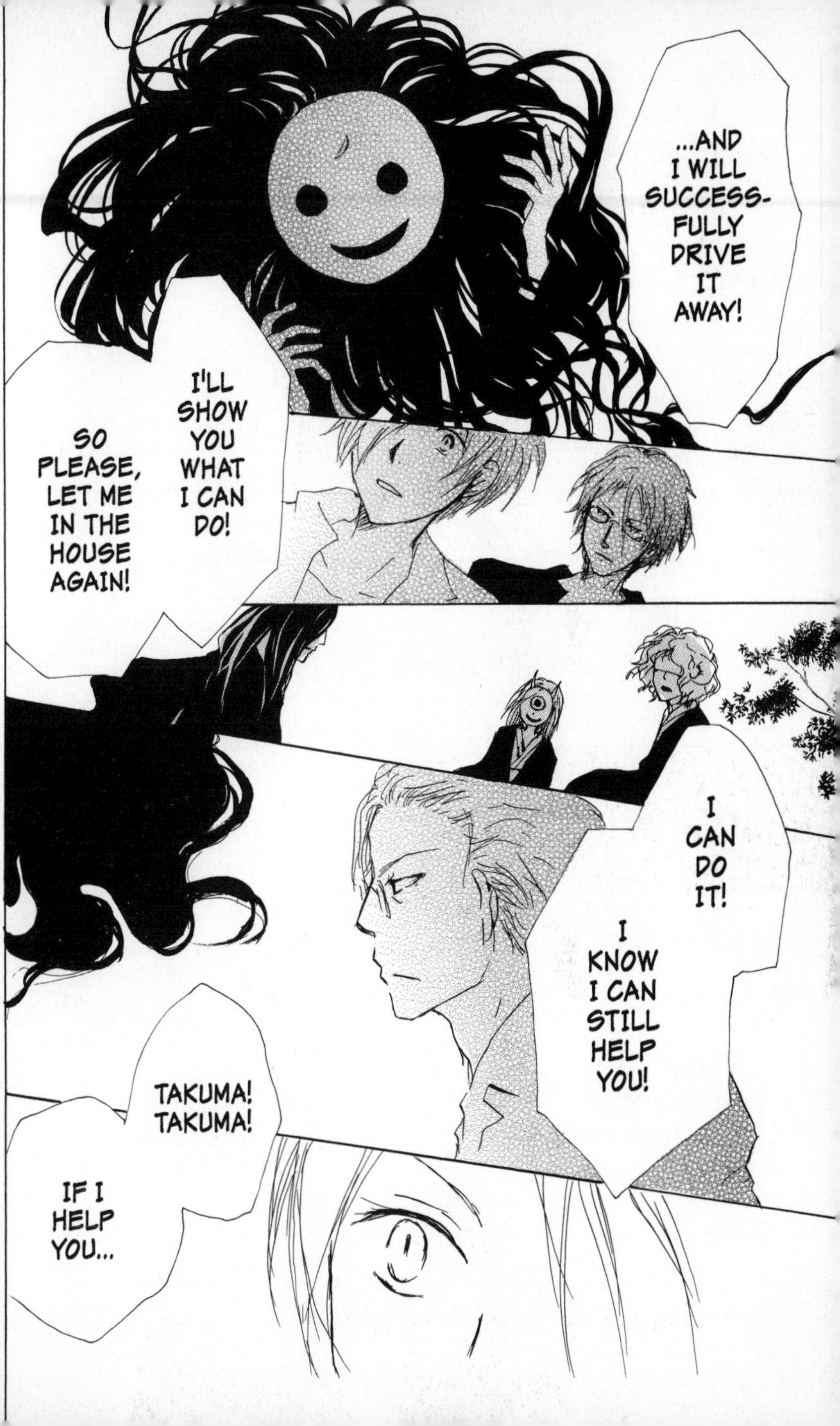
...AND I WILL SUCCESS-FULLY DRIVE IT AWAY!
I'LL SHOW YOU WHAT I CAN DO!
SO PLEASE, LET ME IN THE HOUSE AGAIN!
I CAN DO IT!
I KNOW I CAN STILL HELP YOU!
TAKUMA! TAKUMA!
IF I HELP YOU...

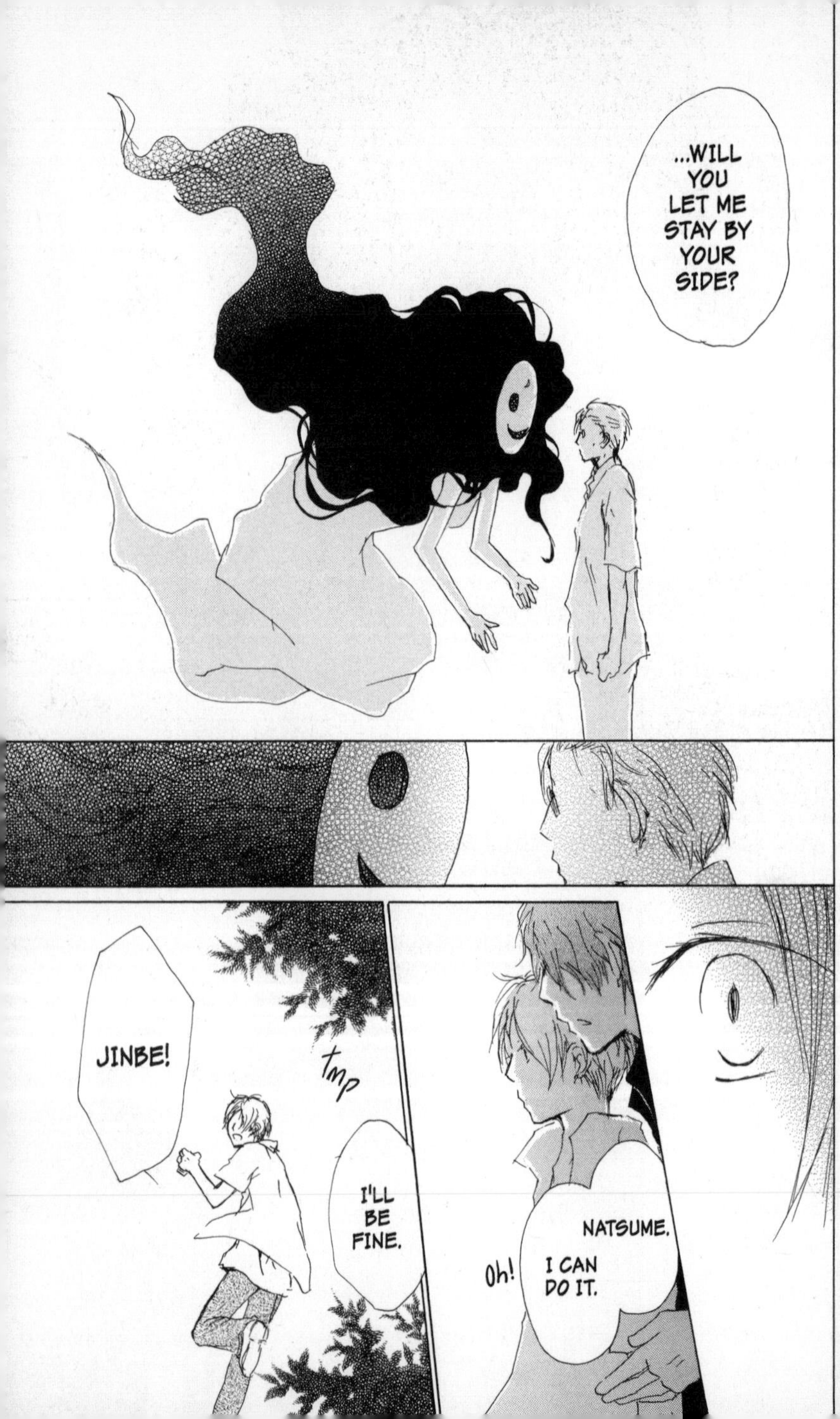
...WILL YOU LET ME STAY BY YOUR SIDE?
NATSUME. I CAN DO IT.
Oh!
I'LL BE FINE.
tmp
JINBE!

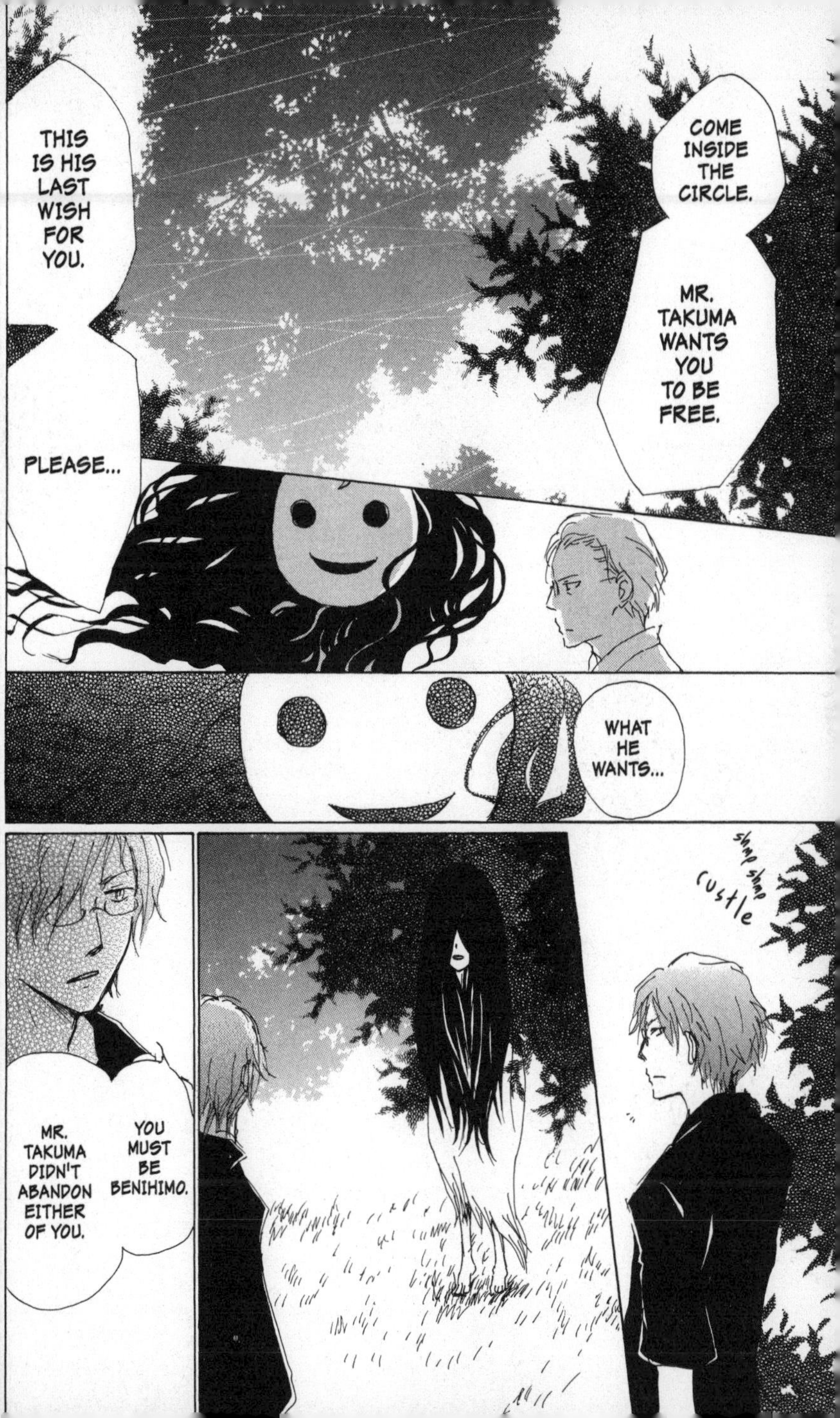
COME INSIDE THE CIRCLE.
MR. TAKUMA WANTS YOU TO BE FREE.
THIS IS HIS LAST WISH FOR YOU.
PLEASE...
WHAT HE WANTS...
shmp shmp
rustle
YOU MUST BE BENIHIMO.
MR. TAKUMA DIDN'T ABANDON EITHER OF YOU.

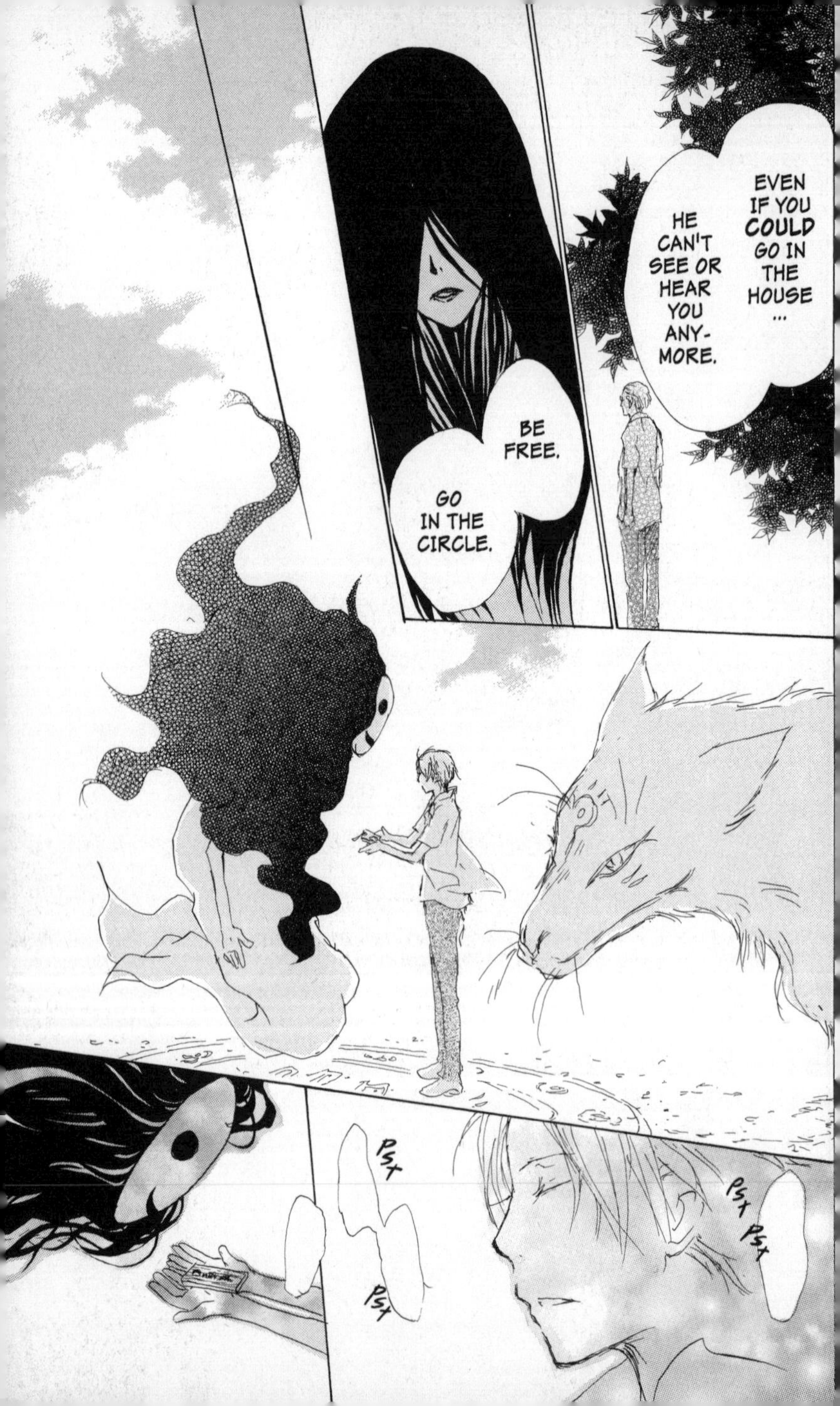
EVEN IF YOU COULD GO IN THE HOUSE ...
HE CAN'T SEE OR HEAR YOU ANYMORE.
BE FREE.
GO IN THE CIRCLE.
Pst
Pst
Pst
Pst

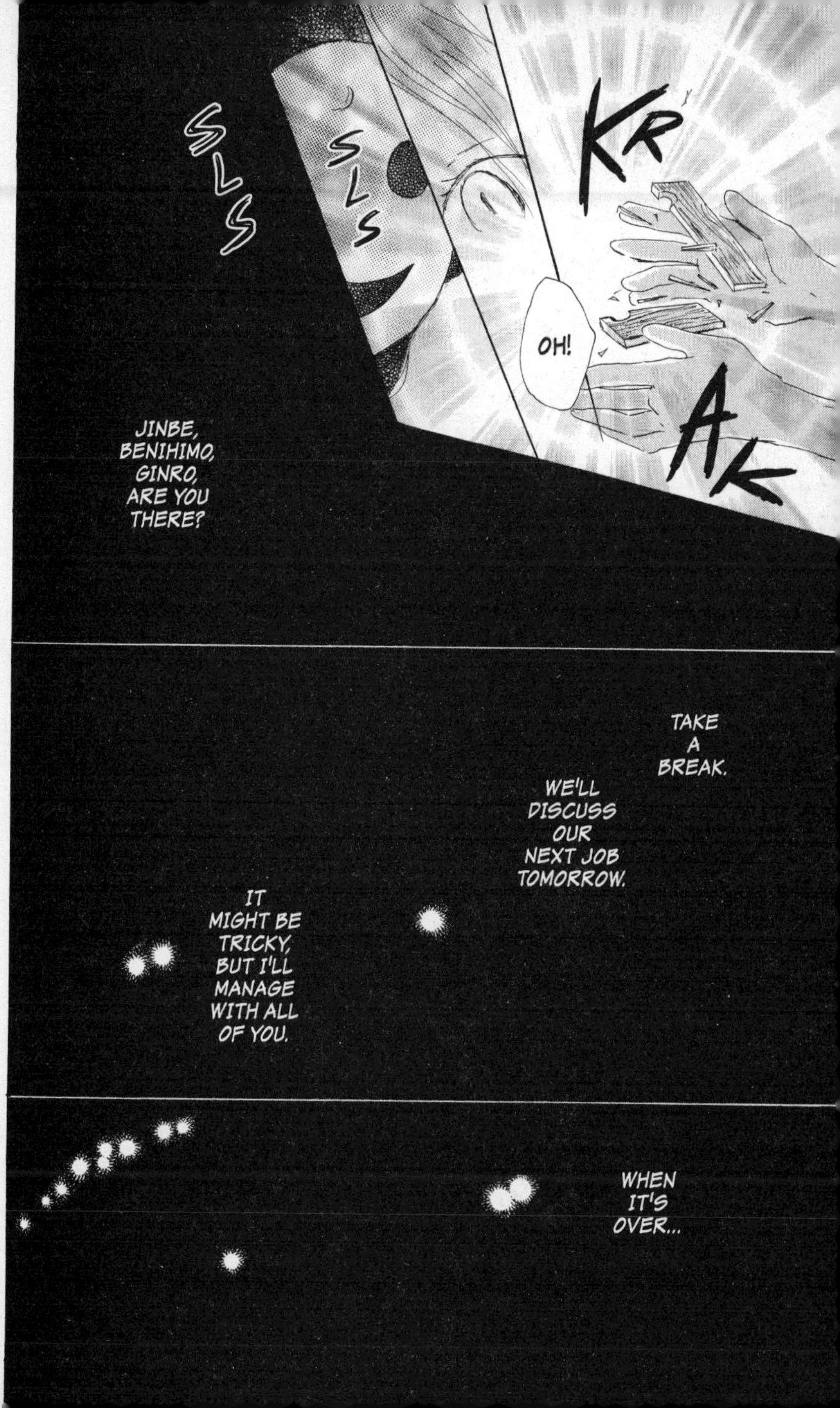
KRAK
OH!
SLS
SLS
JINBE, BENIHIMO, GINRO, ARE YOU THERE?
TAKE A BREAK.
WE'LL DISCUSS OUR NEXT JOB TOMORROW.
IT MIGHT BE TRICKY, BUT I'LL MANAGE WITH ALL OF YOU.
WHEN IT'S OVER...

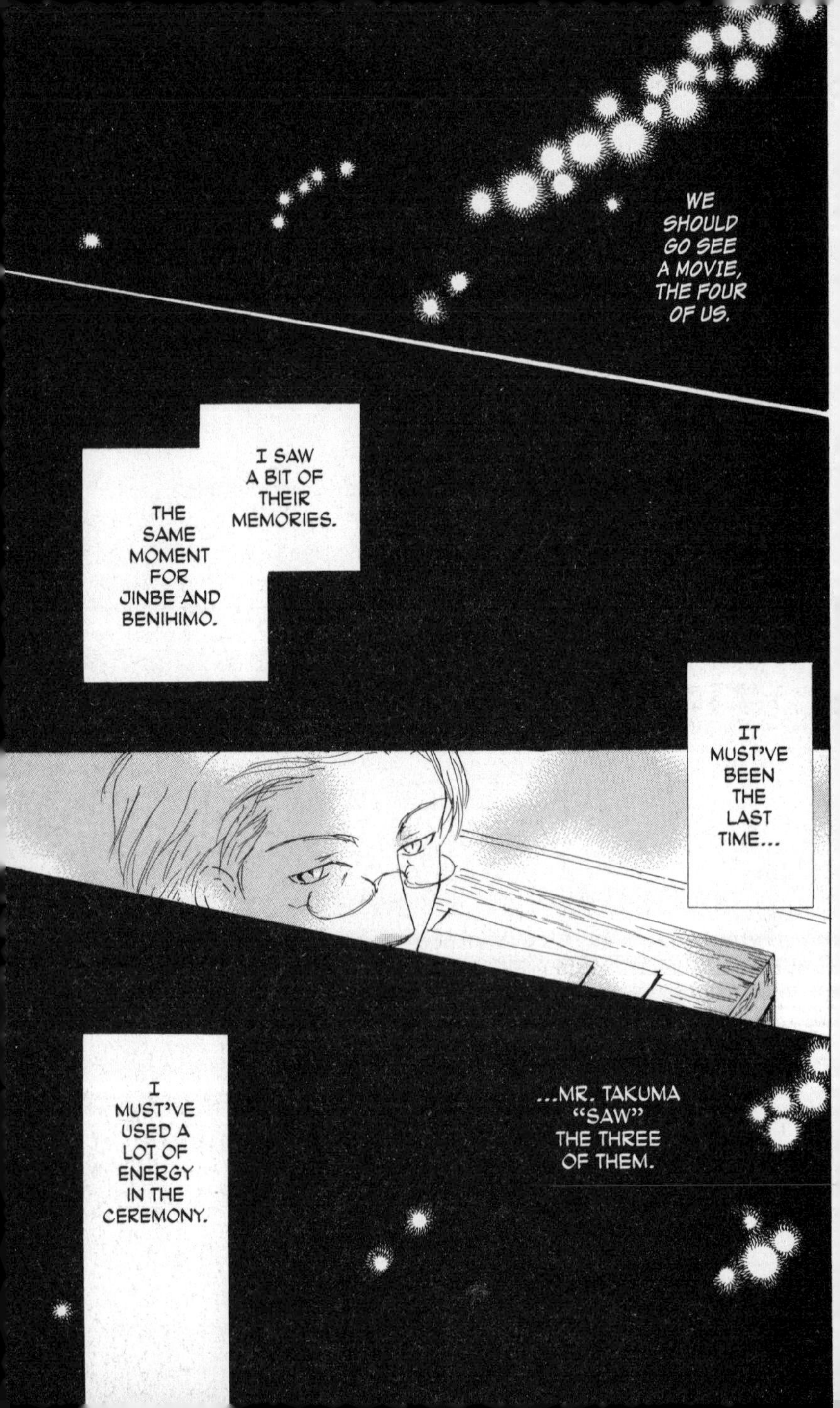
WE SHOULD GO SEE A MOVIE, THE FOUR OF US.
I SAW A BIT OF THEIR MEMORIES.
THE SAME MOMENT FOR JINBE AND BENIHIMO.
IT MUST'VE BEEN THE LAST TIME...
...MR. TAKUMA "SAW" THE THREE OF THEM.
I MUST'VE USED A LOT OF ENERGY IN THE CEREMONY.

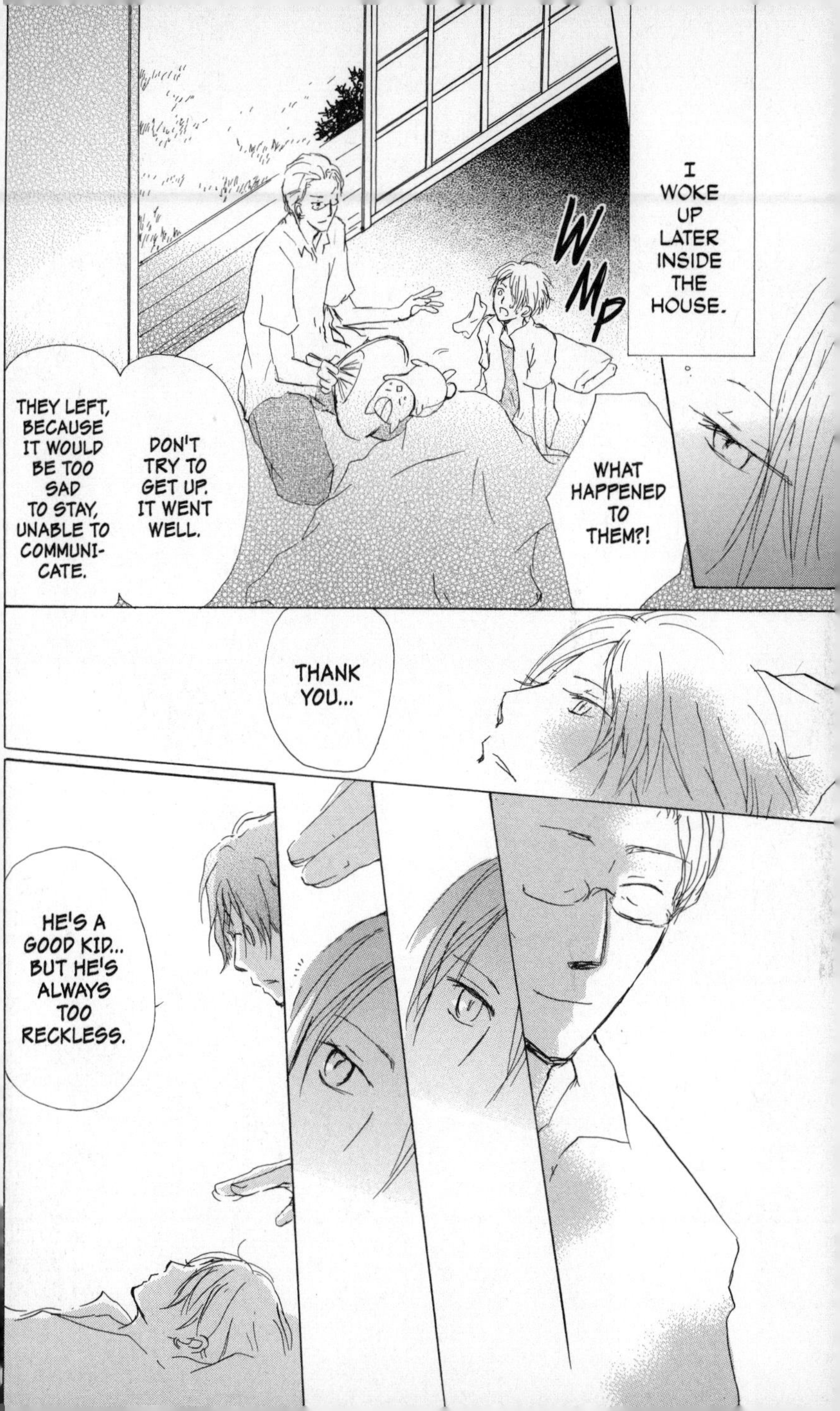
I WOKE UP LATER INSIDE THE HOUSE.
WMP
WHAT HAPPENED TO THEM?!
DON'T TRY TO GET UP. IT WENT WELL.
THEY LEFT, BECAUSE IT WOULD BE TOO SAD TO STAY, UNABLE TO COMMUNI-CATE.
THANK YOU...
HE'S A GOOD KID... BUT HE'S ALWAYS TOO RECKLESS.

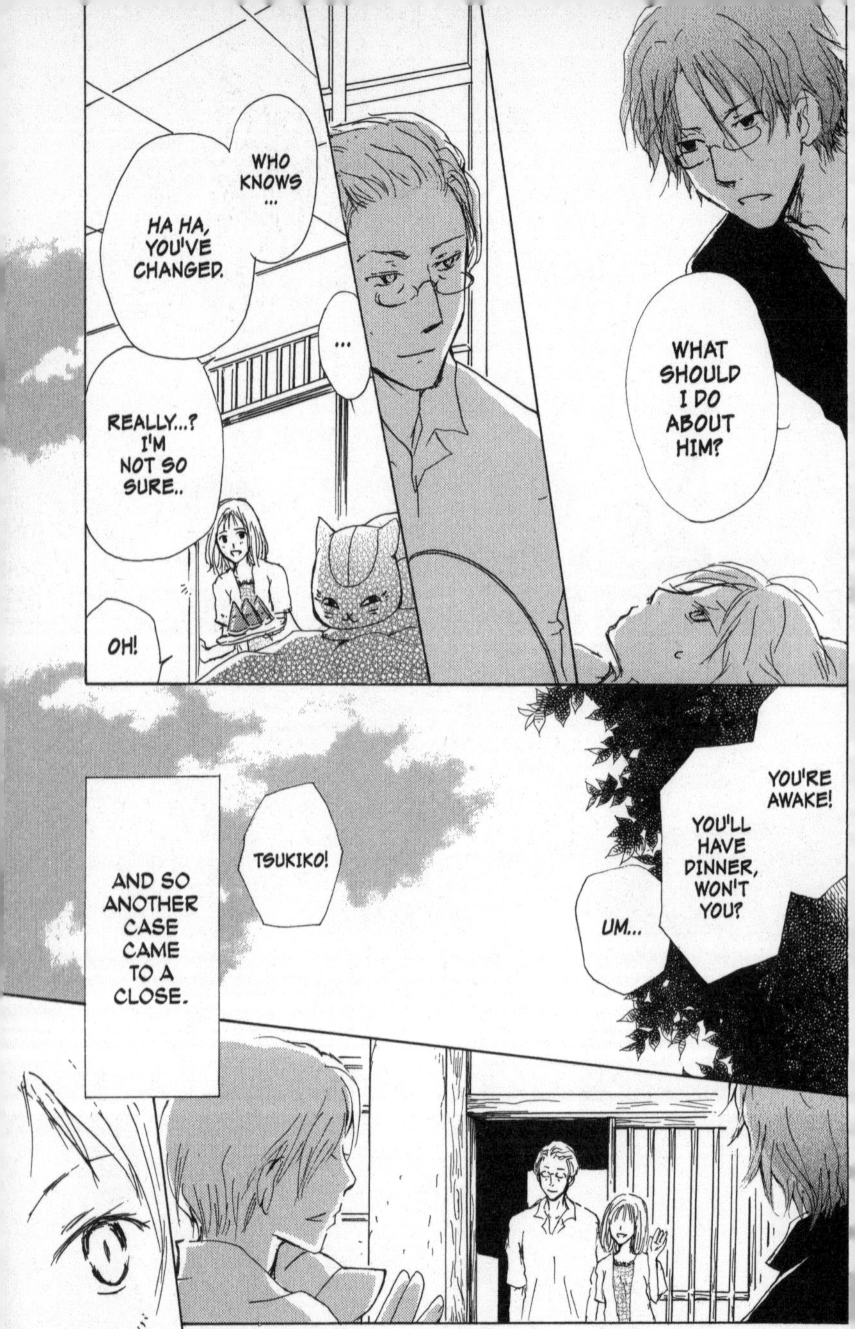
WHAT SHOULD I DO ABOUT HIM?
WHO KNOWS ...
HA HA, YOU'VE CHANGED.
...
REALLY...? I'M NOT SO SURE..
OH!
YOU'RE AWAKE!
YOU'LL HAVE DINNER, WON'T YOU?
UM...
TSUKIKO!
AND SO ANOTHER CASE CAME TO A CLOSE.

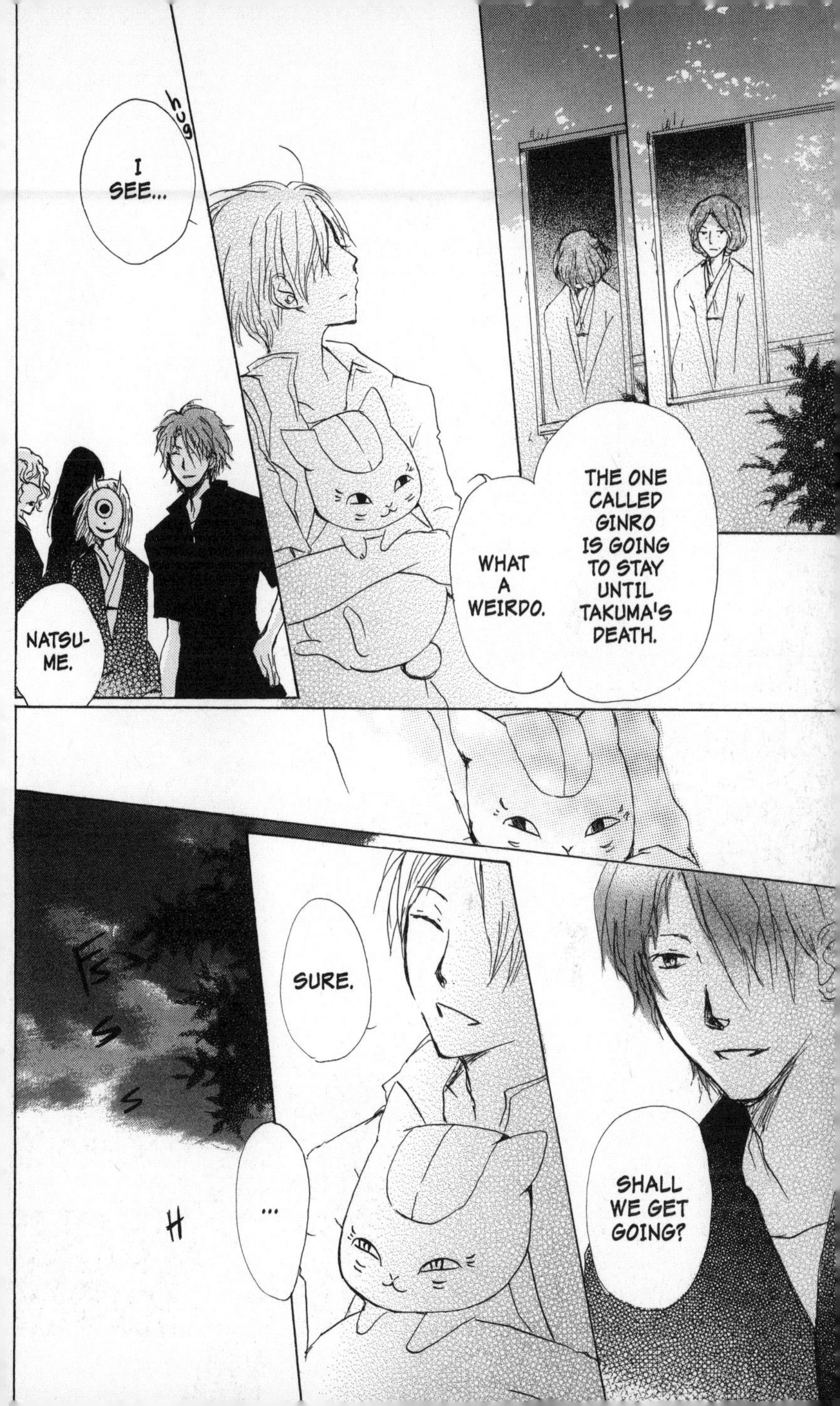
THE ONE CALLED GINRO IS GOING TO STAY UNTIL TAKUMA'S DEATH.
WHAT A WEIRDO.
hug
I SEE...
NATSU-ME.
SHALL WE GET GOING?
SURE.
...
FSSSH

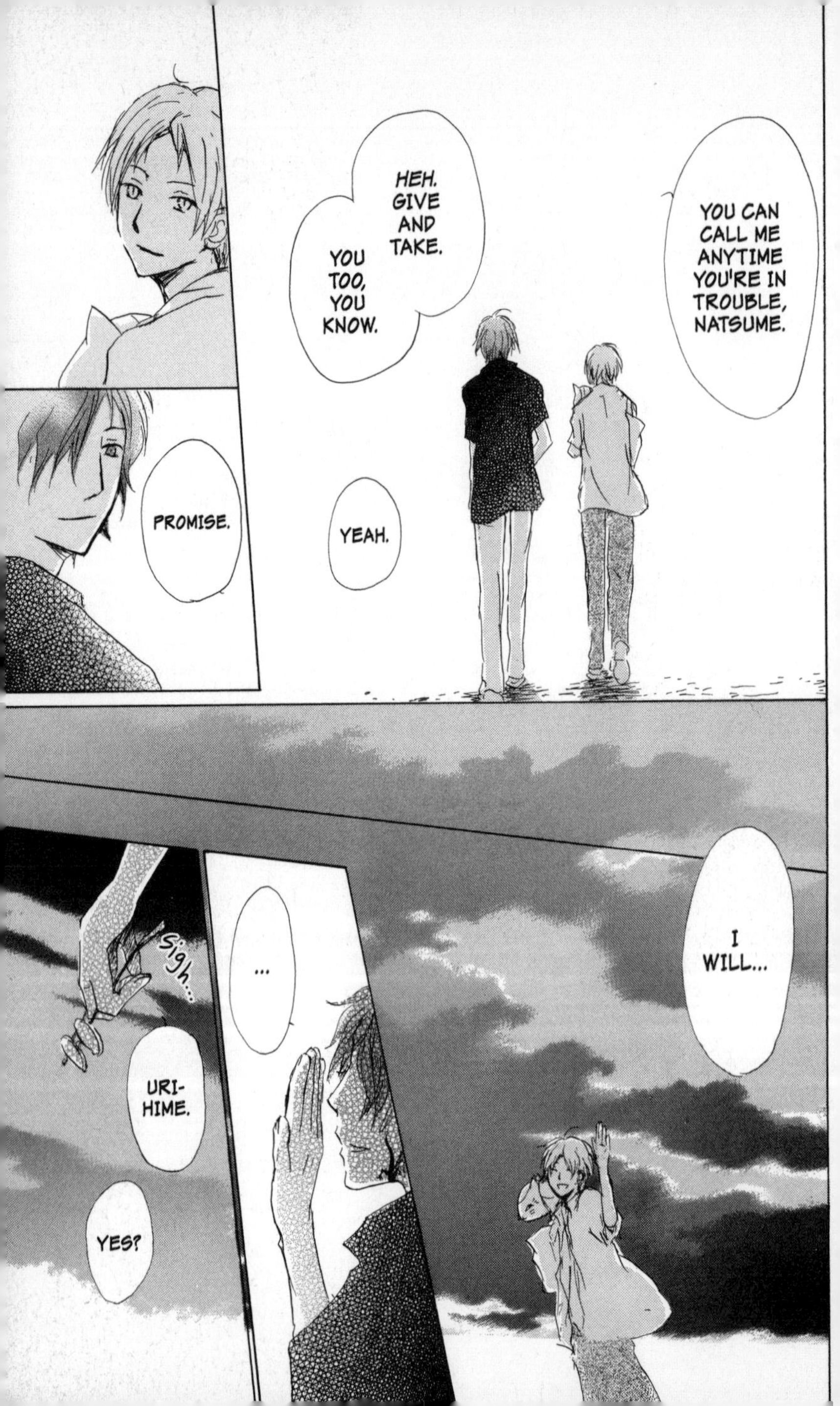
YOU CAN CALL ME ANYTIME YOU'RE IN TROUBLE, NATSUME.
HEH. GIVE AND TAKE.
YOU TOO, YOU KNOW.
YEAH.
PROMISE.
I WILL...
...
Sigh...
URI-HIME.
YES?

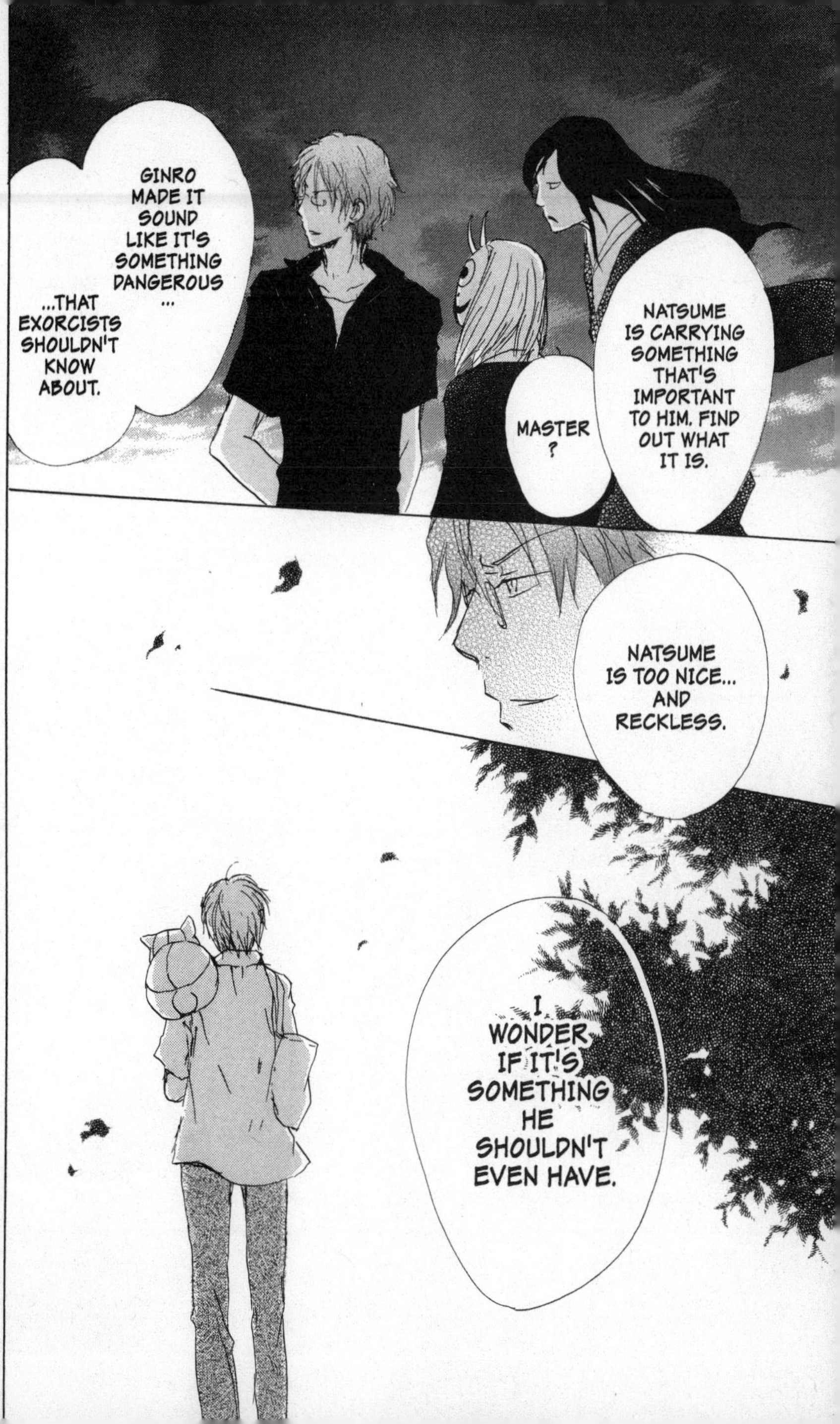
NATSUME IS CARRYING SOMETHING THAT'S IMPORTANT TO HIM. FIND OUT WHAT IT IS.
MASTER?
GINRO MADE IT SOUND LIKE IT'S SOMETHING DANGEROUS...
...THAT EXORCISTS SHOULDN'T KNOW ABOUT.
NATSUME IS TOO NICE... AND RECKLESS.
I WONDER IF IT'S SOMETHING HE SHOULDN'T EVEN HAVE.

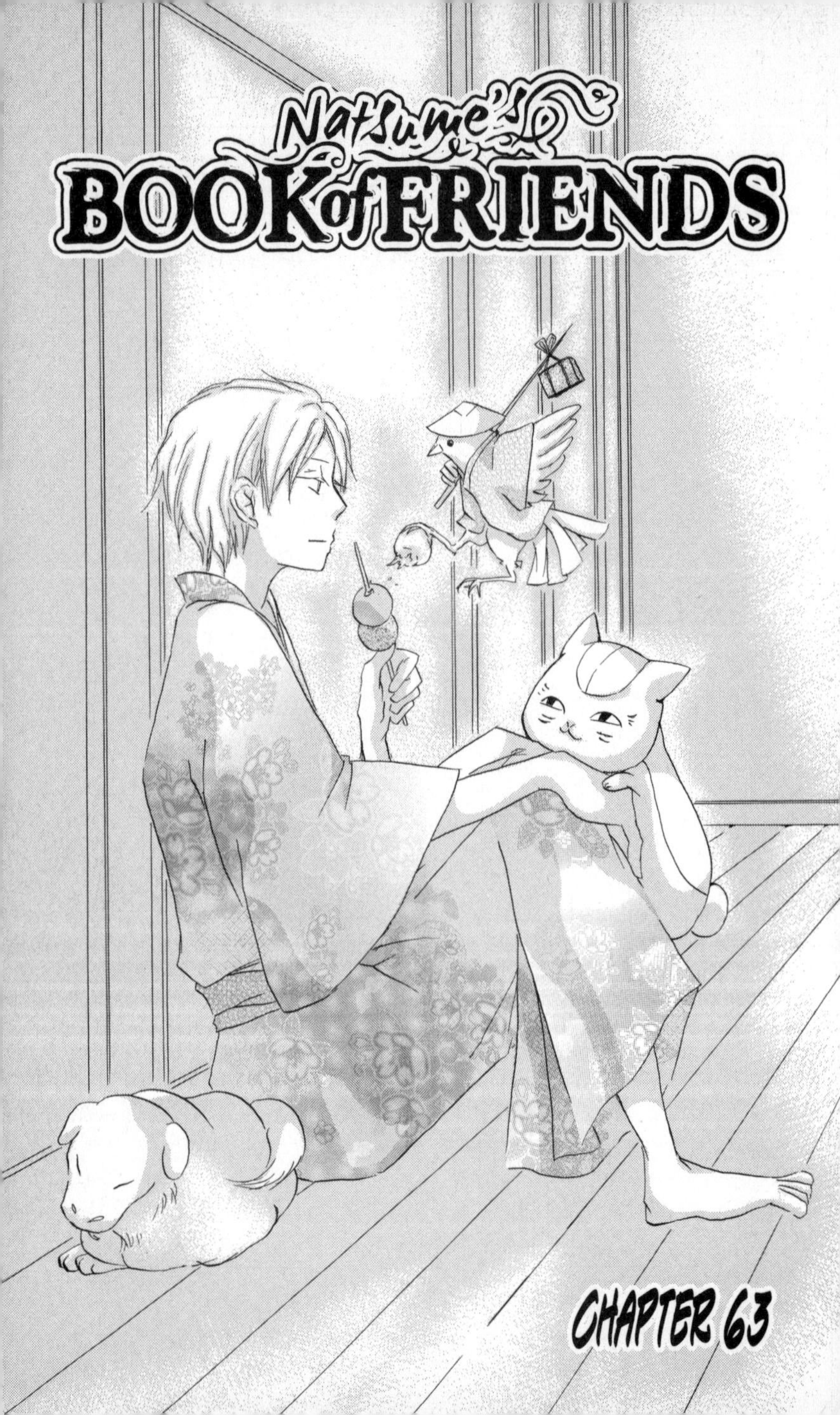

Natsume's
BOOK of FRIENDS
CHAPTER 63

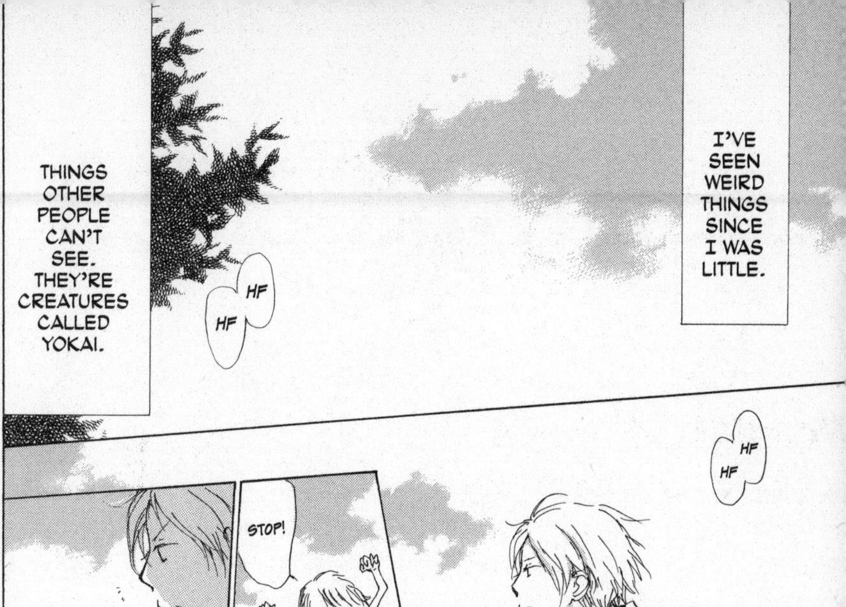
I'VE SEEN WEIRD THINGS SINCE I WAS LITTLE.
HF
HF
THINGS OTHER PEOPLE CAN'T SEE. THEY'RE CREATURES CALLED YOKAI.
HF
HF
STOP!
STOP!

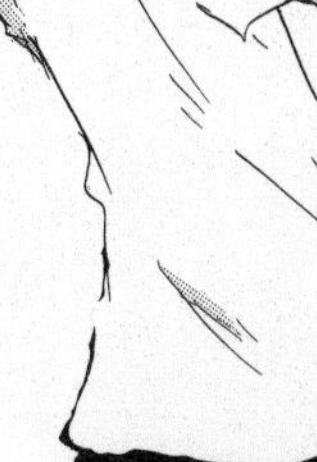

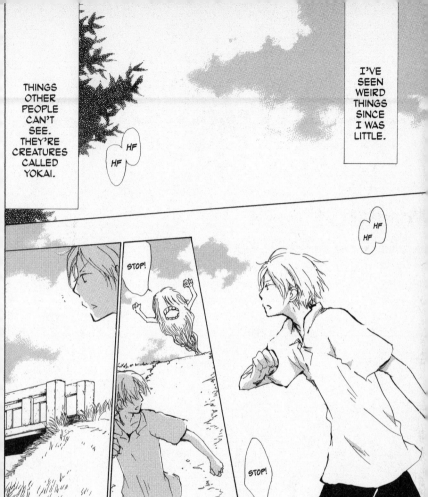

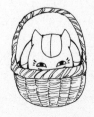

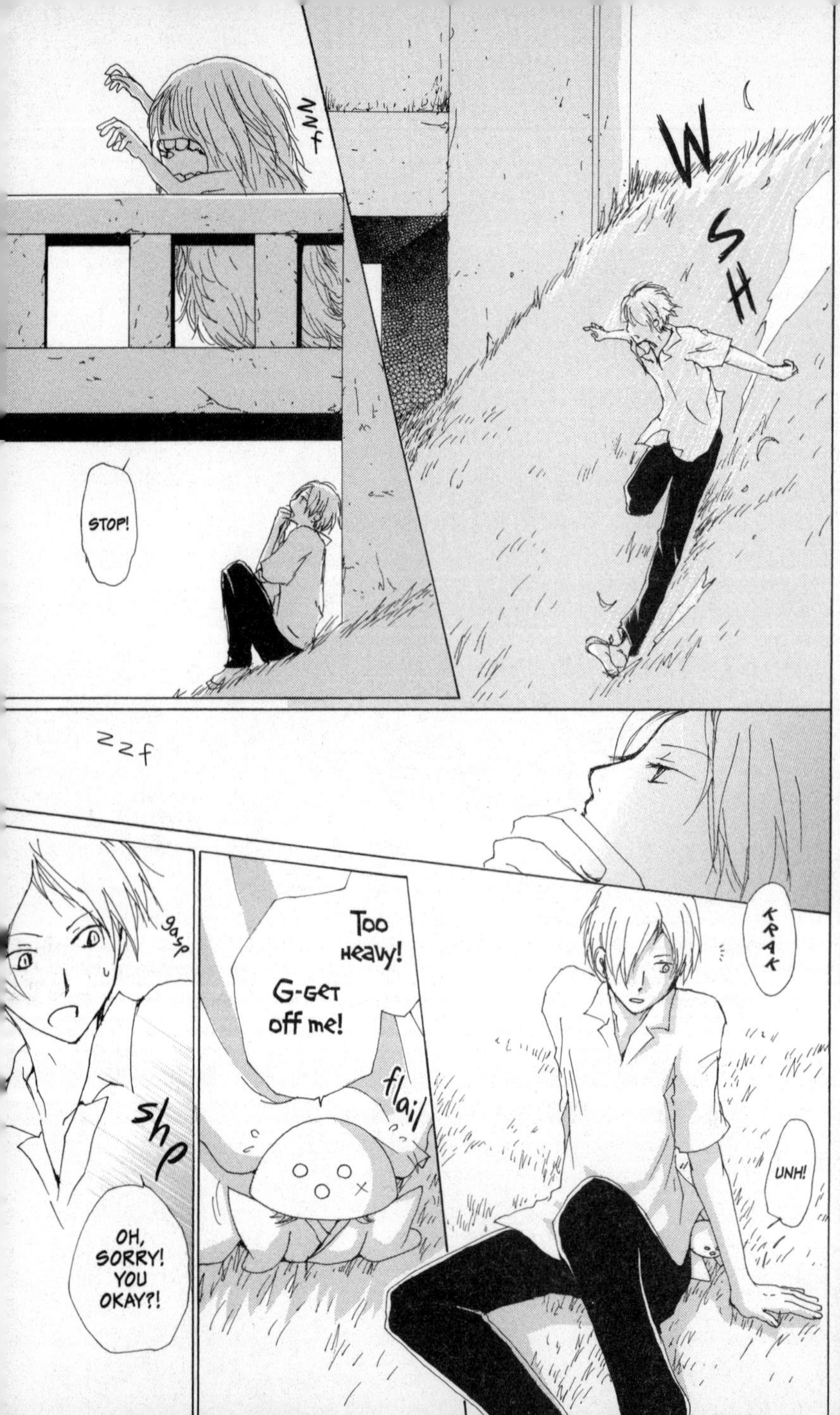
WSH
ZZF
STOP!
ZZF
KRAK
UNH!
Too heavy!
G-get off me!
flail
gasp
shp
OH, SORRY! YOU OKAY?!

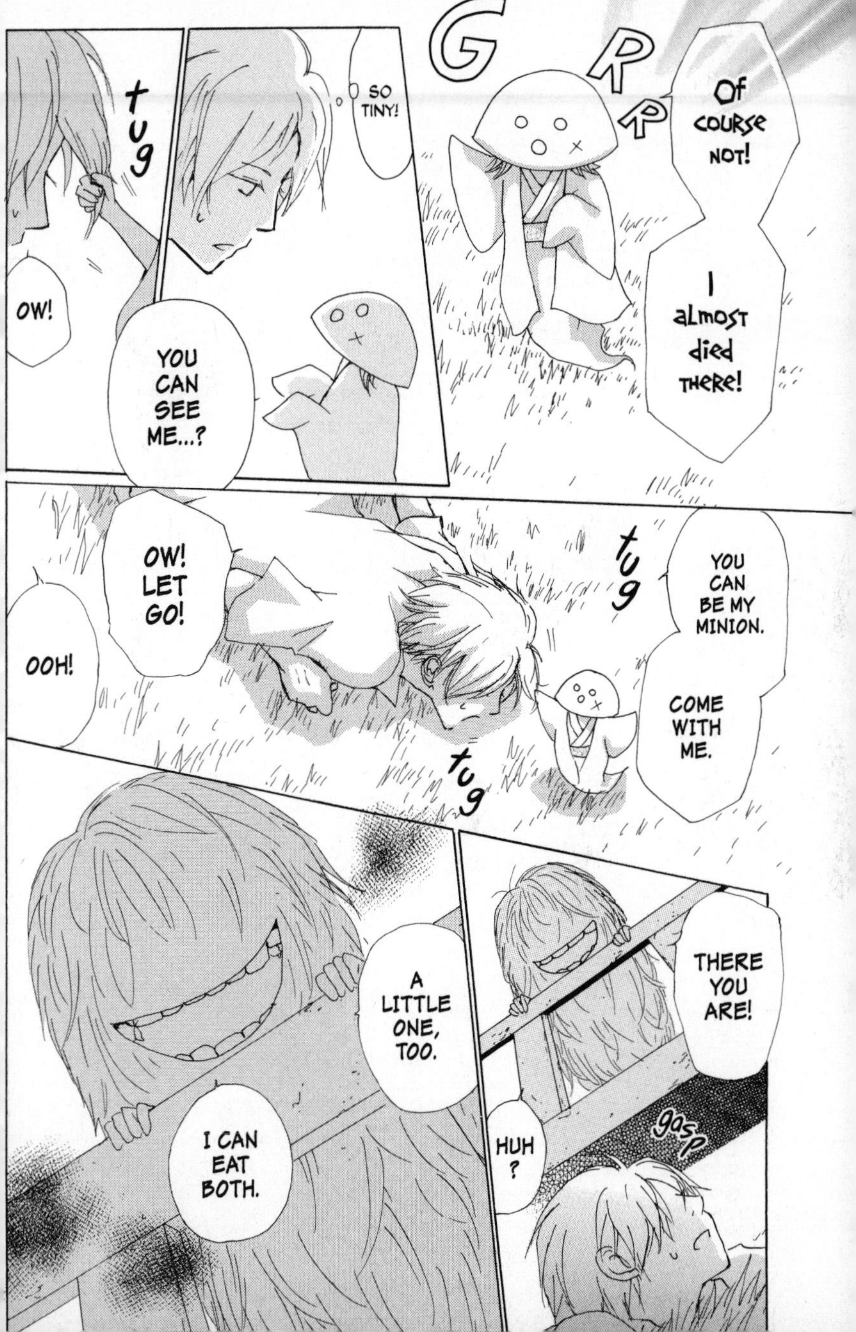
GRR
Of course not!
I almost died there!
SO TINY!
YOU CAN SEE ME...?
tug
OW!
YOU CAN BE MY MINION.
COME WITH ME.
tug
tug
OW! LET GO!
OOH!
THERE YOU ARE!
gasp
HUH?
A LITTLE ONE, TOO.
I CAN EAT BOTH.

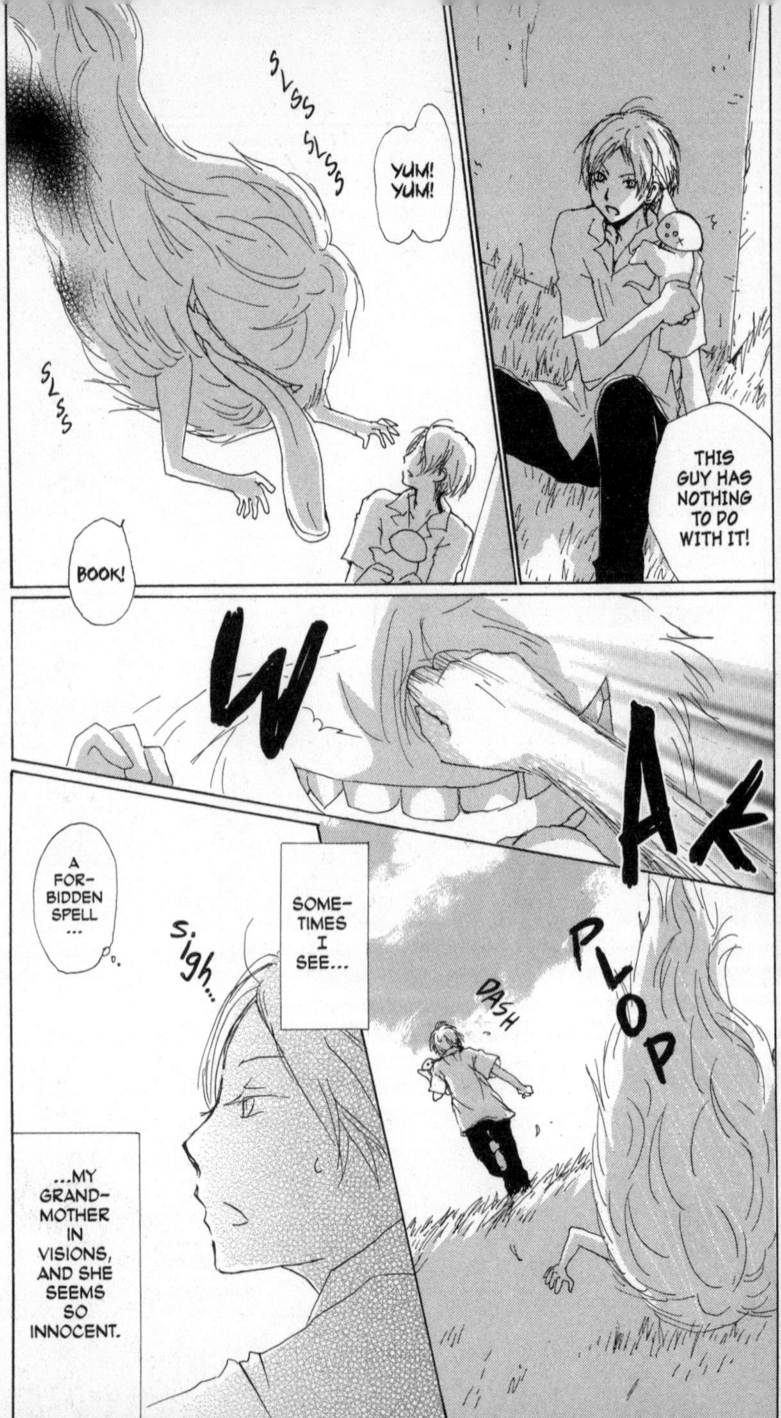
THIS GUY HAS NOTHING TO DO WITH IT!
SLSSS SLSSS
YUM! YUM!
SLSS
BOOK!
WHAK
SOMETIMES I SEE...
PLOP
DASH
A FORBIDDEN SPELL...
sigh...
...MY GRANDMOTHER IN VISIONS, AND SHE SEEMS SO INNOCENT.

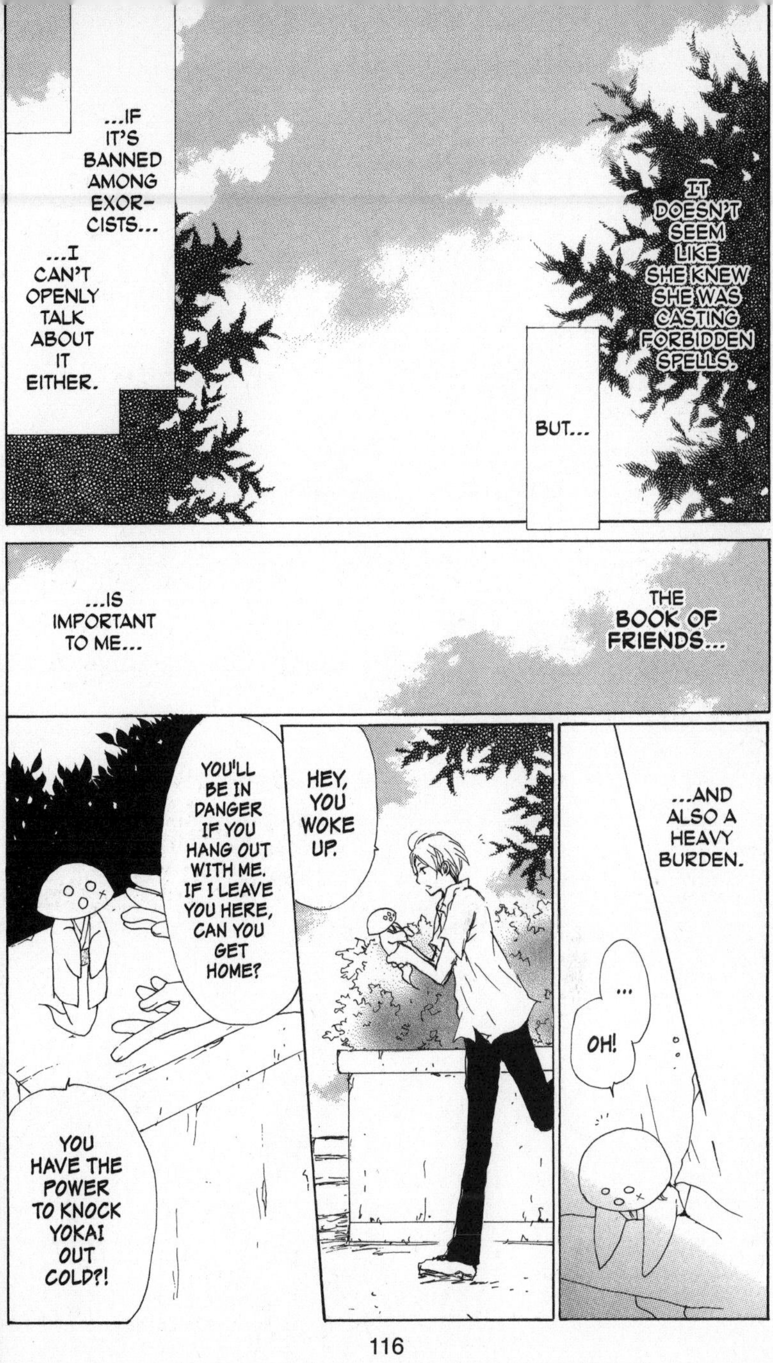

IT DOESN'T SEEM LIKE SHE KNEW SHE WAS CASTING FORBIDDEN SPELLS.
BUT...
...IF IT'S BANNED AMONG EXORCISTS...
...I CAN'T OPENLY TALK ABOUT IT EITHER.
THE BOOK OF FRIENDS...
...IS IMPORTANT TO ME...
...AND ALSO A HEAVY BURDEN.
...
OH!
HEY, YOU WOKE UP.
YOU'LL BE IN DANGER IF YOU HANG OUT WITH ME. IF I LEAVE YOU HERE, CAN YOU GET HOME?
YOU HAVE THE POWER TO KNOCK YOKAI OUT COLD?!

03

❋ Exorcists

People who can see yokai get into scary situations. People who can't see yokai get more scared because they can't see what's happening. It's so fun to think of both sides when I'm drawing a story about exorcists. Takuma must've been a nice mentor for Natori, or at least someone to talk to, since he doesn't get treated very well in exorcist circles.

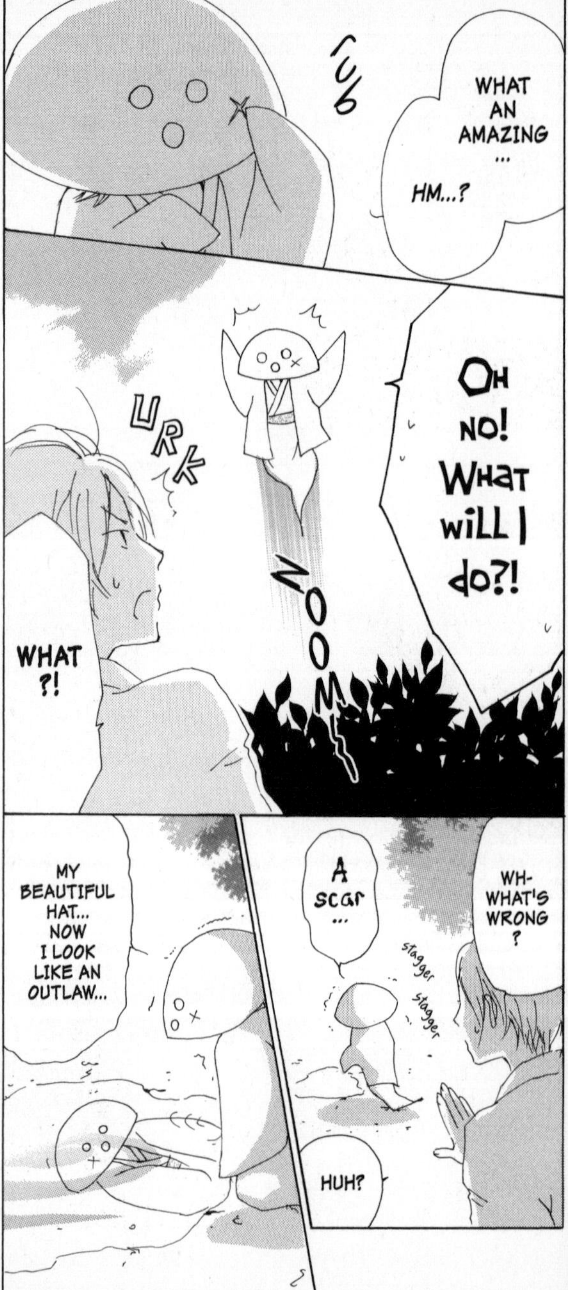
WHAT AN AMAZING ...
HM...?
rub
OH NO! WHAT WILL I DO?!
URK
ZOOM
WHAT ?!
WH- WHAT'S WRONG ?
A scar ...
stagger
stagger
HUH?
MY BEAUTIFUL HAT... NOW I LOOK LIKE AN OUTLAW...

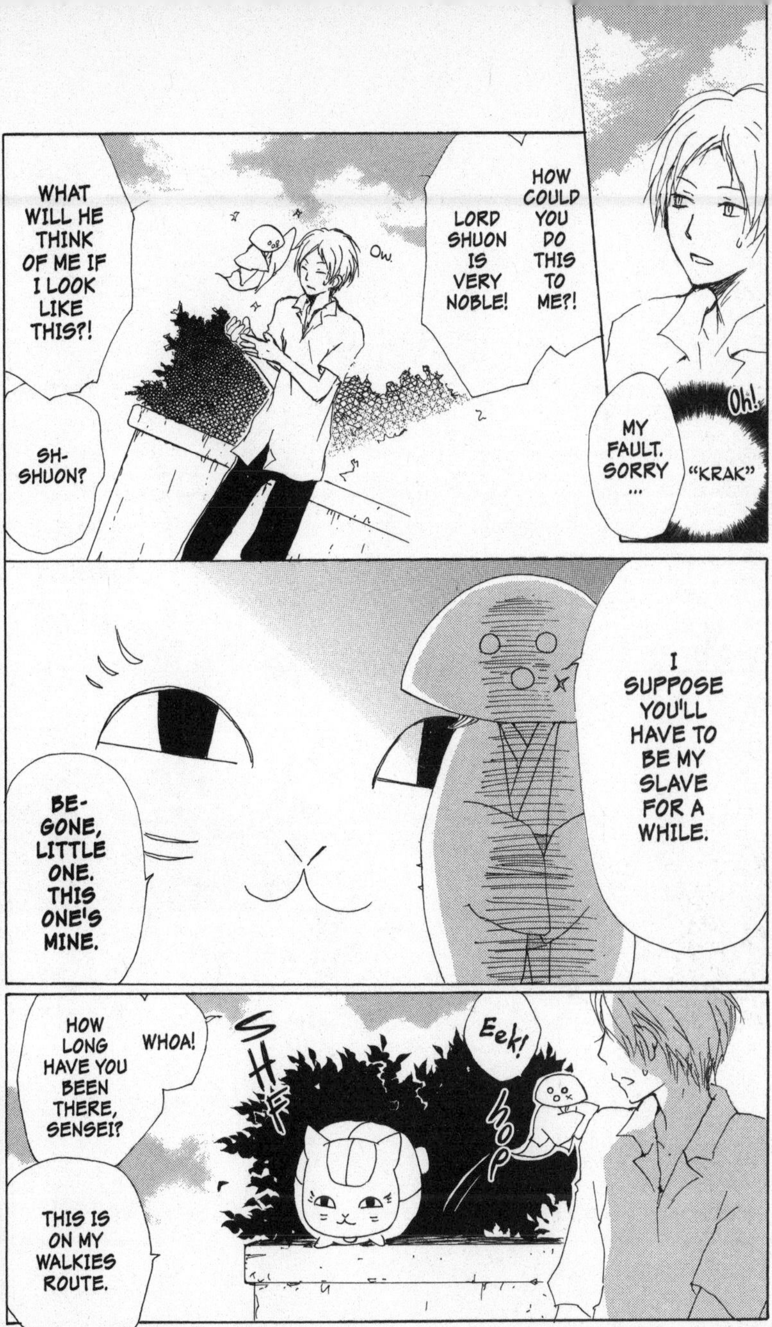
Oh!
"KRAK"
MY FAULT. SORRY ...
HOW COULD YOU DO THIS TO ME?!
LORD SHUON IS VERY NOBLE!
Ow.
WHAT WILL HE THINK OF ME IF I LOOK LIKE THIS?!
SH-SHUON?
I SUPPOSE YOU'LL HAVE TO BE MY SLAVE FOR A WHILE.
BE-GONE, LITTLE ONE. THIS ONE'S MINE.
Eek!
hop
SH
WHOA!
HOW LONG HAVE YOU BEEN THERE, SENSEI?
THIS IS ON MY WALKIES ROUTE.

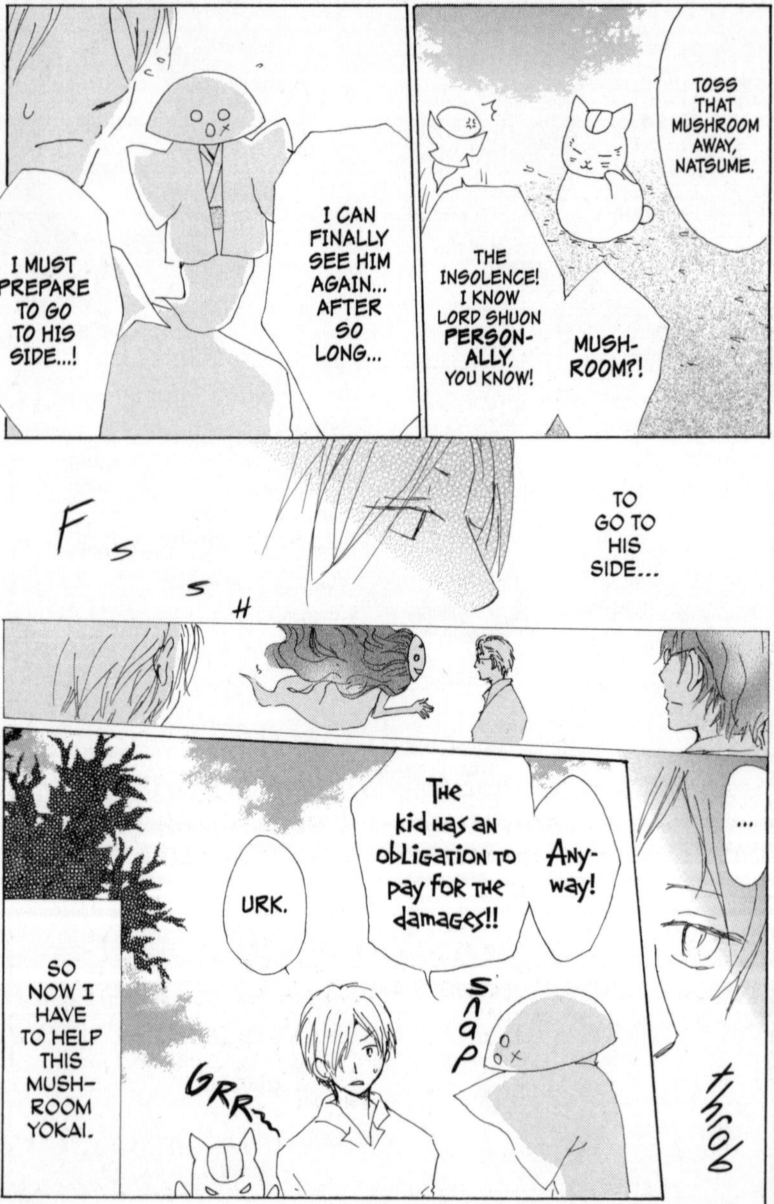
TOSS THAT MUSHROOM AWAY, NATSUME.
MUSHROOM?!
THE INSOLENCE! I KNOW LORD SHUON PERSONALLY, YOU KNOW!
I CAN FINALLY SEE HIM AGAIN... AFTER SO LONG...
I MUST PREPARE TO GO TO HIS SIDE...!
TO GO TO HIS SIDE...
FSSH
...
throb
Anyway!
The kid has an obligation to pay for the damages!!
snap
URK.
GRR~
SO NOW I HAVE TO HELP THIS MUSHROOM YOKAI.

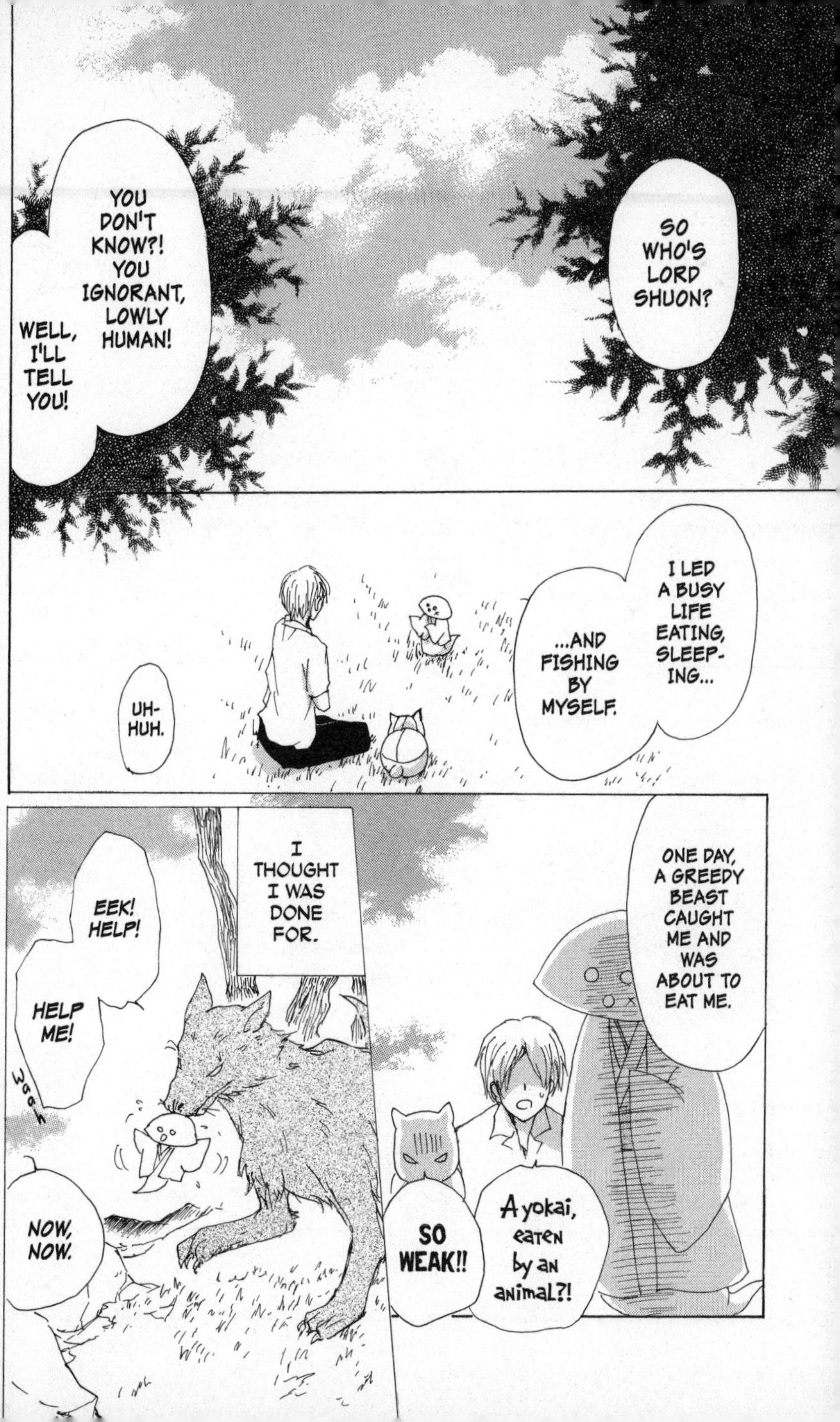
SO WHO'S LORD SHUON?
YOU DON'T KNOW?! YOU IGNORANT, LOWLY HUMAN!
WELL, I'LL TELL YOU!
I LED A BUSY LIFE EATING, SLEEP-ING...
...AND FISHING BY MYSELF.
UH-HUH.
ONE DAY, A GREEDY BEAST CAUGHT ME AND WAS ABOUT TO EAT ME.
A yokai, eaten by an animal?!
SO WEAK!!
I THOUGHT I WAS DONE FOR.
EEK! HELP!
HELP ME!
Waah
NOW, NOW.

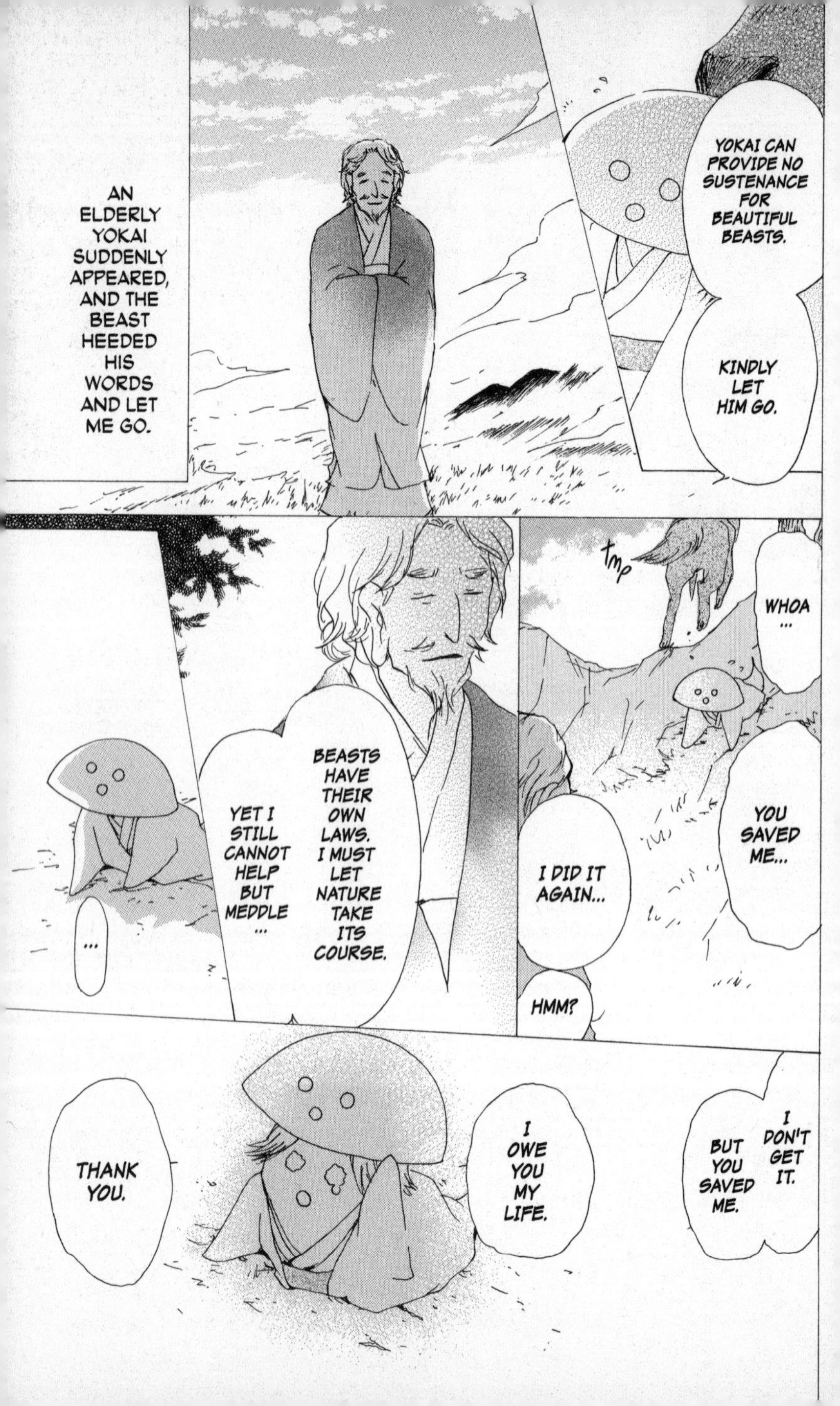
YOKAI CAN PROVIDE NO SUSTENANCE FOR BEAUTIFUL BEASTS.
KINDLY LET HIM GO.
AN ELDERLY YOKAI SUDDENLY APPEARED, AND THE BEAST HEEDED HIS WORDS AND LET ME GO.
TMP
WHOA ...
YOU SAVED ME...
I DID IT AGAIN...
HMM?
BEASTS HAVE THEIR OWN LAWS. I MUST LET NATURE TAKE ITS COURSE.
YET I STILL CANNOT HELP BUT MEDDLE ...
...
I DON'T GET IT.
BUT YOU SAVED ME.
I OWE YOU MY LIFE.
THANK YOU.

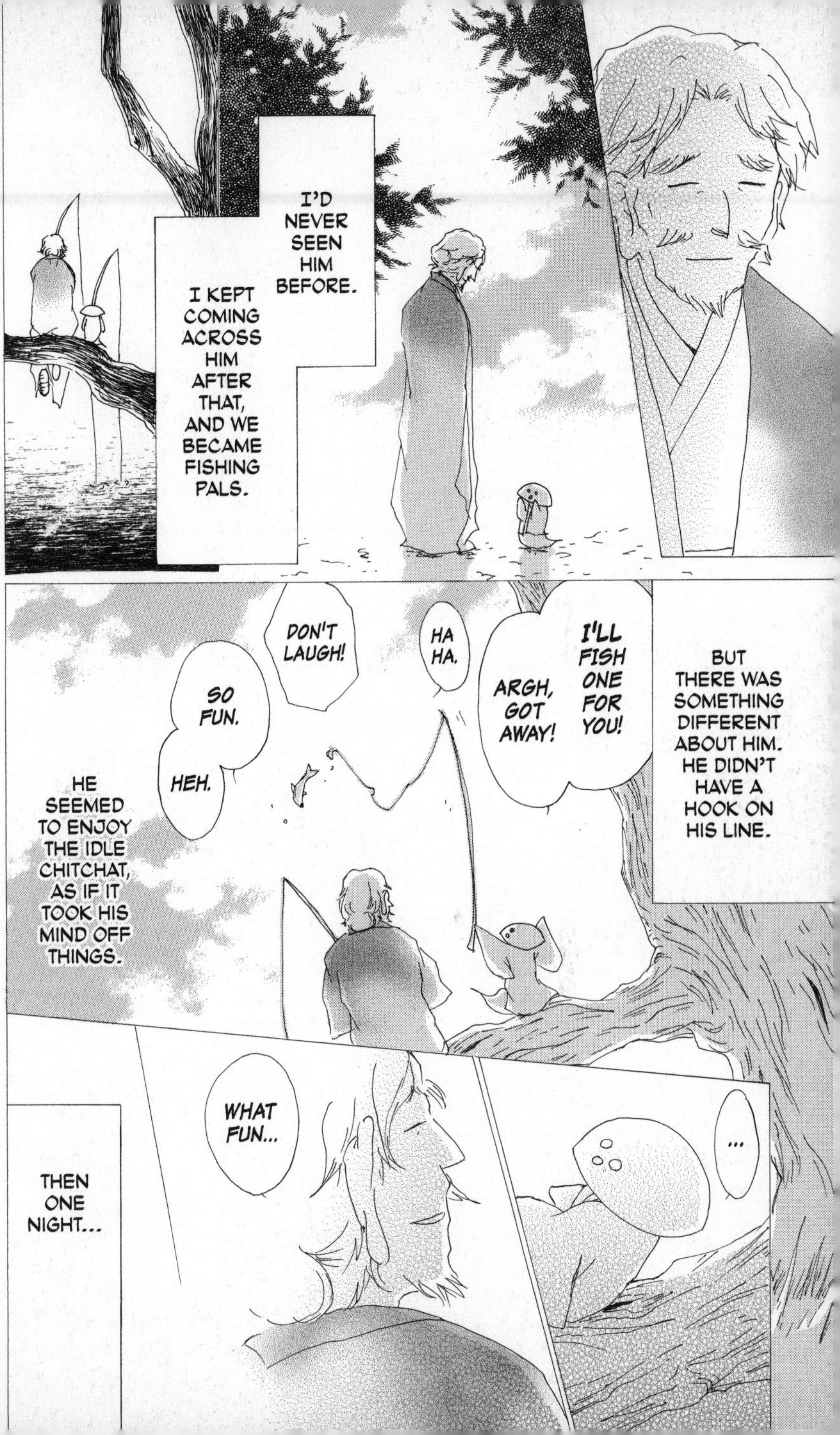

I'D NEVER SEEN HIM BEFORE.
I KEPT COMING ACROSS HIM AFTER THAT, AND WE BECAME FISHING PALS.
BUT THERE WAS SOMETHING DIFFERENT ABOUT HIM. HE DIDN'T HAVE A HOOK ON HIS LINE.
I'LL FISH ONE FOR YOU!
ARGH, GOT AWAY!
HA HA.
DON'T LAUGH!
SO FUN.
HEH.
HE SEEMED TO ENJOY THE IDLE CHITCHAT, AS IF IT TOOK HIS MIND OFF THINGS.
...
WHAT FUN...
THEN ONE NIGHT...

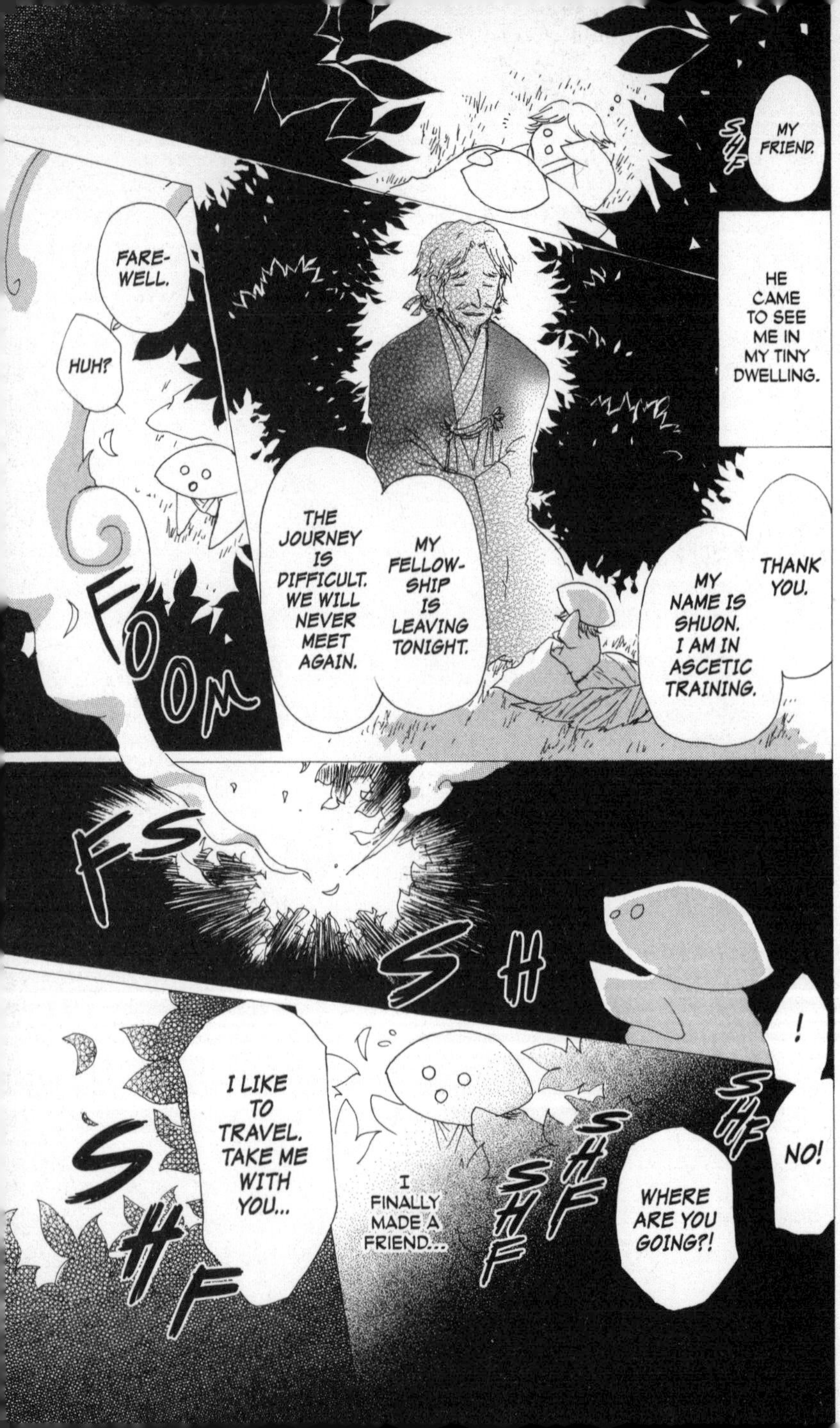
SHF
MY FRIEND.
HE CAME TO SEE ME IN MY TINY DWELLING.
THANK YOU.
MY NAME IS SHUON. I AM IN ASCETIC TRAINING.
MY FELLOWSHIP IS LEAVING TONIGHT.
THE JOURNEY IS DIFFICULT. WE WILL NEVER MEET AGAIN.
FAREWELL.
HUH?
FOOM
FS
SH
!
SHF
NO!
WHERE ARE YOU GOING?!
SHF
SHF
I FINALLY MADE A FRIEND...
I LIKE TO TRAVEL. TAKE ME WITH YOU...
SHF

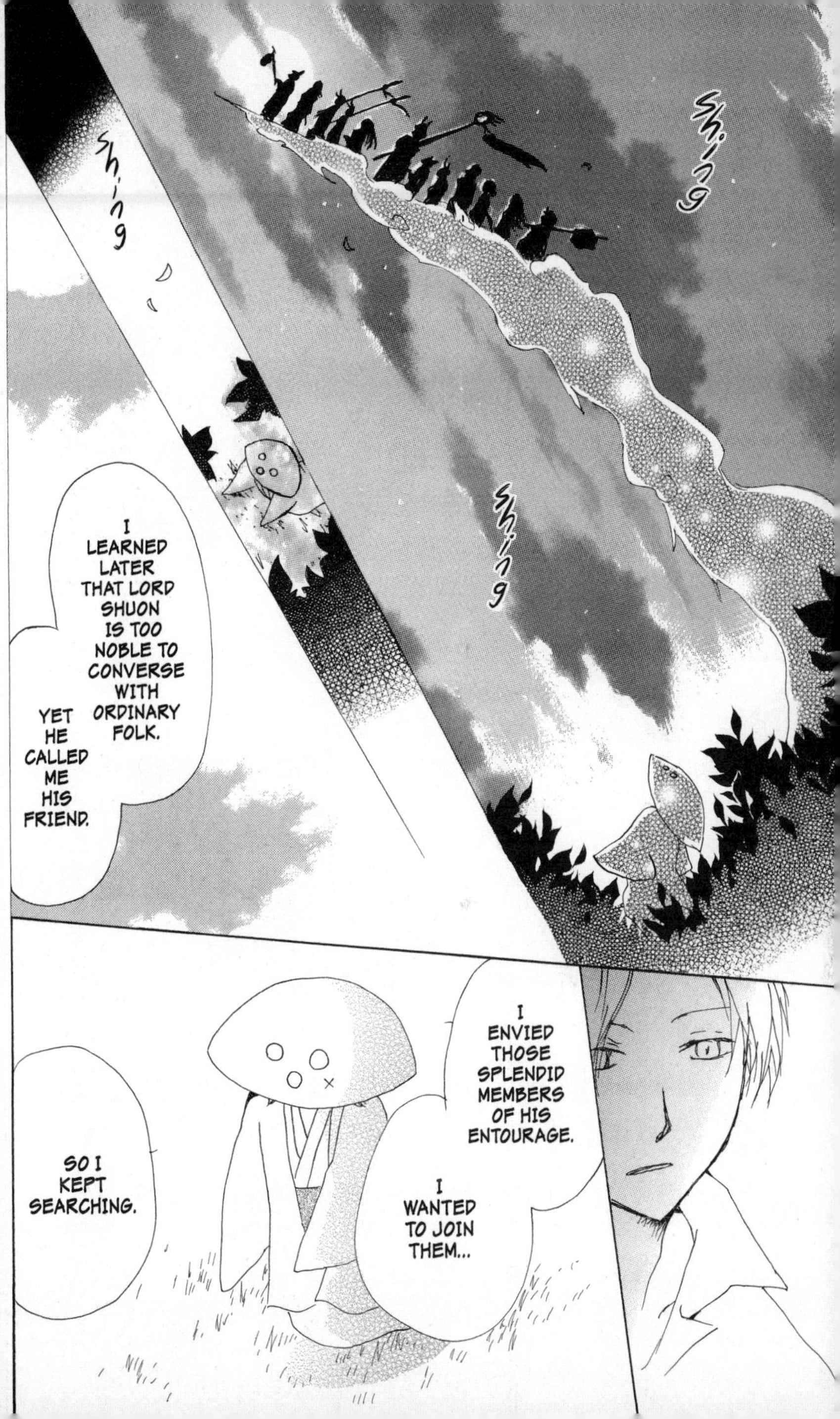
shing
shing
shing
I LEARNED LATER THAT LORD SHUON IS TOO NOBLE TO CONVERSE WITH ORDINARY FOLK.
YET HE CALLED ME HIS FRIEND.
I ENVIED THOSE SPLENDID MEMBERS OF HIS ENTOURAGE.
I WANTED TO JOIN THEM...
SO I KEPT SEARCHING.

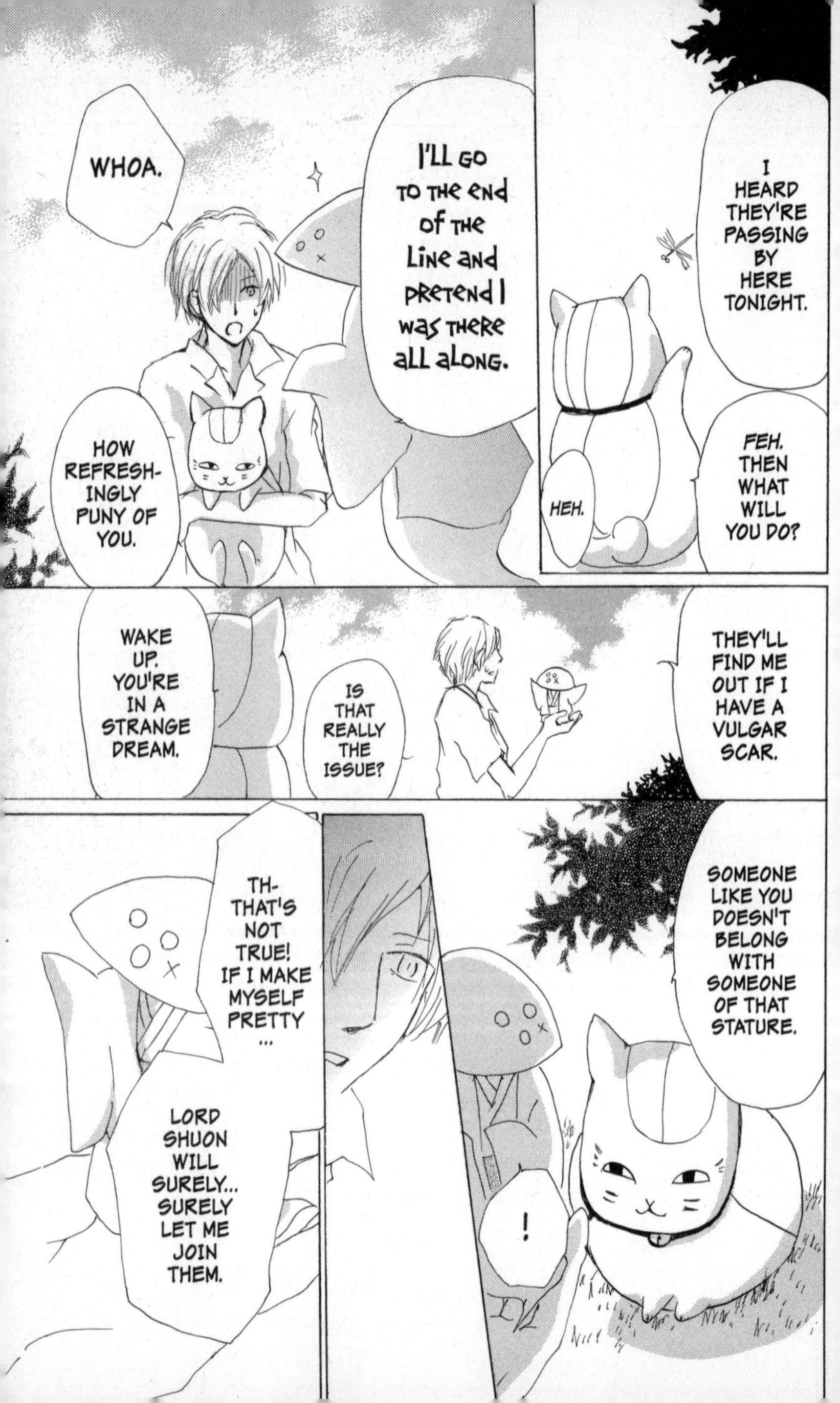
I HEARD THEY'RE PASSING BY HERE TONIGHT.
FEH. THEN WHAT WILL YOU DO?
HEH.
I'LL GO TO THE END OF THE LINE AND PRETEND I WAS THERE ALL ALONG.
WHOA.
HOW REFRESHINGLY PUNY OF YOU.
THEY'LL FIND ME OUT IF I HAVE A VULGAR SCAR.
IS THAT REALLY THE ISSUE?
WAKE UP. YOU'RE IN A STRANGE DREAM.
SOMEONE LIKE YOU DOESN'T BELONG WITH SOMEONE OF THAT STATURE.
!
TH-THAT'S NOT TRUE! IF I MAKE MYSELF PRETTY...
LORD SHUON WILL SURELY... SURELY LET ME JOIN THEM.

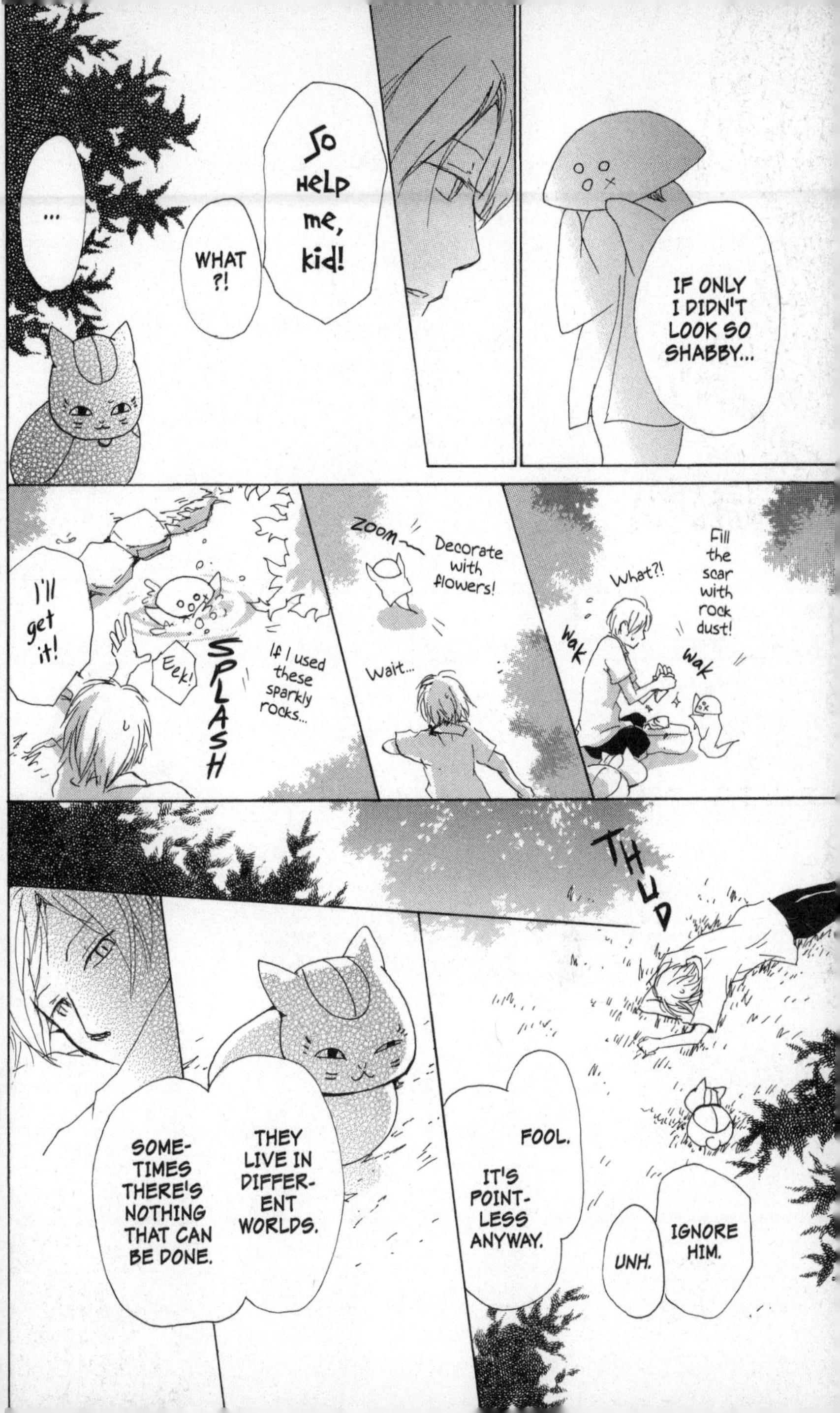
IF ONLY I DIDN'T LOOK SO SHABBY...
So help me, kid!
WHAT?!
...
Fill the scar with rock dust!
What?!
wak
wak
zoom
Decorate with flowers!
Wait...
If I used these sparkly rocks...
SPLASH
Eek!
I'll get it!
THUD
IGNORE HIM.
UNH.
FOOL.
IT'S POINTLESS ANYWAY.
THEY LIVE IN DIFFERENT WORLDS.
SOMETIMES THERE'S NOTHING THAT CAN BE DONE.

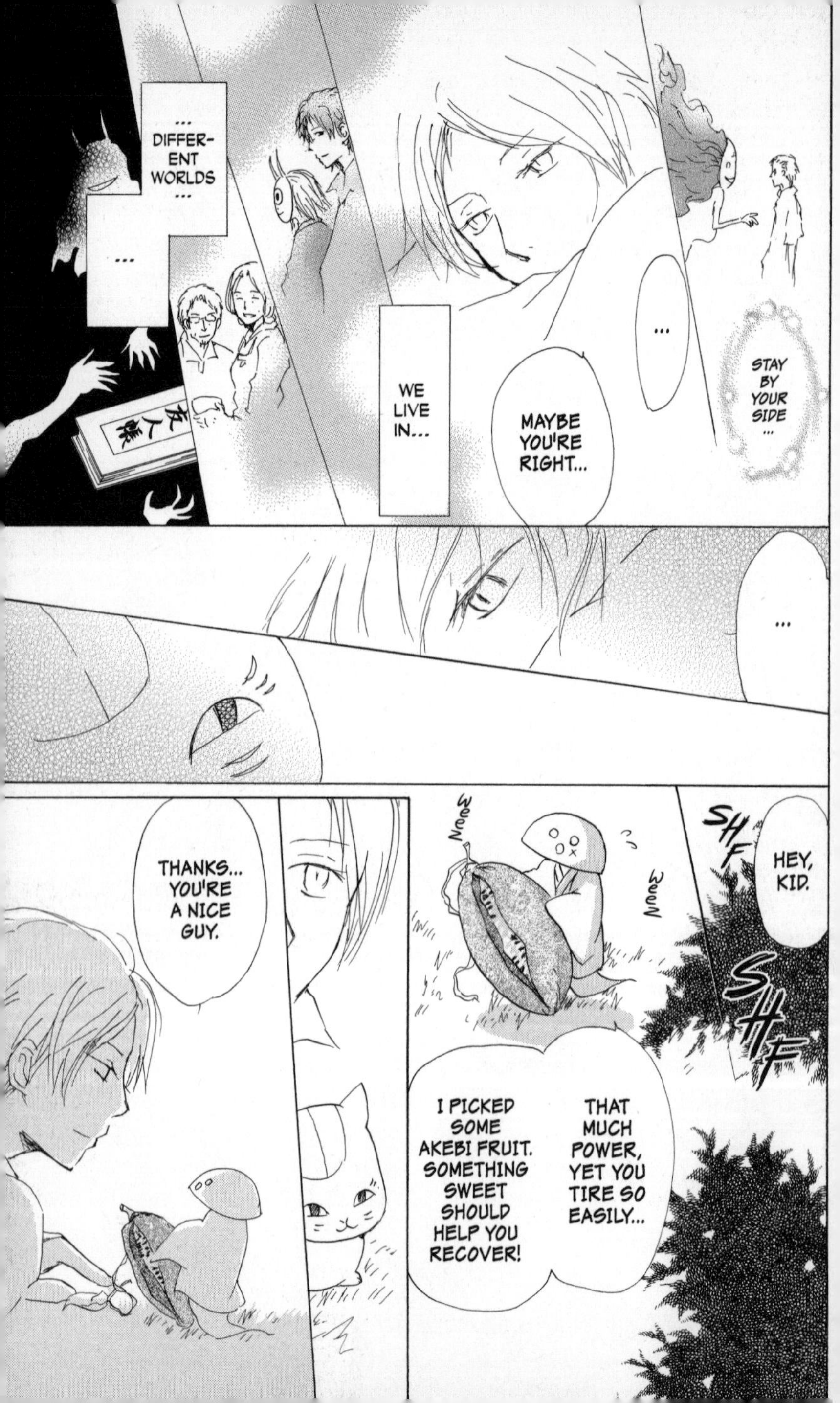

STAY BY YOUR SIDE ...
...
MAYBE YOU'RE RIGHT...
WE LIVE IN...
... DIFFERENT WORLDS ...
...
友人帳
...
HEY, KID.
SHF
SHF
WEEN
WEEN
THAT MUCH POWER, YET YOU TIRE SO EASILY...
I PICKED SOME AKEBI FRUIT. SOMETHING SWEET SHOULD HELP YOU RECOVER!
THANKS... YOU'RE A NICE GUY.

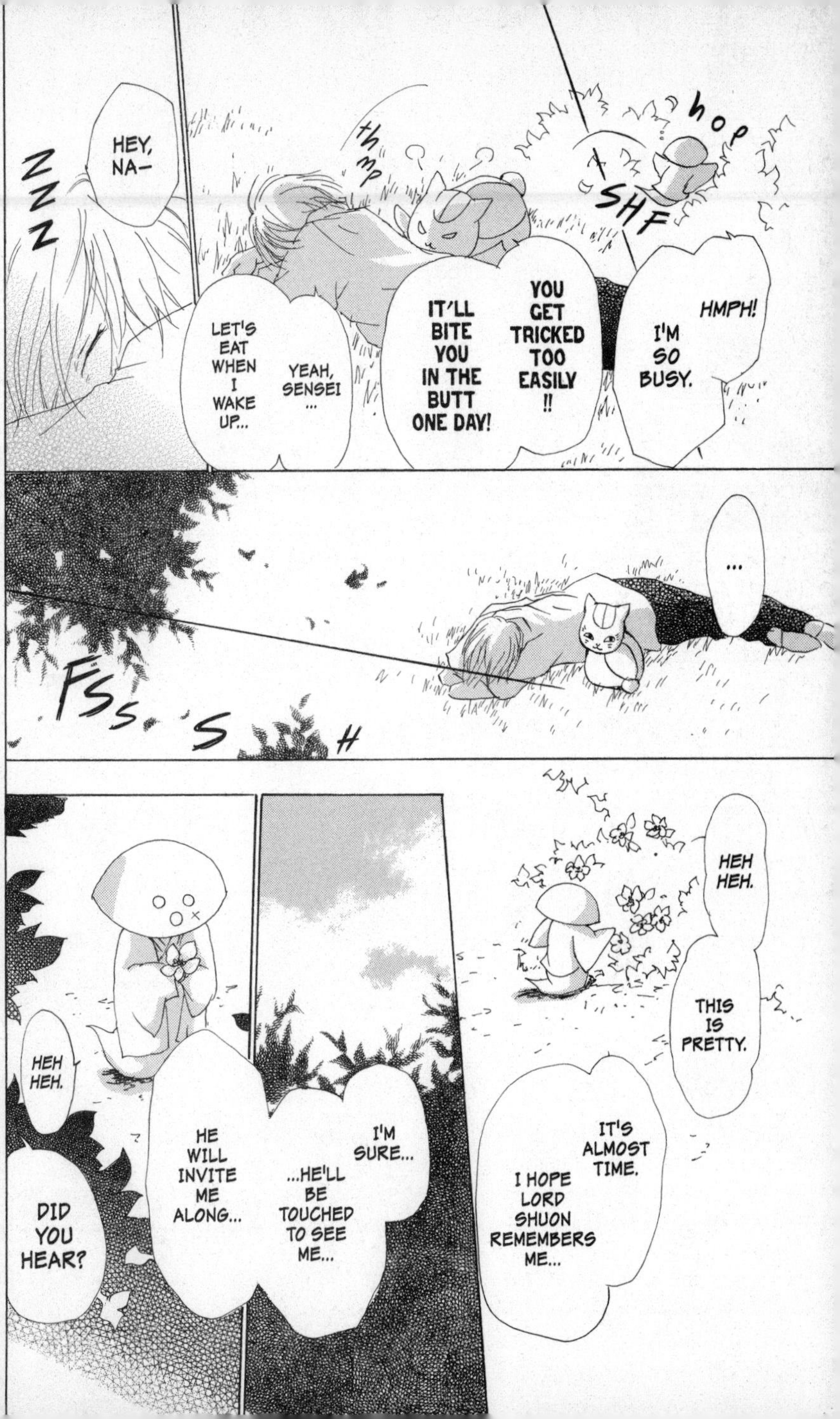
hop
SHF
HMPH!
I'M SO BUSY.
YOU GET TRICKED TOO EASILY!!
IT'LL BITE YOU IN THE BUTT ONE DAY!
thmp
YEAH, SENSEI...
LET'S EAT WHEN I WAKE UP...
HEY, NA–
ZZZ
...
FSSSSH
HEH HEH.
THIS IS PRETTY.
IT'S ALMOST TIME.
I HOPE LORD SHUON REMEMBERS ME...
I'M SURE...
...HE'LL BE TOUCHED TO SEE ME...
HE WILL INVITE ME ALONG...
HEH HEH.
DID YOU HEAR?

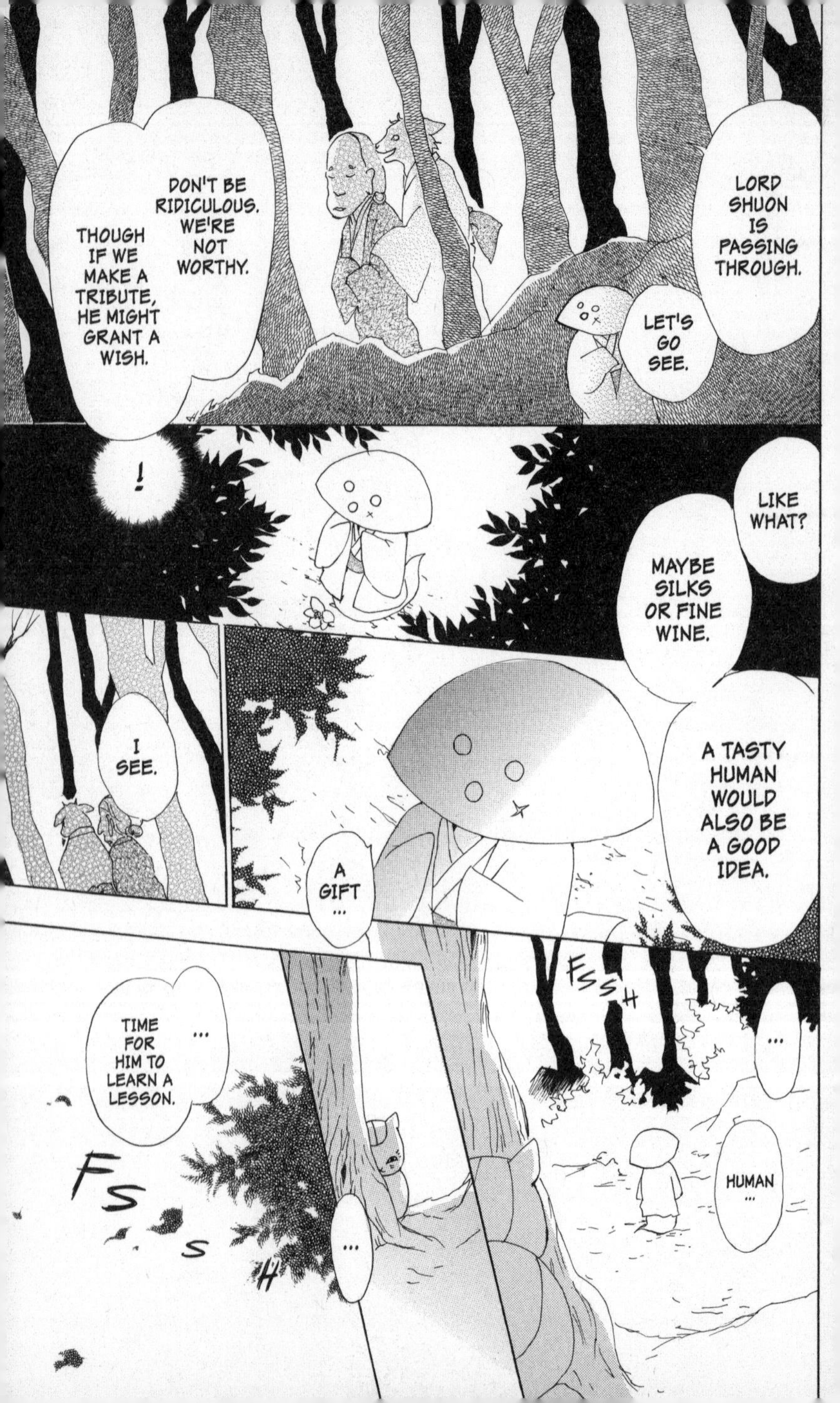
LORD SHUON IS PASSING THROUGH.
LET'S GO SEE.
DON'T BE RIDICULOUS. WE'RE NOT WORTHY.
THOUGH IF WE MAKE A TRIBUTE, HE MIGHT GRANT A WISH.
LIKE WHAT?
MAYBE SILKS OR FINE WINE.
!
A TASTY HUMAN WOULD ALSO BE A GOOD IDEA.
A GIFT ...
I SEE.
FSSH
...
HUMAN ...
...
TIME FOR HIM TO LEARN A LESSON.
...
FSSH

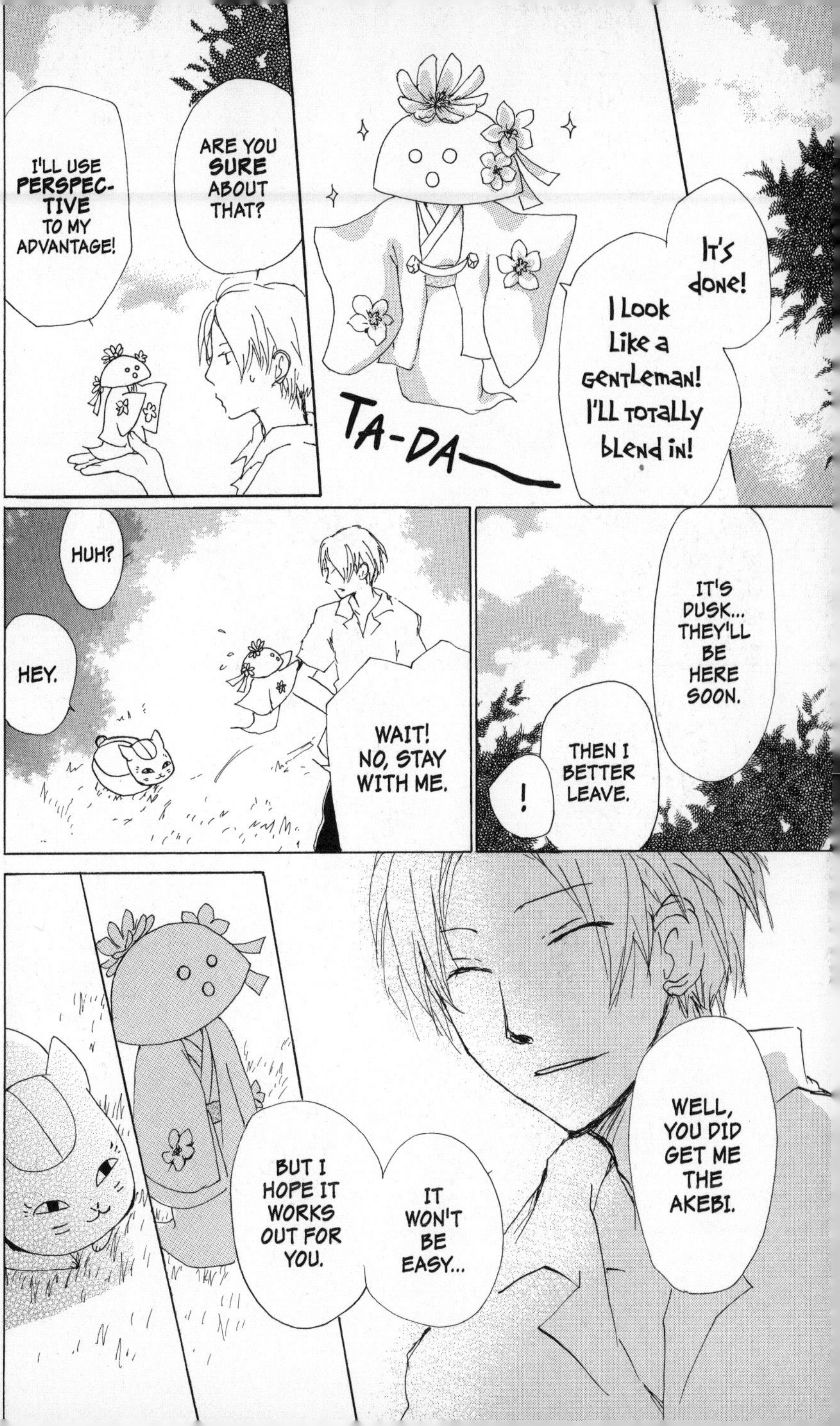

It's done!
I look like a gentleman! I'll totally blend in!
TA-DA
ARE YOU SURE ABOUT THAT?
I'LL USE PERSPEC-TIVE TO MY ADVANTAGE!
IT'S DUSK... THEY'LL BE HERE SOON.
THEN I BETTER LEAVE.
!
WAIT! NO, STAY WITH ME.
HUH?
HEY.
WELL, YOU DID GET ME THE AKEBI.
IT WON'T BE EASY...
BUT I HOPE IT WORKS OUT FOR YOU.

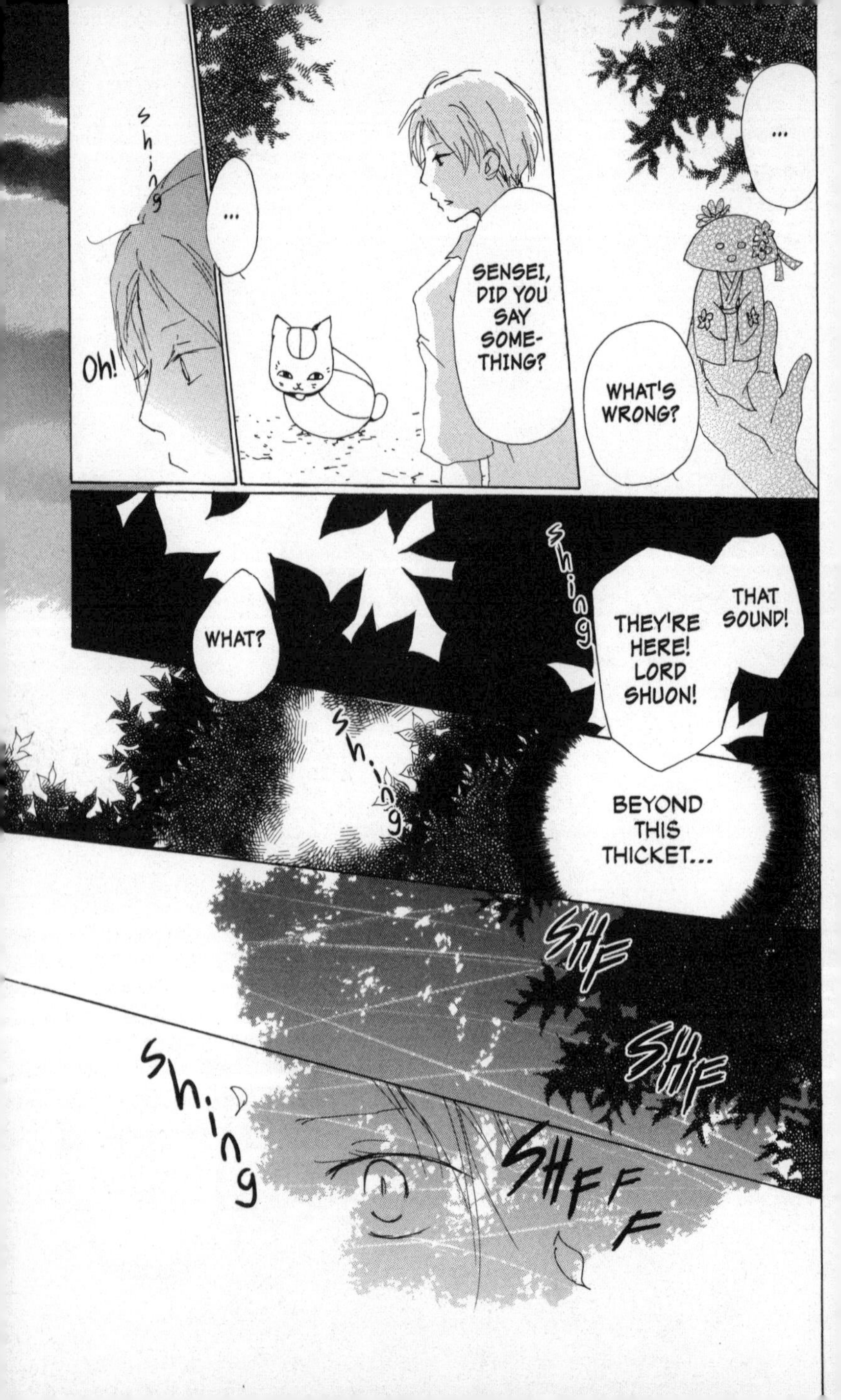
...
WHAT'S WRONG?
SENSEI, DID YOU SAY SOME-THING?
...
shing
Oh!
THAT SOUND!
THEY'RE HERE! LORD SHUON!
shing
WHAT?
shing
BEYOND THIS THICKET...
SHF
SHF
SHFFF
shing

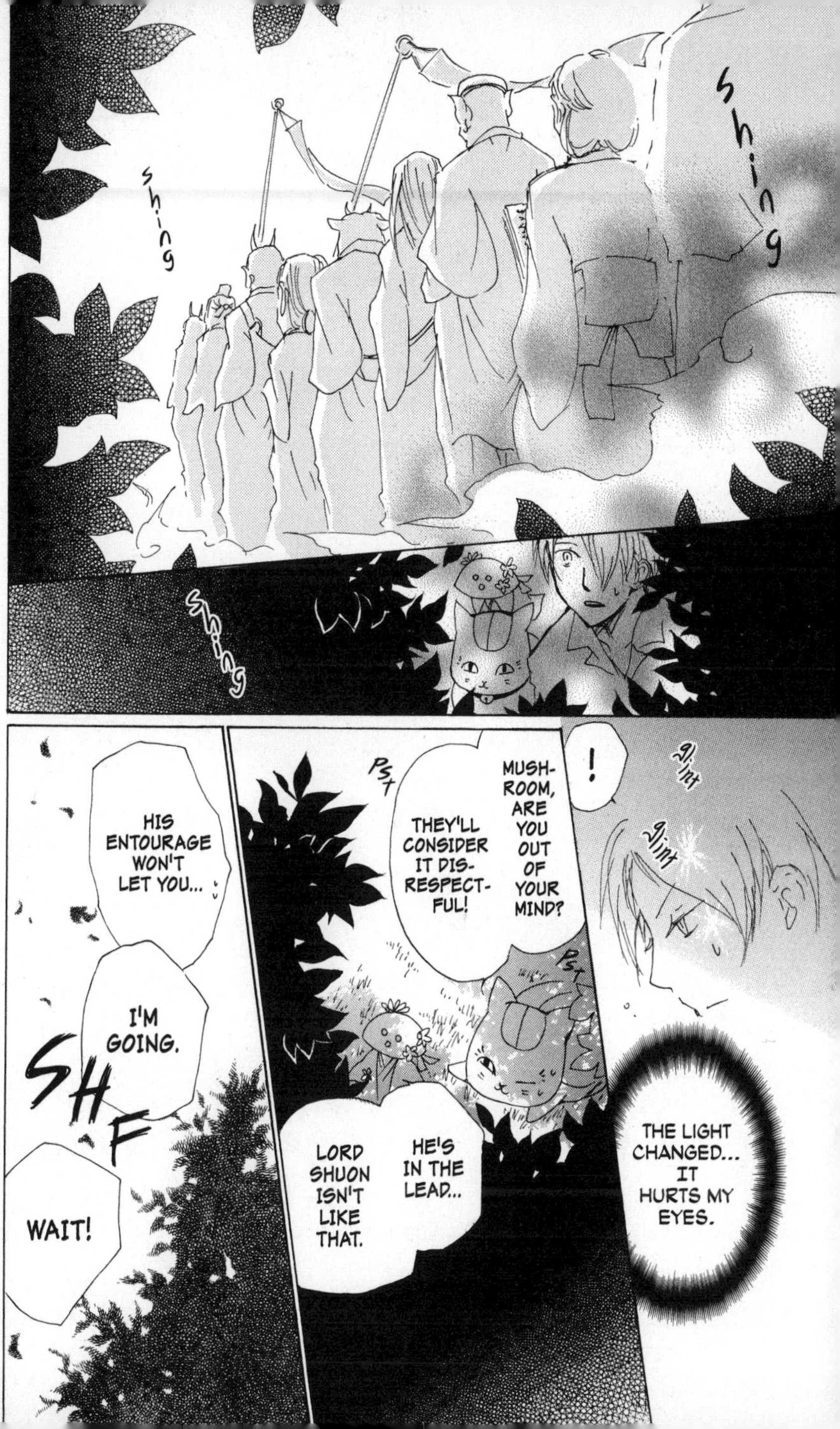
shing
shing
shing
!
glint
glint
THE LIGHT CHANGED... IT HURTS MY EYES.
Pst
MUSH-ROOM, ARE YOU OUT OF YOUR MIND?
THEY'LL CONSIDER IT DIS-RESPECT-FUL!
Pst
HE'S IN THE LEAD...
LORD SHUON ISN'T LIKE THAT.
HIS ENTOURAGE WON'T LET YOU...
I'M GOING.
SHF
WAIT!

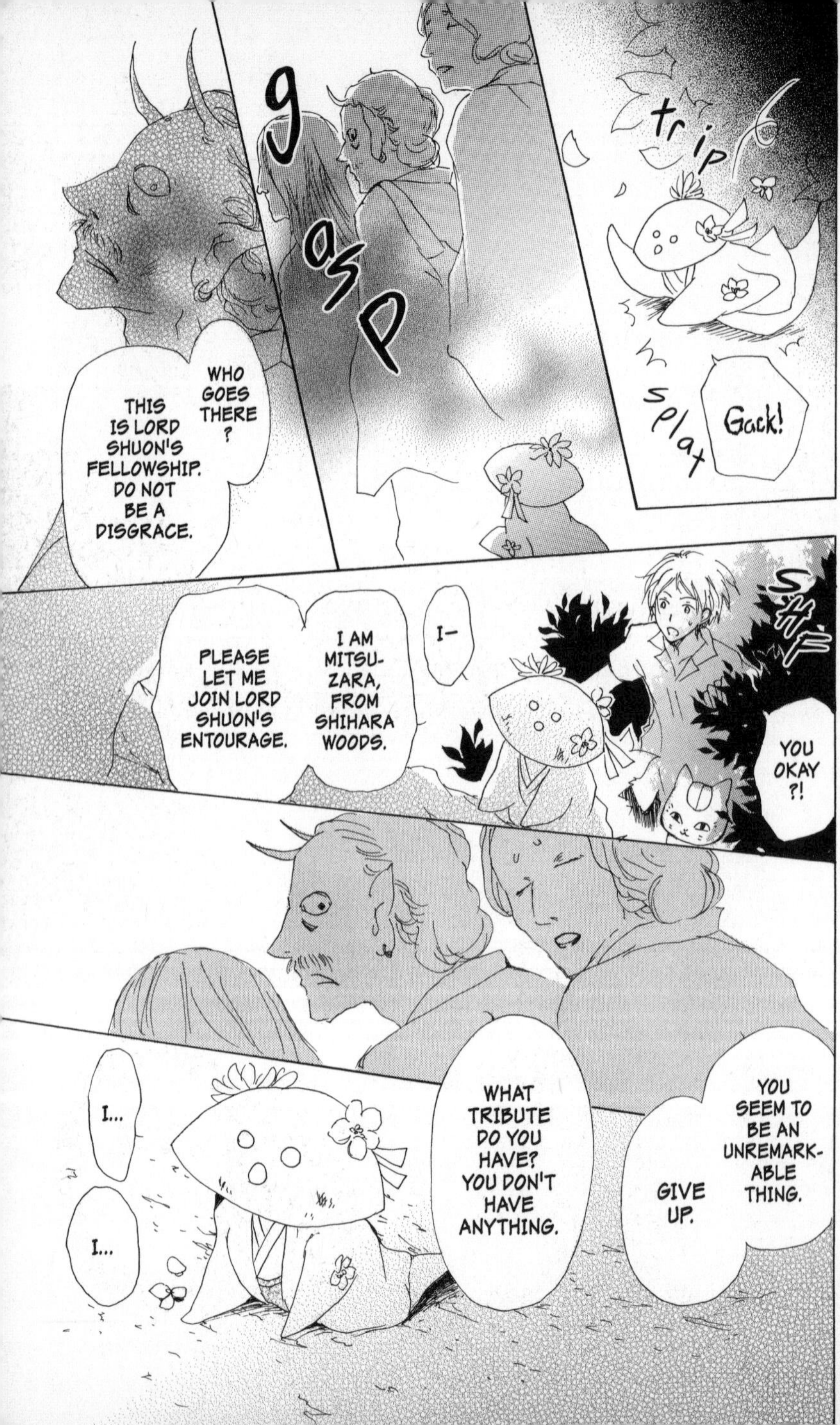
trip
splat
Gack!
gasp
WHO GOES THERE?
THIS IS LORD SHUON'S FELLOWSHIP. DO NOT BE A DISGRACE.
SHF
YOU OKAY?!
I–
I AM MITSU-ZARA, FROM SHIHARA WOODS.
PLEASE LET ME JOIN LORD SHUON'S ENTOURAGE.
YOU SEEM TO BE AN UNREMARK-ABLE THING.
GIVE UP.
WHAT TRIBUTE DO YOU HAVE? YOU DON'T HAVE ANYTHING.
I...
I...

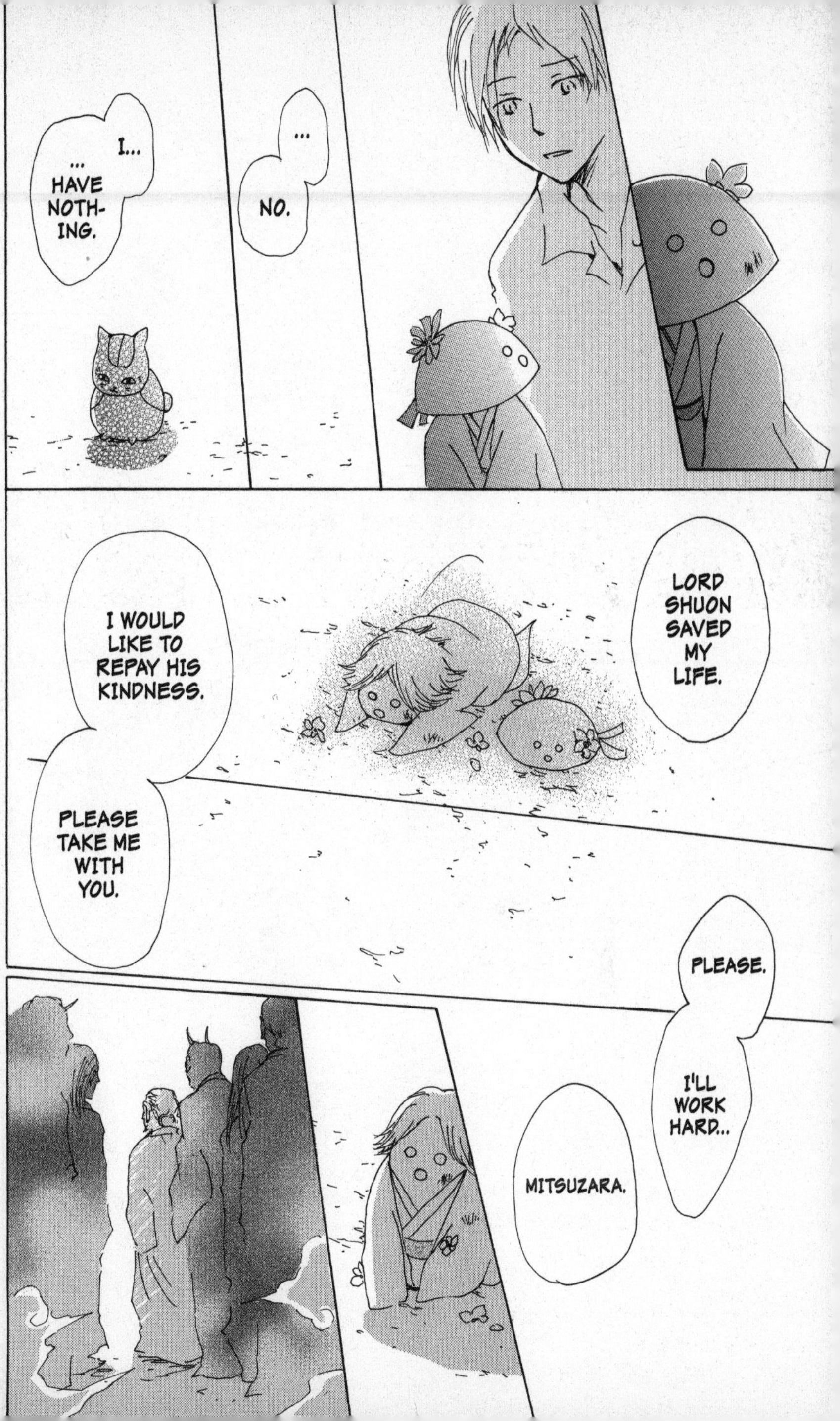
... NO.
I... ... HAVE NOTHING.
LORD SHUON SAVED MY LIFE.
I WOULD LIKE TO REPAY HIS KINDNESS.
PLEASE TAKE ME WITH YOU.
PLEASE.
I'LL WORK HARD...
MITSUZARA.

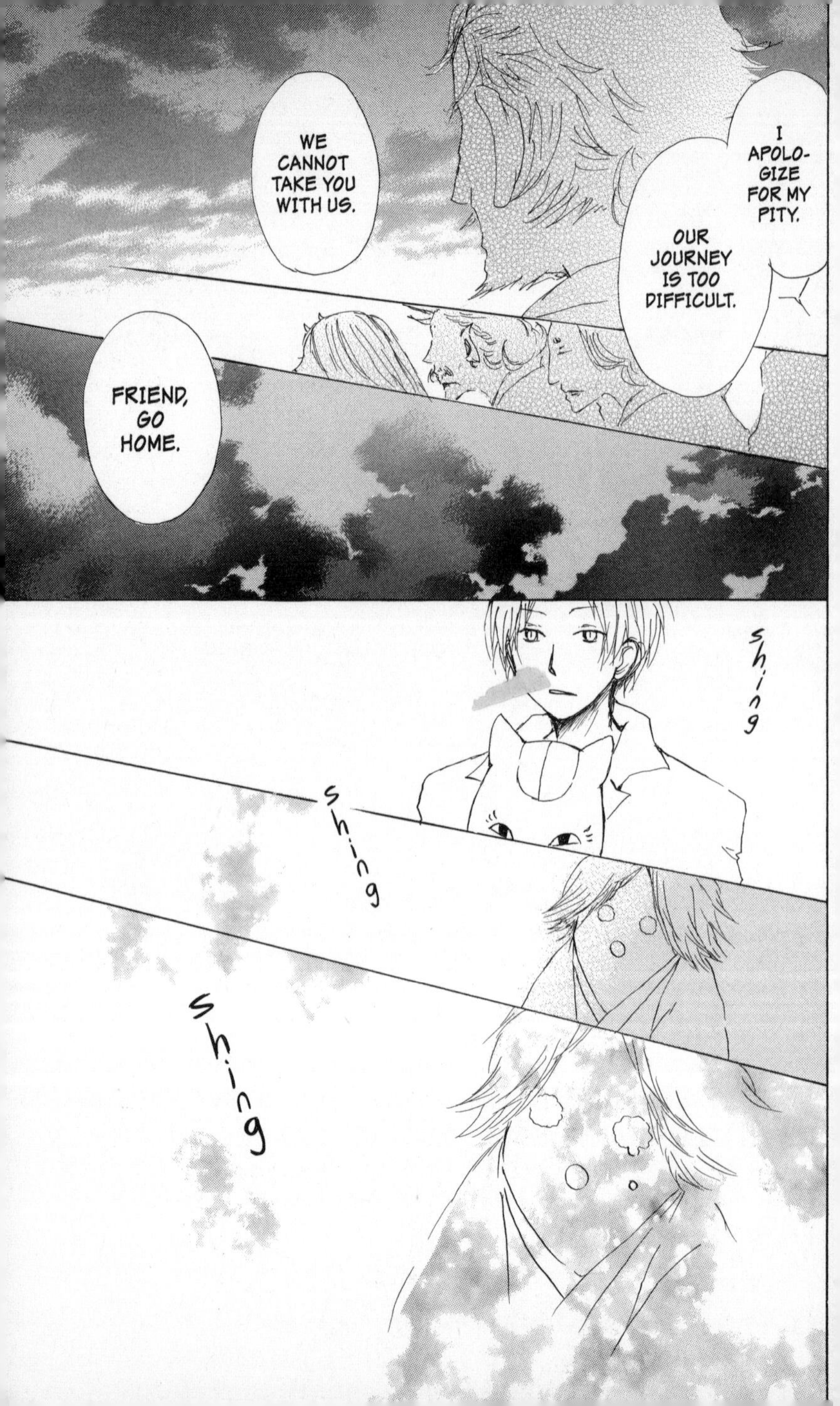
I APOLOGIZE FOR MY PITY.
OUR JOURNEY IS TOO DIFFICULT.
WE CANNOT TAKE YOU WITH US.
FRIEND, GO HOME.
shing
shing
shing

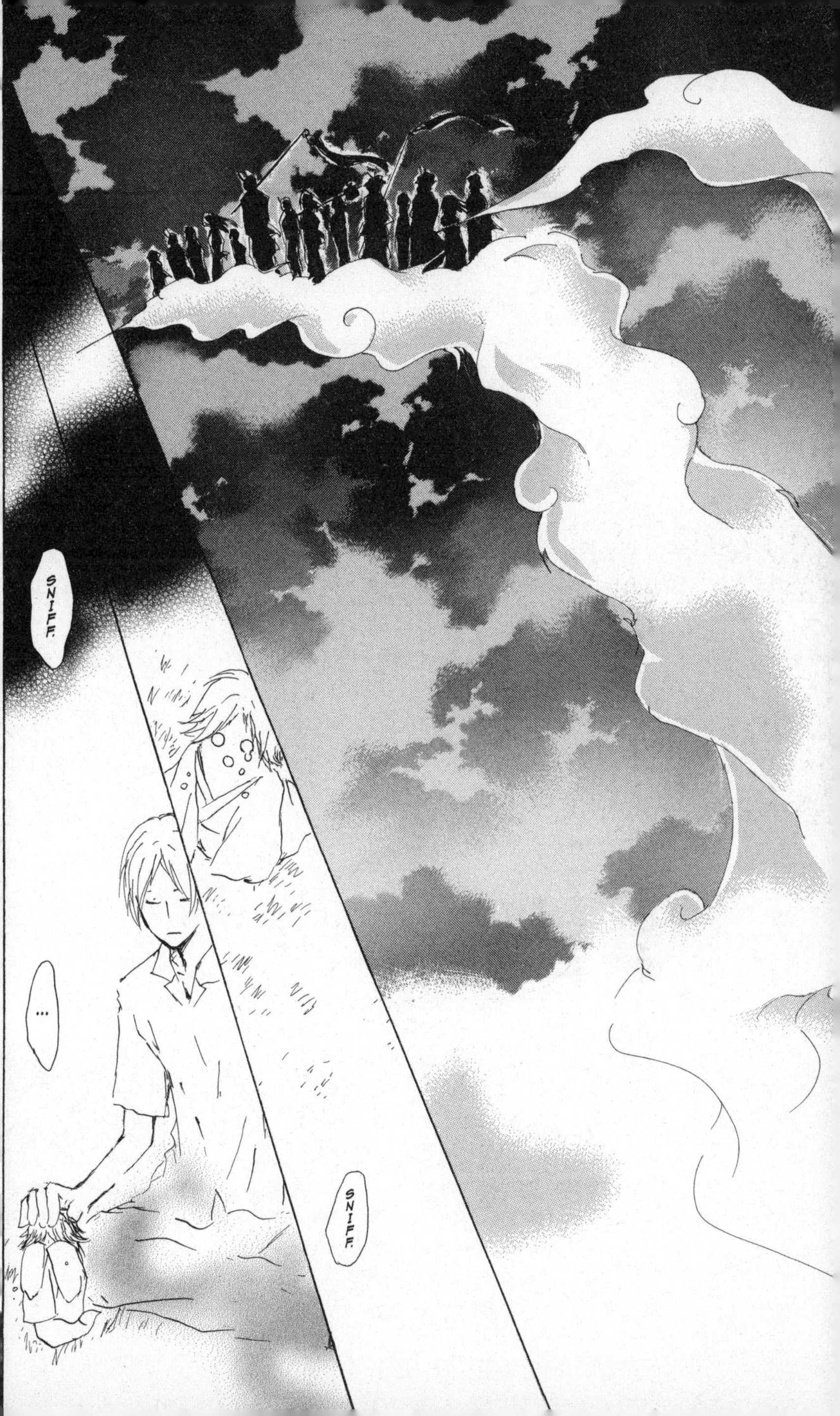
SNIFF.
SNIFF.
...

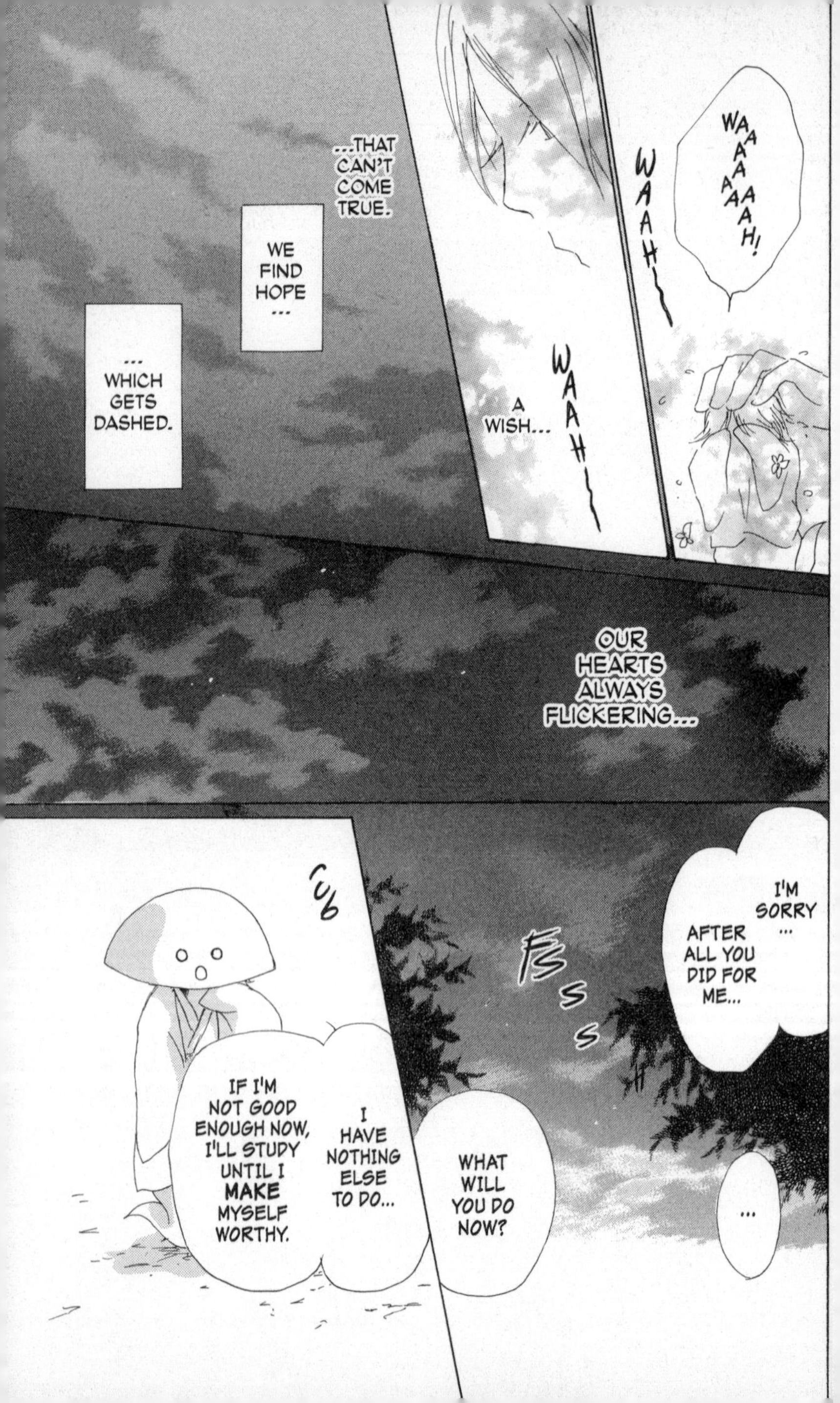
WAAAAAAAAH!
WAAH
A WISH...
WAAH
...THAT CAN'T COME TRUE.
WE FIND HOPE...
...WHICH GETS DASHED.
OUR HEARTS ALWAYS FLICKERING...
I'M SORRY...
AFTER ALL YOU DID FOR ME...
FSSS
...
WHAT WILL YOU DO NOW?
I HAVE NOTHING ELSE TO DO...
IF I'M NOT GOOD ENOUGH NOW, I'LL STUDY UNTIL I **MAKE** MYSELF WORTHY.

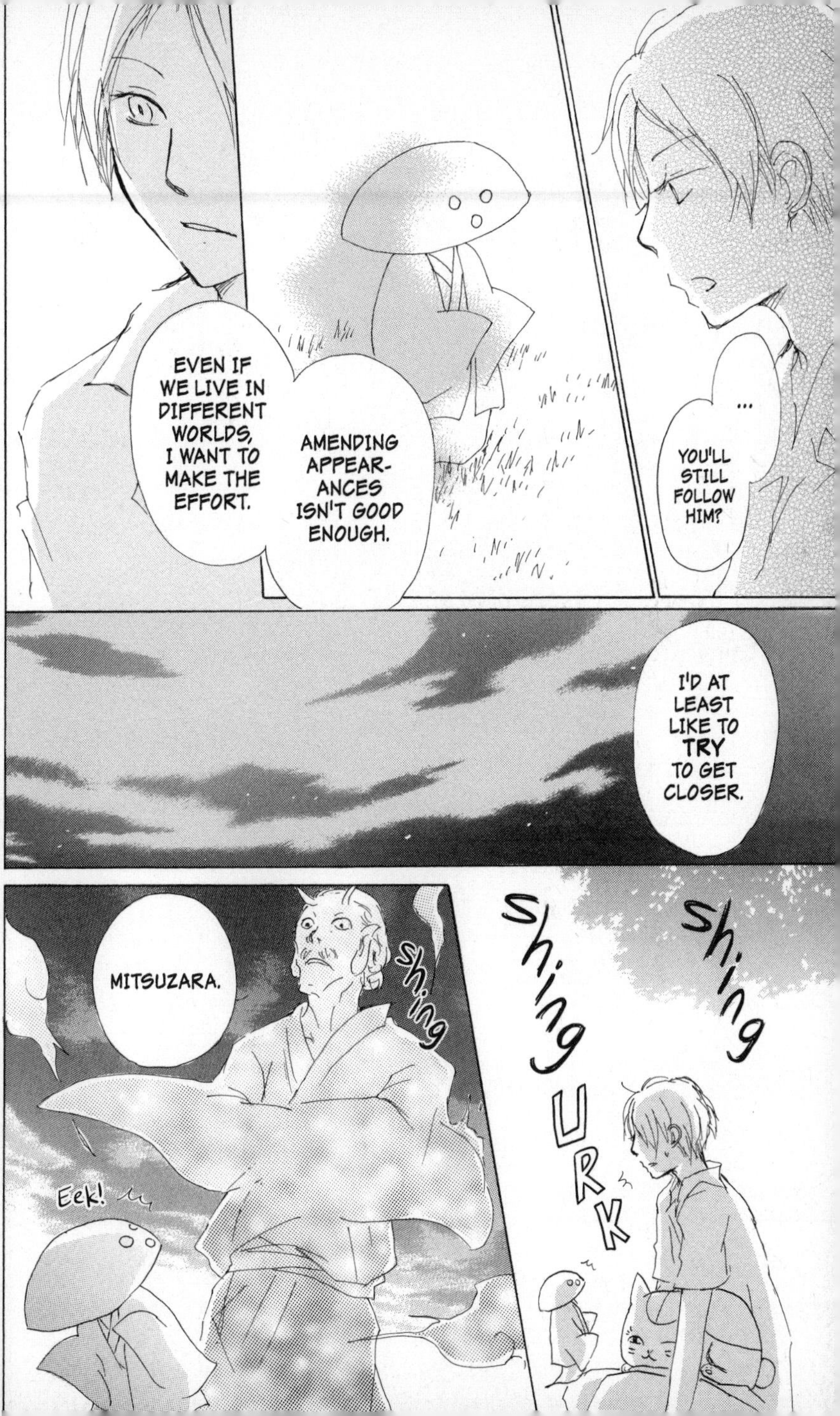
...
YOU'LL STILL FOLLOW HIM?
AMENDING APPEAR-ANCES ISN'T GOOD ENOUGH.
EVEN IF WE LIVE IN DIFFERENT WORLDS, I WANT TO MAKE THE EFFORT.
I'D AT LEAST LIKE TO TRY TO GET CLOSER.
shing
shing
URK
MITSUZARA.
shing
Eek!

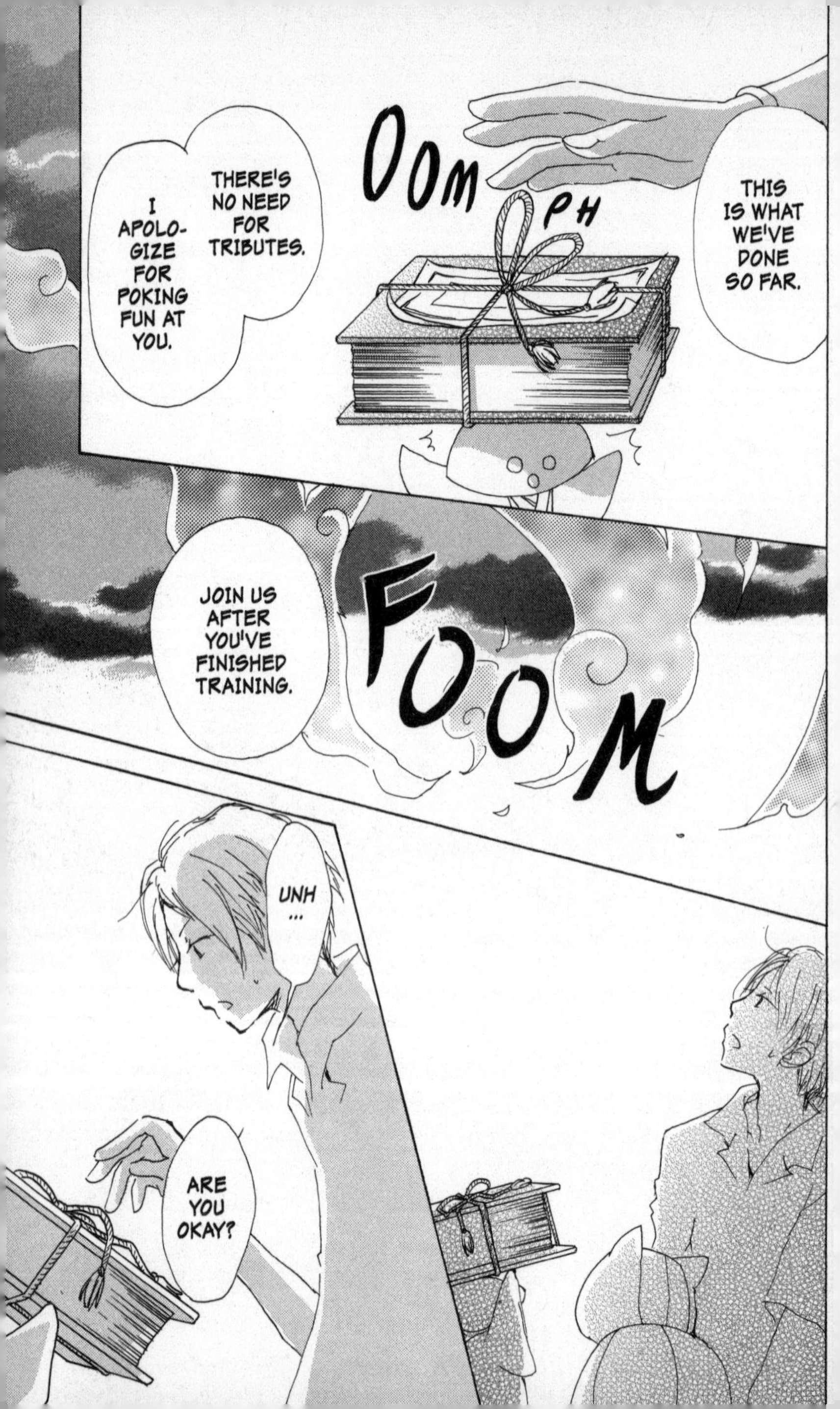
THIS IS WHAT WE'VE DONE SO FAR.
OOMPH
THERE'S NO NEED FOR TRIBUTES.
I APOLOGIZE FOR POKING FUN AT YOU.
FOOOM
JOIN US AFTER YOU'VE FINISHED TRAINING.
UNH...
ARE YOU OKAY?

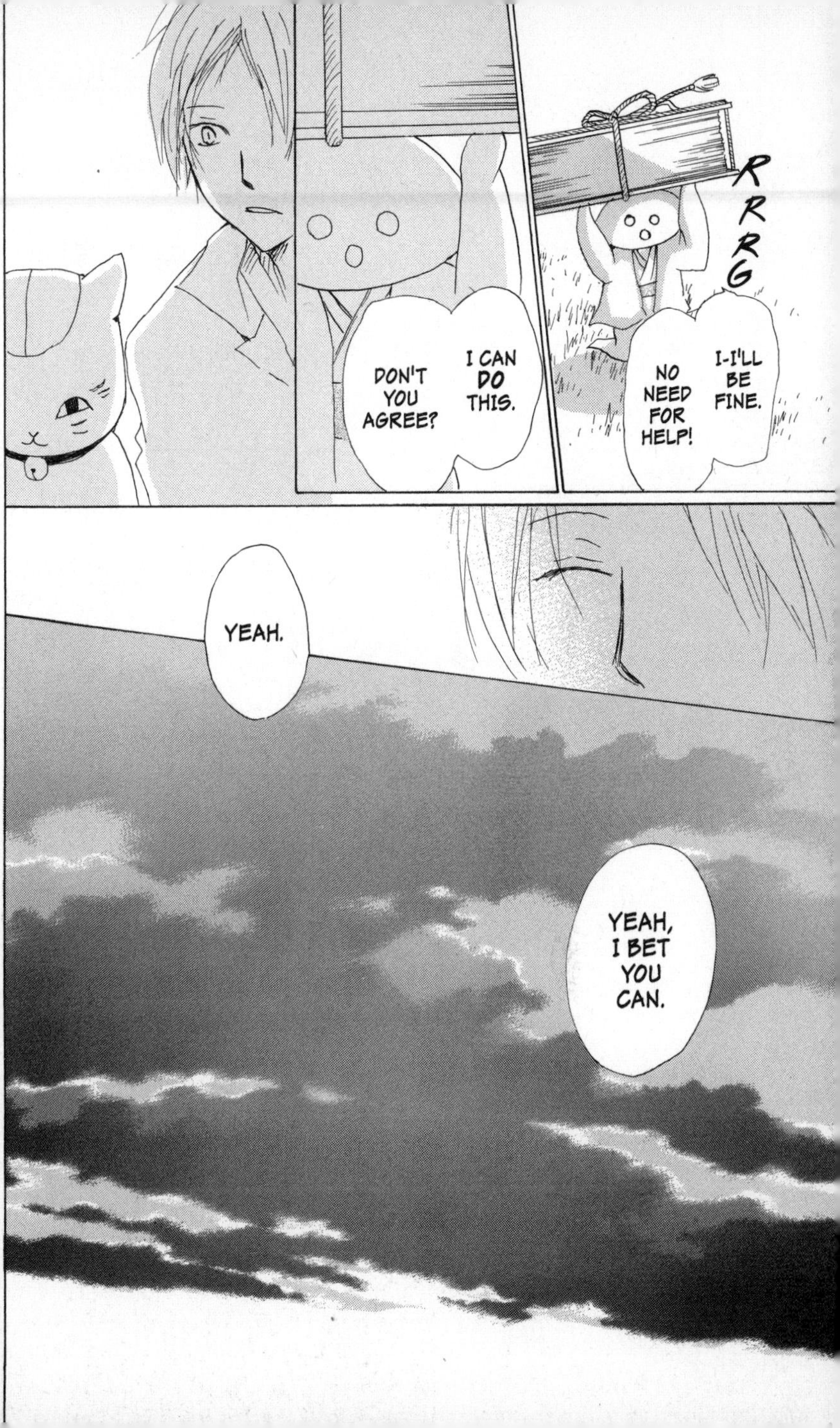
RRRG
I-I'LL BE FINE.
NO NEED FOR HELP!
I CAN DO THIS.
DON'T YOU AGREE?
YEAH.
YEAH, I BET YOU CAN.

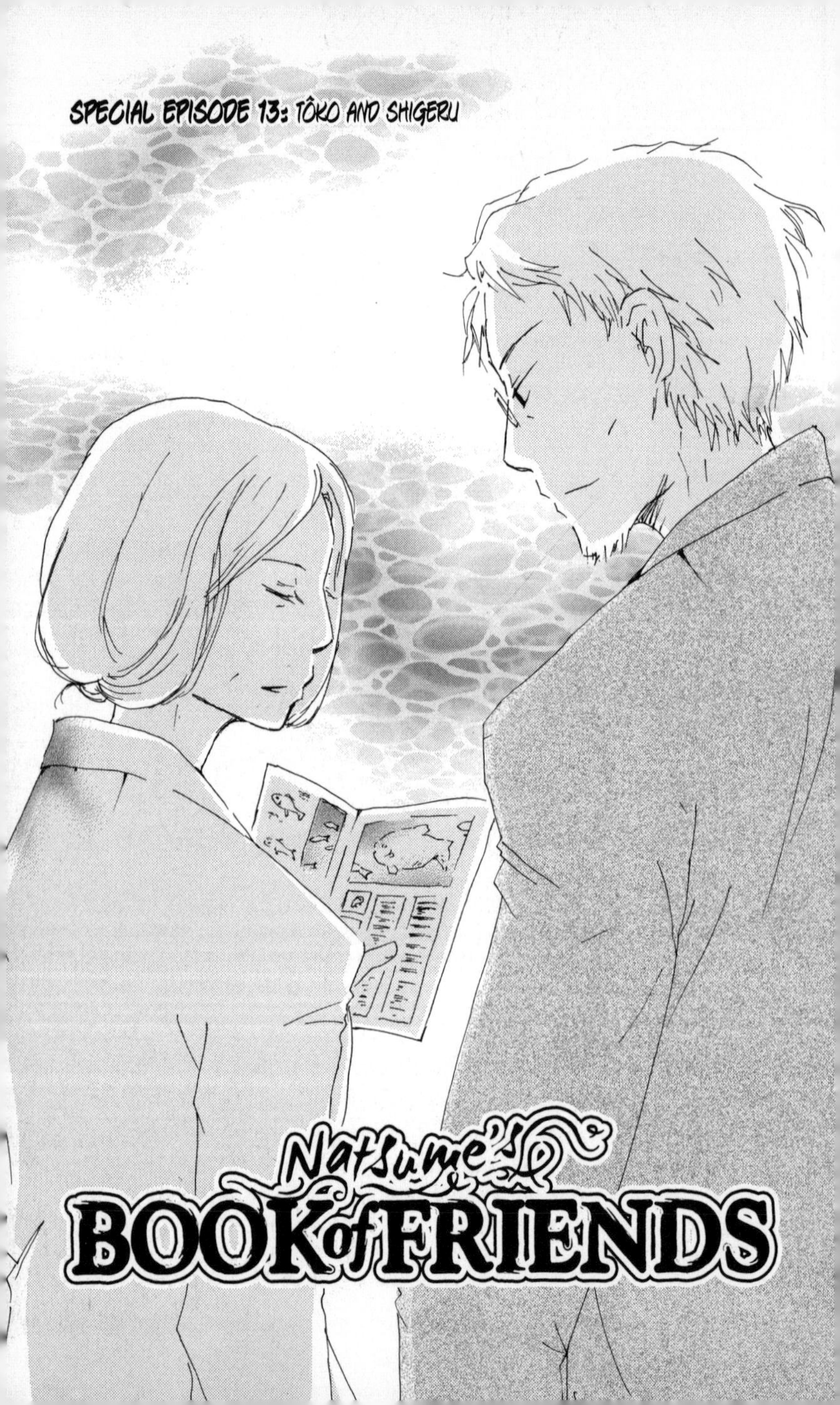
SPECIAL EPISODE 13: TÔKO AND SHIGERU
Natsume's
BOOK of FRIENDS

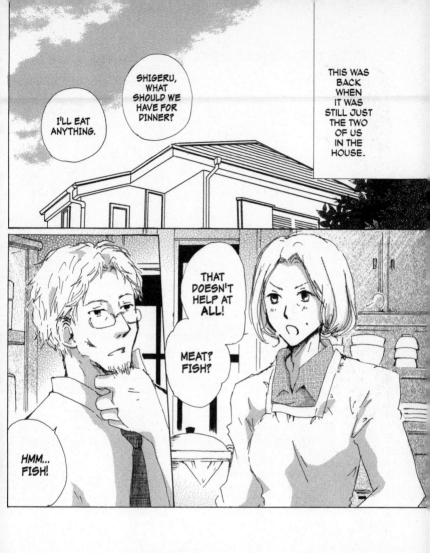

THIS WAS BACK WHEN IT WAS STILL JUST THE TWO OF US IN THE HOUSE.

SHIGERU, WHAT SHOULD WE HAVE FOR DINNER?

I'LL EAT ANYTHING.

THAT DOESN'T HELP AT ALL!

MEAT? FISH?

HMM... FISH!

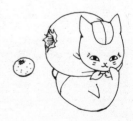

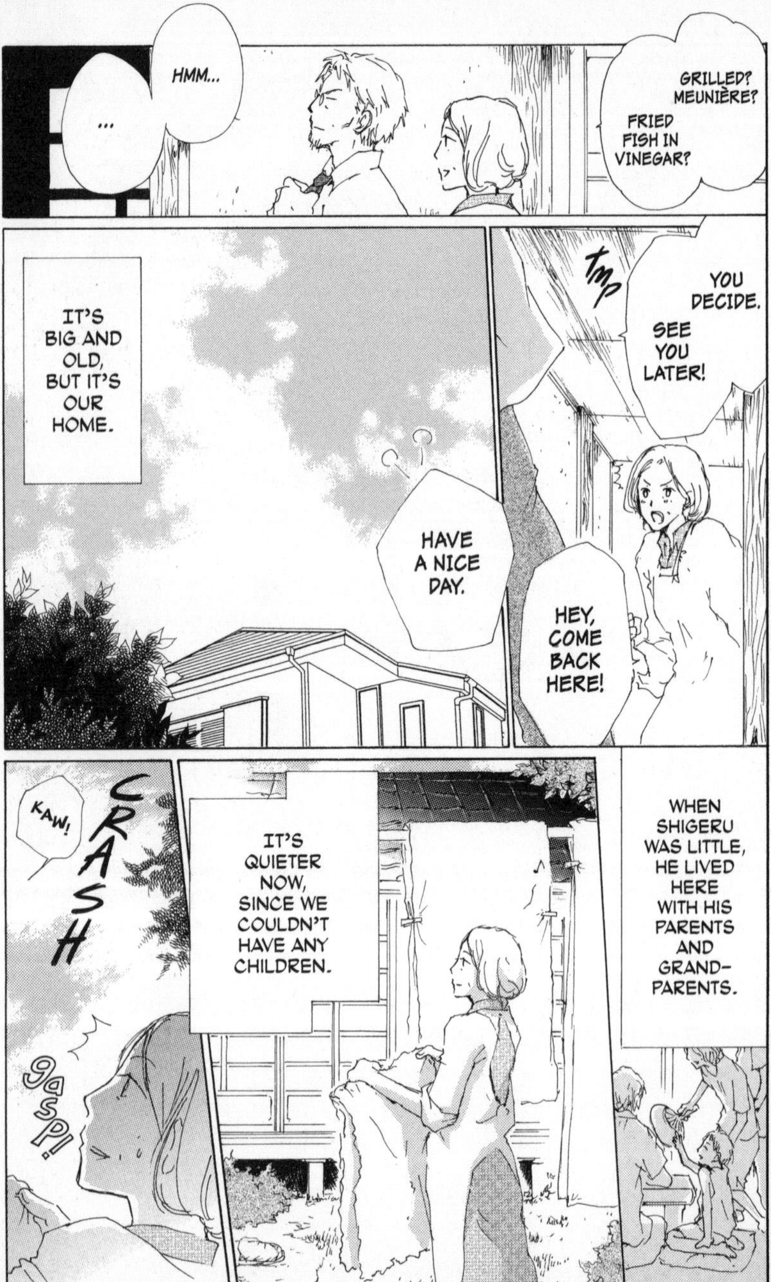
GRILLED? MEUNIÈRE?
FRIED FISH IN VINEGAR?
HMM...
...
tmp
YOU DECIDE.
SEE YOU LATER!
HEY, COME BACK HERE!
HAVE A NICE DAY.
IT'S BIG AND OLD, BUT IT'S OUR HOME.
WHEN SHIGERU WAS LITTLE, HE LIVED HERE WITH HIS PARENTS AND GRAND-PARENTS.
IT'S QUIETER NOW, SINCE WE COULDN'T HAVE ANY CHILDREN.
CRASH
KAW!
gasp!

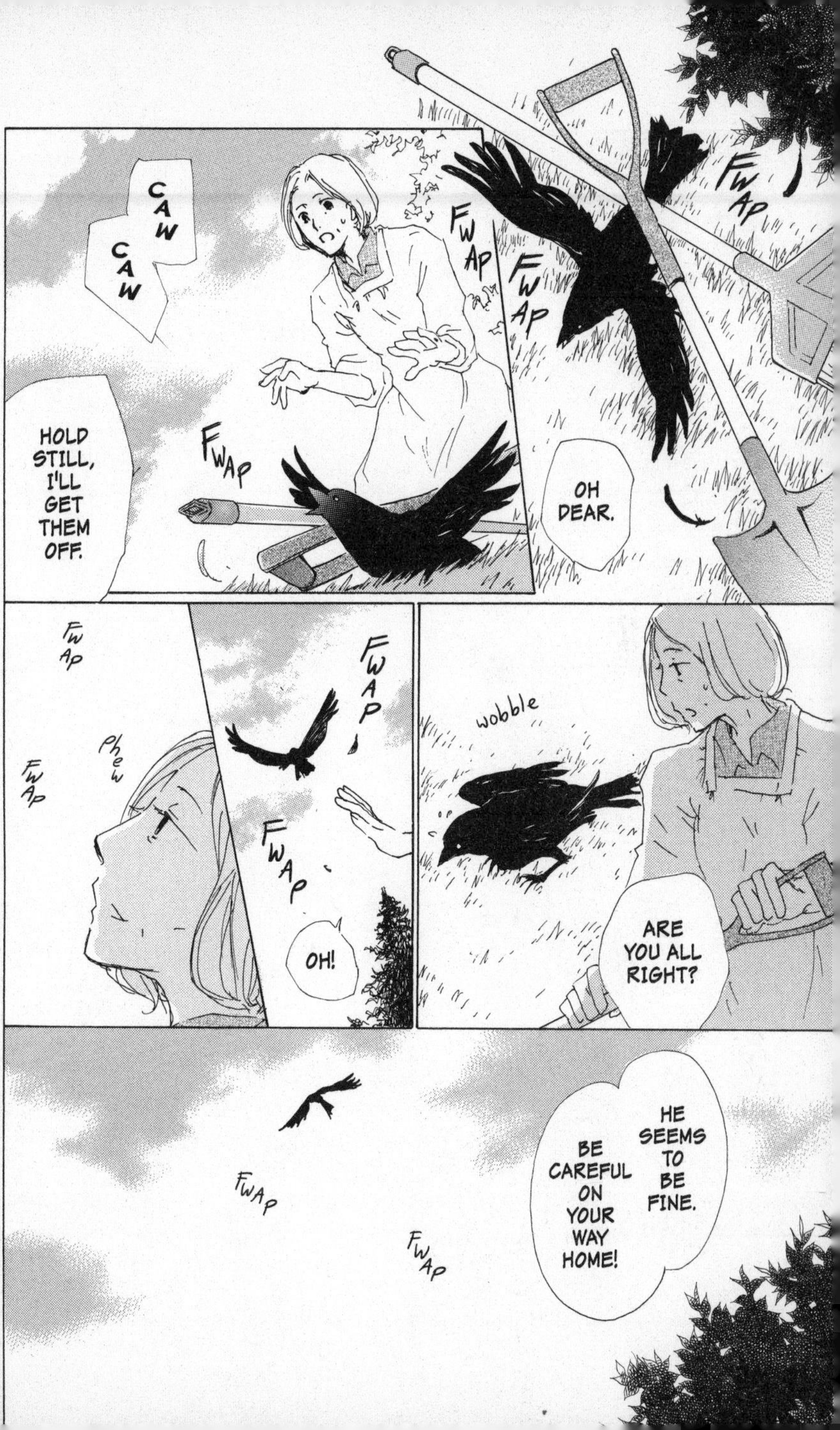
FWAP
FWAP
FWAP
OH DEAR.
FWAP
CAW CAW
HOLD STILL, I'LL GET THEM OFF.
wobble
ARE YOU ALL RIGHT?
FWAP
FWAP
OH!
FWAP
phew
FWAP
HE SEEMS TO BE FINE.
BE CAREFUL ON YOUR WAY HOME!
FWAP
FWAP

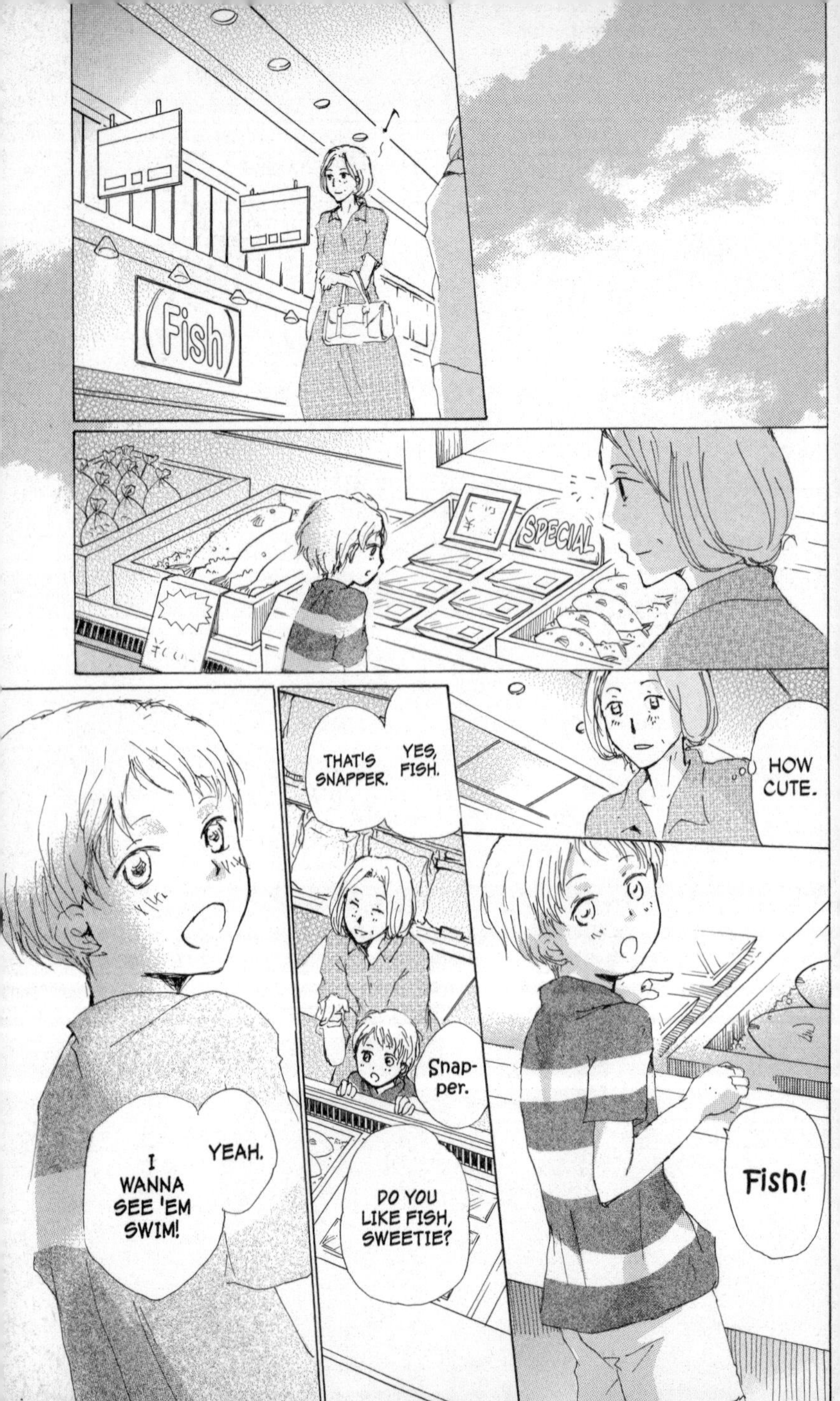
Fish
SPECIAL
HOW CUTE.
Fish!
YES, FISH.
THAT'S SNAPPER.
Snap-per.
DO YOU LIKE FISH, SWEETIE?
YEAH.
I WANNA SEE 'EM SWIM!

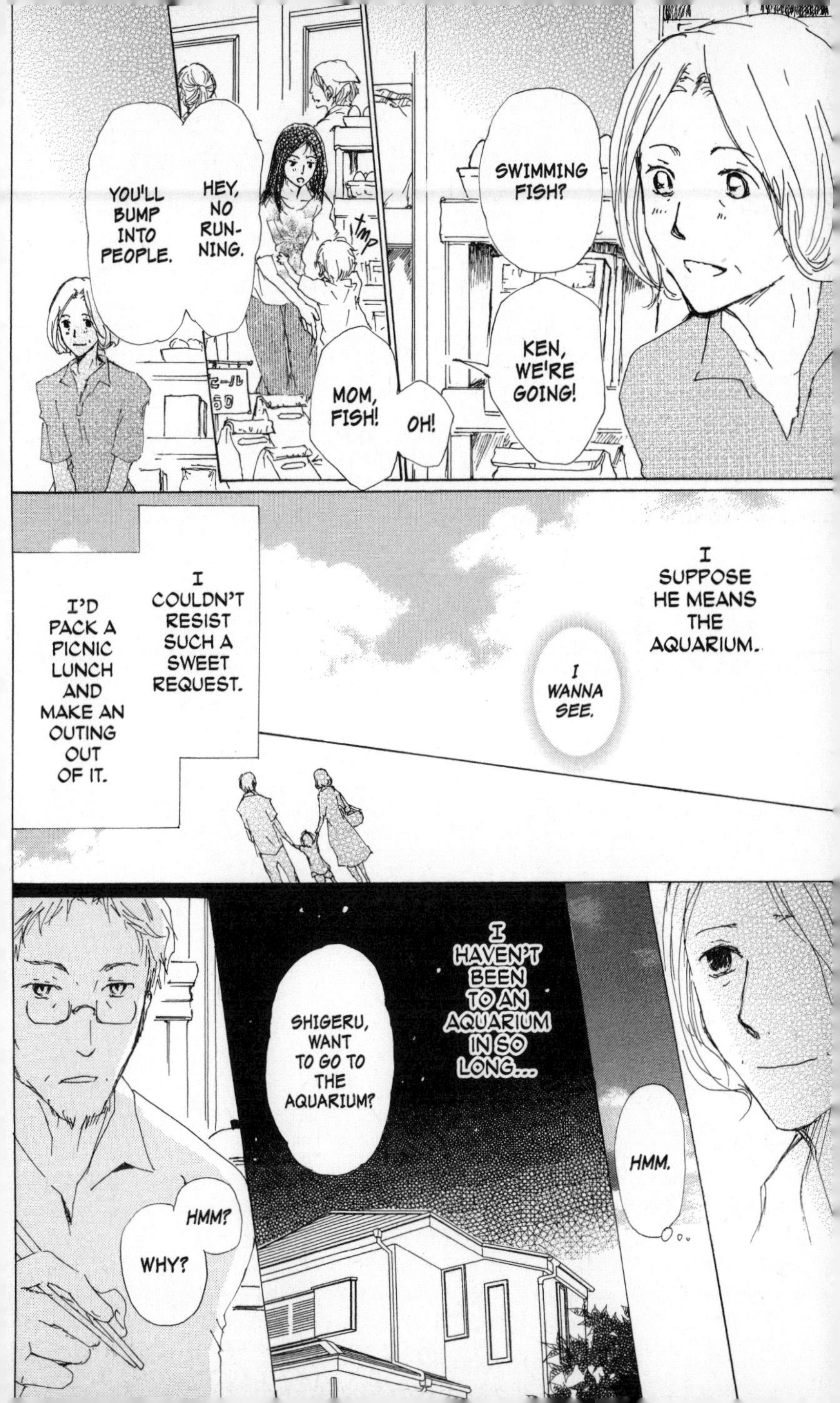
SWIMMING FISH?
KEN, WE'RE GOING!
OH!
MOM, FISH!
tmp
HEY, NO RUN-NING.
YOU'LL BUMP INTO PEOPLE.
I SUPPOSE HE MEANS THE AQUARIUM.
I WANNA SEE.
I COULDN'T RESIST SUCH A SWEET REQUEST.
I'D PACK A PICNIC LUNCH AND MAKE AN OUTING OUT OF IT.
HMM.
I HAVEN'T BEEN TO AN AQUARIUM IN SO LONG...
SHIGERU, WANT TO GO TO THE AQUARIUM?
HMM?
WHY?

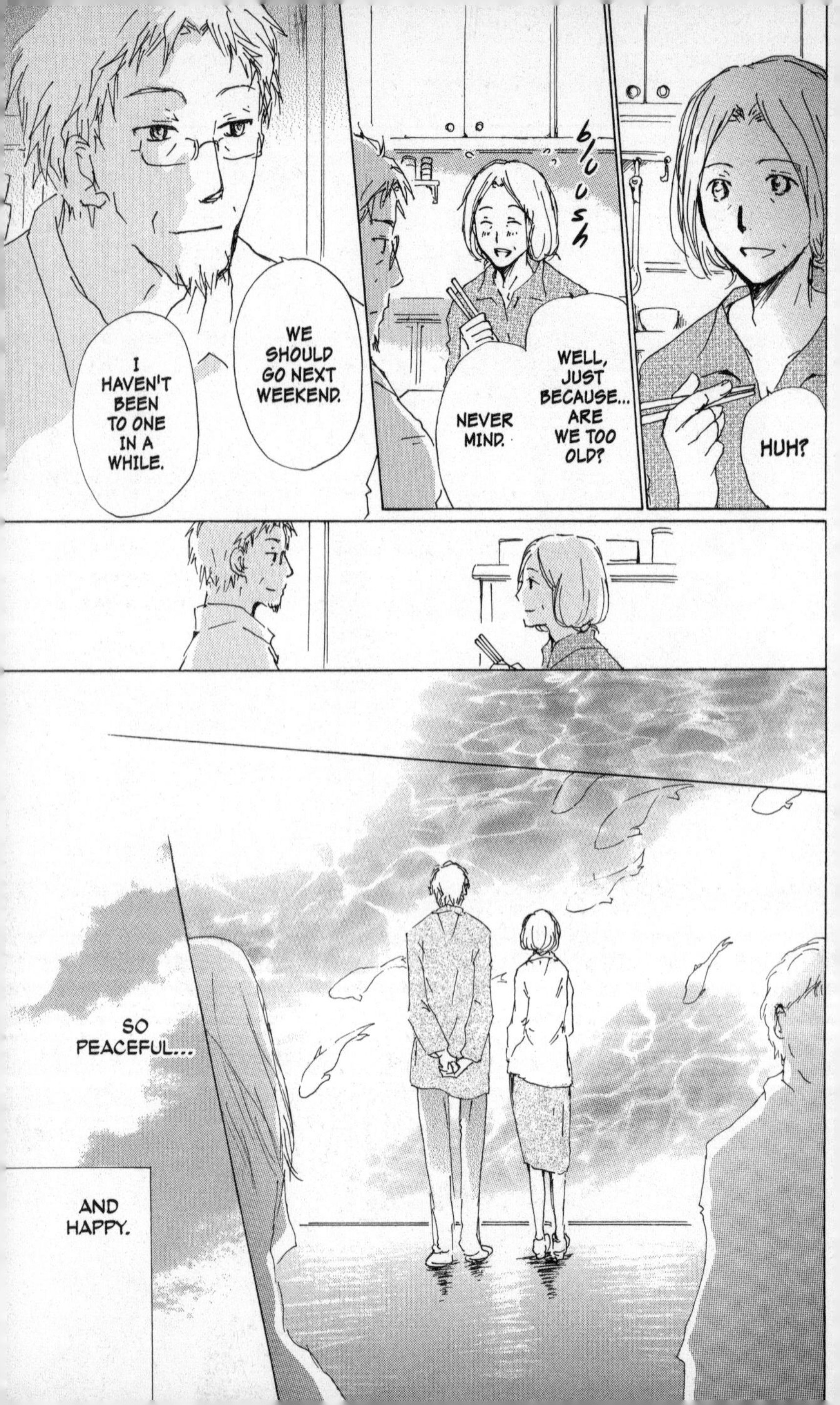
HUH?
blush
WELL, JUST BECAUSE... ARE WE TOO OLD?
NEVER MIND.
WE SHOULD GO NEXT WEEKEND.
I HAVEN'T BEEN TO ONE IN A WHILE.
SO PEACEFUL...
AND HAPPY.

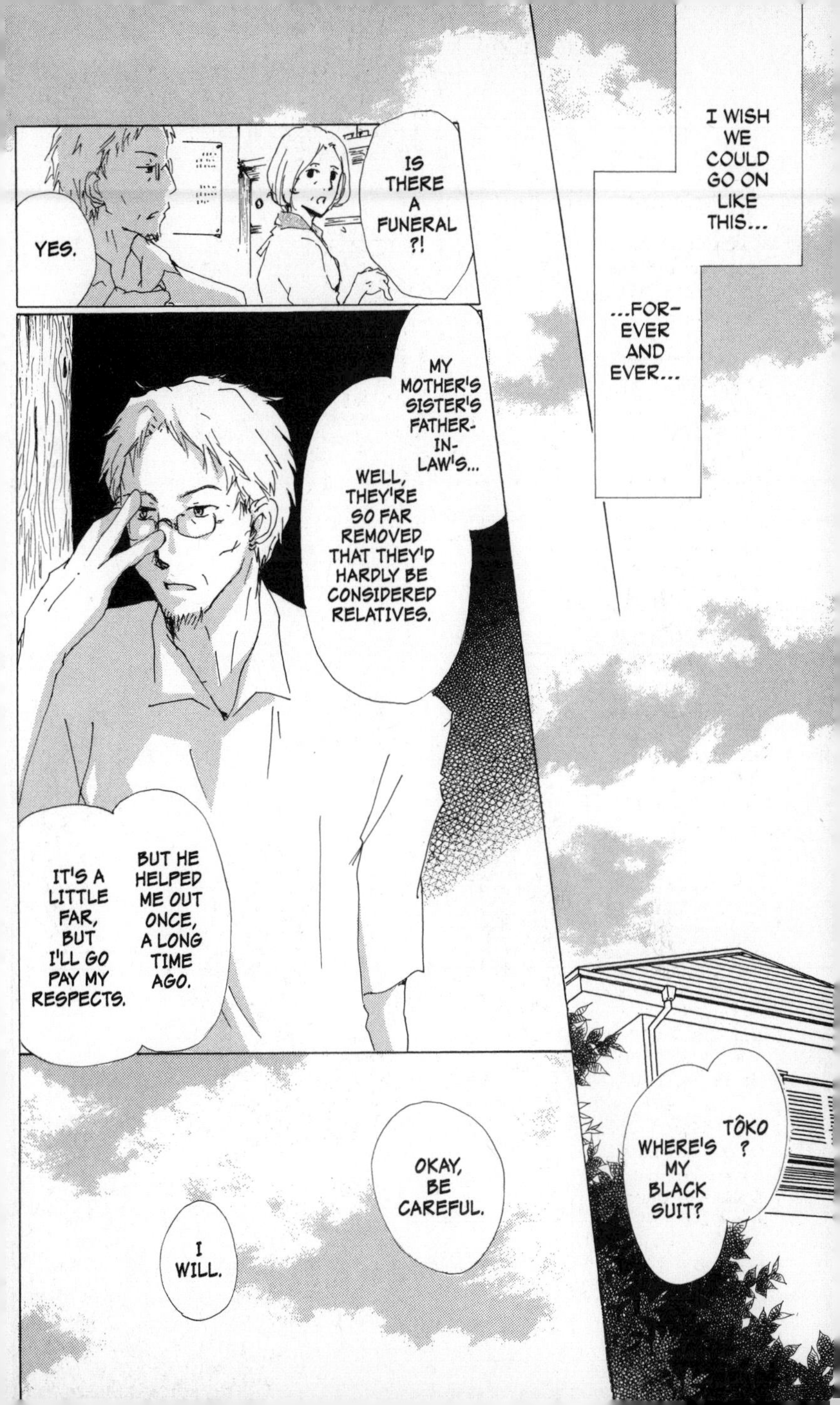
I WISH WE COULD GO ON LIKE THIS...
...FOR-EVER AND EVER...
TÔKO? WHERE'S MY BLACK SUIT?
IS THERE A FUNERAL?!
YES.
MY MOTHER'S SISTER'S FATHER-IN-LAW'S...
WELL, THEY'RE SO FAR REMOVED THAT THEY'D HARDLY BE CONSIDERED RELATIVES.
BUT HE HELPED ME OUT ONCE, A LONG TIME AGO.
IT'S A LITTLE FAR, BUT I'LL GO PAY MY RESPECTS.
OKAY, BE CAREFUL.
I WILL.

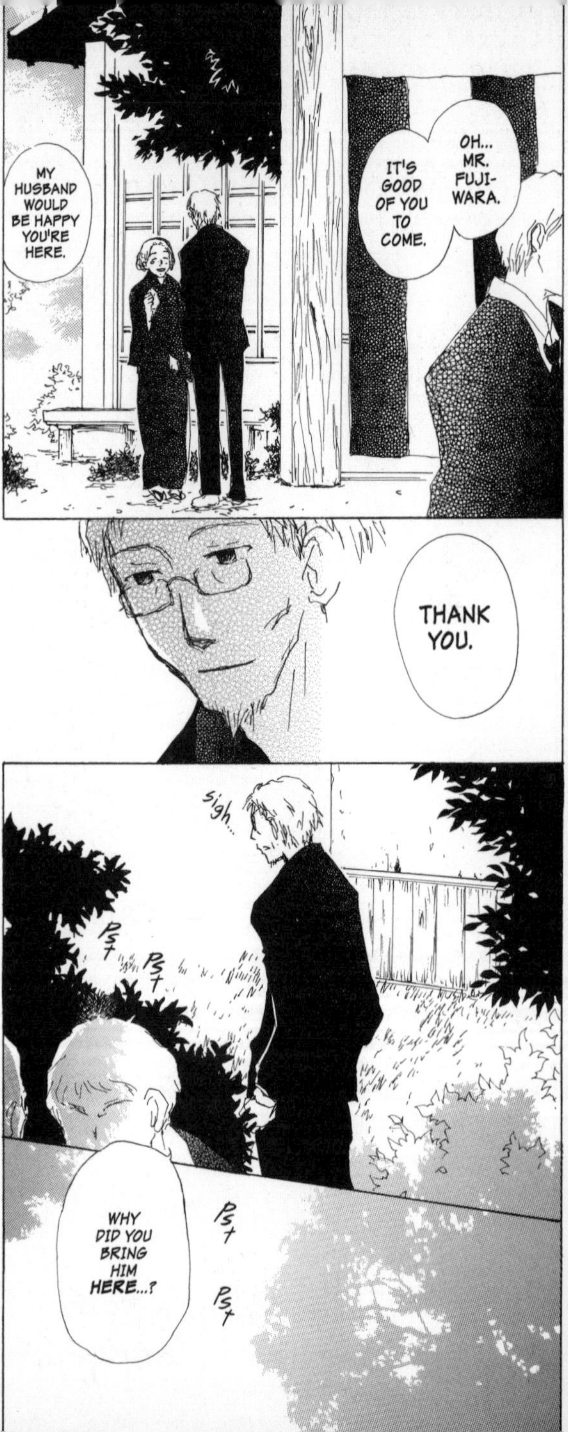
OH... MR. FUJI-WARA.
IT'S GOOD OF YOU TO COME.
MY HUSBAND WOULD BE HAPPY YOU'RE HERE.
THANK YOU.
sigh...
Pst
Pst
Pst
Pst
WHY DID YOU BRING HIM HERE...?

04

❋ Concert

I went to a piano solo concert the other day by Makoto Yoshimori, the composer for the anime *Natsume* and *Hotarubi*. We were all glued to our seats, touched by his performance and the way he opened up the piano in ways I'd never heard before. Director Ohmori, Mr. Yamada, the yokai designer, Mr. Sato from Brains Base Animation Co., and my editor were also there. I hadn't seen them in a while either, so it was a deeply moving day full of pleasant memories.

❋ Hometown

I recently went back to my old hometown. The mountains and rivers hadn't changed much and still displayed their vivid colors. There were changes in the towns and roads, with some places becoming quieter and others more bustling. It was very soothing to see all the old places in a new light.

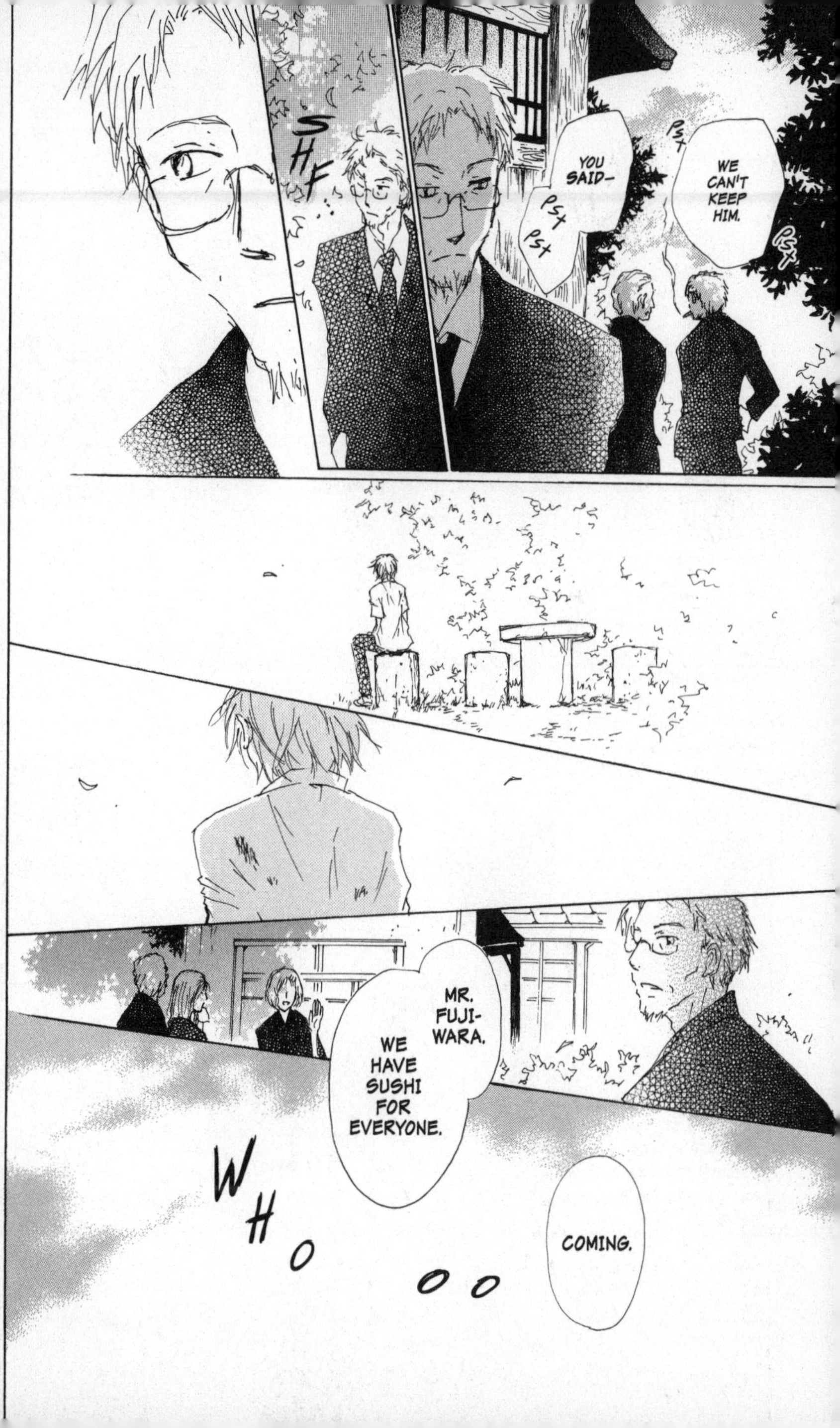
Pst
WE CAN'T KEEP HIM.
Pst
YOU SAID-
Pst Pst
SHF
MR. FUJIWARA. WE HAVE SUSHI FOR EVERYONE.
COMING.
WHOOOO

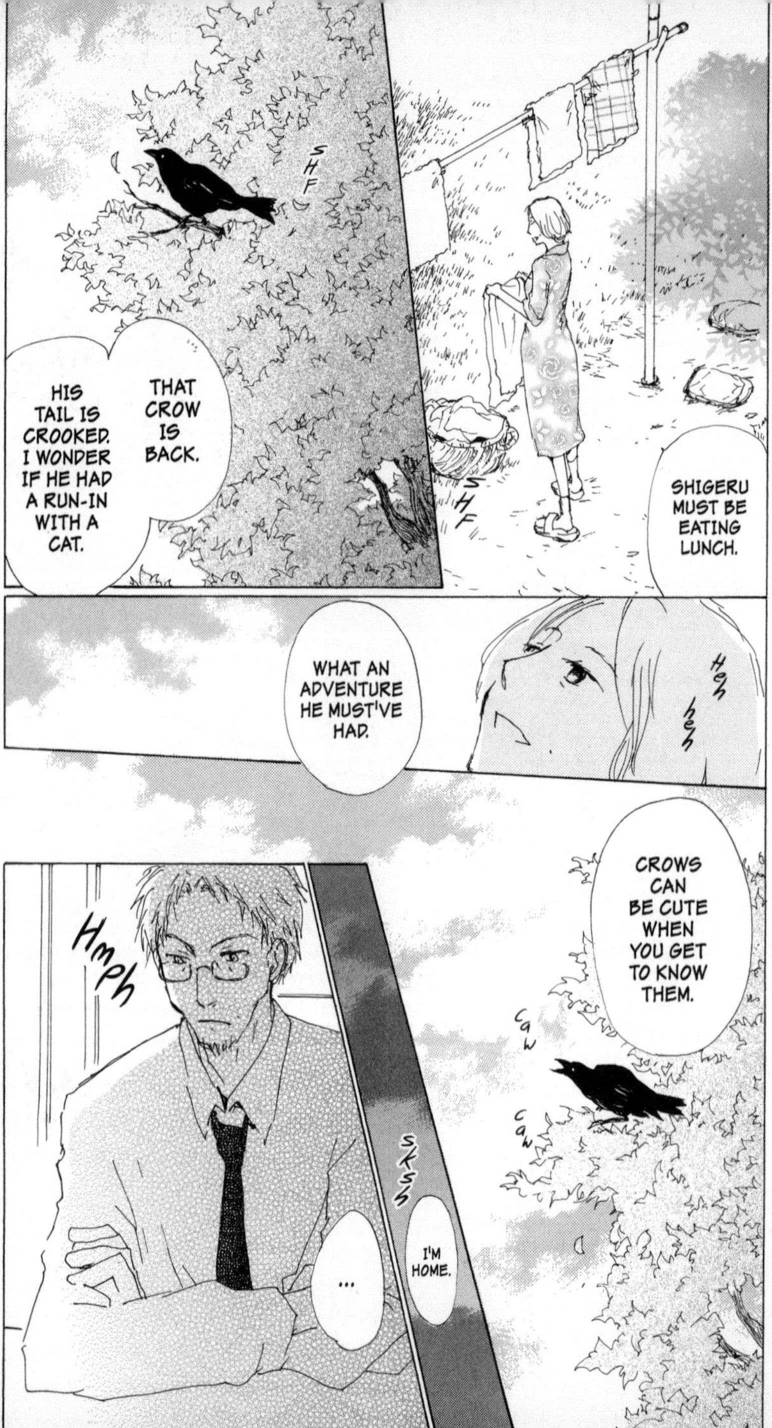
SHF
SHIGERU MUST BE EATING LUNCH.
SHF
THAT CROW IS BACK.
HIS TAIL IS CROOKED. I WONDER IF HE HAD A RUN-IN WITH A CAT.
Heh heh
WHAT AN ADVENTURE HE MUST'VE HAD.
CROWS CAN BE CUTE WHEN YOU GET TO KNOW THEM.
caw caw
SKSS
I'M HOME.
...
Hmph

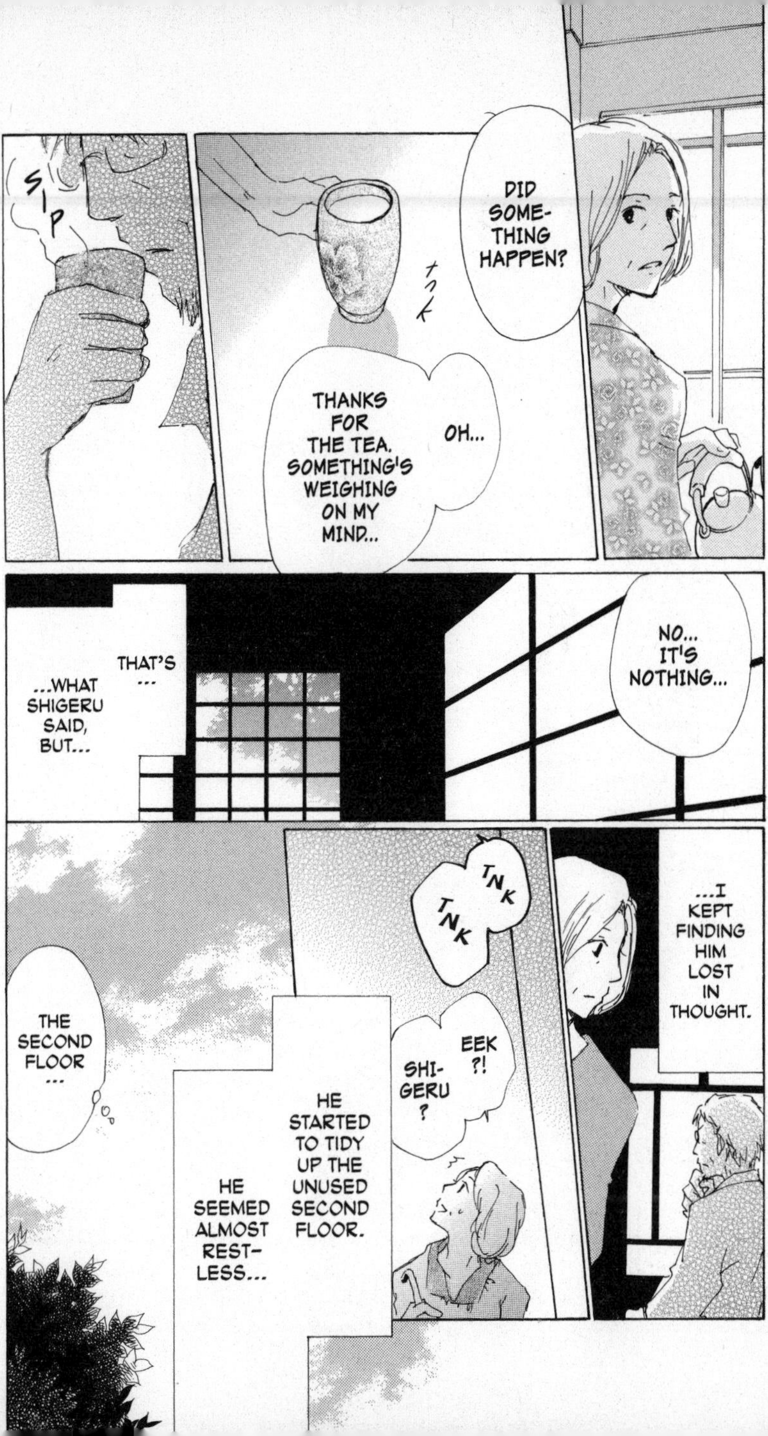
DID SOMETHING HAPPEN?
OH...
THANKS FOR THE TEA. SOMETHING'S WEIGHING ON MY MIND...
SIP
NO... IT'S NOTHING...
THAT'S ...
...WHAT SHIGERU SAID, BUT...
...I KEPT FINDING HIM LOST IN THOUGHT.
TNK TNK
EEK ?!
SHIGERU ?
HE STARTED TO TIDY UP THE UNUSED SECOND FLOOR.
HE SEEMED ALMOST RESTLESS...
THE SECOND FLOOR ...

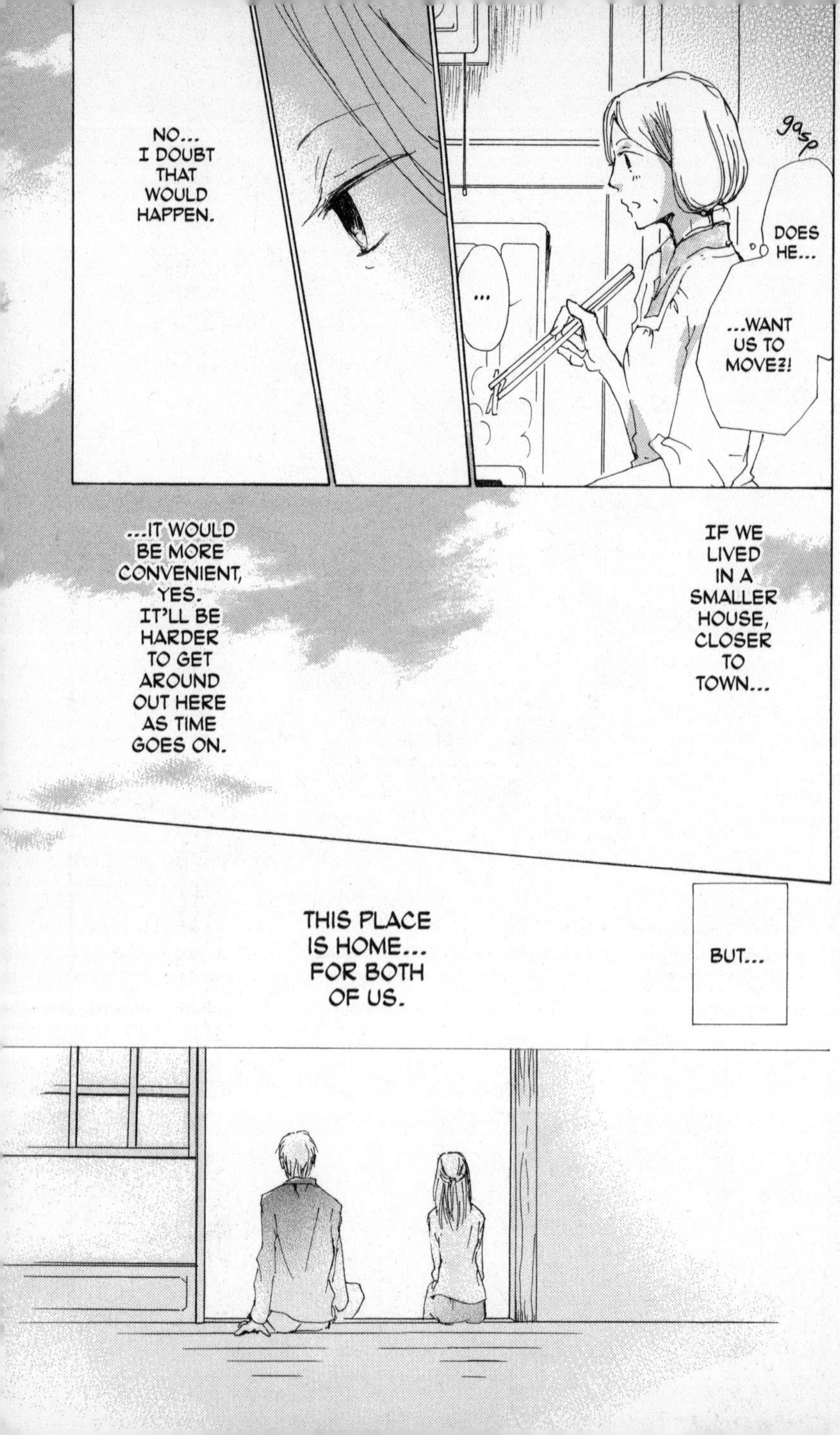
gasp
DOES HE...
...WANT US TO MOVE?!
...
NO... I DOUBT THAT WOULD HAPPEN.
IF WE LIVED IN A SMALLER HOUSE, CLOSER TO TOWN...
...IT WOULD BE MORE CONVENIENT, YES. IT'LL BE HARDER TO GET AROUND OUT HERE AS TIME GOES ON.
BUT...
THIS PLACE IS HOME... FOR BOTH OF US.

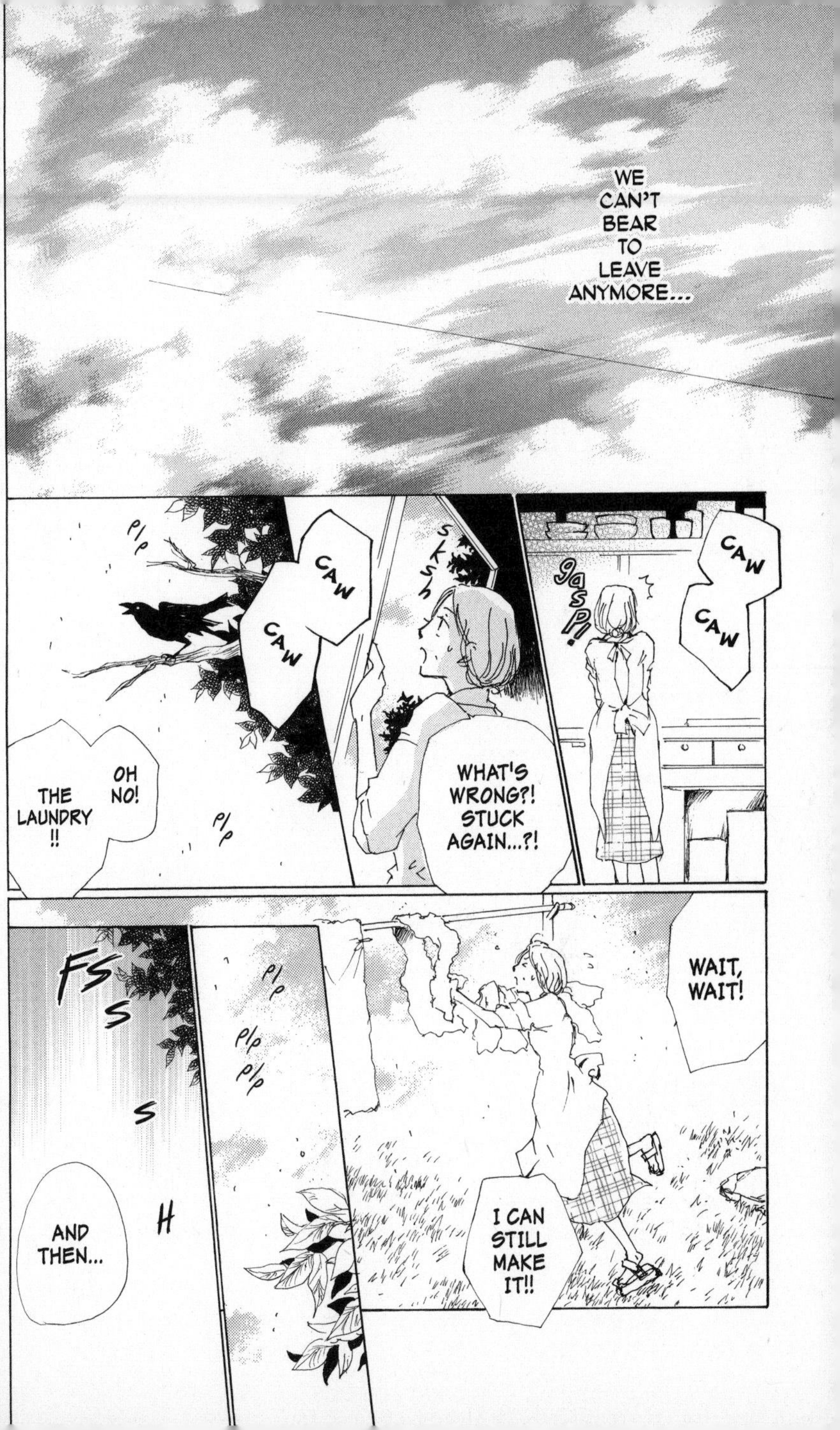

WE CAN'T BEAR TO LEAVE ANYMORE...
CAW
CAW
gasp!
sksh
WHAT'S WRONG?! STUCK AGAIN...?!
CAW
CAW
p/p
OH NO!
THE LAUNDRY!!
p/p
WAIT, WAIT!
I CAN STILL MAKE IT!!
p/p
p/p
p/p
FSSSH
AND THEN...

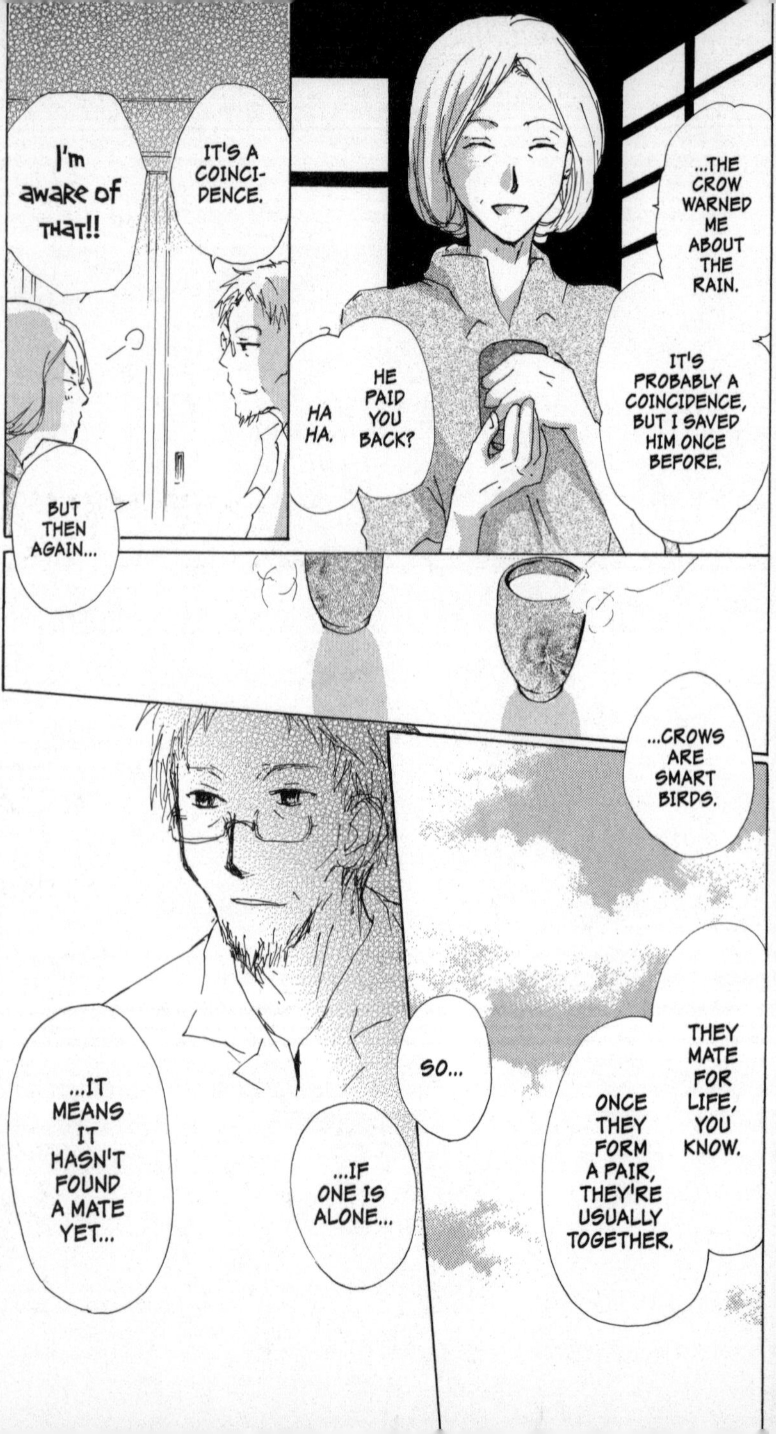
...THE CROW WARNED ME ABOUT THE RAIN.
IT'S PROBABLY A COINCIDENCE, BUT I SAVED HIM ONCE BEFORE.
HE PAID YOU BACK?
HA HA.
IT'S A COINCIDENCE.
I'm aware of THAT!!
BUT THEN AGAIN...
...CROWS ARE SMART BIRDS.
THEY MATE FOR LIFE, YOU KNOW.
ONCE THEY FORM A PAIR, THEY'RE USUALLY TOGETHER.
SO...
...IF ONE IS ALONE...
...IT MEANS IT HASN'T FOUND A MATE YET...

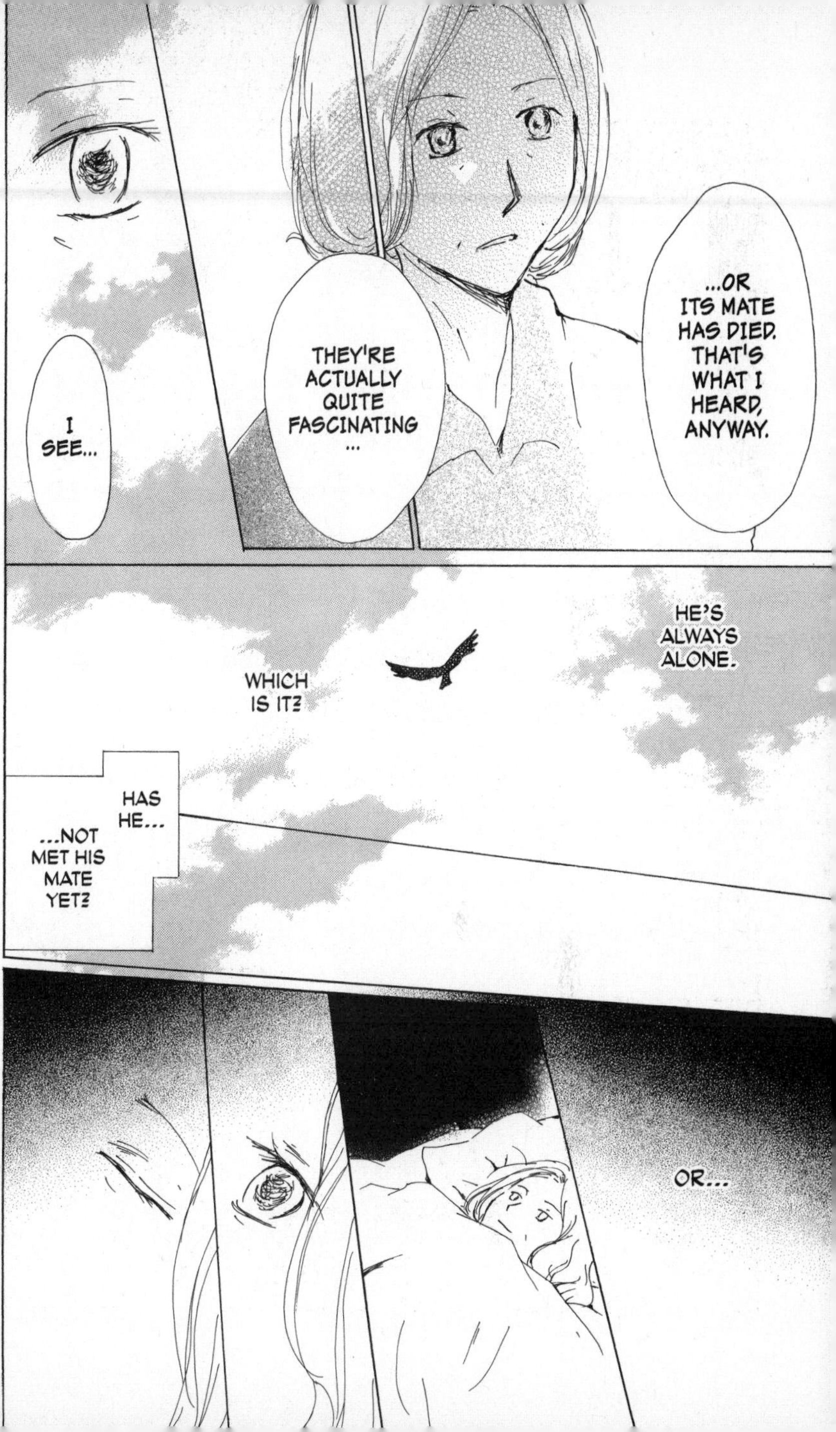
...OR ITS MATE HAS DIED. THAT'S WHAT I HEARD, ANYWAY.
THEY'RE ACTUALLY QUITE FASCINATING ...
I SEE...
HE'S ALWAYS ALONE.
WHICH IS IT?
HAS HE...
...NOT MET HIS MATE YET?
OR...

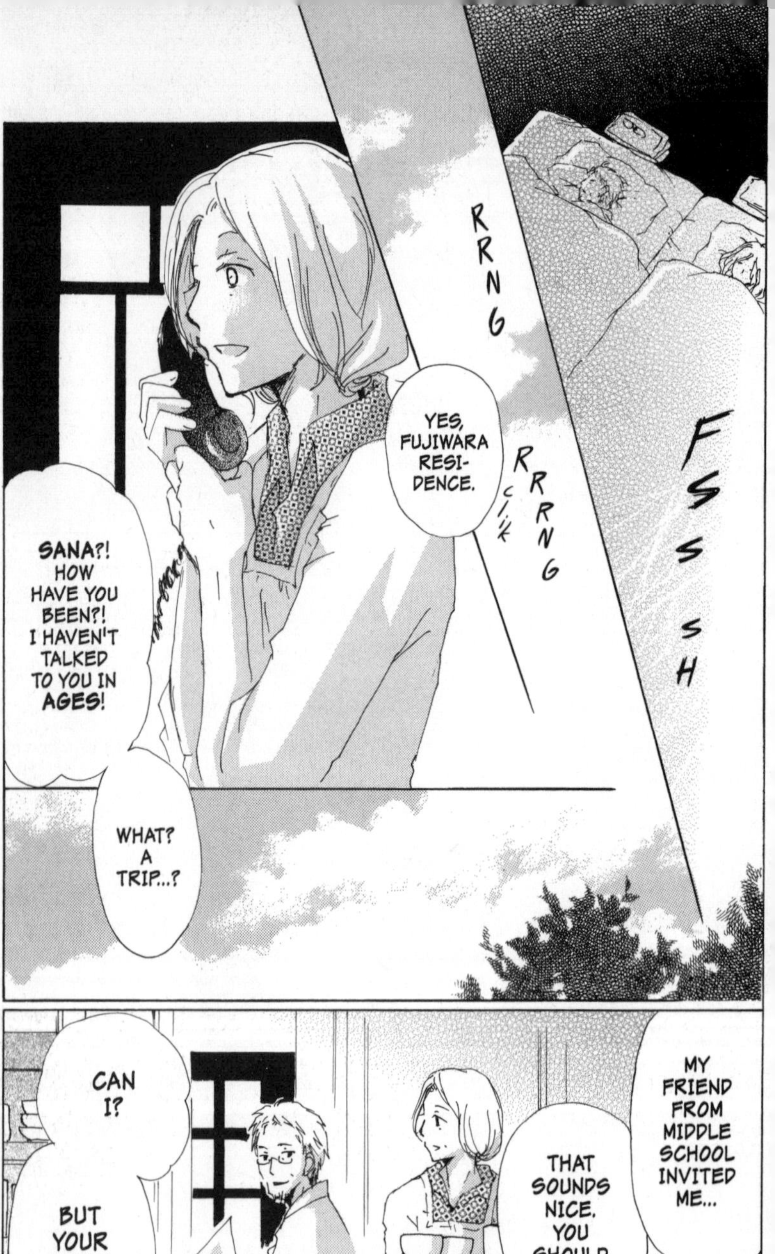
FSSSH
RRNG
YES, FUJIWARA RESI-DENCE.
RRRNG
CLIK
SANA?! HOW HAVE YOU BEEN?! I HAVEN'T TALKED TO YOU IN AGES!
WHAT? A TRIP...?
MY FRIEND FROM MIDDLE SCHOOL INVITED ME...
THAT SOUNDS NICE. YOU SHOULD GO.
CAN I?
BUT YOUR MEALS...

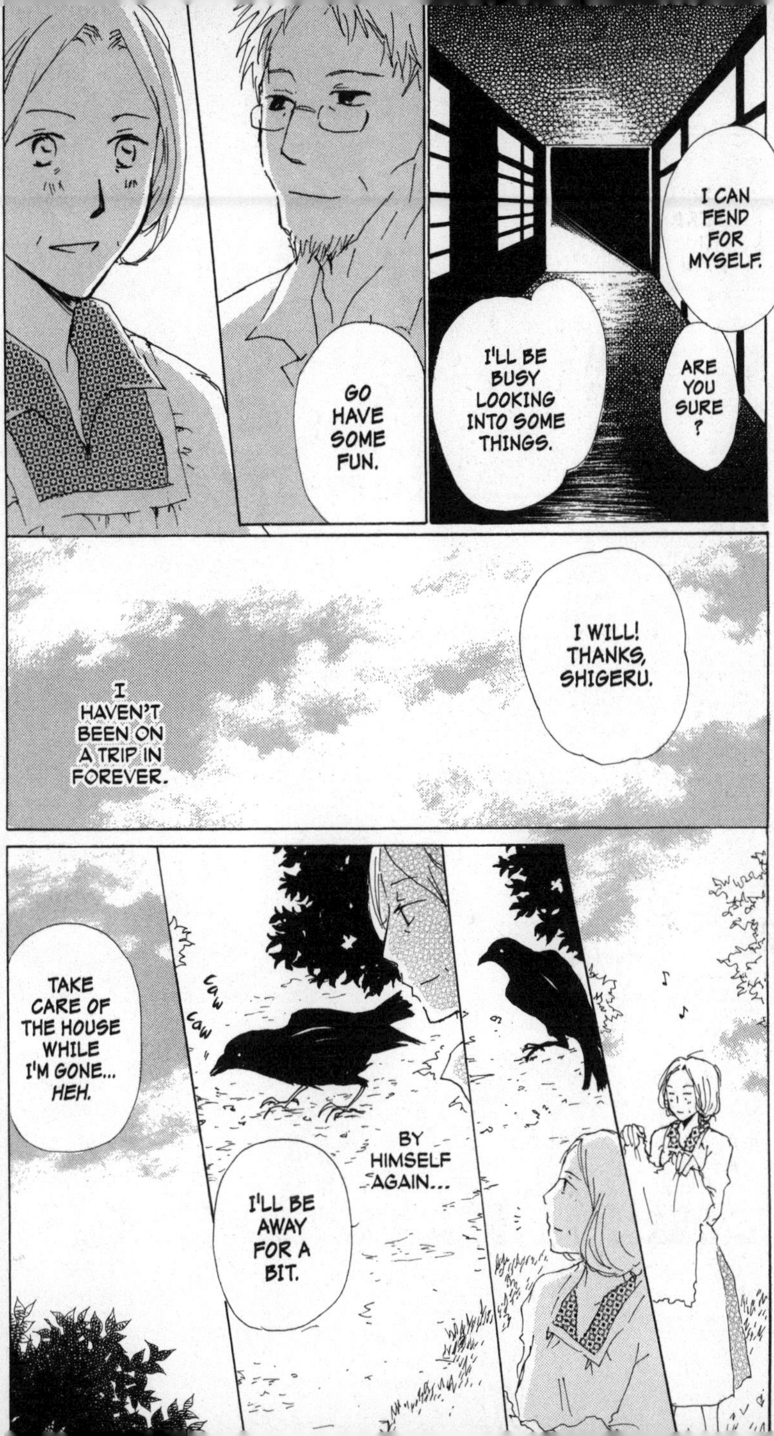
I CAN FEND FOR MYSELF.
ARE YOU SURE?
I'LL BE BUSY LOOKING INTO SOME THINGS.
GO HAVE SOME FUN.
I WILL! THANKS, SHIGERU.
I HAVEN'T BEEN ON A TRIP IN FOREVER.
BY HIMSELF AGAIN...
CAW
CAW
I'LL BE AWAY FOR A BIT.
TAKE CARE OF THE HOUSE WHILE I'M GONE... HEH.

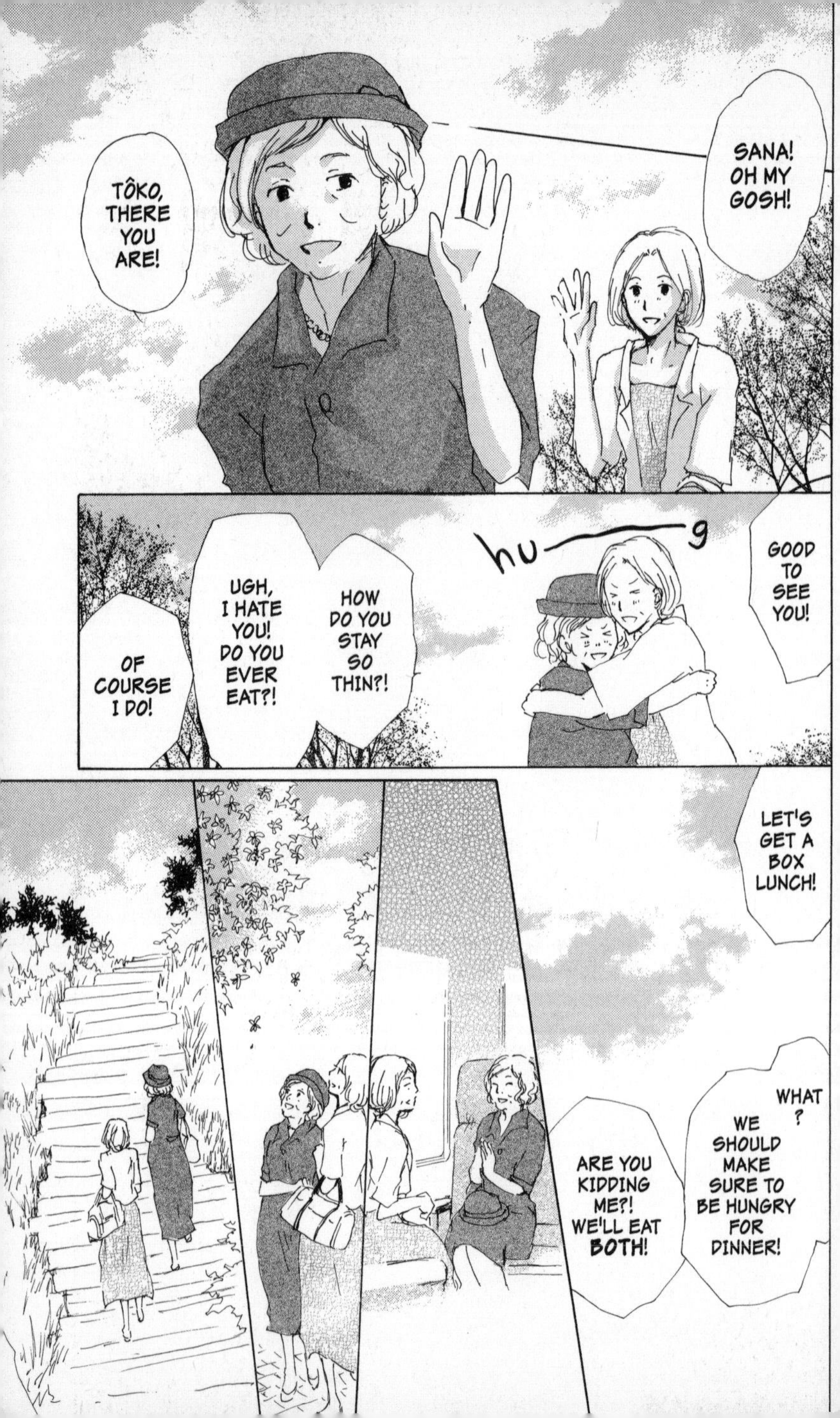
SANA! OH MY GOSH!
TÔKO, THERE YOU ARE!
GOOD TO SEE YOU!
hu——g
HOW DO YOU STAY SO THIN?!
UGH, I HATE YOU! DO YOU EVER EAT?!
OF COURSE I DO!
LET'S GET A BOX LUNCH!
WHAT?
WE SHOULD MAKE SURE TO BE HUNGRY FOR DINNER!
ARE YOU KIDDING ME?! WE'LL EAT **BOTH**!

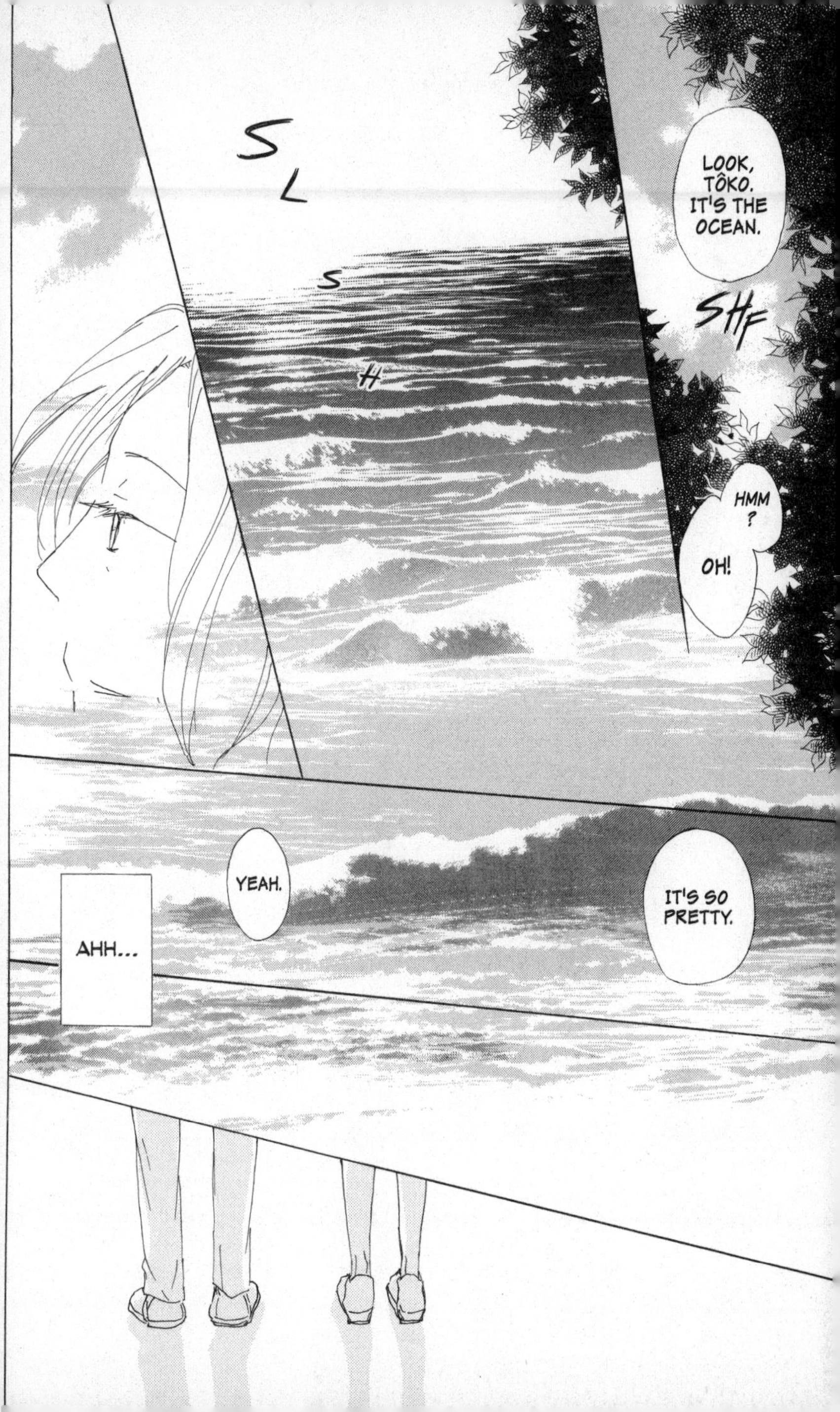
LOOK, TÔKO. IT'S THE OCEAN.
SHF
HMM?
OH!
SLSH
IT'S SO PRETTY.
YEAH.
AHH...

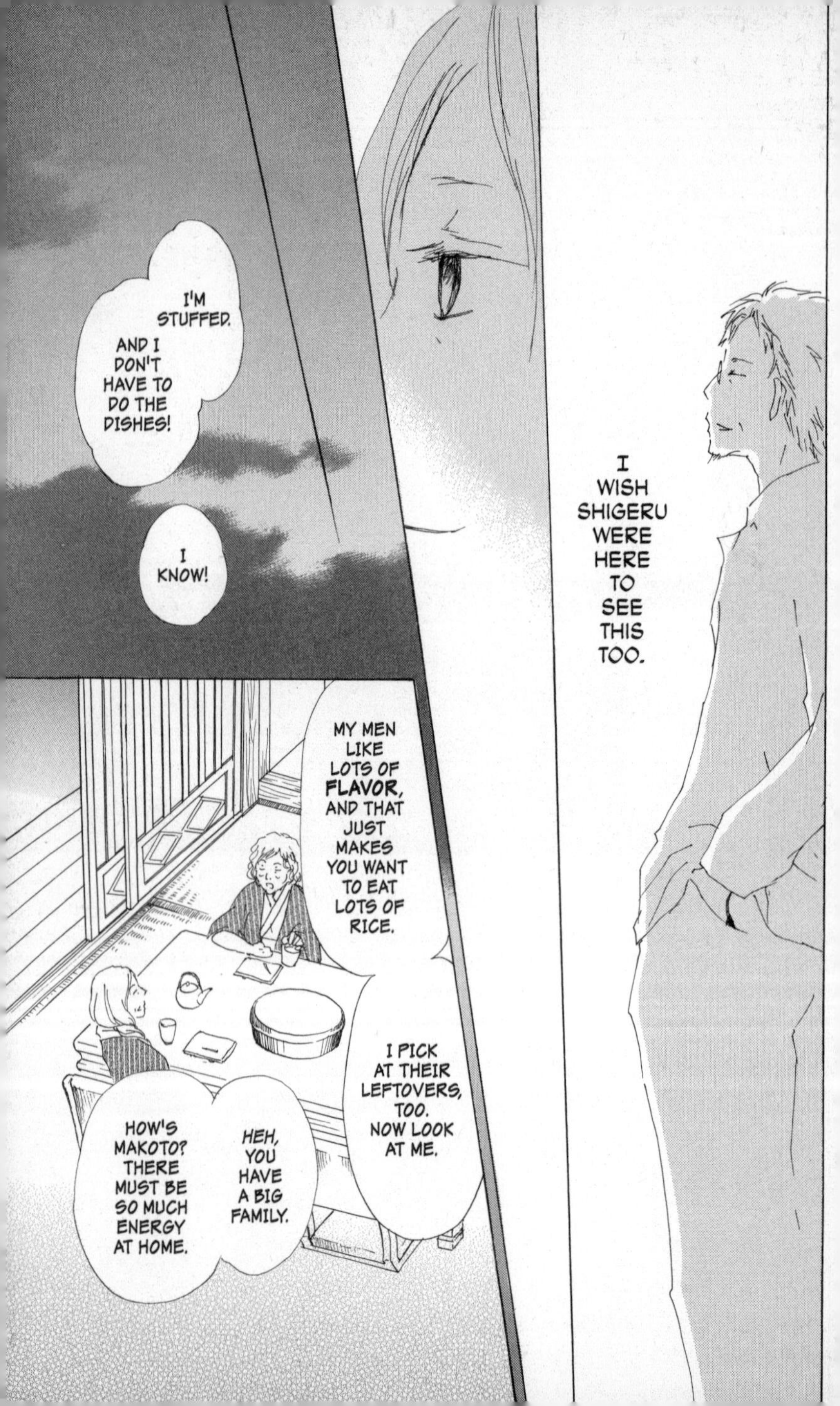
I WISH SHIGERU WERE HERE TO SEE THIS TOO.
I'M STUFFED. AND I DON'T HAVE TO DO THE DISHES!
I KNOW!
MY MEN LIKE LOTS OF **FLAVOR**, AND THAT JUST MAKES YOU WANT TO EAT LOTS OF RICE.
I PICK AT THEIR LEFTOVERS, TOO. NOW LOOK AT ME.
HEH, YOU HAVE A BIG FAMILY.
HOW'S MAKOTO? THERE MUST BE SO MUCH ENERGY AT HOME.

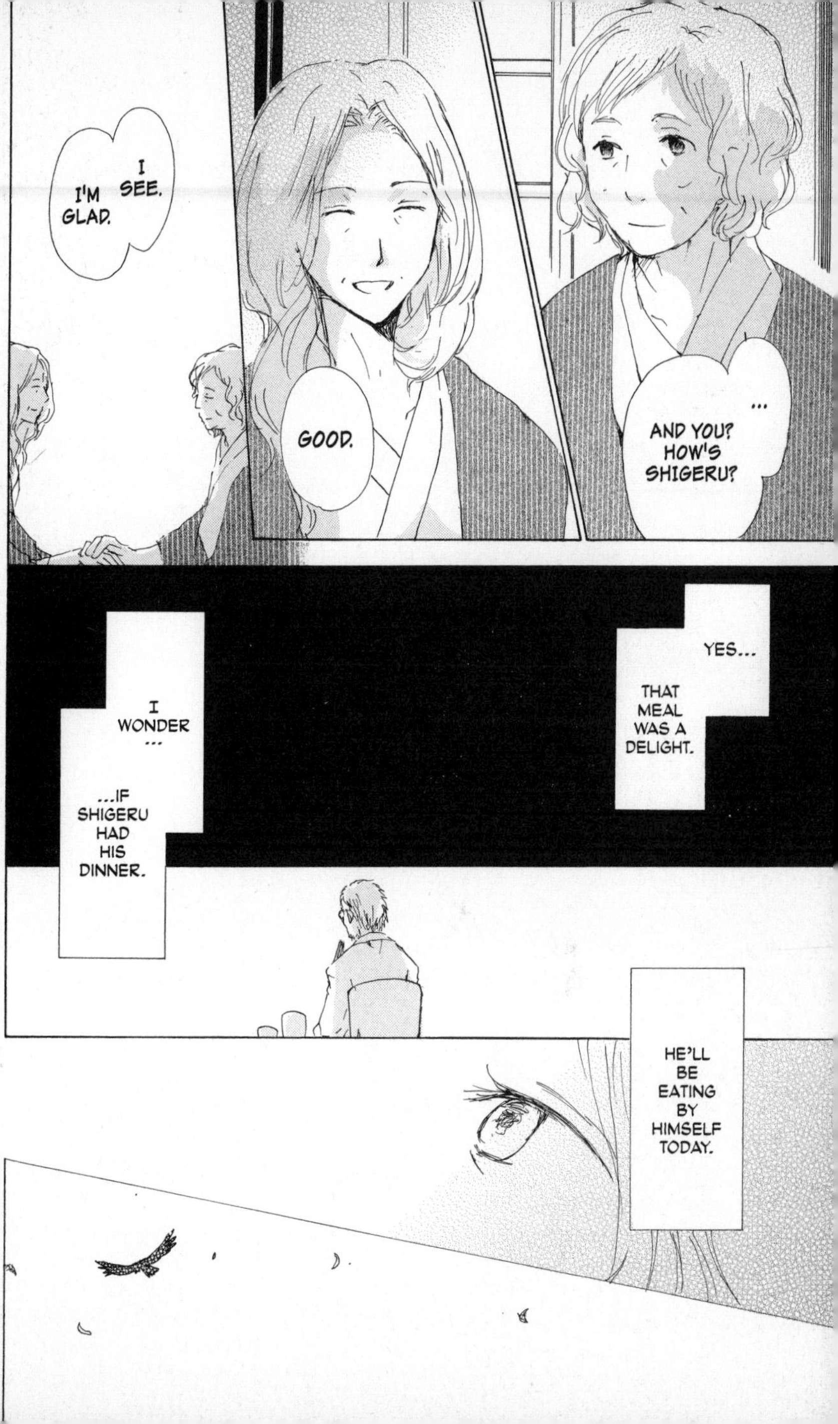
... AND YOU? HOW'S SHIGERU?
GOOD.
I SEE. I'M GLAD.
YES... THAT MEAL WAS A DELIGHT.
I WONDER... ...IF SHIGERU HAD HIS DINNER.
HE'LL BE EATING BY HIMSELF TODAY.

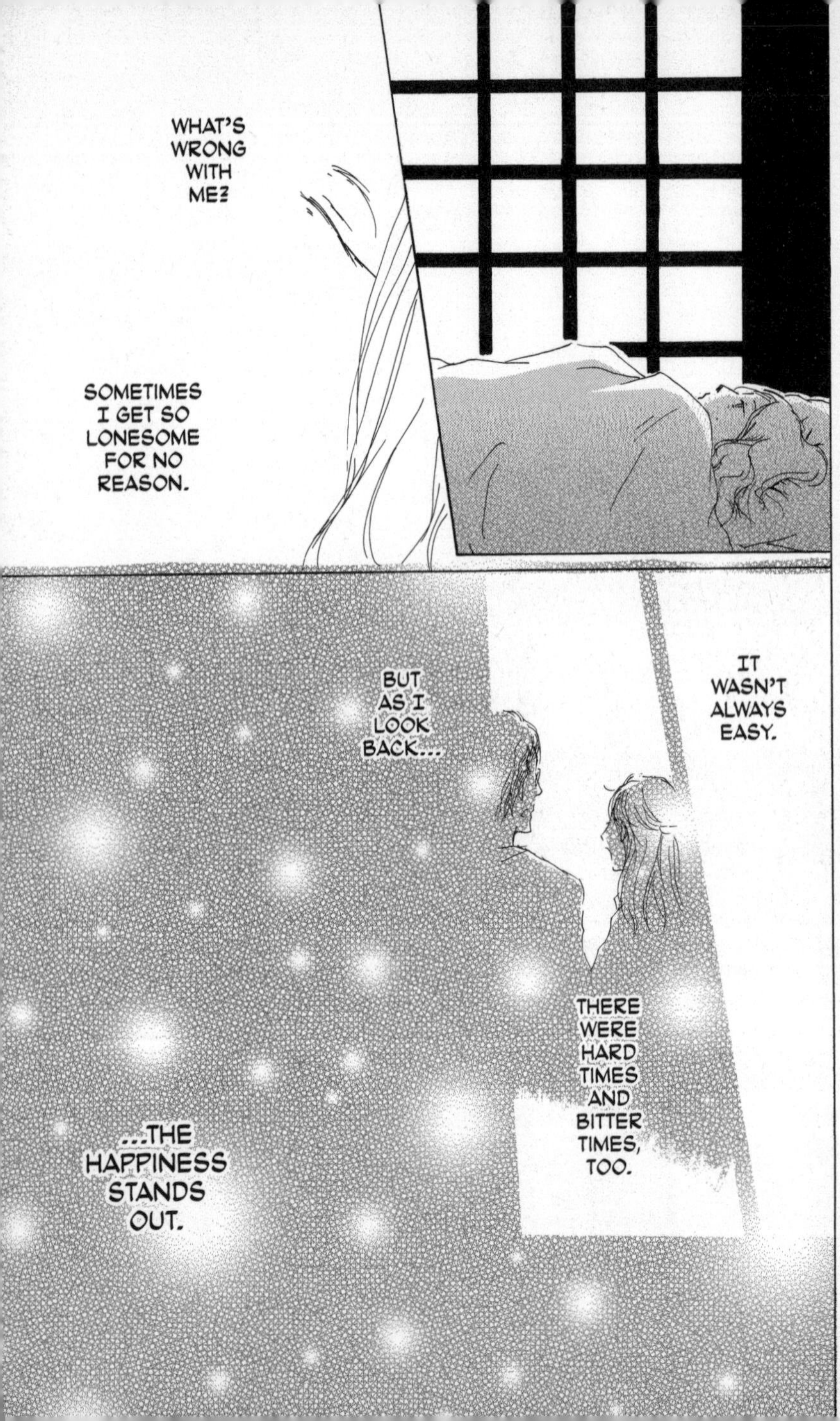
WHAT'S WRONG WITH ME?
SOMETIMES I GET SO LONESOME FOR NO REASON.
IT WASN'T ALWAYS EASY.
BUT AS I LOOK BACK...
THERE WERE HARD TIMES AND BITTER TIMES, TOO.
...THE HAPPINESS STANDS OUT.

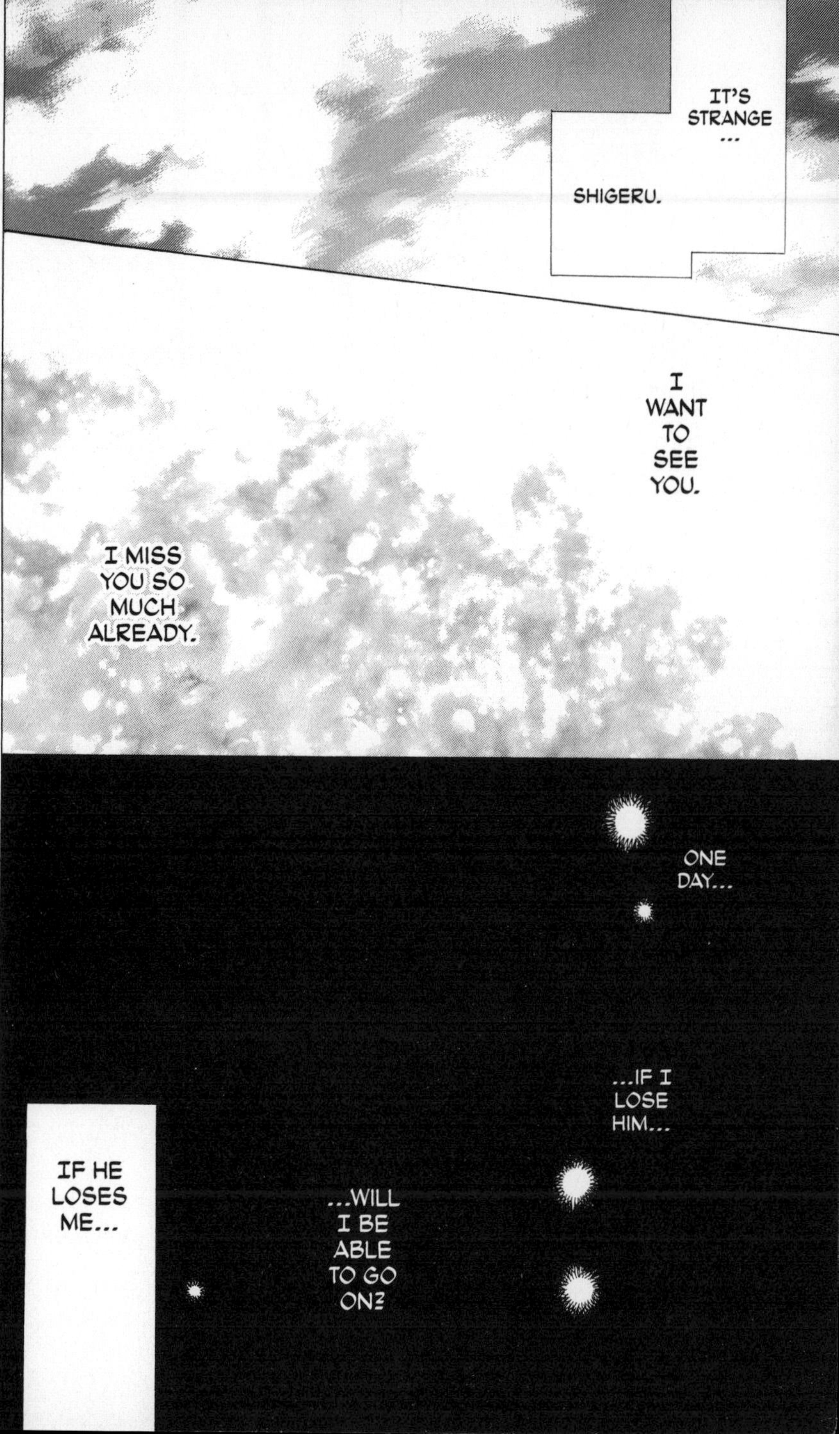
IT'S STRANGE...
SHIGERU.
I WANT TO SEE YOU.
I MISS YOU SO MUCH ALREADY.
ONE DAY...
...IF I LOSE HIM...
...WILL I BE ABLE TO GO ON?
IF HE LOSES ME...

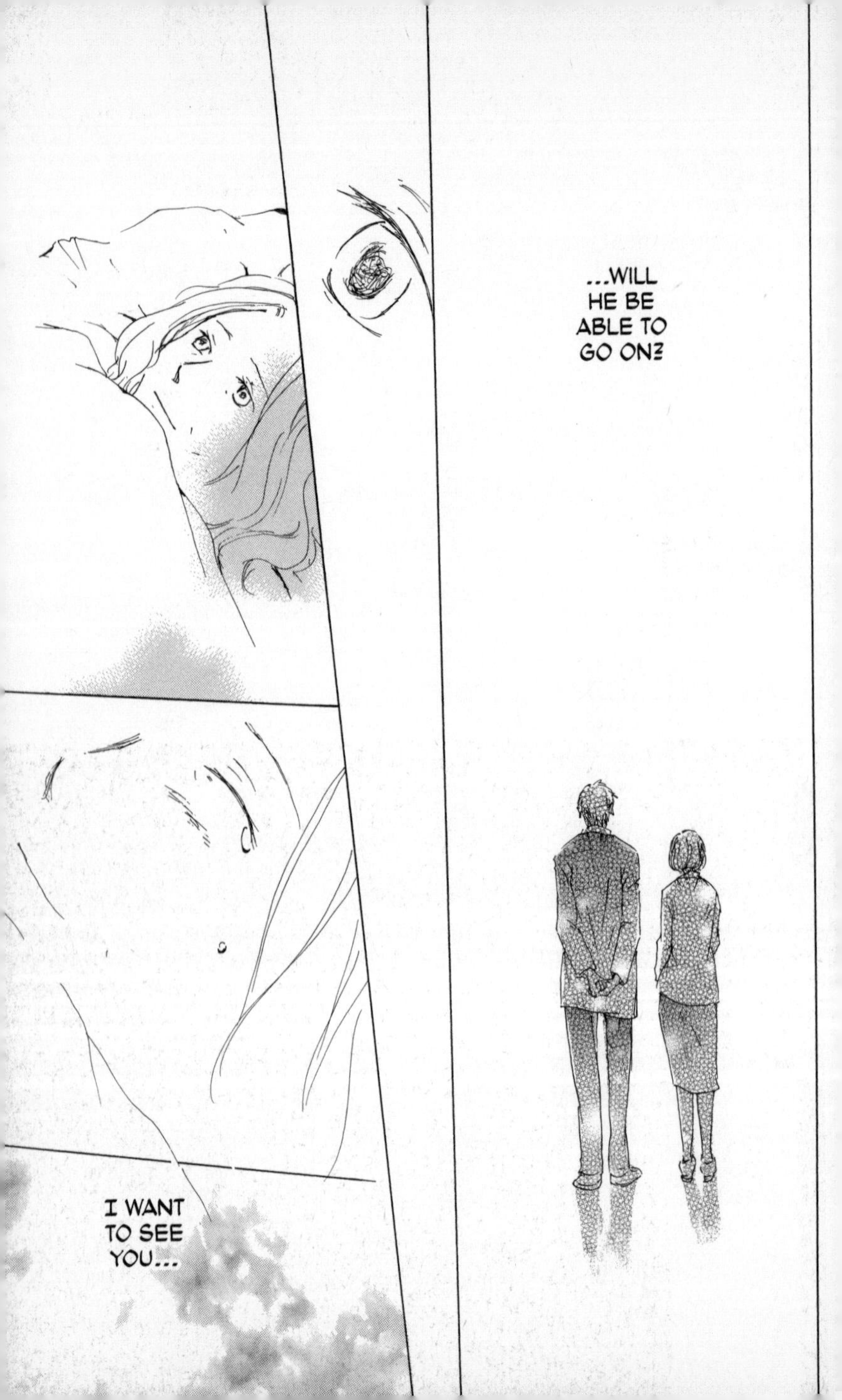
...WILL HE BE ABLE TO GO ON?
I WANT TO SEE YOU...

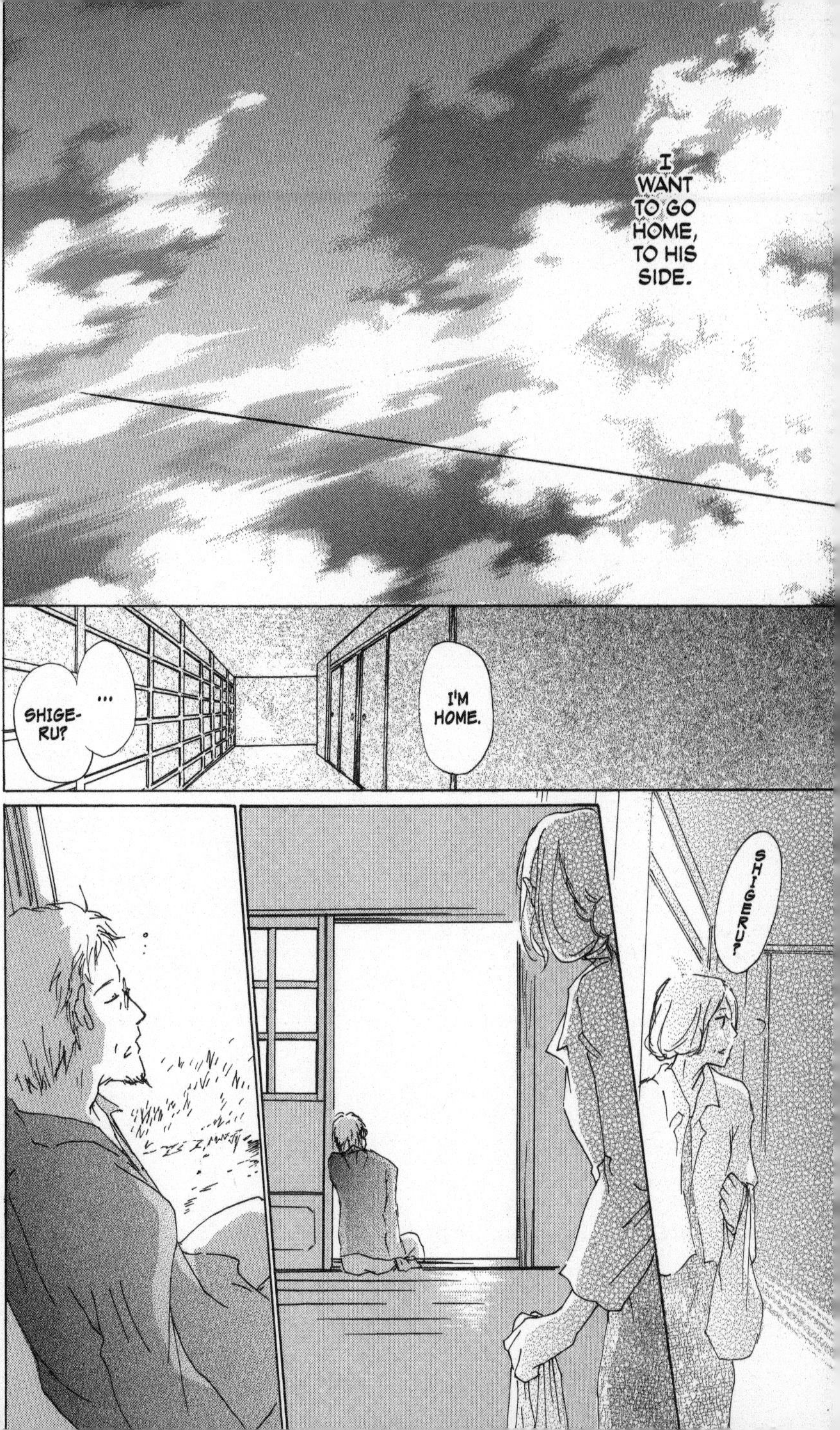
I WANT TO GO HOME, TO HIS SIDE.
I'M HOME.
...
SHIGE-RU?
SHIGERU?

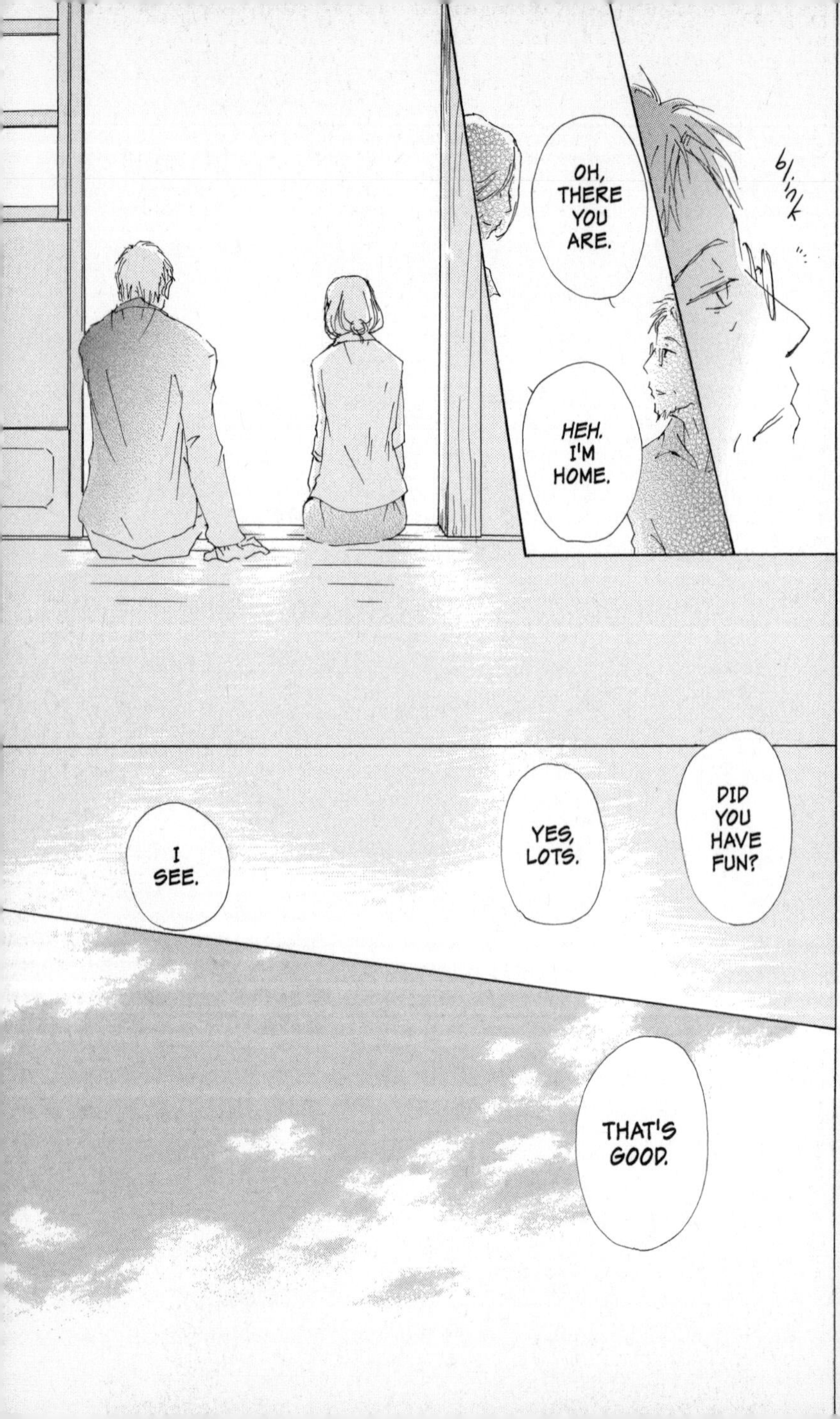
blink
OH, THERE YOU ARE.
HEH. I'M HOME.
DID YOU HAVE FUN?
YES, LOTS.
I SEE.
THAT'S GOOD.

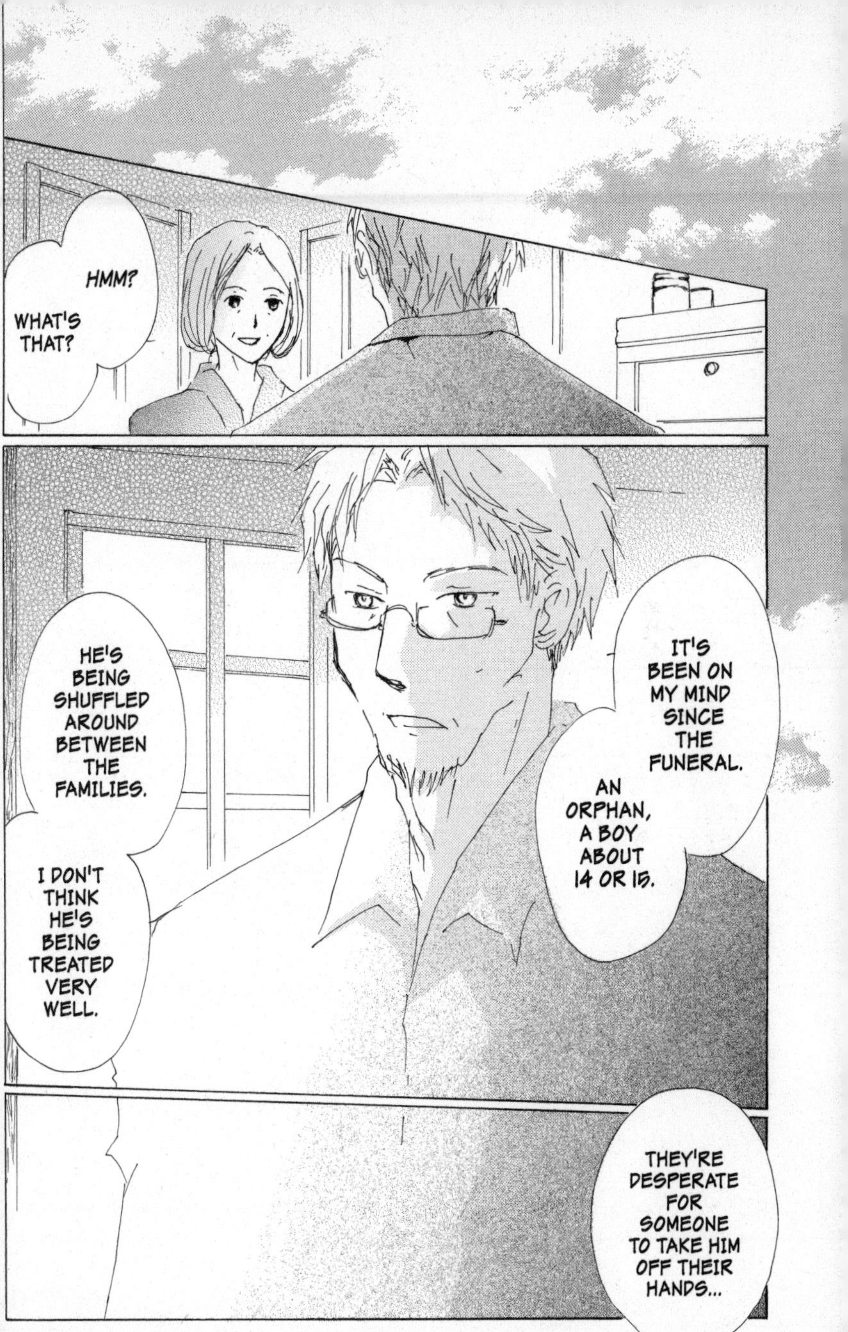
HMM? WHAT'S THAT?
IT'S BEEN ON MY MIND SINCE THE FUNERAL.
AN ORPHAN, A BOY ABOUT 14 OR 15.
HE'S BEING SHUFFLED AROUND BETWEEN THE FAMILIES.
I DON'T THINK HE'S BEING TREATED VERY WELL.
THEY'RE DESPERATE FOR SOMEONE TO TAKE HIM OFF THEIR HANDS...

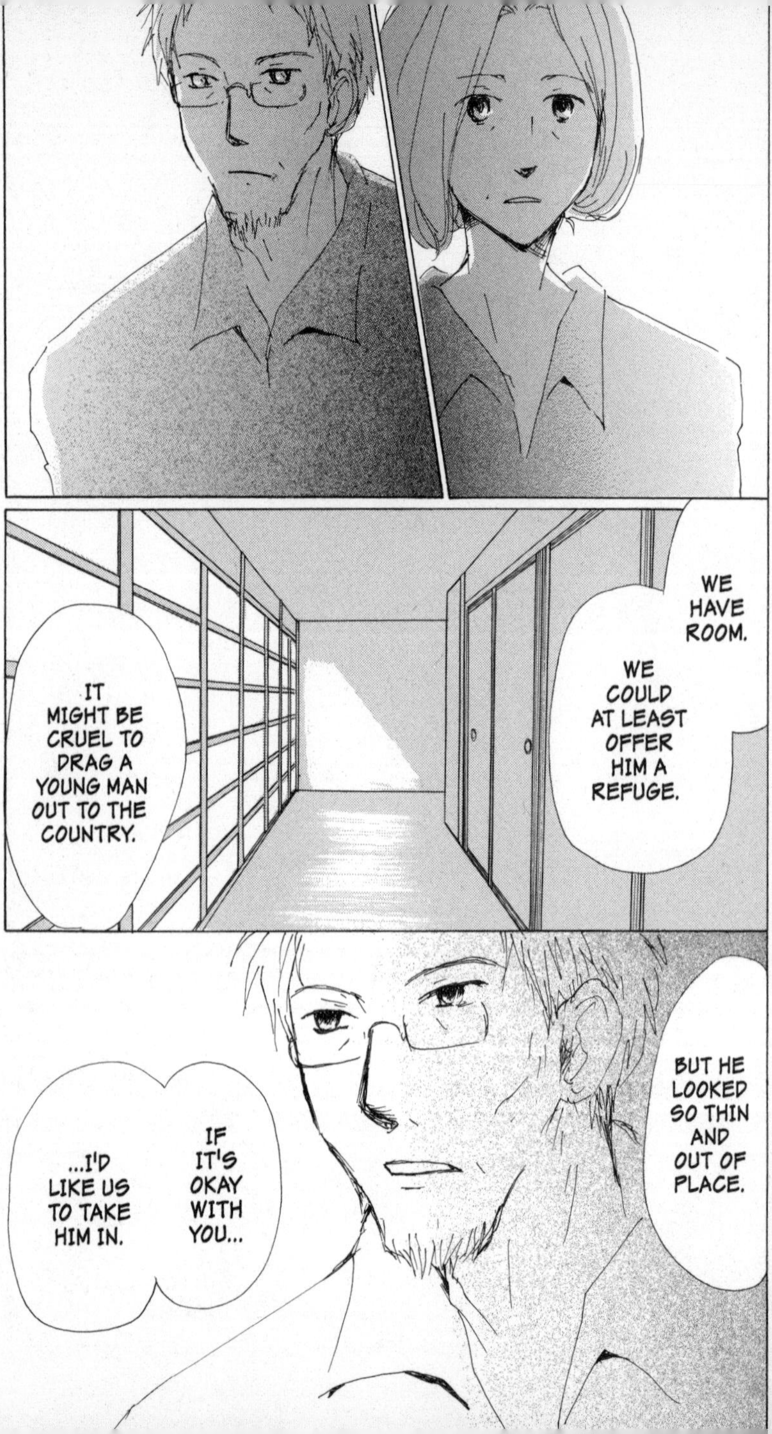
WE HAVE ROOM.
WE COULD AT LEAST OFFER HIM A REFUGE.
IT MIGHT BE CRUEL TO DRAG A YOUNG MAN OUT TO THE COUNTRY.
BUT HE LOOKED SO THIN AND OUT OF PLACE.
IF IT'S OKAY WITH YOU...
...I'D LIKE US TO TAKE HIM IN.

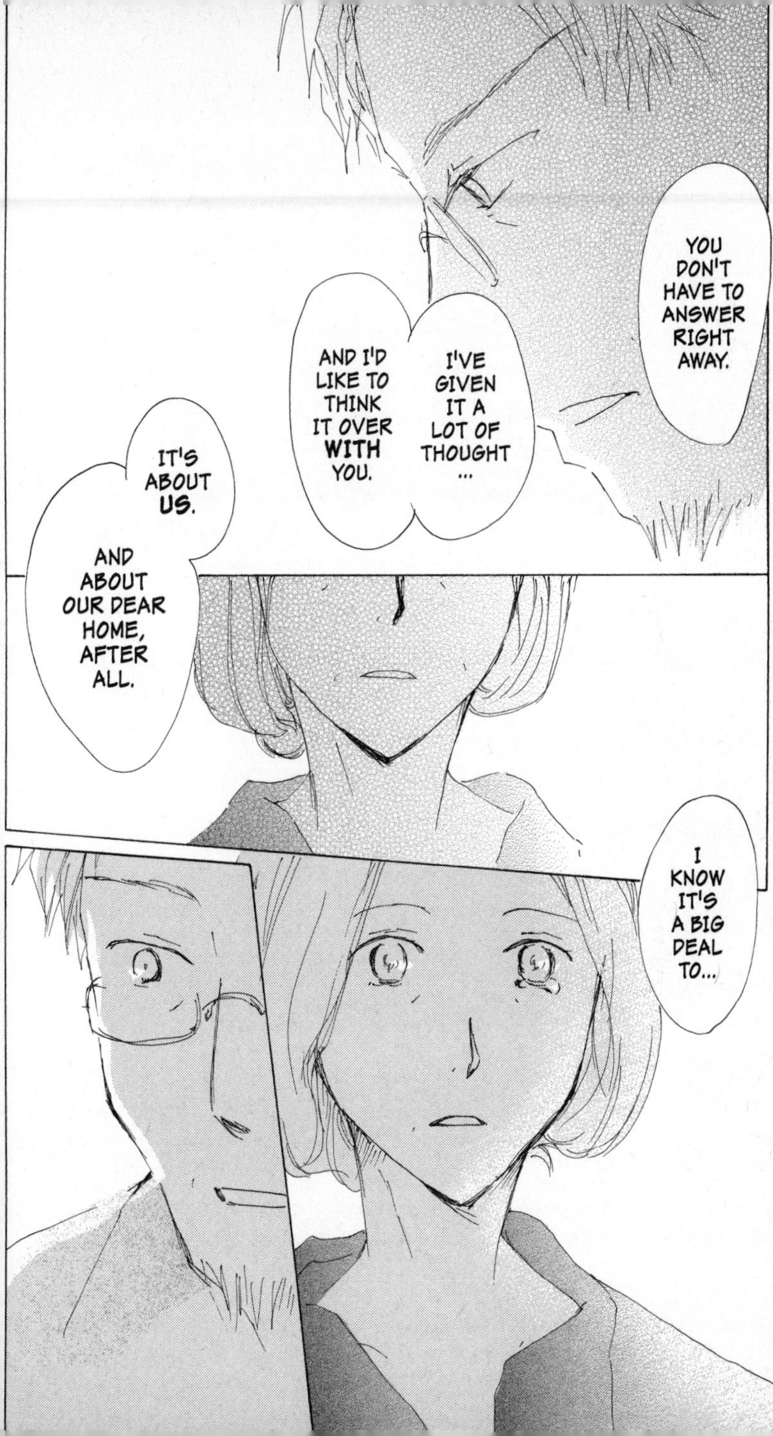
YOU DON'T HAVE TO ANSWER RIGHT AWAY.
I'VE GIVEN IT A LOT OF THOUGHT...
AND I'D LIKE TO THINK IT OVER **WITH** YOU.
IT'S ABOUT **US**.
AND ABOUT OUR DEAR HOME, AFTER ALL.
I KNOW IT'S A BIG DEAL TO...

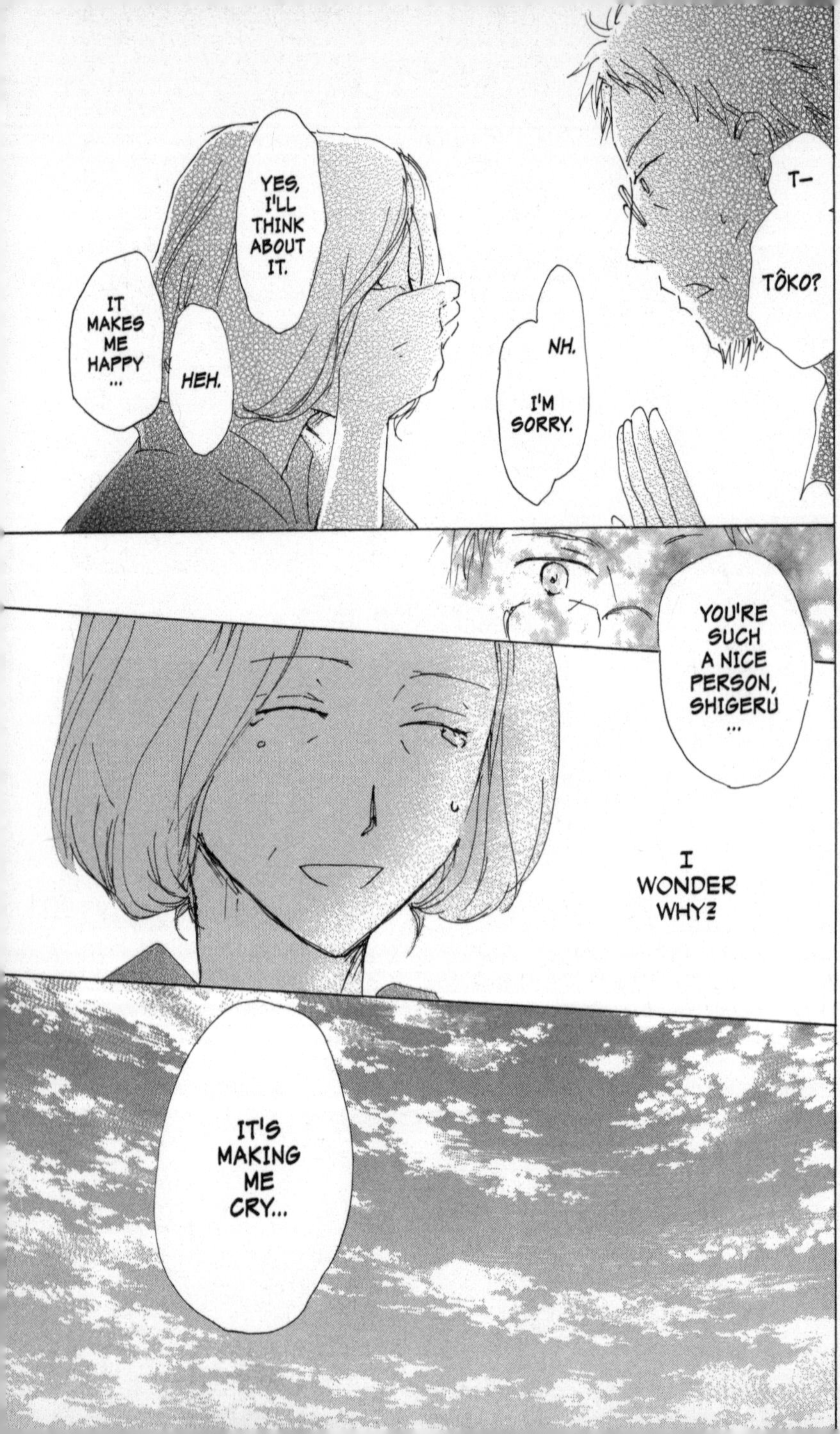
T–
TÔKO?
NH.
I'M SORRY.
YES, I'LL THINK ABOUT IT.
HEH.
IT MAKES ME HAPPY...
YOU'RE SUCH A NICE PERSON, SHIGERU...
I WONDER WHY?
IT'S MAKING ME CRY...

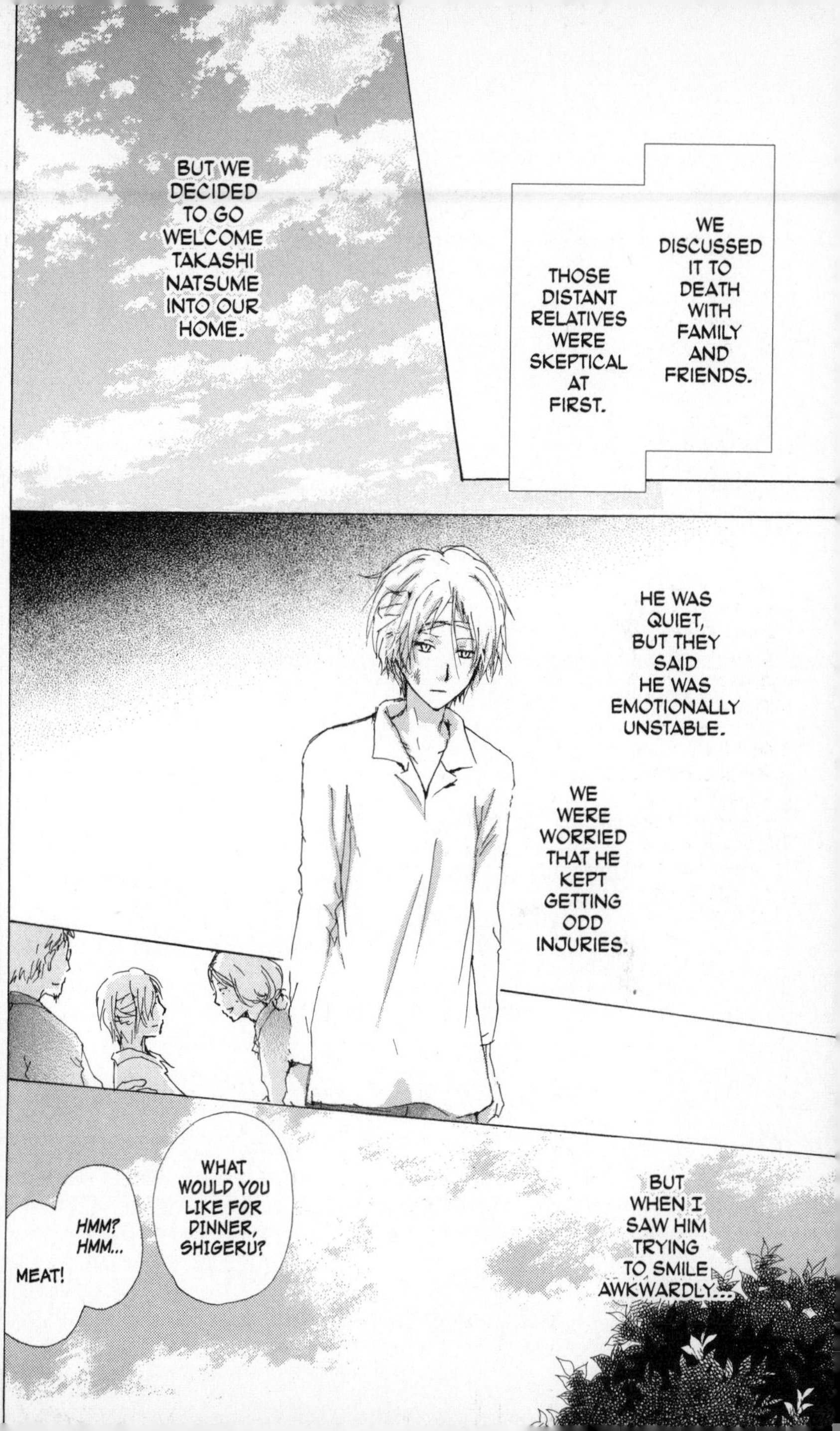
WE DISCUSSED IT TO DEATH WITH FAMILY AND FRIENDS.
THOSE DISTANT RELATIVES WERE SKEPTICAL AT FIRST.
BUT WE DECIDED TO GO WELCOME TAKASHI NATSUME INTO OUR HOME.
HE WAS QUIET, BUT THEY SAID HE WAS EMOTIONALLY UNSTABLE.
WE WERE WORRIED THAT HE KEPT GETTING ODD INJURIES.
BUT WHEN I SAW HIM TRYING TO SMILE AWKWARDLY...
WHAT WOULD YOU LIKE FOR DINNER, SHIGERU?
HMM? HMM...
MEAT!

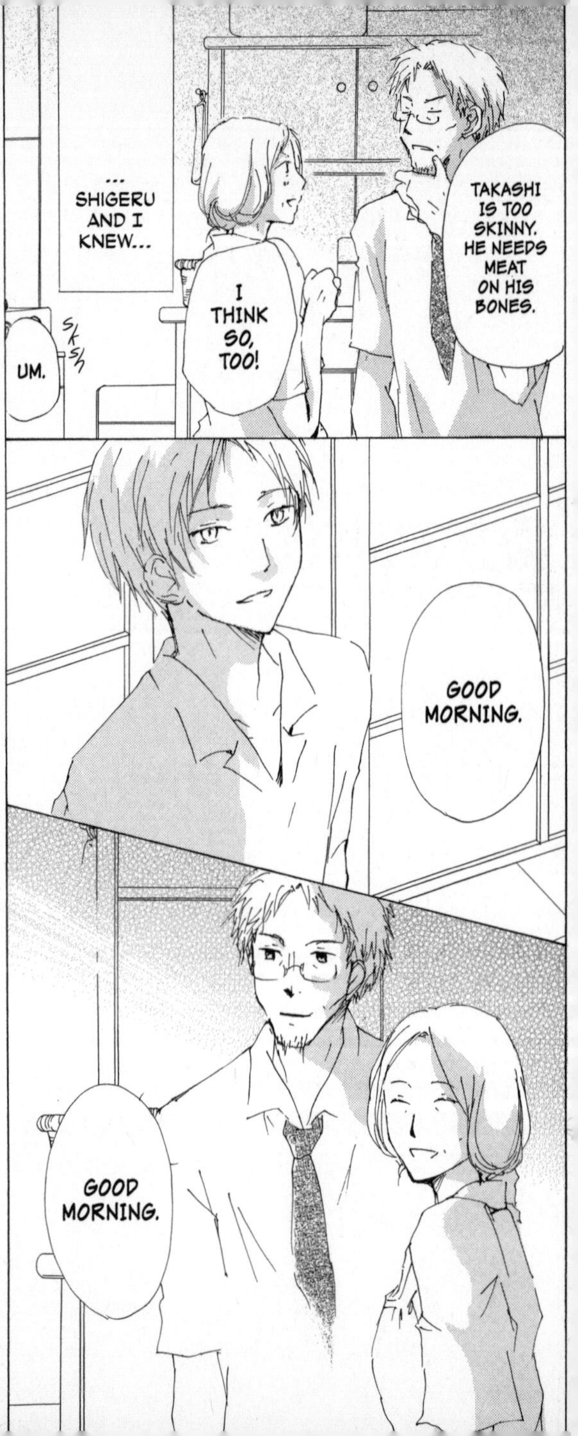
TAKASHI IS TOO SKINNY. HE NEEDS MEAT ON HIS BONES.
I THINK SO, TOO!
...SHIGERU AND I KNEW...
SKSH
UM.
GOOD MORNING.
GOOD MORNING.

05

❋ The Fujiwaras

Tôko is a kind woman, a little overprotective and wide-eyed. Shigeru shows up when there's something important, but you never know if he's in or out of the house. Almost like the yokai.

Natsume isn't used to family, and he's embarrassed to think Tôko and Shigeru notice this. But it's also a new experience for the Fujiwaras. They'll continue to fumble forward in the relationship, alternating between being too reserved and too forward.

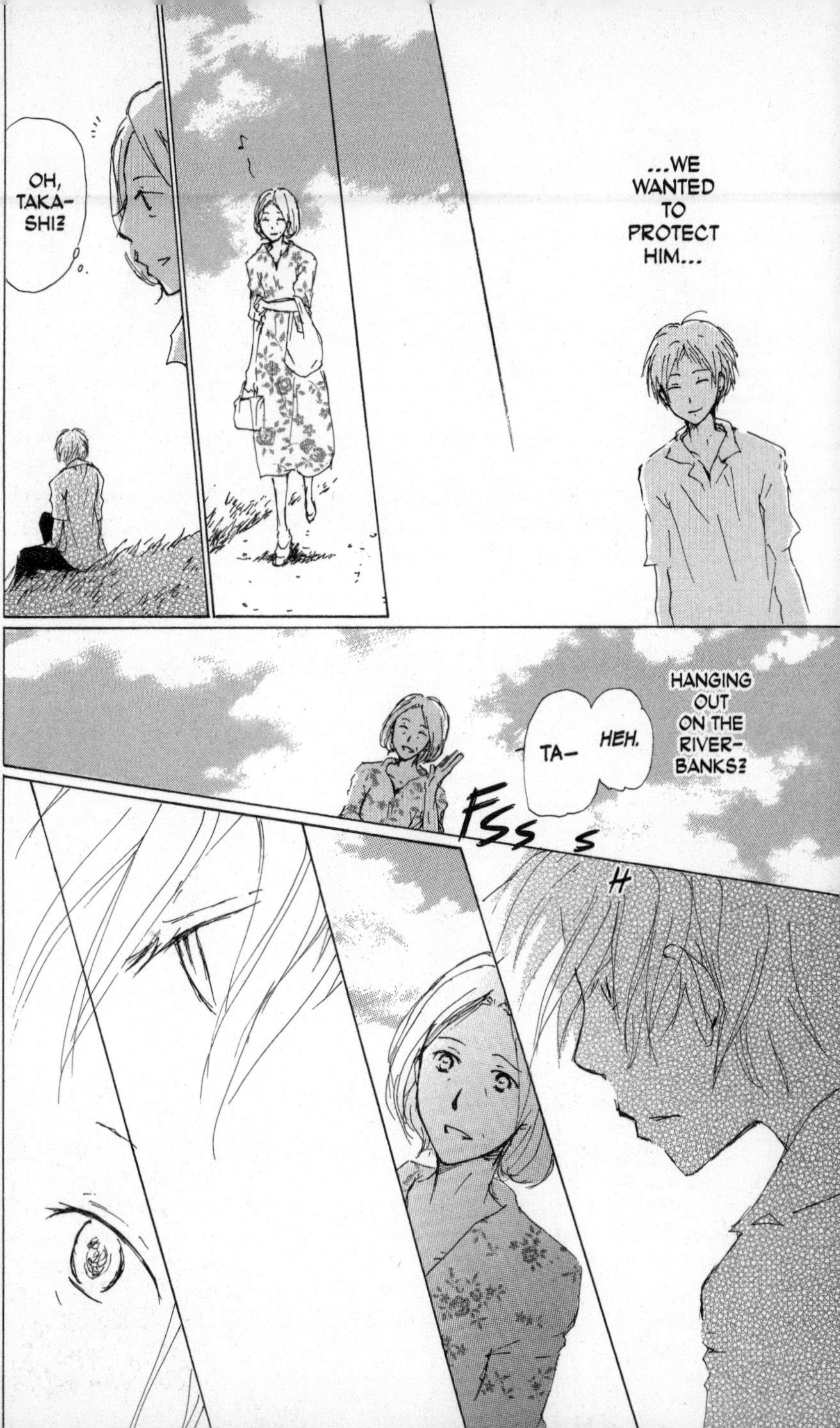
...WE WANTED TO PROTECT HIM...
OH, TAKA-SHI?
HANGING OUT ON THE RIVER-BANKS?
TA- HEH.
FSSS SH

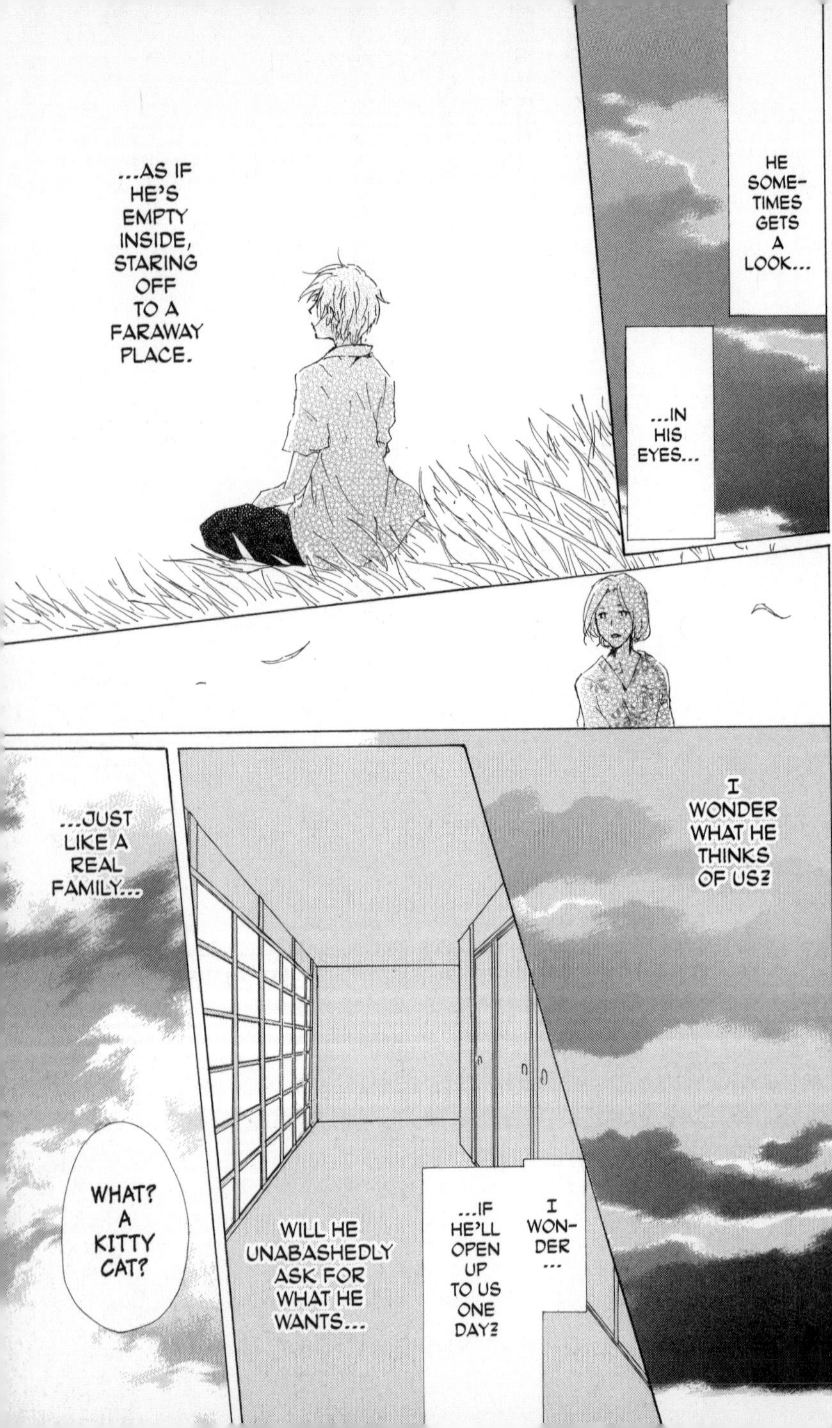
HE SOMETIMES GETS A LOOK...
...IN HIS EYES...
...AS IF HE'S EMPTY INSIDE, STARING OFF TO A FARAWAY PLACE.
I WONDER WHAT HE THINKS OF US?
I WONDER...
...IF HE'LL OPEN UP TO US ONE DAY?
WILL HE UNABASHEDLY ASK FOR WHAT HE WANTS...
...JUST LIKE A REAL FAMILY...
WHAT? A KITTY CAT?

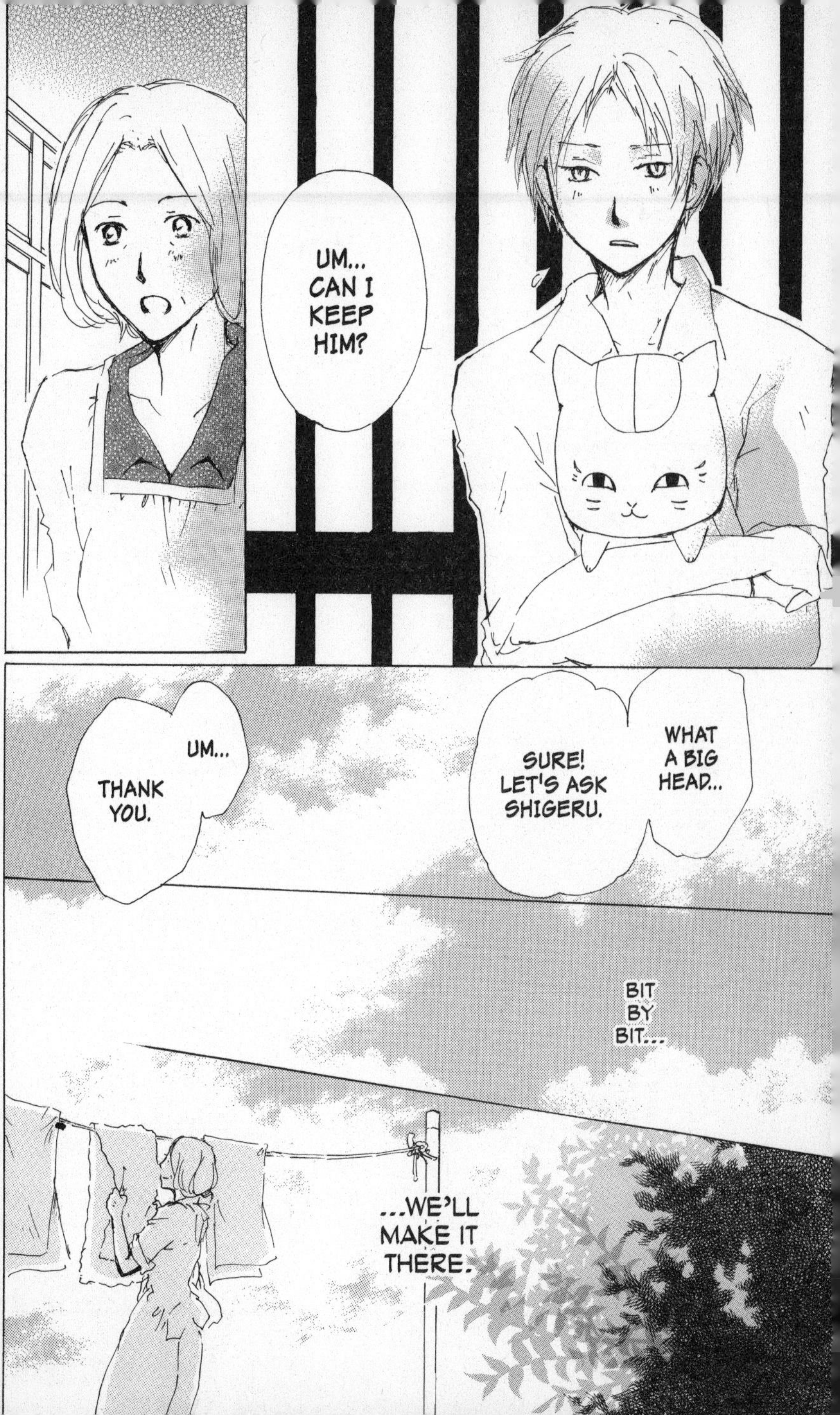
UM... CAN I KEEP HIM?
WHAT A BIG HEAD...
SURE! LET'S ASK SHIGERU.
UM... THANK YOU.
BIT BY BIT...
...WE'LL MAKE IT THERE.

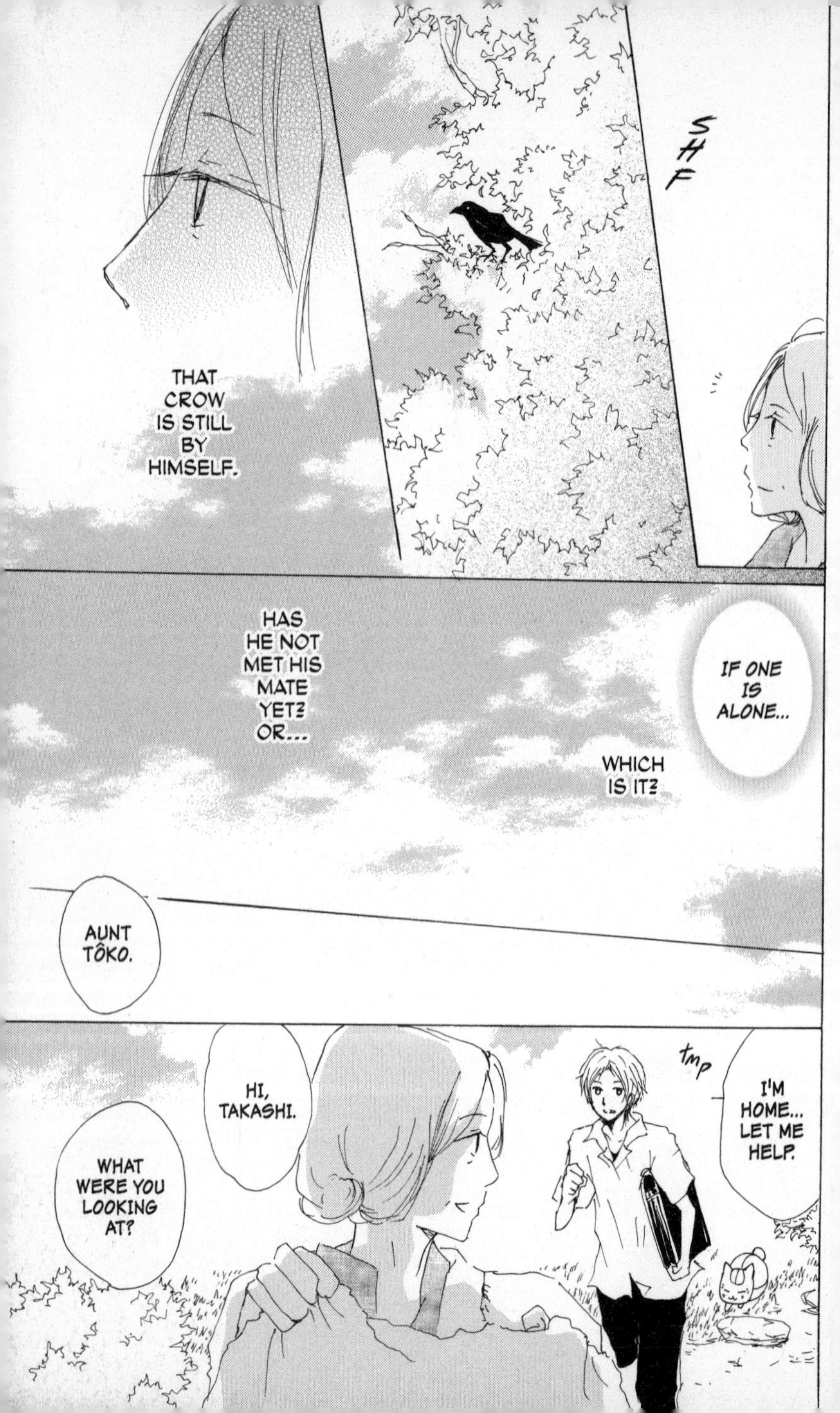
SHF
THAT CROW IS STILL BY HIMSELF.
IF ONE IS ALONE...
HAS HE NOT MET HIS MATE YET? OR...
WHICH IS IT?
AUNT TÔKO.
tmp
I'M HOME... LET ME HELP.
HI, TAKASHI.
WHAT WERE YOU LOOKING AT?

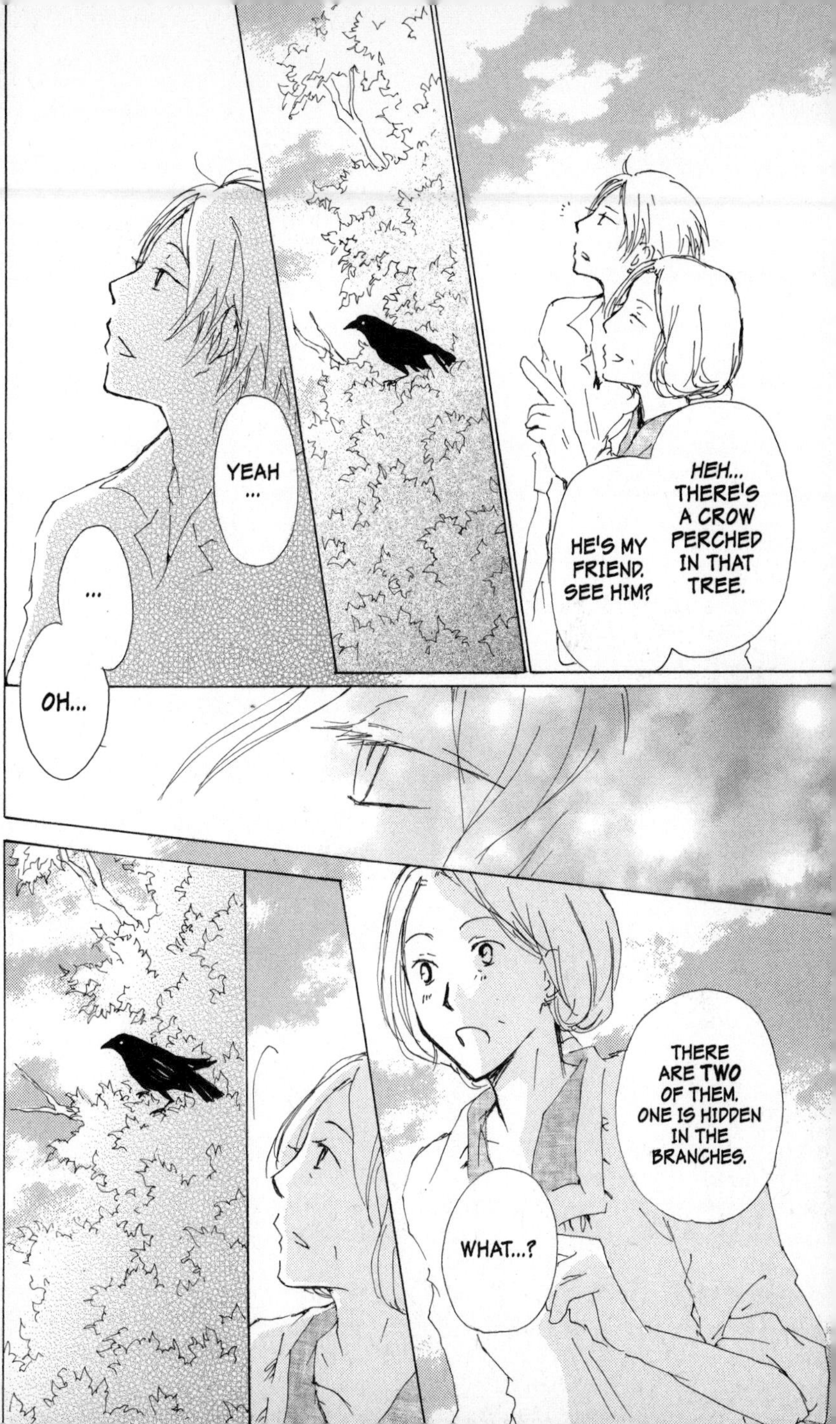
HEH... THERE'S A CROW PERCHED IN THAT TREE.
HE'S MY FRIEND. SEE HIM?
YEAH ...
...
OH...
THERE ARE TWO OF THEM. ONE IS HIDDEN IN THE BRANCHES.
WHAT...?

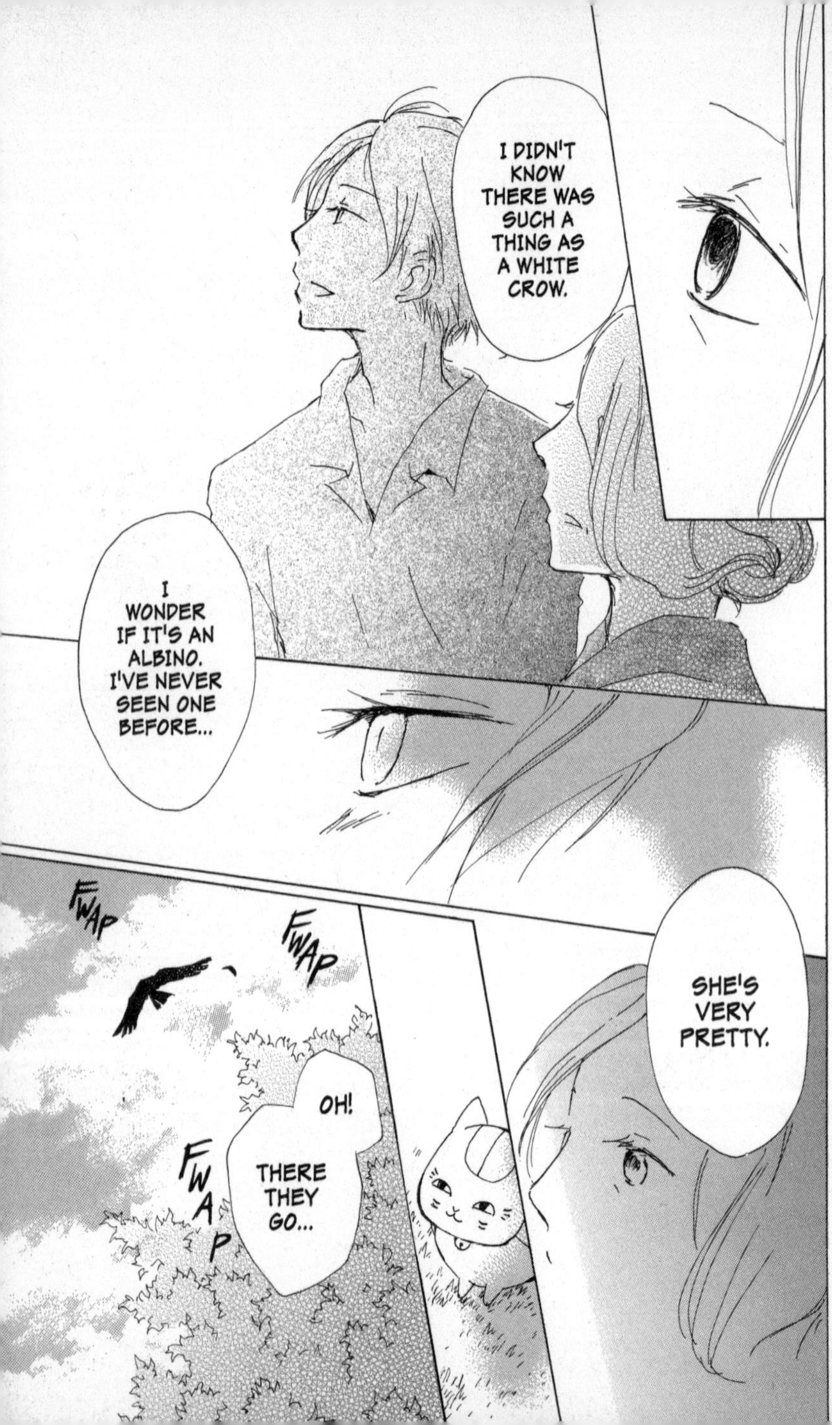

I DIDN'T KNOW THERE WAS SUCH A THING AS A WHITE CROW.
I WONDER IF IT'S AN ALBINO. I'VE NEVER SEEN ONE BEFORE...
SHE'S VERY PRETTY.
FWAP
FWAP
OH!
THERE THEY GO...
FWAP

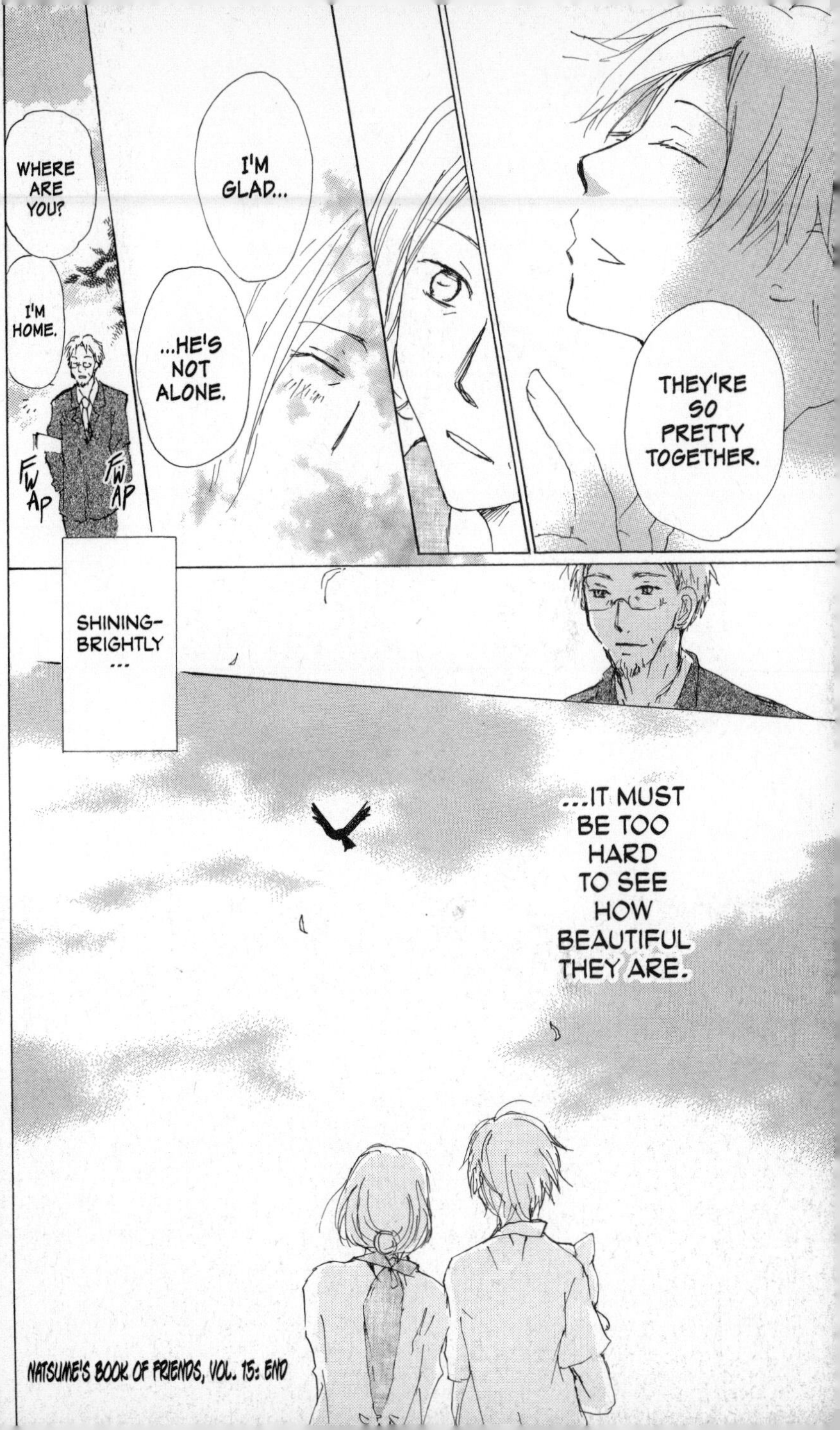

THEY'RE SO PRETTY TOGETHER.
I'M GLAD...
...HE'S NOT ALONE.
WHERE ARE YOU?
I'M HOME.
FWAP
FWAP
SHINING-BRIGHTLY...
...IT MUST BE TOO HARD TO SEE HOW BEAUTIFUL THEY ARE.
NATSUME'S BOOK OF FRIENDS, VOL. 15: END

AFTER-WORD

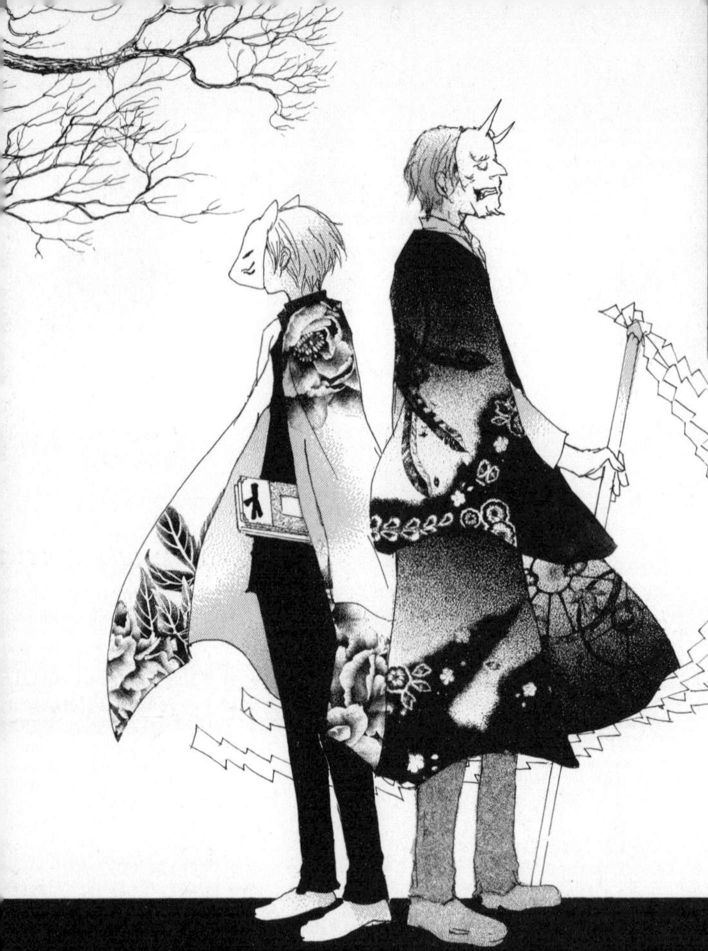

Thank you for reading.

When you grow closer to someone, you might end up growing farther apart from someone else. Natsume always kept his distance from others, so he didn't really understand that before. I hope I'll get to depict these dilemmas that Natsume will face in interpersonal and human-yokai relationships, and the subtle changes in the people around him.

To avoid spoilers please read the rest of this afterword only after reading the entire volume.

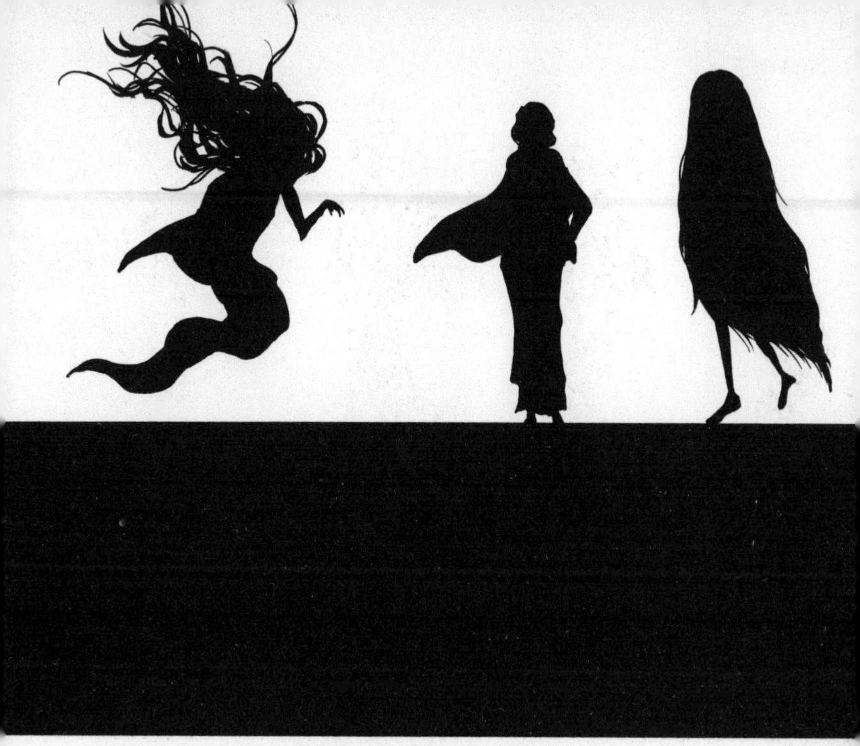

CHAPTERS 60-62 Different Eyes

The **Book of Friends** is the reason yokai come after Natsume. He wants to talk to Natori about it, but since exorcists are a threat to yokai, and since he literally holds the fate of many of them in his hands, he doesn't want to betray them.

Back in volume one, Natsume might've taken the **Book of Friends** and disappeared with Nyanko Sensei somewhere if he really got into trouble. But working on this episode, I don't think he'd be able to do that any longer. How things have changed.

I looked at Natsume trying to understand Tanuma even though they live in different worlds, and I thought he was doing the right thing, but the whole thing also felt comical. I wondered how Natori felt when he saw Matoba making Natsume help with the exorcism work.

This case was frustrating for Natori, who had to witness his old mentor become so oblivious that he could no longer see yokai in his own house. I think the existence of Natsume, with his different opinions, and Hîragi and the others, continue to affect Natori.

I would've liked to draw more about Mr. Takuma and Tsukiko, so I'll do it when I get another opportunity.

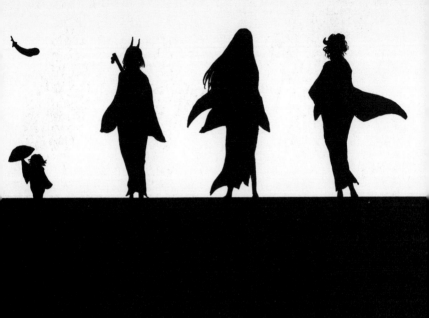

CHAPTER 63   A Difficult Path

This was the episode that came after the exorcism story, so I wanted something without a villain. But then it became a story about the characters feeling impatient with themselves. Natsume can clearly see that Mitsuzara will face huge obstacles in the future, but he sees the little guy flounder about towards his goal and swallows his words. Maybe he sees some hope.

I couldn't decide on what Mitsuzara looked like, then got the idea that he'd take his hat off and his face would look exactly the same. Then it came easily to me that he would look like a mushroom or pancake. I didn't really want to suggest that Mitsuzara's optimism was correct, so I kept revising the story until the very last minute.

CHAPTER 64   Tôko and Shigeru

This was a story I've always wanted to do. Natsume, Nyanko Sensei and yokai don't show up much. I was nervous about whether people would still enjoy the story, but I was happy to have the opportunity.

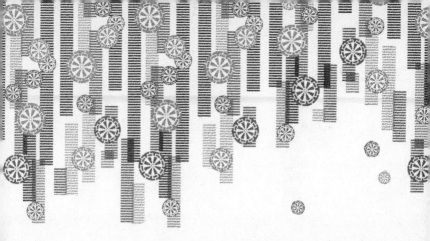

It's been ten years since I did the very first chapter of *Natsume's Book of Friends*. This title gave me my first experiences of chatting with my readers at autograph sessions, and my books getting their own obi ads. When I'm riding the train or a bus, there are moments when I'm awash with happiness, and it almost chokes me up. I will work hard to create manga that people can enjoy, for all my supporters out there!

Thank you very much.

Thanks to:

Tamao Ohki
Chika
Mika
Mr. Fujita
Hinata
My sister
Mr. Sato
Hoen Kikaku, Ltd.
    Thank you.

AFTERWORD: END

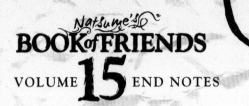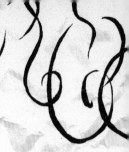

Natsume's
BOOK of FRIENDS
15
VOLUME **15** END NOTES

PAGE 127, PANEL 8: *Akebi fruit*
A purple fruit that grows on vines. When ripe, the pod splits open to reveal seeds surrounded by sweet white pulp.

PAGE 143, PANEL 1: *Meunière*
Fish dredged in flour, then pan-fried in a butter-lemon sauce.

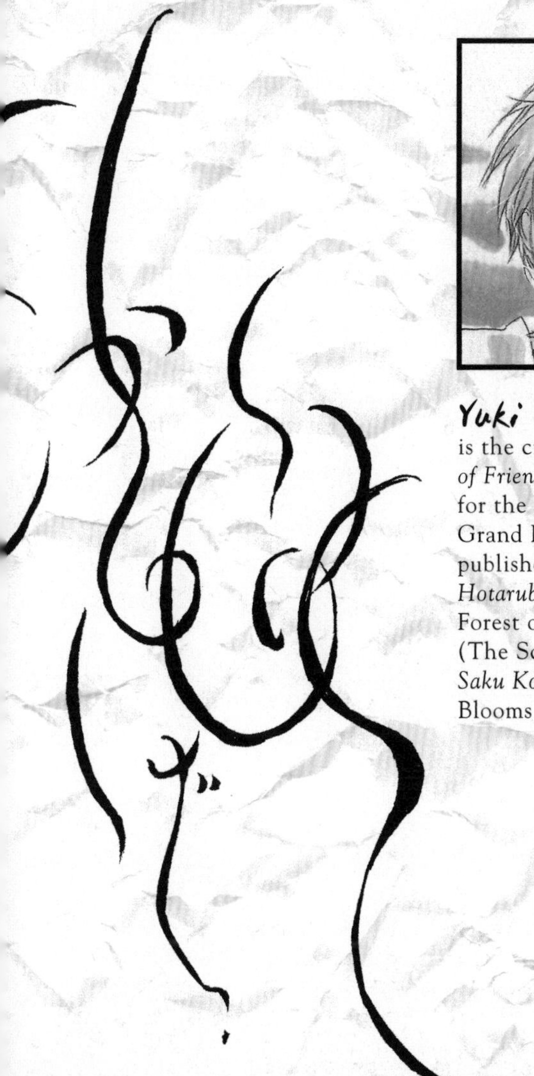

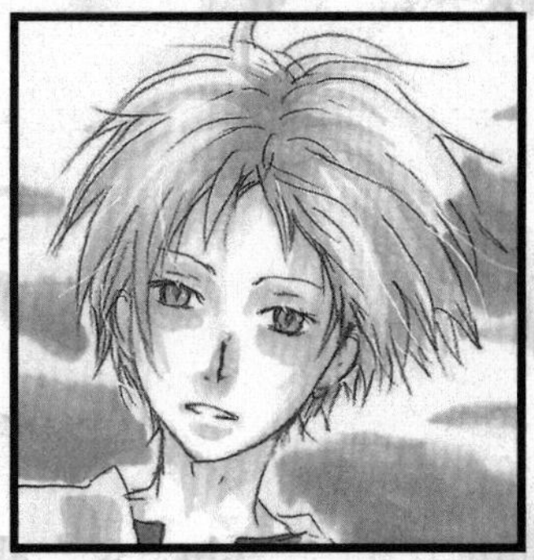

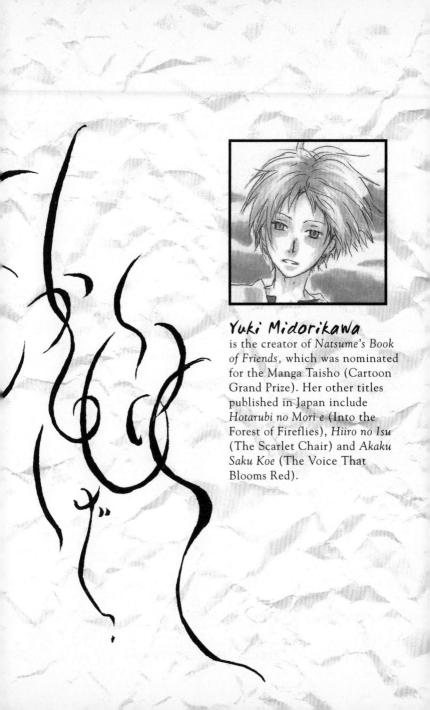

Yuki Midorikawa
is the creator of *Natsume's Book of Friends*, which was nominated for the Manga Taisho (Cartoon Grand Prize). Her other titles published in Japan include *Hotarubi no Mori e* (Into the Forest of Fireflies), *Hiiro no Isu* (The Scarlet Chair) and *Akaku Saku Koe* (The Voice That Blooms Red).

NATSUME'S BOOK OF FRIENDS

Vol. 15

Shojo Beat Edition

STORY AND ART BY **Yuki Midorikawa**

Translation & Adaptation **Lillian Olsen**
Touch-up Art & Lettering **Sabrina Heep**
Design **Fawn Lau**
Editor **Pancha Diaz**

Natsume Yujincho by Yuki Midorikawa
© Yuki Midorikawa 2013
All rights reserved.
First published in Japan in 2013 by HAKUSENSHA, Inc., Tokyo.
English language translation rights arranged with HAKUSENSHA, Inc., Tokyo.

The stories, characters and incidents mentioned in this publication are entirely fictional.

Printed in Canada

Published by VIZ Media, LLC
P.O. Box 77010
San Francisco, CA 94107

10 9 8 7 6 5 4 3 2 1
First printing, January 2014

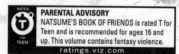

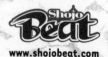

www.viz.com

www.shojobeat.com

Kyoko Mogami followed her true love Sho to Tokyo to support him while he made it big as an idol. But he's casting her out now that he's famous enough! Kyoko won't suffer in silence—she's going to get her sweet revenge by beating Sho in show biz!

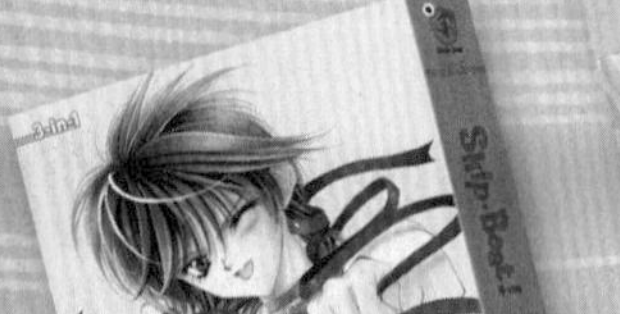

Vol. 1 ISBN: 978-1-4215-4226-3

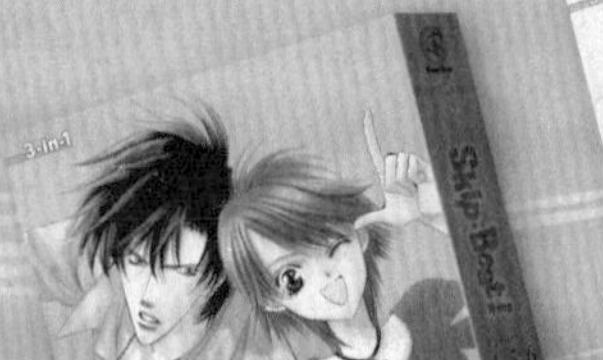

Vol. 2 ISBN: 978-1-4215-4227-0

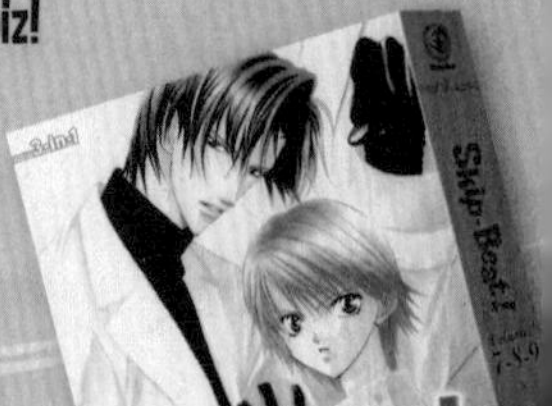

Vol. 3 ISBN: 978-1-4215-422

Show biz is sweet...but revenge is sweeter!

Skip·Beat!

Story and Art by YOSHIKI NAKAMURA

In Stores Now!

Only **$14.99** for each volume (**$16.99** in Canada)

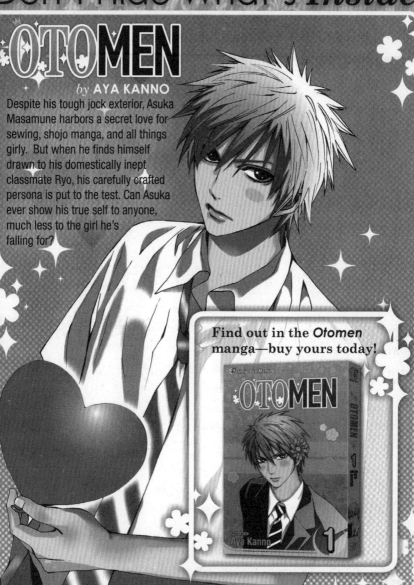
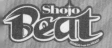
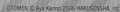

VIZMANGA
Read manga anytime, anywhere!

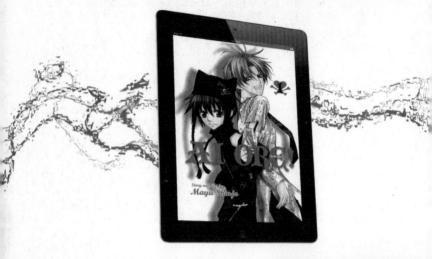

From our newest hit series to the classics you know and love, the best manga in the world is now available digitally. Buy a volume* of digital manga for your:

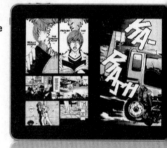

- iOS device (**iPad**®, **iPhone**®, **iPod**® touch) through the **VIZ Manga app**

- Android-powered device (**phone or tablet**) with a browser by visiting **VIZManga.com**

- **Mac or PC computer** by visiting VIZManga.com

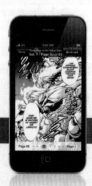

VIZ Digital has loads to offer:

- 500+ ready-to-read volumes
- New volumes each week
- FREE previews
- Access on multiple devices! Create a log-in through the app so you buy a book once, and read it on your device of choice!*

To learn more, visit www.viz.com/apps

* Some series may not be available for multiple devices. Check the app on your device to find out what's available.

SURPRISE!

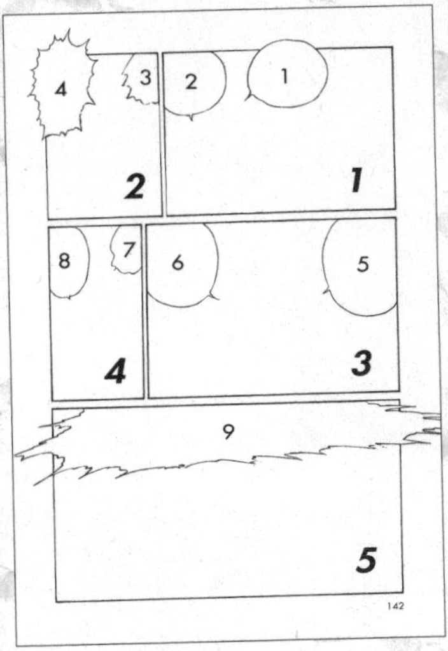
1
2
3
4
1
2
5
6
7
8
3
4
9
5
142

You may be reading the wrong way!

It's true: In keeping with the original Japanese comic format, this book reads from right to left—so action, sound effects, and word balloons are completely reversed. This preserves the orientation of the original artwork—plus, it's fun! Check out the diagram shown here to get the hang of things, and then turn to the other side of the book to get started!

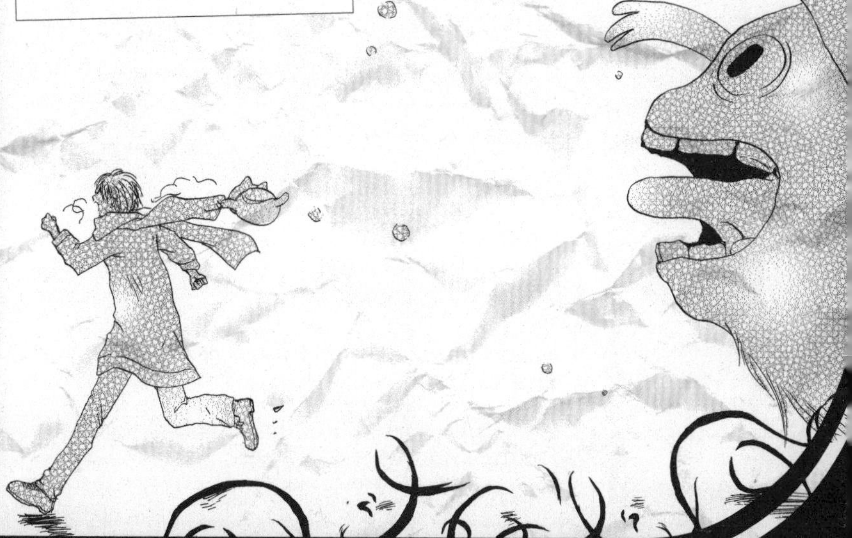